THE COOKBOOK'S COMPANION

By

DR. MYLES H. BADER
(Wizard of Food)

100 YEARS OF FOOD PREPARATION SECRETS YOUR COOKBOOK DOESN'T TELL YOU.

PROVIDES JUST THE SECRETS TO COOKING THE PERFECT FOODS FROM CHEFS AND GRANDMOTHERS WORLDWIDE.

THE MOST COMPLETE "FOOD SPECIFIC" COOKING GUIDE EVER PUBLISHED WITH OVER 9,000 SECRETS REVEALED.

THE COOKBOOK'S COMPANION

By

Dr. Myles H. Bader
(Wizard of Food)

Published By:
Bader Publishing
1818 Industrial Road Ste. 209
Las Vegas, NV 89102
(702) 383-8511
(702) 383-9828 FAX
(800) 717-6001 Order Line
www.wizardoffood.com
www.thecookbookscompanion.com
www.cookbookscompanion.com

Printed in the United States of America
First printing September 2001

ISBN: 0-9646741-8-1

TABLE OF CONTENTS

CHAPTER 3

CHAPTER 4

CHAPTER 5

CHAPTER 6

CHAPTER 7

CHAPTER 12

CHAPTER 13

CHAPTER 14

CHAPTER 15

CHAPTER 16

CHAPTER 17

CHAPTER 21

CHAPTER 22

CHAPTER 23

CHAPTER 24

CHAPTER 25

INTRODUCTION

Not everyone can have the opportunity of going to cooking school and learning the methods, preparation tips and secrets of cooking food. So I thought that it would be nice to write a book that just presented all the little secrets for the preparation of a particular dish, especially the more popular ones.

Since I have been writing kitchen reference books for many years and have learned thousands of individual facts regarding foods, the idea for this book was to provide you with a **totally different book** that contained thousands of actual cooking and food preparation secrets. The tricks, tips and secrets are all **"food specific."** When you want to make a certain food or dish, you can just look up that food or dish and find every tip or secret that pertains to that dish that 25 years of research could come up with.

Kitchen reference books provide in-depth information not found in cookbooks regarding almost every food imaginable, household hints, stain removal information, etc., while *"The Cookbook's Companion"* is related only to food preparation of specific dishes and foods. For example: reference books may only have 4 or 5 facts regarding cooking with cheese, (cookbooks may only have 1 or 2 tips when giving you the recipe) while *"The Cookbook's Companion"* has 35 cooking tips regarding cheeses.

For instance, if you are preparing a roast, the book will provide you with 34 tips and chef's secrets to preparing the perfect roast but not the actual recipe. It is amazing how many secrets there are when cooking different dishes that cookbooks never reveal.

> ### Every cookbook in the world needs "The Cookbook's Companion" to make it a "REAL" cookbook.

This book just goes into the basics of each food or dish and presents the tips (just the facts) that will assist you in general preparation allowing you to prepare the perfect food.

Many of the facts came from chefs worldwide and many from grandmothers and great grandmothers collected and tried over a period of 25 years of research into food and how to prepare a perfect dish.

This is one book that will never leave your home unless you have a very long string on it

...*Getting Started*   ...*Lets Cook*   ...*Preparing to Serve*

Myles H. Bader, DrPH, MPH—Wizard of Food

A WORD ABOUT THE AUTHOR

Dr. Myles H. Bader (Wizard of Food) has been a prolific writer of kitchen reference and cooking secret books for over 10 years. Dr. Bader is a recognized leader in the field of preventive care, weight management, nutrition and wellness and has been a guest on over 5,000 radio talk shows and 135 television shows including Oprah, The Discovery Channel, America's Talking, HGTV, QVC and Smart Solutions.

Dr. Bader received his Doctoral Degree from Loma Linda University and is board certified in Preventive Care. He has practiced weight control, exercise physiology, stress management, counseled in all areas of nutrition and has lectured extensively on supplementation and anti-aging for 25 years. He has also established prevention programs for numerous safety departments, city governments and executive health programs for over 40 major corporations.

A prolific writer, Dr. Bader has authored over 14 books including The "21st Century Reference Guide to Cooking Secrets & Household Hints," "1,001 Secret Household Formulas & Money Saving Tips," "10,001 Food Facts, Chef's Secrets & Household Hints," "To Supplement or Not to Supplement" and many more. Dr. Bader's books are presently, marketed by Barnes & Noble, Reader's Digest, Book of the Month Club and Doubleday.

Presently, Dr. Bader is President of The Family Solution, Inc. of Boise, Idaho, the leading health education and Nutritional-supplement Corporation in the United States, Mexico and Canada. Recently, The Family Solution introduced the most significant development in the weight control field ever formulated. Dr. Bader is presently presenting weight management training seminars nationwide to train consultants.

CHAPTER 1

COOKING VEGETABLES LIKE A PRO

COOKING VEGETABLES

The following are hints and chef's secrets to cooking and preparing the more common vegetables. Some general suggestions, however, are necessary that apply to all vegetables and these include washing the skins with a good quality organic vegetable cleaner before you peel them or even slice in to them, discarding the skins since many contain pesticide or fertilizer residues and inspecting the vegetables for insects.

- When you only want to blanch a small amount of vegetables, just place them into a wire sieve and immerse them in a pot of boiling water for 30-40 seconds, then immediately place them into ice water.
- When you are deep-frying vegetables, the oil should be at 360°F.

ARTICHOKE

Artichoke history can be traced back as far as 250 BC. However, the artichoke; was first brought to the United States by a French immigrant in 1806 who settled in the Louisiana Territory. The first commercial crop was grown in Louisiana. In 1922 artichokes were grown in California, which now produces more artichokes than any other state.

- Never wash artichokes until they are to be used. Artichokes have a protective coating that can be removed by excessive washing.
- Store artichokes in a plastic bag in the refrigerator vegetable storage bin and they will last for 3-4 days, but are best in 1-2 days.
- Make sure the leaves squeak when rubbed together for the freshest artichoke.
- Heft the artichoke, the heavier they are, the better.

Artichoke bottoms may be used as a container for dip or small vegetables.

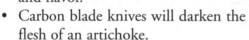

- Never cook in an aluminum pot or the pot will discolor: glass, stainless steel or ceramic is best.
- Keep artichokes covered with water when cooking or they will burn easily.
- Use only stainless steel knives to cut artichokes to retard browning.
- If the artichokes are not "real" fresh, add 1 teaspoon of sugar and $1/4$ teaspoon of salt to each cup of water used. The sugar will add a small amount of sweetness and the salt will help them retain their color and flavor.
- Carbon blade knives will darken the flesh of an artichoke.
- Rub all surfaces of an artichoke with lemon to retard browning.
- Fresh artichoke outer leaves may be tough and should be shortened with a scissors as much as $2/3$ of their height.
- To make the artichokes look shiny, just add 1 tablespoon of extra virgin olive oil to the cooking water.
- To improve the flavor, soak artichokes in a bowl of water with 2-3 tablespoons of lemon juice for 45 minutes.

- A small amount of sugar and salt to cooking water will set the flavor and help retain it. One teaspoon of each should suffice per quart of water.
- Add $1/8$-$1/4$ teaspoon of fennel to cooking water to improve flavor. Fennel will release more, flavor if it is crushed before using.
- Foods consumed after eating artichokes will taste sweet due to a chemical that is released when you are chewing the artichoke.

- Artichokes will remain green and not turn brown if cooked rapidly. The longer it takes the more they will turn brown.
- Cook an artichoke in a covered pot for no more than 30-40 minutes in gently simmering water.
- If grilling an artichoke, cook for only 3-5 minutes on medium coals.
- To microwave an artichoke cook it on high for 5-8 minutes and then allow it to stand for 5 minutes before serving.
- If steaming an artichoke only steam it for 25-35 minutes.

- If artichokes are to be served cold, cool them immediately in cold water; then scoop-out the choke and remove the leaves from around the choke.
- An artichoke is completely cooked when pierced easily with a fork or skewer.

Slicing cooked Artichokes

- Quarter the artichoke lengthwise, slicing through the heart. Next cut across each quarter, at the point where the purple leaves peak. The knife will stop naturally, then peel the heart and choke away from the tougher leaves.
- Next remove the fibrous choke from the heart by cutting down about 1 inch at the base of the choke fibers. Flick the blade up and the choke will lift out, leaving the heart behind.

ASPARAGUS

Asparagus received the name "Food of Kings" by King Louis XIV of France who had special greenhouses made so that he could have the delicacy year round. The male asparagus plant is the sturdiest and most tender, while the female asparagus are week and tougher. The thicker the asparagus stalk: the better.

- Limp asparagus; can be revived by placing the stalks into a bowl of ice cubes and water in the refrigerator for 45 minutes.
- If asparagus is purchased toward the end of the growing season it may be somewhat bitter unless placed in a bowl of water for about 30-60 seconds then placed on paper towel. Growing season is March through June.

- If you are going to store asparagus for a few days, place the bunch under water and slice $\frac{1}{2}$ inch off the bottom, then allow them to remain under water for 1 minute to absorb water. Store standing upright on a damp towel or paper towel. They will not lose flavor.
- Asparagus loses about 10-15% of its sweetness everyday it is stored.
- Keep the tips as dry as possible when storing asparagus, wrap them in paper towel if they are not going to be used for 2-3 days.
- Flavor will be lost if asparagus spears are stored standing in water.

Use a potato or vegetable peeler to remove the outer surface of the stalks to tenderize the stalk

- White asparagus grows underground and is best and more, tender when the stalks are very thin, green asparagus should have thick stalks.

The darker green the stems are, the more flavorful the asparagus

- 50% of vitamin C is lost 2 days after harvesting asparagus, the fresher the better
- Never purchase asparagus if they are sitting in any water

- Cook asparagus only until they are barely tender, since they will continue cooking for about 45 seconds after they are removed from the water. Overcooking will ruin asparagus.
- Wrap the asparagus stalks in damp paper towel when cooking them and only cook them in about 1-1$\frac{1}{4}$ " of water, covered and standing upright.
- To freeze, blanch in boiling water after removing 2 inches off the stems for 2-4 minutes. Freeze in a plastic bag.
- To stabilize asparagus in a tall pot, place a thick ring of aluminum foil around the tied bundle.
- The most common seasonings for asparagus are lemon juice, mustard sauce, parmesan cheese and butter

- Microwave asparagus in a 2-3 tablespoons of water for about 6-7 minutes on high.
- Microwave cooking can also be done in a 12" round microwave-safe dish with all spears aimed toward the center with 2-4 tablespoons of water, then cook on high for about 10 minutes.
- Asparagus can be steamed in about 10 minutes.
- Grill asparagus for 3-5 minutes, precooked and tied in bundles.
- Stir-fry asparagus in 1 tablespoon of olive oil or 1-2 tablespoons of unsalted butter for about 1 minute or until tender.
- Bundles of asparagus should be cooked in about 1" of water: with $1^{1}/_{2}$ teaspoons of salt per quart of water.

BEANS (DRIED)

- Dried beans, such as legumes, peas and lentils contain the chemical "lectin," which is why the bean must be cooked to avoid abdominal discomfort and severe indigestion
- Holes; in dried beans are homes for bugs, throw them away.
- Only two beans are commonly roasted, these are soybeans and peanuts.
- The length of time that beans are stored will affect their cooking time. Best to use the beans within 12 months.

Place a red chili pepper in a bean storage container to keep insects away.

- Dried beans can be frozen in a well-sealed container.

- Beans can be softened by adding $^1/_2$ teaspoon of baking soda to the water beans are soaking in, plus $^1/_2$ teaspoon into the water beans are being cooked in.

To remove the gas problem from dried beans, add 1 teaspoon of fennel seed to the water that the beans are soaking in. The fennel will neutralize the complex sugar causing the gas.

- Another method of softening and reducing the gas problem is to add 2 tablespoons of white vinegar to the cooking water.
- Adding 2 tablespoons of baking soda to the water will also soften beans faster.
- Cook different varieties of beans separately, never together since they soften at different times.
- If any beans float to the surface they should be discarded.
- Add 1-2 teaspoons of olive oil to the cooking water to prevent boil over. You can also rub the olive oil on the inside rim of the pot, about $^1/_2$ inch down.
- Beans will take longer to cook if you add tomato sauce. Acid will slow down the softening process.
- Never allow beans to boil, just simmer or they will come apart or lose their skins.
- Never add salt to the cooking water or it will toughen the beans.
- An uncovered pot will produce firm beans while covered pots produce soft beans.

- If you are cooking beans in a pressure cooker, only cook them for $^1/_3$ of the normal time.
- If you are cooking beans in a pressure cooker, reduce the cooking time to $^1/_3$ of the normal time.
- If you salt beans while they are cooking they will take longer to soften. The salt actually strengthens their cell walls.
- To control the texture of dried beans, cook the beans with the lid on for soft beans and with the lid off for firm beans.

- Never place the beans into a chili sauce until they are finished cooking since the acid level will be too high and the beans will not soften any further and the beans remain hard.
- If you are going to serve beans cold, allow them to remain in the water they were cooked in to cool. This will stop their skins from splitting.
- Beans must be drained as soon as they are soft; further cooking or allowing them to remain in water will turn them mushy.
- Season beans only at the end of the cooking time, salt will prevent the beans from softening.
- Allow beans to cool in their own cooking water to prevent splitting.

Black Beans

Black beans were consumed in Mexico 7,000 years ago and gained popularity all over Central and South America as one of the cholcest beans. In Venezuela black beans are referred to as " creole caviar."

- Uscd cxtensivcly in Mcxican and South American dishes and frequently mixed with rice and spices. One of the tastiest beans.

Black-eyed Peas

- Usually found cooked with collard greens and ham in the South.

Boston Baked Beans

The original recipe for baked beans was brought to Boston by the sea captains who visited Africa in the early 1800's. The dish was composed of navy beans, molasses and salt pork. Boston acquired the nickname of "bean town" and thus Boston baked beans got its name.

- The original recipe calls for the beans to be boiled twice, once for only 2 minutes then allowing them to stand for 1 hour before re-boiling them for another hour.
- The seasonings were $1/4$ cup of molasses, 1 teaspoon of fresh black pepper and 1 teaspoon of dried, finely powdered mustard seed.

If you add molasses to baked beans it will help them retain their shape for a longer period of time.

- When baking the beans they are placed into the pot in layers and the seasoning and layers of salt pork placed on top of each layer.

Chili con Carne

Chili con carne is not a Mexican dish but originated in Spain and was first prepared by Sister Mary of Agreda, Spain in 1618. The legend surrounding the Sister states that she taught the Southwestern American Indians how to make the dish while still in Spain and in a trance. The original recipe called for antelope or venison, onions, tomatoes and chili peppers. True chili con carne does not include beans. The first recorded recipe of chili was in 1850 by a Texas cowboy. The first "chili powder" seasoning: was invented by William Gebhardt in 1890 in New Braunfels, Texas. Beans were finally added in 1922 in Cincinnati.

- Brick chili was the first chili and was prepared from pounded, dried beef, pepper, salt and chili peppers.

Fava beans

- Fava beans should never be pre-soaked, just cover with water, bring to a boil and allow to simmer for 20-30 minutes, drain and peel, then cook as per recipe.
- If the fava beans are large with a tough skin, just place them under cold water as soon as they have finished boiling and the skins will come right off.
- When working with fresh fava beans, snap the pod and remove each bean individually with your thumb and forefinger.
- Chefs use their fingernail to break the skins and push the fava bean out of its sleeve.

Kidney Beans/Red Beans

- Traditional chili bean.

Lentils

To test to see whether lentils have the proper doneness, remove a spoonful from the pan and gently blow on them. If the skin breaks and starts to peel back, the lentils are done. The same test can be done for beans.

Split Pea Soup

Columbus brought peas to the West Indies in 1493 and they were first planted on Isabella Island. Peas were first planted in New England in 1602 by Captain Bartholomew Gosnold on the Island of Cuttyhunk but were not a recognized crop in the United States until 1614 when they were grown in Jamestown, Virginia.

- Be sure and soak the peas for at least 8 hours. Any residue that floats to the top should be skimmed off.
- Retain about 4 cups of the water that the peas were softened in.
- The soup is usually made with the addition of salt pork (optional), onion, celery and 1 bay leaf and salt and pepper to taste.
- The soup is usually brought to a boil and then allowed to simmer for about 2 hours to allow all the flavors to intermingle.
- Drain off the liquid and save. Puree all vegetables and add to the liquid with at least 1-tablespoon of unsalted butter.

BEANS (FRESH GREEN)

- Make sure the beans are crisp and snap when bent.
- Will store for 4-5 days in airtight plastic wrap.

- Frozen beans should be placed in water for no more than 10 minutes, then separate them and prepare.

Never add baking soda to cooking water, it will reduce the nutrient content and give the beans an off-flavor.

- Should only be boiled for 6-10 minutes in about 1" of water.
- Microwave for 5-7 minutes on high in 2-3 tablespoons of water then allow the beans to stand for 2-3 minutes.
- A pinch of granulated sugar in the cooking water will enhance the flavor.

- Keep acidic vegetables, such as tomatoes away from green beans until just before serving to preserve their color.
- Beans should still be crisp after cooking; if overcooked they will lose flavor, become mushy and have an off color.
- The most common seasonings for green beans are basil, oregano, garlic, soy sauce, dill and bacon. These seasonings will enhance the flavor and not detract from the flavor of the green beans.

Haricot Beans

- Haricot beans cook very quickly and will turn a nice emerald green color. They rarely taste like canned beans and are preferred by most chefs.

BEAN THREADS

- These thin; almost transparent bean noodle is commonly used in stir-fry and soups.
- When added to dishes they will cook in about 30 seconds and should be added almost at the end of the cooking time.
- Bean threads can be fried in only a few seconds and the result is a crispy thread used in many oriental dishes.

BEETS

- Beets should not be blemished when purchased.
- Never allow more than 1-2" of the greens to remain after you get the beets home; they will leach liquid from the bulb.
- Beet greens are very high in nutrition and should be prepared similar to spinach.
- Plastic gloves are recommended to keep the beet juice off your hands.
- Beets have the highest sugar content of any vegetable.
- If you use beet, greens in salads, just use the leaves. Remove the stems and discard, since they may be bitter.

- Allowing 1-2" inches of the greens to remain will help conserve nutrients when the beets are cooked.
- Old beets will need to have $\frac{1}{2}$ teaspoon of sugar and $\frac{1}{2}$ teaspoon of salt added to the water.
- If you are preparing whole beets with the skins on, make sure that you do not scrub the skin too hard or you will lose the color.

- Medium size beets need to be just covered with water in a covered pot and cooked for 25-40 minutes or until tender.
- To keep the red color, add 2 tablespoons of lemon juice or 1 table-spoon of white vinegar to the cooking water.
- When you microwave beets, make sure that you pierce the skin.
- Beets can be baked by wrapping them in foil, set the oven for 375°F and bake for about 1 hour or until tender.
- When stir-frying, beets they should be shredded.
- The most common seasonings for beets are allspice, lemon, dill, ginger, cloves and horseradish.
- Try and cook beets of all the same size or at least close.
- If you are not going to use the beet, greens in a salad: leave them on while the beets are cooking to help retain more of the nutrients.

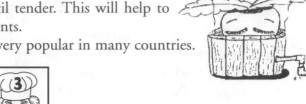

- Beets can be wrapped in tin foil and baked at 350°F for about 1 hour or until tender. This will help to retain most of the nutrients.
- Steamed beet leaves are very popular in many countries.

- To remove the beet skins after cooking, submerse the beets in ice-cold water with ice cubes for 30 seconds to loosen the skin.

Beets will discolor other vegetables and should only be added to them just before serving.

- Try not to use plastic or wood dishes with beets, since they may be permanently discolored.

BOK CHOY

- The chopped stalks can be stir-fried or sautéed for just 1-2 minutes.
- The leaves can be steamed for about 30 seconds.
- Bok choy is easily damaged and needs to handled-with-care.
- Bok choy needs to only be cooked briefly to mellow the flavor. The flavor is similar to cabbage when cooked but with a more, milder flavor.

BROCCOLI

- Store in a well-sealed plastic bag, unwashed and refrigerated for the best results.
- Broccoli should always be blanched before freezing.

- Take at least one layer off the stalks to tenderize them before cooking.
- Cut the heads into about 4 pieces for faster cooking.

- Broccoli must be boiled for no more than 30 seconds to retain its color, when cooked for more than 30 seconds the acid and chlorophyll in the broccoli react changing the color.

Never add any acid to the cooking water, such as lemon juice or vinegar or the broccoli will turn gray.

- If you are planning to cook broccoli with real thick stalks, just drop them in boiling water for about 3 minutes.
- If the green color is weak, try boiling the broccoli for 2-3 minutes and then immersing it in ice-cold water to stop it from further cooking.
- Fresh white bread placed on top of the broccoli while it is cooking will help eliminate the offensive odor.
- Red bell peppers will also absorb the odor from broccoli and is easier to remove from the pot than disintegrated bread, but considerably more expensive.
- A small amount of baking soda added to the cooking water; helps stabilize the color.
- The longer you cook broccoli, the more "isocynates" are released causing a foul odor.

- The most popular seasonings for broccoli are mustard sauce and lemon.

BRUSSELS SPROUTS

- Do not purchase if leaves have any yellow.
- Remove outer leaves, which usually show some damage or discoloration.
- The heads should be very compact and should not be spongy when squeezed
-

- Partially steam the sprouts and then they can be placed in a pan with a small amount of butter and sautéed
- All sprouts should be as close to uniform size as possible so they are all ready at the same time.

Cut an "X" on the bottom of all the sprouts to assure that the heat will penetrate evenly.

- Never add vinegar or lemon juice to the cooking water or the green color will fade.

- Steam for no more than 8-9 minutes over boiling water.
- Boil for about 8-10 minutes in 1" of lightly, salted water; cover the pot after 4 minutes.
- Test during cooking since they become mushy and not very appealing if overcooked.

- Use a skewer to penetrate the stem of the Brussels sprouts to test for tenderness, if tender the skewer should penetrate very easily.
- The addition of toasted almonds to a recipe containing Brussels sprouts tends to enhance the flavor and should only be added during the final 5-10 minutes of cooking to retain the maximum flavor of the nuts.
- The most popular seasonings for Brussels sprouts are cheddar cheese, dill, caraway and Parmesan cheese.

CABBAGE

The Roman Emperor Claudius convened the Roman Senate to vote on whether there was any food dish that was thought to be superior to corned beef and cabbage.

- Heft the cabbage and be sure that it is heavy for its overall size, the heavier, the better.
- Stores well in the refrigerator for up to 2 weeks in a sealed plastic bag.
- Red cabbage will take longer to cook than green cabbage.

To dry cabbage, never press it, always shake it or go outside and swing it around your head.

- When preparing coleslaw, place the shredded cabbage in a bowl of ice water in the refrigerator for 45 minutes before draining and drying. The cabbage will really crisp-up nicely.

- To preserve the color of red cabbage, add about 1 teaspoon of white vinegar or lemon juice to the cooking water.
- Cabbage leaves, can easily be removed if you freeze the cabbage then allow it to thaw just before removing the leaves.
- Shred cabbage when stir-frying in 2 tablespoons of butter for about 1 minute, then add 3 tablespoons of water, cover and cook for 4-5 minutes.
- Before boiling cabbage remove the coarse outer leaves and the stem to reduce bitterness.
- Use young cabbage, the older cabbage gets, the tougher the leaves and the more bitter.
- Soaking cabbage in ice water serves two purposes: it will eliminate the heavy odor that normally develops and tends to make the cabbage very crispy and easier to chew.

- Shredded cabbage should only be boiled for 5 minutes and about 8-10 minutes for larger chunks.
- Overcooking cabbage results in an unpleasant odor.
- When cooking cabbage, add a small amount of vinegar to the cooking water and it will eliminate about 70% of the cooking odor.
- Cabbage wedges cook better and retain their shape if steamed instead of boiled.

- Whole leaves can be easily removed if you remove the core, then place the head into a pot of boiling water, reduce the heat and allow it to simmer for about 1 minute.
- When boiling cabbage change the water once and it will eliminate the problem of flatulence for some people.
- To blanche cabbage, place the head into a pot of lightly, salted boiling water and only allow the cabbage to remain for 50 seconds.
- To boil cabbage only boil wedges for 8-11 minutes in about 1-1^1/$_2$" of water and cover the pot after 2 minutes for the balance of the time.
- To steam cabbage, cut into wedges and steam for 10-12 minutes.
- Stuffed cabbage is normally covered with stock and braised for about 1 to 1^1/$_2$ hours
- Tomato products are high in acid and will extend the cooking time.

Sugar will strengthen the cells and make the cabbage leaves stronger, which is why sweet and sour is so popular.

- Napa cabbage is excellent added to stir-fries since it retains it shape and flavor very well.
- Cooking cabbage uncovered will allow some of the strong flavor to be lost; also using more water that is normally called for will have the same effect.
- When boiling red cabbage add 1 apple cut into quarters to help retain color and add a pleasant flavor.

- To remove the excess moisture from cabbage after boiling, then place the cabbage between two plates and squeeze.
- The tender inner leaves are normally chopped and added to the meat filling, cooked rice and chopped boiled onions can also be added to the meat.
- The large outer leaves are usually used for stuffed cabbage and should be placed on a damp towel since they tend to dry out when working with them
- The most popular seasonings for cabbage are dill, caraway seeds, garlic, celery seed and caraway seeds.

CARROTS

- Never buy carrots with cracks, they are too old and have lost a percentage of their flavor.

  Never store apples near carrots they will make the carrots bitter by giving off ethylene gas.

- Discard the top greens before storing the carrots since they will keep taking fluid from the carrots and cause them to dry out and become limp.

  Never store carrots in a sealed plastic bag or they will turn bitter.

- If carrots get limp, place them in a bowl of ice water for 45 minutes in the refrigerator and they should crisp up like new.

- The best carrots for cooking are the young, thinner carrots.
- If you must use an old carrot, make sure you cut it in half and remove the center core, which causes bitterness.
- Carrot skins can be easily removed similar to potato skins by just boiling them and immersing them into a bowl of ice water while they are hot for a few seconds.
- Carrots will lose their flavor and a good percentage of nutrients in a short period of time if placed in a bowl of water.
- Cooking carrots with either acidic or alkali foods will not alter their color.

- Always boil carrots first when using them for stir-fry then immerse in cold water to stop the cooking before proceeding.

- Cooking carrots allow more nutrients to be easily released.
- Fresh carrot greens may be boiled and are very nutritious.
- It takes 15-20 minutes to boil whole carrots in 1" of water.
- Sliced carrots, take 5-9 minutes to steam, whole carrots take 15-20 minutes.
- Carrot rounds (1-pound) can be placed in a microwave in 2 tablespoons of water for about 7 minutes on high, then allow them to stand for 2 minutes.
- Carrot ribbons, can be prepared by cooking them, then slice them with a potato peeler and drop them into a steamer for 2-3 minutes.
- If carrots are overcooked their color will fade.
- Adding a small amount of orange juice to carrots while they are cooking adds an excellent flavor.
- To retain the flavor of carrots they should be cooked with their skins on.

- The most popular seasonings for carrots are ginger, bay leaves, parsley, dill, tarragon and caraway seeds.

CAULIFLOWER

- The buds should be tightly closed and not brownish or yellow.
- Cauliflower should be stored in the refrigerator in a large sealed plastic bag.
- The green leaves at the base of the cauliflower are edible and nutritious.
- If you plan on serving cauliflower raw be sure and soak it in salted water for about 10-15 minutes to get rid of any bugs.
- The greener the leaves, the fresher the cauliflower.

- Always remove tough part of stalk and leaves.
- Soak in lightly salted water to remove any insects.
- Separate bundles of florets leaving a small part of the stalk on each section.
- Center stalk should be removed for more even cooking.

- Lemon juice or white vinegar added to cooking water will help keep cauliflower white.
- Cauliflower may be cooked in a small amount of milk to help them retain their color and as a mild sweetener.
- Only cook cauliflower until it is just tender since overcooking will turn it somewhat bitter.
- Chunks of stale bread added to the cooking water; should eliminate most of the odor.

Cooking odors: can be reduced by changing the water during cooking.

- Never cook cauliflower in an aluminum or iron pot, this will turn the cauliflower yellow, brown or a nice blue-green.
- If you are going to cook a whole head all at once, be sure and cook it stem side down in about 3 quarts of water.

- In England, cauliflower is served on a bed of toast to absorb the excess water.
- Parmesan cheese and melted butter on cauliflower are European favorites.
- The most popular seasonings for cauliflower are tomato sauce, nutmeg, dill, and cheese sauces.

CELERY

- Never purchase celery that is limp.
- Crisp up celery by placing it in a bowl of ice water in the refrigerator for 45 minutes.
- Celery contains the oil "limonene" that may cause skin irritation in susceptible individuals. Limonene is also found in lemon and lime rinds.
- To store celery for a prolonged period of time, wrap the stalks tightly in aluminum foil
- The more white inner stalks are the most tender and flavorful.

- Soak celery in a bowl of lemon juice and water for 5 minutes and   it slow down the browning for a long period of time.
- Celery "strings", do not break down easily and should be removed with a potato or vegetable peeler before cooking or serving.

Always remove the "strings" before stuffing celery with cream cheese or peanut butter.

- The pectin in the celery cells break down easily when cooked producing a soft food in a very short period of time.
- Cooking celery in boiling water for about 2-3 minutes should suffice.

- The most popular seasonings for celery are onion powder, tarragon, parsley and red peppers.

CORN

Blue corn was the most popular corn of the American Indians of the Southwestern United States. Most of their bread staples were blue.

- Corn silk is actually the fertilizer for the corn kernels. If it is brown, don't buy the corn.
- When purchasing corn, the silk should be dry and never soggy.

- Corn kernels should be in even rows and the same size. If frost or disease has damaged the ear of corn, the rows will be uneven and the kernels will be different sizes.
- Never buy corn that has already been husked by the market, it is usually old corn and not very sweet.
- As soon as corn is picked its sugar starts converting to starch and loses its sweetness very quickly.
- Corn should be eaten fresh and not stored for more than 2 days. The fresher the corn is, the sweeter.

To remove the silk, try using a new plastic hairbrush.

- If you want creamed corn, just slice through the middle of each row before removing the kernels.
- To remove corn kernels from a cob, try using a shoehorn.
- Never add salt to the boiling water or it will toughen the corn.
- If you are going to barbecue corn, wrap it in tin foil and add a sprig of marjoram next to the ear of corn.

- When boiling corn-on-the-cob the corn kernels should be somewhat milky when pierced.
- A small amount of sugar in the water will help activate the natural sugars in the corn and provide a pleasant sweet flavor. The rule of thumb is 1 teaspoon to 1 quart of water.
- Best to place the corn into boiling water and never place corn in cold water waiting to boil.

- Corn cobs can be cooked in water and the liquid used for a soup base.
- The pot should be covered allowing steam to cook the corn that may not be covered with water.
- Corn-on-the-cob (1) can be placed in a microwave with husk removed by brushing with butter and wrapping in wax paper, twisting the ends.
- Corn-on-the-cob; can be roasted by rubbing the corn with butter then wrapping it in aluminum foil and baking at 375°F for 30-35 minutes.
- Never add salt to the cooking water, this will toughen the corn.
- Cooking corn in half milk and half water will produce a tender, sweet ear of corn.

Corn has the tendency to become tough the longer you cook it.

- When you sauté corn it only takes 3-4 minutes and should be stirred continually.
- One of the best methods of cooking corn is to steam it for 7-10 minutes.

Cooking corn in the husk

- In America the standard method is to remove the husk and stems before cooking, however, corn will be more tender if cooked in the husks.
- Corn-on-the-cob (1) can be placed in a microwave with the husk on for $3^1/_2$ minutes.
- Cook the corn on a grill.
- Corn can be grilled in the husks for about 20-30 minutes. Before placing on the grill it is best to soak the corn for 15 minutes so that they won't burn.
- It is best to soak the corn with the husks on, in a bowl or large pot of cold water for 15 minutes before peeling the husks halfway down and discarding the silk.

Corn can be grilled and should be removed from the grill when the kernels just start to swell or you will have popcorn. If you leave the husks on, soak the corn in water so that the husks will not burn before the corn is done.

- The exposed kernels should be rubbed with butter and the husks replaced.
- Wrap each ear in aluminum foil and place on medium hot coals.
- Grill the ears for 30-40 minutes turning a quarter turn every 10 minutes.

- Cooked corn may be chilled and used in salads.
- The most popular seasonings for corn are bacon bits, chili powder, flavored butter or a mild cheese.

Polenta

- If you can buy "fine-ground" cornmeal it will work better than the coarse. The "finc-ground" cornmeal is actually called polenta in Italy.
- Polenta can be purchased in most supermarkets if you don't have the time to make it.

  A wooden spoon is preferred when making polenta.

- When making polenta, to avoid lumps, just use cold water instead of warm or hot water, which are what most recipes call for. Cold, lightly salted water will not cause the starch to lump together. As the polenta cooks, the starch in the corn will remain in a state of semi-separation and will remain that way.
- The cornmeal needs to be added slowly in a thin steam and whisked continually.

Popcorn

The first recorded history of popcorn in the form we know it today can be traced back to the American Indians about 500 years ago, who tossed whole ears of corn into a fire and caught the popcorn as it popped. Early explorers purchased the popcorn, which was strung and worm as a necklace.

Popcorn is composed of a complex carbohydrate (starch), and includes insoluble fiber (cellulose), which may help prevent constipation. It is always best, however, to drink plenty of fluids when consuming any large amount of insoluble fiber. Insoluble fiber tends to absorb water from the intestinal tract and will add bulk. The only risk that might exist would be if you ate a large tub of popcorn without drinking any liquids, then you may have a major traffic jam.

- Raw corn for popping is sold in many different grades. Most of the corn products sold in the supermarkets to produce popcorn have an expansion ratio of only 28:1, while those sold to movie theatres have an expansion ratio of 42:1. The oil to corn ratio of quality popcorn should be about 3 parts corn to 1 part of polyunsaturated oil.
- Old maids are kernels of corn that are too pooped to pop. These kernels usually have lost sufficient moisture and can be revived by just placing a handful of them into a sealed container with 1-2 tablespoons of water, then shake for at least 3-4 minutes. The container should then be placed in a cool (not cold) location for about 3 days. This should revive them and you should have no problem popping them.
- When making popcorn, the oil to corn ratio should be three parts of corn to one part of oil.
- Salt should only be added to fully cooked popcorn or it will become tough.

When the popcorn kernel is heated, the moisture inside turns to steam and as the pressure builds it has to vent and bursts the kernel. The explosion forms a fluffy white starch. Normal corn will not explode because it does not have as high moisture content as special popcorn. As soon as the popcorn is popped it is best to open the bag or remove the lid as soon as possible to avoid the popcorn absorbing the steam and becoming soggy. Popcorn should always be stored in a well-sealed container so that it will retain as much of its moisture as possible.

- Salt should never be included in packaged popcorn or placed in a popcorn popper. Salt should only be added after the popcorn has fully popped to keep the popcorn tender. Salt will cause the popcorn to become tough.
- It may be healthier to air pop your popcorn; however, all this does is make larger blossoms that are tougher and not as crispy.

CUCUMBER

- Make sure that the cucumber does not have any soft areas and is firm.
- The larger the standard cucumber, the more pithy it will probably be.

Large cucumbers tend to be more bitter than smaller cucumbers.

- English cucumbers are usually wrapped in plastic and are not bitter nor do they have any seeds. They are grown in hot houses and are sometimes called "hot house" cucumbers.

- Standard cucumbers may be waxed to prolong their shelf life by reducing loss of moisture.
- If the skin is waxed the cucumber should be peeled before use and it may also be bitter.
- Once a cucumber is peeled it will lose a high percentage of its vitamin C very quickly.

Since cucumbers do not have any starch, they do not sweeten and produce a sugar.

- If you are going to use cucumbers for pickling, never store them below 50°F or they will deteriorate.
- Only use glass, ceramic or plastic containers when pickling to avoid an acidic reaction that may ruin the pickles.
- Cucumbers should be stored in a plastic bag with holes and never stored in the coldest part of the refrigerator.
- Most cucumbers do not need to be peeled unless you are running into bitter ones. Fresh ones are the best and are rarely bitter.
- The best pickling cucumber is the Kirby. The smallest are the gherkin.

- To eliminate the bitterness, just cut about 1" off either end and rub the two exposed surfaces together in a circular motion and pull them apart to neutralize the chemical that causes bitterness.
- To remove the seeds, just slice the whole cucumber lengthwise and use a spoon to remove them.
- A layer of salt can be placed on the top of cucumber slices that have been placed on a dish in the refrigerator for 30 minutes to drain some of the moisture out and crisp them up. The salt can be removed with a piece of paper towel before adding to a salad.
- Hollowed out cucumbers make an excellent holder for dips.
- Salting a cucumber is another method of neutralizing the bitterness.
- To remove the seeds from a cucumber, try using a melon scoop.
- Save pickle juice and place a layer of cucumber slices on a dish covered with the juice in the refrigerator for 3-4 days to make cucumber pickles.
- Cucumbers used for pickling should be used within 24 hours of harvesting.

- Remove a small piece from the blossom end of the cucumber before pickling to avoid the pickle becoming soft and mushy.
- Cooking cucumbers with fish dishes adds an excellent flavor treat.
- If you are going to sauté cucumber, they are best, sautéed in unsalted butter with a small amount of dill.

- The most popular seasonings for cucumbers are mint, garlic and dill.

Marinating Cucumbers

- Cucumbers are marinated best in tarragon vinegar with fresh dill and kosher salt. Black pepper is sometimes added for taste.

EGGPLANT

- Eggplants get bitter the older they get, try and buy a young, fresh one.
- Never purchase an eggplant that has soft spots.
- May be called "aubergine" or "morelle" in some cookbooks.

Male eggplants are sweeter than female eggplants since males have less, seeds that are bitter. To tell them apart, the make has a well-rounded bottom and a smooth, even stem area. The female has a narrow bottom with an indentation in the stem area.

- Try not to buy eggplants with an indented base, these will have more bitter seeds.
- Eggplants should be used 1-2 days after purchase and stored in a cool, dry location.

- If the eggplant is young, the skin will be tender and can be left on.
- After peeling an eggplant, spray with a solution of powdered vitamin C and water to slow down the discoloration. Lemon juice may also be brushed on.
- If you batter eggplant it will reduce the amount of fat it will absorb.

- Any coating placed on vegetables will adhere better if the battered food is placed in the refrigerator for 30-40 minutes before frying.

If you go to the Near East, every household has a wooden knife or one carved from bone, which is only used to cut eggplant. If a metal knife (except for stainless steel) is used it will turn black as well as turning the eggplant black.

- For quick-cooking eggplant dishes you may want to salt the eggplant slices, allow it to sit for a few minutes then drain off the juices. This will eliminate the bitterness that may occur.
- In almost all instances it is best to place the eggplant slices in a colander and lightly salt them all and allow them to sit for 30 minutes to remove some of the excess water before preparing.
- The eggplant needs to be thoroughly dried before preparing it.
- If you are going to grill or bake eggplant slice, place an "X" with a sharp knife in the center of each slice to assure even grilling or baking.

Eggplant will absorb more cooking or frying fat than any other vegetable.

- To reduce the absorption of fat, place the slices on a cookie sheet and lightly salt, then cover each layer with wax paper, place another cookie sheet on top and add a bowl filled with water as a weight for about 30 minutes, wipe with paper towel before frying
- Eggplant cooks fast and should only be added to cooking dishes during the final 8-10 minutes.

- The most popular seasonings for eggplant are oregano, garlic, marjoram, and Parmesan cheese.

FENNEL

- For a unique pleasant flavor when baking whole fish, try placing thin fennel strips under the fish.
- Has a slight flavor of aniseed, which is similar to licorice.
- Don't purchase fennel if there is any browning.

- The fennel core is normally removed before cooking.

Fennel provides an excellent flavor for soups when pureed.

- The stalks and greenery should be removed before cooking fennel.

- The flavor of fennel becomes more delicate, the more it is cooked.
- If fennel is halved lengthwise it should be boiled for about 8-10 minutes in 1" of water.
- Fennel slices should be steamed for about 10 minutes; halves will take 20 minutes.
- Fennel can be placed in a microwave if you cut it into quarters lengthwise and place the equivalent of 2 bulbs in $1/4$ cup of water for about 7 minutes.
- Pre-cooked fennel bulbs can be grilled if you boil them for 10 minutes, cut them into wedges and then grill for about 7 minutes
- To stir-fry fennel, cut into $1/4$" slices and stir-fry for 1 minute in 1 tablespoon of olive oil
- Fennel adds excellent flavor when added to other dishes about 15 minutes before they are done cooking.

- Fennel greens can be used as a garnish.

GREENS (SALAD)

There are thousands of varieties of green salads and hundreds of ingredients that can be added. The base of the salad is lettuce or a similar green leafy vegetable. However, you need to take care when using certain leafy vegetables since many have a somewhat bitter flavor and not too desirable when too much is added to a salad. Salads should also never be piled high over the rim of a salad bowl and should be complimented with a variety of other vegetables depending on the type of salad.

- For in-depth information about individual salad ingredients and how to choose them in the supermarket, see "Grandmother's Kitchen Wisdom or The 21st Century Reference Guide to Cooking Secrets & Helpful Household Hints" by Dr. Myles H. Bader.

- When possible avoid using iceberg lettuce as much as possible due to its very low nutritional levels
- Make sure whatever lettuce you are purchasing is free of blemishes and that the stem is white and that there is no hint of brown.
- Use stainless steel knives to cut greens to reduce the risk of browning.
- Fresh lettuce or greens always smell fresh and never have a sour smell.
- Salad greens will last for a longer period of time if they are washed and placed in the crisper, drawer in the refrigerator with a piece of paper towel under them. Make sure the greens are good and dry before storing.
- If you need to store the greens for a few days, remove any leaves and the stem before storing them.
- If you are using iceberg lettuce, tap the bottom core hard on the counter and twist it out before storing the lettuce since the core tends to increase the loss of liquid.
- When making Caesar salad with a bottled dressing, place the romaine lettuce pieces in a large plastic bag, then add the dressing and shake just before serving.

Any pasta that is added to salads should be washed first to stop the pasta from sticking together.

- Always serve salad on a well-chilled plate to keep the salad crisp.
- Wooden salad bowls should be wiped off with pieces of waxed paper after being washed and dried to seal the surface and preserve the wood.
- The greener the salad greens, the higher the nutrient value.
- Salt causes greens to wilt; never salt before serving.
- Most salad greens have a protective coating that keeps water from entering but allows oils and salad dressing to stick to the surface.
- Place a small inverted bowl on the bottom of your large salad bowl so that the excess water from washing will run under the bowl and allow the greens to remain dry.
- Salad greens must be completely dry before using them in a salad.
- A salad spinner should be used to remove excess water from greens, then dry the greens in paper towel.
- If your lettuce gets droopy, just place the head into a large bowl with very hot water then immediately remove and plunge the head into a bowl of ice water. Cold water will enter the cells easier and crisp up the lettuce.

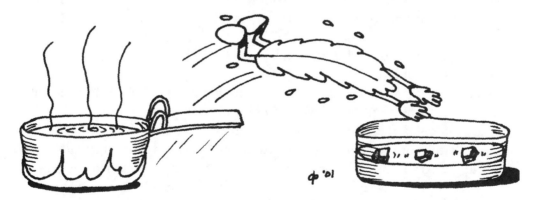

- Never use chicory, endive or escarole by themselves or the salad will be bitter. They should be mixed with sweeter greens for the best results.
- Croutons should added just before serving and included in the final toss.
- Try and balance different textures.
- When tossing a salad, make sure that the heavier vegetables are placed on the bottom and the lighter lettuce on top, toss and serve immediately.
- Greens can be stored for 2-3 days in a salad spinner if it is covered.
- Allow $1/4$ medium head of lettuce per person.

- If you add nuts to a salad, add them just before serving.

  Tomatoes used on green salads should be at room temperature when added to the salad and always last, just before serving.

- When using wine vinegar on salads, be sure that it is of a good quality. Poor grades of wine vinegar tend to turn some greens bitter.

Arugula

- Provides a peppery flavor and goes well with grilled portabello mushrooms.
- Arugula has high iron content.

Belgium Endive

Endive was accidentally grown when a farmer in Belgium hid chicory root in his cellar in 1840 so that he would not have to pay the chicory root tax. Chicory root was used to prepare coffee and was taxed. When he eventually found it, it had sprouted and was popular since fresh leafed vegetables were scarce.

- Has a slightly bitter flavor, but lots of crunch

Bibb

- Bibb lettuce can be purchased in two varieties Boston and Kentucky. Both arc excellent and should not be overpowered with dressing.

Boston

- Boston lettuce bruises easily and needs to be handled with care.

Dandelion Greens

- If dandelion greens are used they should be young leaves since as they age they tend to get bitter with age.

  Don't harvest this green at home if you have any outside pets.

Escarole

- Has a tart flavor.

Iceberg

- Iceberg lettuce has less, flavor than any other lettuce and should have other lettuce added.

Radicchio

- Radicchio can be added to green salads for color, but only use a small amount since it is a little bitter.

  Sea salt tends to bring out the flavor of many foods much better than table salt. If your dish is a little bitter, sea salt can remove the bitterness, especially from dishes that contain mushrooms or radicchio.

Romaine

- Romaine lettuce has a somewhat sweet flavor and is used in Caesar salads.

Watercress

- When using watercress, be sure and remove the thick stem.
- Has a somewhat peppery crispness.

Cobb Salad

The Cobb Salad; was invented at the brown Derby Restaurant in Los Angeles in 1926 by Bob Cobb who found a way to use leftovers. The Cobb Salad; was popularized by Sid Grauman, the owner of Grauman's Chinese Theatre.

- The original salad was composed of avocado, celery, tomatoes, chives, watercress, chicken, hard-boiled eggs, bacon and Roquefort cheese.
- Blue cheese is usually substituted for the Roquefort cheese since it less expensive and a vinaigrette salad dressing.

EDIBLE FLOWERS FOR SALADS

Historical records date flower consumption, back thousands of years to the Chinese, Greeks and Romans. Even if a flower is not poisonous it may not be edible since many can cause allergic reactions and illness.

Anise hyssop flowers	• Anise flavor (similar to licorice) used on salads and fruits.
Arugula flowers	• Has a mild peppery flavor in salads and sandwiches.
Basil	• Different varieties have different flavors. • Most taste like lemon mint.
Bee Balm	• Frequently used to replace bergamot. • Can be used to make tea.
Borage	• Has a mild cucumber flavor and is used on salads and in drinks.
Calendula	• Has a slight peppery flavor, petals are great in salads. • Tastes a little like saffron. • Somewhat spicy, peppery taste
Carnation	• Tastes like spicy peppery cloves.
Chamomile	• Used on salads mostly for garnish. • Has a mild apple flavor.
Chive flowers	• Has a mild, onion flavor.
Cornflower	• Sweet, spicy clove-like flavor.
Daisies	• Only use the petals, the centers are too hard and not too tasty.

Dandelion flowers	• Somewhat bitter taste. • *Commonly fried in butter similar to mushrooms in the Southern United States.* • Used for making a potent wine.
Day lilies	• Used to garnish salads and decorate cakes. • Many species are not edible and have a laxative effect
Fennel	• Sweet licorice taste.
Gardenia	• Light, sweet flavor.
Hollyhocks	• Can be stuffed with salad for a different treat. • Flavor is very bland.
Honeysuckle	• Tastes just like the aroma. • The berries are poisonous.
Jasmine	• Has a sweet flavor. • Used in teas.
Lavender	• Has a strong flavor and needs to be used sparingly. • Lavender oil is poisonous to some individuals.
Marigold	• Use the petals only in salads. • Has a somewhat spicy, bitter flavor.
Mustard flower	• Has a somewhat mild taste. • Some people are allergic to it.
Nasturium	• Buds are often used in place of capers. • Has sweet, peppery flavor.

Okra	• Similar taste to squash blossoms
Pansies	• Usually has a mild grape-like flavor. • Some are a little too tart.
Radish	• Sweeter than the radish.
Rose petals	• Has a very delicate taste and can be used in salads and other foods. • Remove the bitter white portion of the petal.
Rosemary	• A somewhat pine-like, sweet savory flavor.
Safflower	• Similar to saffron but without the aroma or the strong flavor.
Squash blossoms	• Has a mild flavor similar to zucchini and can be sautéed. • Squash blossoms are edible and make a great garnish for many dishes. • Squash blossom can be battered and fried. • Squash blossoms will always be soft and somewhat limp.
Thyme	• Taste is similar to lemon and has a nice aroma.
Violets	• Excellent: in salads or honey.

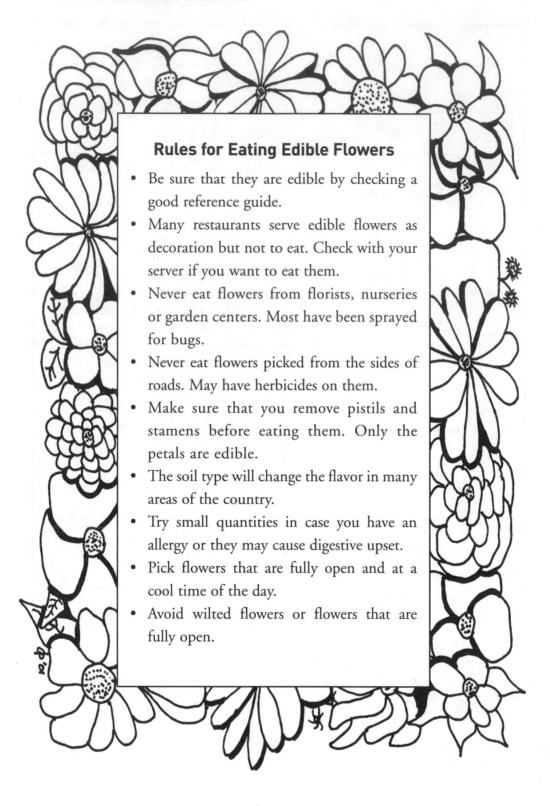

Rules for Eating Edible Flowers

- Be sure that they are edible by checking a good reference guide.
- Many restaurants serve edible flowers as decoration but not to eat. Check with your server if you want to eat them.
- Never eat flowers from florists, nurseries or garden centers. Most have been sprayed for bugs.
- Never eat flowers picked from the sides of roads. May have herbicides on them.
- Make sure that you remove pistils and stamens before eating them. Only the petals are edible.
- The soil type will change the flavor in many areas of the country.
- Try small quantities in case you have an allergy or they may cause digestive upset.
- Pick flowers that are fully open and at a cool time of the day.
- Avoid wilted flowers or flowers that are fully open.

HORSERADISH

- Make sure that you remove the fibrous core before using it.
- The fumes from grating horseradish can irritate your eyes and nose.•
- The color of horseradish is determined by the medium it is sold with. White will have vinegar in it and red had beet juice.
- Horseradish will only remain fresh for 3-4 weeks before turning bitter.
- For a quick roast beef, horseradish sauce: mix 1 cup of sour cream with 2 tablespoons of white horseradish.
- For a professional horseradish sauce use the following recipe:

Roast Beef Horseradish Sauce

1 cup of heavy cream
¼ cup of prepared horseradish (drained well)
Dash of salt

The cream should be whipped until it is just barely stiff. Do not make whipped cream. Temper the horseradish with a small amount of the whipped cream by mixing it into the horseradish, then adding the balance of the whipped cream and the dash of salt.

KALE

- Kale should be used as soon as possible since it becomes bitter when stored.

   Use only the kale leaves; discard the tough stem and ribs.

- Flowering kale (salad savory) is best used for decoration than in a salad.

KOHLRABI

- Before preparing, peel and shred the kohlrabi bulbs and squeeze out any excess moisture.

LEEKS

- Leeks were originally cultivated from Oriental garlic.
- The white area should never be fibrous.
- Never buy leeks if they have yellow-spotted leaves. The leaves should be bright and crisp.

Leek bulbs may be planted and the green shoots used as chives.

- Wash thoroughly since dirt tends to get between the leaf layers, split the leek and spread out the layers for a thorough rinsing.

- May be cooked whole or sliced and used in soups.

- The green leek ends are usually tough and should only be placed in a cheese-cloth bag and used to flavor soups.
- Leeks are closely related to the onion family but with a milder flavor.
- If the leeks are split lengthwise it will take about 5-8 minutes to cook them in boiling water or to steam them.
- Leeks can be prepared by slicing them and sautéing in a small amount of butter and seasoning with coriander.
- The entire leek can be cooked in a pot of boiling water for about 10-12 minutes or until tender.

- If you are going to use leeks in another dish after they have been boiled, then rinse them under cold water to stop the cooking.

MUSHROOMS

Mushrooms have been cultivated by Asian civilizations for 2,000 years and evidence has proven that the Romans and Greeks cultivated mushrooms. Commercial mushroom growing began in France in the 17th century. It takes between 9-12 weeks for a mature mushroom to grow big enough to harvest.

- Always choose fresh mushrooms; never buy pre-packaged.
- Never store; mushrooms in a plastic container or wrap them in plastic wrap since both tend to retain moisture.
- The outer skin of a mushroom contains a large percentage of the flavor. Never peel a mushroom.

Never store mushrooms on top of each other or they will develop mold very quickly.

- Dried mushrooms; will last 3-4 months if stored in a cool dry location.
- Wild mushrooms tend to dry out faster than most other mushroom varieties and should be used as soon as possible after harvesting.
- Fresh mushrooms have a shelf life of only 2-3 days and should be stored in an open container. Containers that retain moisture with a lid will cause mushrooms to go bad in a few hours.

- Never clean or remove the stem before you are ready to use them and be sure that the gills on button mushrooms are not showing when you purchase them. Sealed up mushrooms will last longer.
- Mushrooms should not be washed until just before being used and if covered with a damp paper towel will last about 3-4 days under refrigeration.
- Never peel the mushroom cap or you will lose 40% of the flavor.
- Chef's use an egg-slicer to slice mushroom caps only and should be performed in one quick motion or the cap will fall apart.
- To keep mushroom caps white, just wipe the cap with a piece of paper towel that has been dipped in lemon juice.
- When washing mushrooms, it should be done by hand and never allow them to soak or they will become mushy, dry immediately before cooking.

- Stems should be discarded or at least $1/4$ inch cut from each stem before using since they contain "hydrazine," which in large quantities is not healthy.
- Spraying the surface of mushroom caps with a solution of vitamin C (ascorbic acid) and water will keep the mushrooms white.
- Dried mushrooms; can be plumped up by immersing them in boiling water for about 1 minute.
- Raw stems especially should not be eaten since they contain the majority of the "hydrazine," however cooking tends to neutralize the chemical.

Braised Mushrooms

Braised mushrooms are cooked over low heat and in a liquid with seasonings and usually a few vegetables. The mushrooms are porous enough to absorb flavors, which gives them a great flavor. Use a deep 8-10 inch skillet and be sure that the lid fits tight. Prepare a normal sauté using clarified butter and add the mushrooms as soon as has heated up. Stir until the mushrooms are just starting to brown (about 3 minutes), then add $1/3$-cup of chicken broth (or wine or tomato juice) and $1/4$ cup of finely diced onions and carrots, then bring to a boil. Cover the skillet and just simmer until the mushrooms and vegetables are tender, which usually takes about 3-5 minutes more.

- Mushrooms should be removed and cooking discontinued as soon as they start to darken.
- Sautéing mushrooms in olive oil will make the flavor more intense.
- When sautéing mushrooms and they are steaming in liquid and not browning, the heat is too low or the pan is too small. Transfer the mushrooms to a larger pan or raise the heat.

Oven-Roasted Mushrooms

Use a baking dish that is just big enough to hold the mushrooms in a single layer. Lightly brush the bottom of the dish with clarified butter or spray with vegetable oil (not olive). Heat the oven to 450°F; then add 3 partially crushed garlic cloves to the dish and place in the oven. Sprinkle the mushrooms with salt and pepper to taste and mix the

mushrooms with the garlic and seasoning. Stir occasionally until the mushrooms are browned and the garlic has softened. Cooking should take about 20 minutes.

- It takes about 4-6 minutes in 2 tablespoons of butter to cook 1 pound of mushrooms.
- Large mushroom caps can be grilled in about 8 minutes on medium hot heat.
- When broiling mushrooms, brush them with olive oil.

- The best herbs to compliment the flavor of mushrooms are parsley, nutmeg, dill, cayenne and paprika.

TYPES OF MUSHROOMS

Angel Trumpet

- Best sautéed in unsalted butter with a small hint of fresh lemon juice.

Button

The button mushroom: was first developed in France by Oliver de Serres, who was an agronomist in the court of Louis XIV. It was called champignon de Paris and in France is also known just as the Parisian mushroom.

- Very versatile cooked almost any way and used raw in salads.
- Button mushrooms that have a closed stem should be cleaned with a damp piece of paper towel to avoid water retention.

Make sure that the caps are closed and the gills are not showing.

Cepe (porcino)

- Cepe mushrooms have a spongy surface and a solid brown cap instead of gills and are one of the best tasting mushrooms.
- This the best tasting wild mushroom, which is imported from either France or Italy.

Chanterelle

- Chanterelle mushrooms; should be a bright yellow to somewhat orange color with no soft spots.
- Goes well with poultry dishes.
- Best sautéed with unsalted butter and shallots.

Cremini

- Best grilled and sprinkled with olive oil and lemon juice.

Enoki

- Enoki mushrooms have a small cap and long thin stems. The caps should be white and not yellowish. Separate the mushrooms at the stem end before using.
- Used in salads or stir, fries.
- Will provide mild, sweet flavor.

Fairy Ring

- Best when cooked with poultry, stews and soups.

Hen-of-the-Woods

- Needs long, slow cooking to give it the right, tender texture.

Matsutake

- Best sautéed or grilled.

Morel

- Morel mushrooms are more cone-shaped and have a light brown cap. They should be slightly spongy.

  Best in cream sauces: or sautéed with butter and garlic.

- They will have a very intense flavor.

Oyster

- Oyster mushrooms have a fan-shaped cap that is a more grayish-brown color. They should be no more than about 1¹/₂-inches in diameter. Large ones are not as flavorful.
- Best used in cream sauces and gratins.
- Have a dense, chewy texture.
- Can be used raw in salads, but are best in dishes.

Portobello

- Portobello mushrooms have a very hearty flavor and a large circular cap with a long stem which, tends to get a little woody and is usually removed and not used.
- Never wash them until you are ready to use them.
- The stems are best for soups and stews.
- Never freeze portobello mushrooms.
- Cooked portobello mushrooms can be frozen for about 2-3 months. Make sure they are sealed in as airtight a bag as possible.
- Never peel the skin off a portobello since it has the ability to retain flavor and spices.
- To sauté, just pace the whole or pieces in a skillet with a small amount of oil or clarified butter. It only takes about 6 minutes to cook them. Make sure that you leave adequate space around each mushroom or they will not brown evenly.
- To roast them, just place the caps on a cookie sheet gill side down and roast for 20 minutes at 425°F.
- Gently wipe the mushroom with a damp cloth and do not immerse in water. If you feel that there is too much grime, place the mushrooms in a colander and quickly rinse them.
- The longer you cook, the more, firm the mushroom will become.
- Needs a good cleaning since most tend to retain the black soil they are grown it and will be gritty.

Shiitake

- Shiitake mushrooms have a dark brown cap that is somewhat floppy and can be about 8-9 inches in diameter. The edges should curl under. Stems should be removed.
- Best cooked with poultry, stir-fry or grilled.

  The stems are tougher than the cap and many chefs will not use them in dishes.

- The stems can be used to flavor stock but should then be strained out and discarded.
- Provide a rich flavor to sauces.

Truffles

Truffles are considered one of the world's most expensive foods at close to $500 per pound.

- Impossible to cultivate they must be found in the wild.
- Have a somewhat garlicky flavor, which is why they are so prized.
- Very expensive, but worth it.
- You can purchase two types: the black from France and Italy or the white from Northern Italy.
- They are usually sliced or grated raw over foods to retain their intense flavor.

  Recently truffles have become available in cans and as a paste in tubes.

- Be sure and peel black truffles before using. The peelings can be used to flavor soups, stocks and stews.

Wood Ear (black tree fungus)

- Used in Chinese soups and stir-fries.
- Sold mostly as dried.
- Best in casseroles and stews.

Stuffed Mushrooms

For stuffed mushrooms, break away the stalk from the cap and clean out the cap. Wash out the inside and dry with paper towel. Arrange the caps on a cookie sheet that has been oiled and lightly moisten them with butter or spray oil. Cook in oven for no more than 5 minutes at 325°F then stuff.

OKRA

- The smaller the pod, the more tender. The larger the pod, the more fibrous and tough.
- Okra compliments tomatoes, corn and onions.
- Okra should be as fresh as possible for the best results.
- Ideally, okra should be blanched in salted water before being used in salads or other dishes.
- Always remove a portion from the stem end before cooking whole or in lengthwise strips.

Okra can be used as a thickening agent for soups and stews since it tends to produce a thick carbohydrate substance that also contains pectin and gums from seed capsules.

- Okra can be grilled by brushing with olive oil and cooking an medium-high heat turning and grilling for 3 minutes on each side.
- To avoid "roping," add one teaspoon of white vinegar to the cooking water. Okra tends to become stringy very quickly when cooked.
- To boil okra, cover whole okra with water and boil covered with a lid for 8-10 minutes.
- To steam okra it will take about 15-20 minutes.
- The best spices to compliment okra are coriander, garlic and sage.

ONIONS

- Always purchase heavy onions for their size with no soft spots
- If you only need $1/2$ and onion, use the top and leave the skin on the root end then store in a glass jar in the refrigerator. Should last for 4-5 days.
- Lemon juice or white vinegar will remove onion odor from your hands.
- Plastic bags are somewhat porous and onion aroma will leak through.

- Leeks may be substituted for onions in most recipes.
- One tablespoon of onion powder may be substituted for 1 medium onion in most recipes.
- Store onions in a cool, dry location and if they touch each other be sure that the skins are intact.
- Wet necks on onions possibly indicate decay.

- Another method of preparing fried onion rings is to season them with salt and pepper then sprinkle a small amount of oil and vinegar on them and allow them marinate for 30 minutes before dipping in batter and frying them.
- When you slice an onion hold the onion from the stem and only cut the root end off.
- If the onion has a strong flavor, just soak the onion in ice water for about 45 minutes and change the water twice.
- To peel a standard onion, just cut off the root end and peel under cold running tap water.

When onions sprout, the sprouts can be cut off and used in salads. The main part of the onion will not be very good to use.

- Onions occasionally become bitter when added to salad dressings. To avoid this problem, just place the sliced onions in a small bowl of ice water with 1-2 teaspoons of apple cider vinegar.
- Onion juice is an excellent flavoring for many dishes. Place the onion in a blender or food processor and puree.
- To eliminate tearing, just place the onion into the freezer for 5-10 minutes before slicing.

- When cooking onions and garlic together, always cook the onions first for about $1/2$ of their cooking time before adding the garlic or the garlic will overcook.

- When you cook onions, the sulfur turns into sugars. This process is called "Maillard Reaction."
- Prepare dried onions by thinly slicing onions and place the rings on a cookie sheet. Place the pan into a pre-heated 275°F oven for about 45 minutes or until they are dry. They will stay under refrigeration in a well-sealed container for about 3-4 weeks.

If you want to keep whole onions whole while boiling, just cut an "X" about ¼ inch deep on the stem end to release the steam that builds up and tears the onion apart.

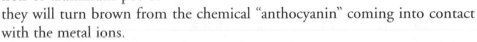

- If you want to keep onions white, never cook them in an iron or aluminum pot or they will turn brown from the chemical "anthocyanin" coming into contact with the metal ions.
- To improve the flavor of onions that will be used in casseroles or similar dishes, just sauté the onions in corn or olive oil for a few minutes to sweeten them up.

Rapid boiling will cause onions to fall apart. Best to just simmer them.

- When sautéing onions the best way to tell if they are cooked is when the onion liquid stops evaporating and the oil used for sautéing starts to separate out.
- To roast onions place them into a baking dish so that they stand upright, butter lightly and bake at 350°F for 30-40 minutes, basting occasionally with melted butter.
- To reduce the intense flavor of a pungent onion just change the water once or twice during the cooking process.

- If onions become too soft during cooking, just immerse them in a bowl of ice cold water and refrigerate for 45 minutes.
- The best seasonings for onions are sage, nutmeg and thyme.

- Onion juice from $1/2$ an onion can be added to many dishes to provide the onion flavor without adding the onions.

Bermuda

- Mild onions are the yellow, Bermuda and the purple-skinned.
- Bermuda onions are the most popular for salads and hamburgers.

Caramelizing Onions

- When onions are cooked, the sulfur in the onions evaporates.
- The sulfur gives the onions its pungency that makes you cry.
- Some of the onions complex carbohydrates (starches) break down and turn into sugars causing sweetness.

Caramelizing browns the sugar in onions. If you have patience, the result will be great caramelized, onions.

- To caramelize 2 pounds of onions it should take $1^1/2$-hours.
- The onions need to release their liquid and soften slowly before you attempt to brown them.
- The pan should be covered with a tight-fitting lid and on a low flame.
- Make sure that there is enough fat in the pan so that they do not dry out too much and start to stick.
- If you are using a 10-inch pan you will need about 2-3 tablespoons of butter or a combination of butter and extra virgin olive oil.
- Check the onions after 45 minutes to be sure that they are not drying out.
- After about an hour, remove the lid and increase the heat to medium (not high) at which time the sugars should start to brown.
- After the lid is removed, you may want to add some stock or white wine.
- Continue cooking until the liquid has completely evaporated.
- For every pound of onions you will get 1 cup of caramelized onions.

Onion Rings

- After breading onion rings place them in the refrigerator for 30 minutes so that the breading will adhere better.

Make sure they are very dry before breading them.

- Great onion rings should be made from thick slices of onions, preferably Maui, Walla Walla or Vidalia onions and not sliced thin.
- Slice the rings $^1/_4$ inch thick and then soak them in ice water in the refrigerator for 2 hours.
- Onion rings should be fried at 375°F and never any more for the best results.
- It should take about 4-5 minutes to fry the onion rings.

Pearl Onions

- Pearl onions; can be easily peeled by boiling for about 1 minute them immediately immersing them into a bowl of ice water for a few seconds. Pinch the root end and pull and the skin will come off in one piece.
- When adding pearl onions to a pickling solution, be sure and prick them all over with a long sewing needle so that they will absorb the pickling solution.
- Pearl onions are the choice for making cream sauces.
- Commonly used in stews dropped in about 15 minutes before the stew has finished cooking.

Purple Onion (Red)

- Best for salads or on sandwiches since it is relatively mild.
- Best not to cook purple onions with other foods since the color fades and turns everything red.

Shallots

- Very versatile cooking onion used in many dishes.
- Shallots should be plump with dry skins and no signs of mold.
- If your recipe calls for shallot, it is referring to 1 clove (or section). Do not put the whole shallot in the recipe.

Spanish Onions

- Spanish onions are light brown and will caramelize more easily than most other onions.
- These are mild enough to eat raw and are frequently used on hamburgers.

Sweet Onions

- Sweet onions are the Maui, Walla Walla and Vidalia.

  All sweet onions have high water content and will not last very long.

- They are naturally sweet and can be used in any dish, especially salads.

White Onions

- White onions are usually used in soups, stews or dishes that are creamed.

PARSNIPS

- Do not purchase if blemished or limp.
- Have a celery-like, nutty flavor.

  Large parsnips are usually somewhat woody and not that good.

- Basic preparation is the same as carrots for all dishes.
- Have a strong cell wall and are more easily digested if at least blanched or cooked.

- Can be used in salads if blanched first.
- The ends should be cut off before preparing.

- Parsnips can be steamed to soften for 15-20 minutes.
- If peeled and cubed parsnips can be placed in the microwave in 2-3 table-spoons of water for about 10 minutes on high.
- Be careful not to overcook since they turn mushy very easily.
- Whole parsnips can be boiled for 12-20 minutes to soften.

- Very popular cooked, placed through a dicer and mashed.
- Add to stews or soups while they are fairly firm.
- In France, parsnips are a favorite for flavoring stocks.

PEAS (DRIED)

- Dried peas are specially grown and can be frozen for 10 years.
- Dried peas are actually mature seeds that contain twice the starch of fresh peas.
- Peas are an excellent source of protein.
- Make sure there are no worm holes in any of the beans and that they are not all shriveled up.
- When split peas are used in soups the water will be a good source of B vitamins.

- The yellow dried beans are preferred in France and are always prepared pureed.
- Re-hydrate the beans by soaking overnight and changing the water twice to eliminate an intestinal gas problem in susceptible individuals.
- Dried beans can be more easily re-hydrated by placing the beans in a pot of water, then bringing to a boil and allowed to stand for about 2 hours.

Never cook the beans in the same water that they have been soaking in since soaking can release a complex sugar that causes flatulence.

- Never salt the water the beans are cooking in or it will toughen the beans.

- Beans will retain heat after they have finished cooking and if used cold should be placed into a bowl of ice water for a few seconds. If used for soups or stews there is no problem.
- Cooked dried beans will last for 4-5 days in the refrigerator after they have been cooked.

PEAS (FRESH GREEN)

- Never buy peas if the pods are shriveled.
- The pods have flavor and are frequently used by European chefs to flavor soups and stews.
- Pods can be frozen in a well-sealed plastic bag for up to 3 months.
- Do not wash the pods if you are going to store them.

- Peas should never be cooked with an acidic vegetable such as tomatoes or they will lose their color.
- Peas are easy to overcook and will lose their flavor and color.
- Remove the peas from the pods just before using them, then just pop the pod open after snapping off the stem and run your fingers under the peas to dislodge them.

Never add baking soda to the cooking water or it will reduce the nutrient value of the peas about 35% and reduce the flavor.

- Peas can be soaked in sugar water for 15 minutes and used in salads.
- Snow peas are not removed from the pods. The complete pod is served in salads or steamed.
- Most frozen peas do not have to be de-frosted if used in stews or soups.

- Peas can be boiled in a full pot of water for 30 seconds.
- Peas can be cooked in their pods. The pods will open and release the peas to float to the surface.
- Peas take about 4 minutes to steam.

- A sprig of fresh mint is an excellent flavoring for peas.
- Peas can be removed from the water with a strainer.
- The best seasonings for peas are dill, basil, mint, and onion powder.

PEPPERS (HOT)

- Peppers should be firm and not mushy.
- Red peppers are more nutritious than green peppers.
- Rubber gloves should be worn when working with hot peppers.

Capsaicin can be neutralized with almost any dairy product, which is why sour cream is sometimes used on extra spicy Mexican dishes.

- Mole is made with chili peppers and spices, some of which may actually sweeten the sauce.
- The color should not be dull.

- To reduce the hotness in hot peppers, just remove the ribs and seeds then wash out the inside with cold water. The seeds and ribs contain about 80% of the capsaicin that causes the hotness.
- To reduce the hotness you can also soak the peppers in salt water after you remove the seeds and ribs.

- When peeling peppers make sure that you do not wash them or you will lose about 35% of the flavor.
- To keep peppers crisp when canning, place a grape leaf or two into the jar.

- Green peppers may lose their color when cooked, since the chlorophyll fades. Red and yellow peppers rarely lose their color due to the carotenoids.
- One method of roasting peppers is to place them on a cookie sheet that has been foil-lined, then place the cookie sheet under the broiler at 450°F for about 10 minutes.
- If you roast them on top of a burner, just remove them when the skins start to turn black.
- Never breathe the fumes when roasting chili. The fumes will irritate your throat, eyes and nose.

- If you over spice a dish with hot peppers, just add a few slices of raw potato and simmer for 15-20 minutes, stirring occasionally.

Common Hot Peppers

Anaheim peppers — can be purchased either red or green and are only moderately hot.

Ancho peppers — are usually found dried and flat, are moderately hot and ground up for salsa and sauces.

Cascabel peppers — are moderately hot with seeds that rattle.

Cayenne peppers — are one of the hottest and usually dried and made into chili spice.

Habanero peppers - are the hottest peppers grown with a bite that does not go away quickly unless you drink milk.

Jalapeno peppers — are usually fairly hot and almost always sold green. If you find a red one it will curl your toes.

Scotch Bonnet peppers — are very, very hot and are yellow and lantern-shaped.

Serrano peppers — are very hot and used in Mexico to prepare chili.

PEPPERS (SWEET, BELL)

- Make sure that the peppers are heavy for their size, have a shiny skin and a vivid color (not faded).
- Red bell peppers are actually green peppers that have ripened for a longer period of time.

- Bell peppers make an excellent dip or small pickle holder.
- Remove the ribs and seeds using the side of a tablespoon.
- The stem end can also be hit against a hard surface thus loosening the seed core and making it easy to just pull out.

To eliminate the "burp" factor related to bell peppers, just use a vegetable peeler to remove the skin before using the pepper. The complex sugar is more concentrated in the skin, which is the main cause of people burping.

- If you are canning peppers, add a grape leaf or two and it will keep them crisp.
- When chopping or slicing bell peppers always cut from the fleshy inside not the shiny skin side. The skin is tough and hard to cut evenly.

- Purple peppers will not stay purple if heated; they will turn back to their original color, green.
- If you wish to roast bell peppers, just slice them in half, remove the ribs and seeds and place them on a cookie sheet that has been lined with tin foil. Place

the cookie sheet under the broiler until the skins just turn black. Remove and place them into a plastic bag for 15 minutes before peeling to allow the steam to loosen the skins.

- When stuffing peppers you can keep the skins soft and more pliable by just rubbing olive oil on the skins and allow the skins to rest for 1 hour.
- Stuffed peppers should be cut crosswise, not lengthwise to support the filling better.
- Pepper seeds do contain flavor that can improve the dish and a few seeds should be added.

SCALLIONS

- Scallions usually have a somewhat milder flavor than standard onions.
- The white portion of the scallion is a little more potent than the green tops and can be mixed to provide a somewhat stronger seasoning.

Scissors are the best method of cutting scallions.

- When scallions are mixed with sour cream the mixture should be used and not stored.
- Before you slice a scallion crosswise, it is best to make one vertical cut all the way down starting at the root to the tip. This will allow all the rings to separate easily providing you with additional pieces.

SPINACH

- The darker the leaves the better and the more nutritious. Be sure that they are crisp and do not have yellow spots.
- When storing spinach, always remove the stem.
- Always leave the pot uncovered when cooking spinach or the steam buildup will cause the leaves to lose color.
- Spinach releases more nutrients for absorption when cooked.

Spinach should be used within 2 days of purchase.

- Spinach leaves need to be stripped and washed thoroughly then parboiled in salted water. Parboil as quickly as possible to retain the color. Wash under cold water before using. Drain and dry well before using.
- Popular spices used on spinach are nutmeg and garlic. The French tend to use nutmeg on almost every spinach dish.

The thick center rib should be removed from all leaves as well as the small stem before adding raw spinach to a salad.

Creamed Spinach

- Your recipe should call for white bread, if it doesn't, get a different recipe.
- The bread should be soaked in milk after the crusts are removed.
- The spinach should be cooked in lightly, salted boiling water for 5 minutes. Drain and cool with cold water.
- The spinach needs to be chopped very fine.
- Add 1 egg to the white bread soaked in the milk and mash together.
- Garlic may be mashed and added if you desire along with the balance of the ingredients in your recipe, which may include chicken broth or water, flour and salt.
- Follow directions per your recipe.

The milk soaked bread thickens the spinach and acts as mild filler, which improves the flavor of the spinach.

- Flour is also used to thicken the spinach, but without the bread the flavor would be somewhat floury.

SPROUTS

- Always purchase crisp sprouts with the buds attached.
- Sprouts tend to get slimy easily and should be used within 2-3 days of purchase.
- All sprouts should be washed and dried before using.

Never freeze sprouts they become mushy.

- The roots should be removed; however, the bean or seed end is edible.
- Sprouts do not cook well and lose their enzymes. Best to eat them raw in salads or on sandwiches.

Mung Bean Sprouts

- Mung bean sprouts are a little heartier and are sometimes used in stir-fries.
- The shorter the tendril, the more tender.

SQUASH

- When pureeing squash the strings will be trapped by the blades and easily removed.

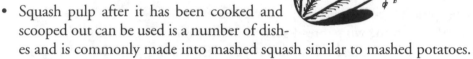

Some squash will explode if they are not punctured before being placed into a microwave.

- Squash pulp after it has been cooked and scooped out can be used is a number of dishes and is commonly made into mashed squash similar to mashed potatoes.
- The heavier the squash the better.
- The best spices for winter squash are allspice, cinnamon, ginger and nutmeg.

Acorn Squash

- A popular method of preparing acorn squash is to slice a squash in half and remove the seeds and fiber, then place the halves cut-side down on a pan with 1-2" inch side and add about $^1/_4$ " of water then bake at 400°F for about 25 minutes.
- After cooking acorn squash, it can be stuffed if desired.
- Make $^1/_2$ inch incisions in the flesh of the acorn squash so that the butter can be absorbed when baking cut-side up.
- Acorn squash is the number one choice for baking and always comes out moist and tender.

Butternut

- Second only to acorn squash in popularity. Bakes moist and very sweet.

Hubbard

- Usually sold by the piece because of their large size.

- The flesh is a bit stringy and drier than other types of squash but they are tasty steamed or baked.

Pumpkin

- When preparing pumpkin pie filling, add a small amount of banana squash to give the pumpkin better flavor.
- Pumpkin does not have a strong enough flavor when prepared alone.

Summer Squash

- Summer squash can be baked or steamed easily due to its high water content.
- The best spices for summer squash are cumin, oregano, rosemary, garlic, onion and basil.

Spaghetti Squash

- Spaghetti squash is done when the shell gives under pressure.

Yellow Crookneck

- Yellow crookneck squash when split lengthwise can be grilled on medium hot for about 8 minutes.

Zucchini

- Zucchini slices can be steamed for 5 minutes to tenderize them.
- Always leave the stem on when grating zucchini to get a better grip.

SUNCHOKES (Jerusalem Artichokes)

- If they have a hint of green, do not buy them.

   The skin can be left on and does not have to be removed. If you wish to remove the skin, just use a vegetable peeler.

- Can be used raw in salads or cooked.
- Commonly used in stews and soups to add a nutty, somewhat sweet flavor.

TOMATOES

The French were the first to utilize tomato sauce in recipes after the tomato was discovered in Peru and brought to France by the Spanish Moors in the 1500's. If you are going to use fresh tomatoes in a recipe, be sure they are at room temperature for the best results.

- Tomatoes should only be refrigerated for storage purposes.
- If tomatoes are refrigerated they should be allowed to remain at room temperature for 20-30 minutes before slicing or serving to regain their aroma and flavor that has been lost.
- Yellow tomatoes will be slightly sweeter than red tomatoes.
- Plum tomatoes should be used if you are preparing tomato sauce. They are not as juicy, however, they have a more, intense tomato flavor and does not turn into mush as easily allowing the sauce to have more, body.
- If you are using canned tomatoes, be sure they are a good red color not a pinkish color or they will have lost a good percentage of their flavor.
- Canned Italian tomatoes are preferred when good fresh tomatoes are out of season.
- When using tomato paste in a recipe use the paste that comes in a tube instead of a can. The flavor will be more, intense in most instances and it keeps longer.
- Some tomato pastes contain MSG, so it would be wise to read the labels.
- When tomatoes are called in recipes, they should be peeled and seeded unless the recipe says otherwise.

Aluminum foil should never be placed on a tomato product. The acid in the tomatoes will cause the aluminum to break down and place aluminum in the food. This is a real health hazard!

- When tomatoes are refrigerated the flesh may become somewhat pulpy after 4-5 days.
- Never ripen tomatoes in direct sunlight or they will lose a high percentage of their nutrition.
- If you desire a silky, smooth tomato sauce: use a puree of tomatoes.
- Tomato sauce should not be cooked for an extended time or it will lose flavor.

Tomato sauces tends to stain plastic ware. Spray the inside of the container with vegetable oil and it won't stain.

- Tomato sauce will burn easily and should be stirred frequently.

- Whole canned tomatoes can be easily sliced with a kitchen scissors.
- Chopped or grated carrots can be added to tomato dishes to reduce the acidity.
- Tomatoes should never be added to a salad until just before serving to avoid the juices from making the salad soggy.
- Sun-dried tomatoes are easily cut with kitchen scissors.

- Tomatoes should never be cooked in aluminum pots or they may taste bitter.
- Chefs normally add a pinch of sugar to cooked tomatoes or tomato sauce to intensify the flavor.
- Broiled tomato halves are made by seasoning with salt, pepper and butter; then placing under the broiler on low heat for about 8-10 minutes or until heated through.

- When diced tomatoes are called for in a recipe, the tomatoes should be peeled and the seeds and liquid removed by squeezing the tomato.
- The best spices for tomatoes are garlic, celery seed, basil, oregano, dill and chili powder.

Fried green Tomatoes

- Fried green tomatoes can be made with very firm green almost; mature tomatoes. Slice the skinned tomatoes about $1/3$ inches thick and season with butter and a small amount of soy sauce then pan fry in olive oil, keeping the temperature below the smoke point.
- Another method is to just dip the tomatoes in cornmeal, brown in bacon drippings and layer in a sandwich with very crisp bacon and lettuce.

The original fried green tomatoes from the South were just sliced and fried in bacon fat.

Removing the skin

- Use a foil-lined cookie sheet and place one single layer of tomatoes on the sheet but make sure that they do not touch each other. Place the cookie sheet under the broiler as far from the heat as possible and as soon as they blister and start to blacken remove them. Allow the tomatoes to cool before removing the skins.
- To peel a tomato, just skewer it and turn it over a low flame until the skin crinkles and cracks.

Never place a whole tomato in the microwave or it will explode.

- Tomatoes can also be peeled by placing them into boiling water, remove from the heat and allow to remain for 1 minute before plunging them into ice cold water for 15 seconds.
- If you wish to use a microwave to loosen tomato skins, just place the tomato in and turn on high for 15 seconds then allow it to remain in the microwave for 1 minute before peeling.

Tomato Paste

- Tomato paste can be purchased in a tube so that a small amount can be used since it is highly concentrated and a small amount goes a long way.

To spice up and add more flavor when using canned tomatoes add a small amount of tomato paste.

Tomato Sauce

- Homemade tomato sauce can be stored in the refrigerator for 2 days and will freeze for 3-4 months.

Hot Garlic Tomato Sauce Recipe

1 Tablespoon of extra virgin olive oil (cold pressed)
¹/₂ teaspoon canola oil
1 cup of chopped red onion
6 Large peeled and seeded ripe tomatoes or
one 16 ounce can of peeled whole tomatoes
3 cloves of finely minced garlic
2 Tablespoons finely chopped fresh basil (or ¹/₂ tsp. dried basil)
3 Tablespoons finely chopped fresh thyme (or ¹/₂ tsp. dried thyme)
Salt and fresh ground black pepper as desired

The olive and canola oil should be heated in a large pan on medium heat. When slightly heated, add the onions and sauté for about 3 minutes or until the onions are soft, then add the garlic and stir for 2-3 minutes. Place the heat on a low setting and slowly stir in the tomatoes, basil and thyme. Simmer the sauce while breaking up the tomatoes for 10 minutes if using fresh tomatoes or 6 minutes if you are using canned tomatoes. Add the salt and ground pepper to taste. If you wish to spice it up a little, just sprinkle ¹/₈ teaspoon of powdered red pepper over the sauce as it is simmering.

Tomatillos

- Can be purchased in yellow or green and wrapped in a peppery husk.
- They are used in Mexican cooking and have a somewhat lemony flavor when cooked in dishes.

Yellow Tomatoes

- All yellow tomatoes lack the flavor of red tomatoes.
- Yellow tomatoes are used to provide color for salads more than for cooking.

TURNIPS

- When choosing a turnip for a dish, always choose the smallest ones. They will be the sweetest.

Turnip greens should never be cooked in an aluminum pot. The chemicals in the turnip greens will react with the aluminum and turn them very dark as well as giving them a slight metallic taste.

- Large turnips should be peeled and sliced before cooking. Always remove the stem and root tip.
- Turnips are commonly mashed and served similar to mashed potatoes.
- Boil or steam them for the best results.

CHAPTER 2

COOKING POTATOES

POTATOES, WHITE

- Never store potatoes near onions, since onions give off a gas that will alter the flavor of the potato.
- Store potatoes in a cool dry location with a small piece of gingerroot to stop the potatoes from sprouting.
- Potatoes tend to lose flavor and nutritional value when frozen for more than 1 month.
- Potato skins should be avoided since the latest studies show that they are the only vegetable-skin that tends to hold pesticide and fertilizer residues.
- Potatoes with a green tint should be discarded.

Baked

- Russet (Idaho) potatoes are best for baking.

- Steam needs to be released from a baked potato. Use a skewer to make several punctures at least $1/2$ to 1" deep.
- Potatoes will bake faster and have a crisper skin if you brush to skin with corn or canola oil before baking.
- If you desire a soft skin on the potato, just wrap it in aluminum foil and keep the steam in.
- To bake a potato faster in a standard oven (not a microwave), insert an aluminum nail through the potato.

To reduce the baking time in the oven, just pierce the potatoes and place them in the microwave for about 3-4 minutes for one potato. Increase the time 1-2 minutes for every other potato.

- Best not to fully cook potatoes in the microwave, since they tend to be too moist and soggy.
- Baking a potato in aluminum foil tends to steam the potato, making the center moist and very dense.
- To revive leftover baked potatoes that have been stored in the refrigerator, just soak the potato in hot tap water for about 1 minute, wrap in aluminum foil and bake at 350°F for 20-25 minutes.
- Potato will cook in about 1 hour at 400°F and will yield to gentle pressure when done.

- A baked potato is done at 210°F if you wish to take its temperature.
- To test if a potato is fully cooked, just insert a skewer completely into the potato. If there is no resistance, the potato is fully cooked.

Boiled

Never boil potatoes in an aluminum or iron pot or they will turn yellow.

- Boiled potatoes will lose 90% of their nutrient value if stored in the refrigerator for 3-4 days. The life of a boiled potato is only 1-2 days.
- To boil potatoes in less time, just remove a small strip of skin from one side. After they are cooked, the balance of the skin will be more easily removed.
- Boiled potatoes should be started in cold water to allow more even heat penetration.
- To keep boiled potatoes white after they are cooked, just place then in a bowl of cold water with a few drops of white vinegar then refrigerate.
- When boiling potatoes add a small amount of white sugar to the water to

help restore the flavor that may be lost from boiling.

- Never cool potatoes in cold water, always hot tap water otherwise they may become soggy.
- To keep potatoes firm while boiling, just cook them in 2 parts of water to 1 part of white vinegar and a small amount of kosher salt.
- When boiling potatoes, place them into a metal mesh basket for easy removal and avoid them becoming mushy.

French Fries

The word French has nothing to do with the country France when used in the words "French fries." Frenching means cutting potatoes into narrow strips. The origin of French fries can be traced back to 1894 when the words "french-fries" were mentioned in an English dictionary. The actual potatoes as we know them today are actually attributed to an American origin in the 1920's.

- Older potatoes are best for fries since they tend to have lower water content and will splatter less.
- The rule of thumb when frying potatoes is 1 medium potato per person.
- The more starch a potato has, the less fat it will absorb.

To be sure that the potatoes you are using have a high starch level, prepare a large pot with 1 cup of salt to 11 cups of water. Place the potatoes in, if they float, the starch content is too low for French fries and they will absorb too much oil.

- Never re-use frying oil. The more oil is used the more trans-fatty acids that build up.
- If excess residue builds up while frying batches, just place a piece of raw potato in the oil and swish around then remove and discard.
- Russet potatoes are the best for frying; they are low-moisture and high-starch.
- Thin potatoes will absorb more oil than thick potatoes.

- French fries should be crinkle-cut using a special tool. This allows more of the surface to be fried and makes a thicker fry.
- Never slice fries with a carbon-steel knife or they may turn yellowish.

Excess starch is released when a potato is sliced and should be removed before frying by soaking the potatoes after they have been sliced in ice cold water for 20-30 minutes. Make sure the potatoes are dry before frying.

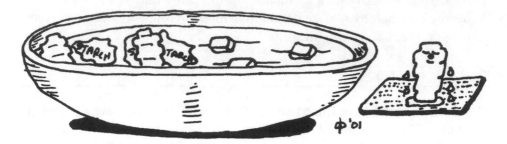

- The thinner the fry, the faster it will cook. Typical of fast food chains, but the thinner fry does not make for a very appetizing fry.

- Fries should be fried at 375°F in canola oil, which has a high smoke point.
- If the oil is over 380°F, it is too hot and the fries will burn.
- Make sure that the oil remains at 375°F between batches.
- Never place too many fries in the deep-fat fryer at one time or it will lower the temperature and cause excess oil to enter the fries.
- Overcrowding also causes uneven cooking and a poor product.
- Pre-heat the oven to 250°F, turn the oven off and keep the fries warm by placing them on a cookie sheet that has been lined with paper towel.
- For crispier fries the fries need to be fried twice. Once at 340°F until they just become brown and then removed and dried on paper towel for about 10 minutes. Allow the fries to remain at room temperature for 3 hours before you need to fry them for the meal and then fry them at 375°F until they are browned. Place on paper towel and dry before serving.
- To make oven fries, just place the potatoes on a cookie sheet after they have been washed in ice water and dried. Brush or spray a thin layer of oil on the fries and bake in a pre-heated 400°F oven for 15-20 minutes or until brown. Turn the fries over and repeat.

Always use a deep-fat thermometer when frying.

- If oil smokes discard the oil and start over, the oil will be high in trans-fatty acids and very unhealthy.

SOLVING FRENCH FRY PROBLEMS

THE FAT SMOKES WHEN I FRY

- Use fat with a higher smoke point, such as canola
- There is too much food residue in the frying vat
- The fat has deteriorated and should be replaced
- Utensils are being placed into the oil with baked-on polymers

THE FRIES ARE TOO GREASY

- The fat is too old and needs to be changed
- The water content of the fries is too low
- The fries are too skinny
- The temperature is not high enough

SOME OF THE FRIES ARE COOKED AND OTHERS ARE NOT

- The fries are not uniform in size
- Some of the fries were not dry enough before being placed in the fryer

Hashed Brown Potatoes

- Potatoes need to be chopped or grated into fine pieces.

A small amount of onion will add a great flavor to hashed browns.

- Potatoes need to be shaped into a patty of irregular sizes and placed into a skillet with a layer of oil.
- The patties need to be browned on each side then seasoned with a small amount of salt and pepper to taste.
- Hashed brows should always be served very crisp, not half raw.

Mashed

- Russet (Idaho) potatoes make the lightest mashed potatoes. However, if you can obtain a Yukon Gold potato they are even better than the russet for mashed potatoes and baking.
- Baked potatoes can be used to make mashed potatoes.
- The Yukon Gold potato actually tastes somewhat buttery and has a natural creamy texture.
- Schmaltz is made by rendering the chicken fat from the belly, which is at the end of the breast and around the upper part of the thigh.
- Best not to add potato skins since they may contain pesticide or fertilizer residues and not everyone like the consistency.

- Never add cold milk to mashed potatoes since it mixes with the starch and makes them heavy and possibly lumpy.
- Always use warm or hot milk in mashed potatoes.

A pinch of baking powder will fluff the potatoes up, never use baking soda that will turn the potatoes black.

- Potatoes should only be cooked until a skewer can be inserted and removed easily. Overcooking will turn the potatoes somewhat gritty.

- To reduce the water content of the potatoes either cook them with the skins on or put them back into the pot after the water has been drained and place them over the hot burner, which has been use to cook them for about 1 minute. Do not turn the heat on.

- Use a "ricer" to squeeze the potatoes through and you will never have lumps.
- The more you beat mashed potatoes the more likely they will become sticky and release too much starch.
- A small amount of chicken fat (schmaltz), butter or onion will give a great flavor to mashed potatoes.
- If adding butter, add the butter and mix well before adding any milk or sour cream.
- A small amount of white pepper is excellent in mashed potatoes.
- When mashed potatoes are used for decoration, try adding a lightly beaten egg to the potatoes while you are beating them to make them more firm then place in a pastry bag and squeeze.

A small amount of cheese that melts easily may be added to mashed potatoes to give added flavor.

- To peel a cooked potato easily, just drop it into a bowl of ice water when it is still very hot to loosen the skin.

Garlic Mashed Potatoes

- Peel a whole head of garlic and wrap it in aluminum foil, then roast it for 1 hour at 350°F.
- Remove the cloves and let them cool for a few minutes before pressing them to release all the pulp.
- Mash the pulp into 2 pounds of mashed potatoes and add butter and milk to taste. Be sure that the milk has been warmed before adding it and that the butter has been softened at room temperature and not in the microwave.
- If you prefer just a hint of garlic, rub the garlic clove around the inside of the serving bowl before adding the mashed potatoes.

Pan Roasted

- The potatoes should be peeled and washed, then washed again and sliced into cubes about 1" each.
- Cook them in a pot with barely enough water to cover them plus 1" more. Add some caraway seeds and 1 teaspoon of salt to the water.

Grandma used a combination of butter and lard but you can use any oil with the butter.

- Use a heavy frying pan to heat the oil then add the cold potatoes. The potatoes should be cooked slowly turning occasionally.
- Allowing the potatoes to return to room temperature before cooking them assures that they will not fall apart when cooked.
- Paprika is usually sprinkled on while they are being cooked to give the potatoes a great brown color.
- Heat over medium heat only until boiling begins then remove from the heat and allow potatoes to stand for 5 minutes.

- Pour off the water and place the potatoes in a bowl and allow the potatoes to cool to room temperature.
- Mix any seasonings you will be using in a separate dish.
- The potatoes should not be greasy if prepared right and will retain a natural potato flavor.

BAKED, POTATO CHIPS

Homemade potato chips; can be made by cutting the potato in half exposing the two flat surfaces, then using a very wide potato or vegetable peeler to slice thin slices. The slices are sprayed with vegetable oil and placed on a cookie sheet and baked at 450°F for 10-12 minutes or until they are a golden brown. After they are browned, place the chips in a brown paper bag with $1/4$ teaspoon of salt or salt substitute for each potato and shake. The paper bag will absorb some of the fat.

Potato Salad

- Use new red potatoes for the best potato salad.
- Make sure that the potatoes are not overcooked or undercooked.
- Whole potatoes take about 15-20 minutes to become firm and tender.
- After they are cooked, slice them and lightly sprinkle them with white vine-gar, olive oil, salt and pepper to taste.
- Additional ingredients will depend on your recipe.

If you don't want to add mustard to your potato salad but want the nice yellow color, just add a small amount of yellow food coloring.

- Best to use fresh new potatoes that will absorb less moisture when boiled.
- New potatoes will also absorb less mayonnaise.
- New potatoes are stronger and won't break down when stirred.

Potato Pancakes (latkas)

- If you add 1 teaspoon of baking soda to the batter you will eliminate anyone having indigestion after eating the pancakes. Only add it if there is a problem.
- Grate 3 pounds of potatoes and $1/2$ pound of onions, squeeze out the excess starch using a China cap.

Use a stainless steel bowl and the potatoes will not discolor as fast.

- Use about 1 ounce of all-purpose flour, 3 eggs and 1 teaspoons of salt to help bind the batter.
- A small amount of lemon juice added to the batter will help avoid discol-oration if desired.
- Pan fry in about $1/4$ inch of corn oil at 325°F and only turn once. Place on paper towel and pat dry before serving.
- Store in warm oven (200°F) on a cookie sheet lined with paper towel. Be sure and turn heat off before placing the cookie sheet in oven with paper towel.

Potato Puree

- Potato puree is used as a base for many potato preparations.
- Starchy potatoes are always used, preferably russets.
- Potatoes should be eyed, washed and peeled.
- Simmer until done and a skewer can be easily inserted. Do not allow pota-

toes to boil and be sure that they are fully cooked for the best results.
- Place the cooked potatoes in a metal colander in the oven for a few minutes to dry out.

Use a ricer that has been placed under hot water to puree. A cold ricer will cool the potatoes too much and may make them grainy.

Roasted

- The best potatoes for roasting are small red potatoes. If red potatoes are too sweet, they are probably frost bitten. When red potatoes freeze, the carbohydrate turns to sugar.
- Larger potatoes can also be used for roasting if they are quartered or halved.
- Place halved or quartered potatoes on a pan and brush with oil and roast at 400°F for 1 hour or until skewer can be inserted easily and potatoes are crisp and brown.
- Roasted potatoes should be turned about every 15-20 minutes for the best results.

Scalloped

- The potatoes should be dropped into boiling, salted water for 8 minutes. Slice the potatoes about $1/4$ inch thick and place about $1/3$ of them on a 10" square baking dish with sides. Use about $1/2$ tablespoons of butter to lightly dot and sprinkle on about 2 tablespoons of all-purpose flour. Make one or two more layers in this manner. Heat $1^1/4$ cups of low fat or regular milk with $1^1/4$ teaspoons of table salt added and pour over the potatoes. Place in 350°F oven uncovered for 30 minutes or until a skewer can be inserted easily through all layers.

Grated cheddar or Swiss cheese can be sprinkled on top a few minutes before removing from the oven to give the cheese time to melt.

- Breadcrumbs are also popular when sprinkled on top of the scalloped potatoes

POTATOES, SWEET

Sweet potatoes originated in Peru and records date the tuber back as far as 750 BC. The reason sweet potatoes became associated with the yam was due to the American slaves calling the sweet potato by an African name, "nyami."

- Sweet potatoes are preferred over yams, which have more reddish meat instead of orange.
- Sweet potatoes have a richer flavor and should never be stored in the refrigerator or any location where the temperature may go below 40°F or they will become bitter.
- Yams will do as a replacement and can be prepared in the same manner.
- Yams require more sweetening than sweet potatoes.

Best to avoid making dishes with sweet potatoes or yams in June and July. The potatoes will have been stored in cold storage and may be stringy and somewhat dried out.

Baked

- Baked sweet potatoes get sweeter the more they are cooked.
- The skins tend to break away from the meat more easily when baked.
- Can be frozen without becoming mushy unlike white potatoes.
- Bake at 350°F for 1½ hours or until skewer can be inserted and be removed clean.

Boiled

- When sweet potatoes are boiled they tend to absorb water easily and need to be dried before using them in some dishes.
- Dry sweet potatoes in a colander in the oven for 1-2 minutes.

To peel a boiled sweet potato, just take it from the boiling water and immerse it in very cold water for about 15 seconds.

- A 3-4" inch sweet potato will take 25 minutes to boil in about 2 inches of water.
- To shorten cooking time. Parboil the potatoes for 20 minutes before baking.
-

Candied

- Slice potatoes in $1/4$ inch slices, boil and peel.
- The syrup is prepared by mixing 1 cup of brown sugar with $1/4$ cup of water, $1/4$ cup of unsalted butter and $1/2$ teaspoon of table salt.
- Place the slices next to each other in a pan with about 2-inch sides and baste with syrup during cooking process on moderate heat, about 350°F for 45 minutes.
- Mini-marshmallows may be added during the last 7 minutes of cooking time.

French Fries

- Sweet potato fries are best when sliced into thin strips then soak for 20 minutes in ice water, then drain and dry thoroughly on paper towel.
- Fry small batches only at 370°F until just barely brown; drain and dry them. When ready to serve place the fries in the fryer basket at 390°F and continue frying until done.
- These fries do not need salt and will have a somewhat sweet flavor.
- Sugar is often sprinkled on sweet potato fries.

Mashed

- Slice whole sweet potatoes in 1-1$1/2$" circles and drop in boiling water until you can insert a skewer easily.
- The skins should come off easily, if not place the potatoes in ice water for about 15 seconds to loosen them.
- Use a ricer to mash the potatoes and add a small amount of milk and salted butter as needed then blend by hand.

Sweet Potato Pie Recipe

2 cups of sweet potatoes (not yams)
4 Tbsp. unsalted butter
3 large eggs
1 cup granulated sugar
1 tsp. cinnamon
$1/4$ tsp. grated fresh nutmeg
$3/4$ cup whole milk (not low fat)
1 tsp. quality vanilla extract
$1/4$ cup chopped pecans (optional)

Use a 9" pie shell. Boil the sweet potatoes with their skins on; then mash the sweet potatoes together with the melted butter. Blend in the eggs, sugar, cinnamon and nutmeg. Add the milk and vanilla then pour into the baked pie shell. Bake in oven for 35-45 minutes at 375°F or until you can insert a metal skewer into the center and it comes out clean.

CHAPTER 3

COOKING AND PREPARING FRUIT

COOKING & PREPARING FRUIT

Fruits can be more difficult to cook since many have higher water content (80-90% in most fruits) than most vegetables. Fruits also have a higher acid content than most vegetables making it more difficult to control the over-acidity and color of the final dish.

APPLES

- Apples float because of air pockets between the cells.
- If apples are somewhat dried out, just place them into a small bowl with ice water for 30 minutes in the refrigerator.
- Apple seeds do contain cyanide, a deadly poison; however, they are harmless if swallowed since the body cannot break the seed open. If the seeds are crushed and ingested you will get very ill.
- Mature apples are less likely to brown easily. The younger the apple the faster it will brown when sliced.
- If you soak sliced apples in a very mild solution of salt water they will not turn brown until you are ready to use them.
- Keeping apples chilled below 40°F after they are cut will slow the browning.
- Golden Delicious apples will not brown as fast as most other apples.
- Any salad dressing that is acidic will keep apples and other fruits that turn brown easily their natural color for a long period of time.

- To keep apples from browning after they have been sliced, just dip them in a solution of 4 tablespoons of powdered vitamin C (ascorbic acid) and 1 quart of water for a few seconds.

Lemon juice and water will also keep apples from browning but tends to impart a sour taste.

- Muffin tins are the best method of keeping baked apples in good shape.
- Gala, Johnathan, Rome Beauty and Elstar apples tend to hold their shape well for baking.
- Apple butter should be prepared with no added fat, just cinnamon and allspice.
- Apples can be pared easily if you pour scalding water on them just before peeling. This loosens the skin.
- When juicing apples, try adding a handful of raspberries to increase the nutritional content and add a nice flavor.

Applesauce

- If you prefer a smooth applesauce, add the sugar after the apples have been cooked and mashed.
- Tart cooking apples are best for applesauce since it will help you control the sweetness.
- If you have oversweet applesauce, just add a small amount of lemon juice until you like the taste.
- If you prefer chunky applesauce, add the sugar before cooking and the cells will be more firm.

A small amount of honey is an excellent sweetener for applesauce.

- If you would like your applesauce to have a reddish tint, add a small amount of 100% pure cranberry juice.
- If the applesauce is too thin, just allow it to simmer until it reaches the right consistency.
- Apples can be cooked in the microwave by peeling them and placing them into a baking dish and cook for about 20 minutes or until soft and tender.

Baked Apples

- If you leave the skin on baked apples just make a few slits around the apple to release the steam. The steam causes the expansion of the skin and subsequent bursting.

  If you sprinkle a small powdering of calcium on the apples they will retain their shape by strengthening the cell walls when they are being baked.

- A "canelle" knife works really well for taking a small strip off apples, making them easier to peel after they are cooked.
- Condensed milk makes an excellent sweet glaze for baked apples when brushed on 15-20 minutes before the apples are done.
- Sprinkle a small amount of apple juice in the pan to keep the apples from drying out during cooking.
- Bake the apples covered at 350°F for 30 minutes, then remove the cover and bake about 60 minutes more or until tender.
- Apples can be cooked in the microwave by coring them, placing them into a custard cup and pouring a small amount of cider or apple juice over them, cover them with waxed paper and cook 2 apples in 4 minutes or until tender.
- Check the apples with a skewer, it should insert very easily when they are done.

Sautéed Apples

- Peel the apples; core and slice them, then sauté in apple juice with a small amount of unsalted butter or clarified butter. Takes about 3-5 minutes.

APRICOTS

- Apricots can be grilled by placing them on a skewer, brush them with honey and place on a grill.
- You can oven-broil apricot halves, by placing them in the broiler, cut-side up and broil for about 7 minutes. Be sure they are 4 inches from the heat.
- To poach apricots, place them into a pan after peeling and halving them into simmering fruit juice. Add any spices you desire and cook until tender.
- Dried apricots can be reconstituted by placing them into a pan with fruit juice and water for about 15 minutes.

AVOCADO

- To ripen avocados faster, place them in a wool sock in a dark location for 1-2 days. You can also place them into a brown paper bag with an apple for 1-2 days.
- To remove the seed, just slice the avocado lengthwise and hit the seed with the blade of a heavy knife and gently twist.

Avocados cannot be heated or they will release a chemical compound that turns them bitter.

- To retard the browning, just spray the surface with a solution of powdered vitamin C and water and place a piece of plastic wrap directly on the surface to stop air from hitting the flesh.
- The brownish discoloration can easily be scraped off and will not affect the balance of the avocado.
- Always add avocado to a dish just before serving.
- Avocados that are not completely ripe can be placed in a microwave on high for 1 minute then turned for another minute to soften them, however, they will not be ripe.
- To remove the skin after the avocado pit has been removed, just make a slice through the middle of the skin on each half and peel the skin down.
- The best seasoning when using avocados in salads is vinaigrette because of the acid content.
- Avocado is often used as a substitute for butter in some countries, since it has about a 20% fat content.
- Avocados will not ripen on the tree and must be harvested before it will ripen.

Never store avocados in the refrigerator or it will affect their flavor.

- Avocados should never be placed on a window in full sunlight. They ripen better between 60-70°F. Higher temperatures will result in brown spots appearing and a loss of nutrients.
- An avocado mousse; can be prepared by pureeing an avocado and adding some sugar and a small amount of lemon juice.

BANANA

- Green bananas will ripen quickly at room temperature. They can also be placed into a brown paper bag with an apple.

  When bananas are green they must be cooked to be edible.

- Whole bananas if left in their peel can be frozen for 4-6 months.
- Plantains are large, starchy bananas that are fried or used to replace potatoes in South America.
- After ripening, place the bananas that will not be used immediately into the refrigerator to slow the ripening process. The skin will turn brown but it will not affect the flesh.

- When preparing dishes that call for bananas to be cooked; always choose bananas that are not quite ripe. The ingredients will provide the additional sweetening and the bananas will not fall apart and become mushy.
- Overripe bananas can be pureed with a small amount of lemon juice and frozen for 4-6 months. The puree can be used in many dishes such as cakes, daiquiris, puddings, etc..

- When banana chips are fried, they are not a healthy food. However, they can be made in the oven.
- If banana chips (1oz) are fried, they contain about 8 grams of fat compared to the same weight of potato chips that have 5 grams of fat.
- To pan-fry bananas, just slice the banana into thick slices and sauté in unsalted butter and 2 tablespoons of brown sugar for about 1-2 minutes. Remove, place on paper towel and sprinkle with a few drops of orange juice or powdered sugar (and rum if desired).
- To bake bananas, just halve them lengthwise without peeling and place them into a baking dish. Brush them with a fruit juice of your liking and a small amount of honey and bake until hot, which takes about 15 minutes at 350°F.

Bananas Foster

The dish was created in 1954 in New Orleans at the Brennan's Restaurant. It was originally part of a breakfast promotion and was named after Richard Foster, a frequent visitor to the restaurant and owned Foster Awning Company. The chef who made the first Banana Foster dish was named Paul Blange.

- Mix the banana cordial and good quality rum together in a bowl and set aside.
- The butter should be allowed to soften at room temperature, then melted in a double boiler.
- Mix the brown sugar into the melted butter and place the sliced bananas into the mixture, making sure that they are well, coated.

Arrange the bananas on a flat dish and sprinkle them with cinnamon; then cook for 1-2 minutes as per the recipe.

- Drizzle the rum mixture over the bananas and cook per recipe.

Banana Fritters

- To make banana fritters, slice the bananas into quarters then dip into batter and fry at 375°F until brown. Batter is made by beating 2 eggs and stirring in $1/2$ cup of milk. In a separate bowl, sift together 1 cup of all-purpose flour, 1 tsp. of baking soda and 1 tsp. of salt. Add the sifted mixture to the eggs and milk then beat in 1 tsp. of corn oil.

Dip each piece into flour before placing the banana slices into the batter or the batter will separate from the bananas when they are frying.

BERRIES

- Never wash berries until just before using them, they tend to retain water and get mushy.

If you add large berries to a cake batter be sure that the batter is thick enough to support the berries or they will sink to the bottom.

- If you use frozen berries in pies or cobblers decrease the thickener since frozen berries release more liquid than fresh berries.

- If the berries being used for baking are not sweet enough, try adding 1 tablespoons of sugar per cup of berries then allow the berries to remain at room temperature for 45 minutes and only stir once.
- When you use sugar to sweeten berries, especially strawberries, they tend to get somewhat soggy and should be consumed or added to dishes very shortly after sweetening.
- Lemon will remove berry stains from hands.
- Sorbet can be made from berries by pureeing them and adding confectioner's sugar to taste.

Never hull berries unless you are going to use them immediately.

- To defrost berries, just place them into a plastic bag and immerse in cold water for 10 minutes.
- A small amount of lemon juice will improve the flavor if sprinkled on berries.
- Frozen strawberries should be defrosted slowly in the refrigerator to help retain their shape.
- To hull a strawberry use flat-end tweezers.
- If you are making blueberry muffins and the recipe calls for 1 cup of berries, only use $^3/_4$ cup if the berries are canned.
- Wash berries in a colander allowing the water to gently wash them in a slow stream.
- When preparing gooseberries, use a scissors to remove the tops before preparing.

CHERRIES

- Cherries will last longer if you don't wash them or remove the stem.
- When preparing any dish that calls for cherries, always add about $^1/_4$ teaspoon of pure almond extract to bring out the cherry flavor.
- Cherries tend to lose their color when cooked in a dish. Try adding a few drops of red food coloring to most cherry dishes or cakes.

Dried cherries can be used to replace raisins in most recipes.

- Cherry jam uses $1^1/_2$ pounds of sugar to 2 pounds of cherries.
- Puncture cherries with a pin in the opposite end from the stem, leaving the stem attached. Allow the cherries to soak overnight in a solution of a good quality brandy with 2-3 tablespoons of sugar. Dip in semi-sweet chocolate and serve the following day. They can also be frozen and dipped at a later date.

- The shelf life of canned dark cherries is only 1 year.
- The shelf life of canned light-colored cherries, such as Queen Ann's is 3 years.
- Use a bent paper clip to remove cherry pits.
- Poaching cherries works great, they retain their texture and flavor.

CITRUS FRUITS (general)

The first citrus trees were grown in Southern China over 4,000 years ago and were called "citron." The citrus fruit; was brought to the United States by Columbus in the late 1400's. They were extensively grown in Florida as early as the 16th century and have been their major crop ever since.

Segmenting Citrus fruits

- Cut off both ends first so that you have two flat surfaces. Next work the knife down along the shape of the fruit removing the peel and the bitter pith. Firmly hold the fruit and cut straight down between the membranes to allow the segments to free up.

Zest

- The outer peel is the zest and is called for in a number of recipes.
- Fresh zest is very potent and a small amount goes a long way.
- A special tool is available that is called a citrus zest stripper.
- Always remove the zest if you need to use it before squeezing the fruit.
- Citrus zest can be frozen for later use.
- Before removing zest from citrus fruit, make sure you wash them thoroughly to remove any pesticide or fertilizer residue.

COCONUT

- If you are not going to use all the coconut meat, it must be stored in its own milk, in the refrigerator, and will last for about 4-5 days.
- Dried out shredded coconut can be soaked in milk for 20-30 minutes before using.

Food coloring can be added to shredded coconut for desserts or vegetable garnish.

- To prepare coconut cream, just use 1 part of water or milk mixed with 4 parts finely shredded coconut.
- To toast coconut, spread the coconut out on a cookie sheet and bake at 325°F turning 2-3 times for about 10-12 minutes or until it has browned.

CRANBERRIES

Cranberries seemed to originate in the United States in the New England states around the Cape Cod area and grow well in sandy soil. The "cranberry bogs" of New England have a story attached that says that in the late 1700's Reverend Richard Bourne made an Indian medicine man mad and he placed a spell on him before placing him into quicksand. The Reverend spent 15 days buried in the quicksand and this aggravated the Indian who thought that he would die fairly quickly.

While unable to move: the Reverend lived on berries that were dropped over him by a white dove. The medicine man became frustrated and released him from the spell and the quicksand. One of the berries is supposed to have fallen into the sand and rooted starting the cranberry bogs of New England.

- Only cook cranberries until they "pop" or they will become bitter and require a lot of sugar.
- Fresh cranberries should bounce if they are fresh; they should be very firm, even hard.
- Cranberries were once called "bounce berries."

Grandma's Cranberry Sauce Recipe

2 cups fresh cranberries (frozen if necessary)
1^1/$_2$ cups granulated sugar
1 cup dry, white wine (optional)
1^1/$_2$ cups pure water
^{1}/$_2$ cup dark rum (optional) or a small amount of rum extract
^{1}/$_4$ pound of unsalted butter

Using a large saucepan, combine the cranberries, sugar, water and wine and simmer over medium heat. Stop the cooking process as soon as the cranberries pop, which means that they are done. If they are cooked any further, they will be too bitter. Add the rum and room temperature butter and mix well. The heat should melt the butter and create an excellent sauce. The sauce should gel in the refrigerator in about 3 hours and may be served hot or cold.

Leah's Thanksgiving Cranberry Jell-O

2 small packages of raspberry Jell-O (or 1 large package)
1 8 ounce can of Ocean Spray whole cranberries
2 cups boiling water
1 small can crushed pineapple
^{1}/$_2$ cup of quality rose wine
^{1}/$_2$ cup of walnuts

Dissolve the Jell-O in the boiling water; then add other ingredients except for the nuts. Mix all the ingredients well then add the nuts. Allow the Jell-O to set in the refrigerator.

GRAPES

- Grapes should be served at around 60°F for the best flavor and should be removed from the refrigerator about 20 minutes before serving.
- For a great snack food, dip grapes in cherry juice and freeze.

  To frost grapes, just dip them in slightly beaten egg white and immediately in granulated sugar.

- To remove the skins from grapes, just drop them in boiling water for a few seconds them immediately immerse them in ice water and you should have no trouble removing the skins.
- Grapes will go very well with fish or chicken dishes that are cooked in wine.
- When using grapes in dishes, they should be added into the cooking liquid just before serving.

FREEZING FRUITS

- A mixture of 40% syrup is recommended for most fruits; however, mild-flavored fruits are better when packed in lighter syrup.

Type of Syrup (%)	Cups of Sugar	Cups of Water	Cups of Syrup
30-percent	2	4	5
40-percent	3	4	$5^1/_2$
50-percent	$4^3/_4$	4	$6^1/_2$
60-percent	7	4	$7^3/_4$

LEMONS AND LIMES

- If you just need a small amount of fresh lemon or lime juice, puncture a small hole with a skewer in the bottom and remove the desired amount then store in the refrigerator and the hole will seal up.
- Acids have a tenderizing effect on the meat of fish and when placed in lime or lemon juice for about 10 hours, the meat will turn white instead of translucent. There is no heat generated, however, the meat will look as if it were cooked. Two foods that utilize acidic cooking are pickled herring and seviche.
- When using lemon wedges that will be used on fish or shellfish dishes, remove the white pith that remains after you quarter them and the slices won't spray when squeezed.

- To prepare limeade, just squeeze $^1/_3$ cup of lime juice into 1 cup of water and add 5 teaspoons of sugar or the equivalent of an artificial sweetener.
- Both lemon and lime juice are natural tenderizers for any type of fowl dish.
- To obtain more juice from lemons and limes, just immerse them in very hot water for 15 minutes.
- Lemon juice is an excellent flavoring for many dishes and can replace salt in most of them. The high acid content tends to mask the need for the salty taste.

To make pink lemonade, use a small amount of grenadine syrup.

- Both lemon and lime have the ability to blend well with a number of foods such as: potatoes, rice, all types of salads and most cooked vegetables. When the juice is processed it does tend to lose a good percentage of its flavor, so try and use the juice from fresh-squeezed for the best results and taste.

OLD FASHIONED LEMONADE RECIPE:

Using a medium saucepan on low heat, combine 1 cup of water with 1 cup of granulated sugar and the cut up rind from 2 lemons. Stir until the sugar has melted, then boil for about 6 minutes. Remove from heat and allow it to cool, then add 4 cups of pure water and juice of 6 fresh lemons (not reconstituted lemon juice). Serve over crushed ice. For limeade just replace the lemons with lime zest and the juice of 8 limes.

MELONS

- Cut melons should be consumed within 1-2 days since they will absorb odors and have an off taste.
- Allow the seeds to remain in a halved melon and it will keep its flavor longer and store better.
- Melons (except for watermelon) will have a better flavor if served at room temperature. Cold tends to reduce the flavor by 40% in most melons.
- Melons with poor flavor can be soaked in a mixture of 1 cup of orange juice, $1/4$ teaspoon of cinnamon and $1/8$ teaspoon of finely ground ginger.
- Watermelon should be served cold for the best flavor.
- If you purchase $1/2$ melon in the supermarket and the seeds have been removed it should be consumed the same day.

One average size cantaloupe will provide about 45-50 melon balls or about 4 cups of diced melon.

- Watermelon seeds can be salted and roasted in the oven at 400°F for 15-20 minutes.

NECTARINES

- Best not to slice nectarines until you are ready to prepare them since they turn brown very easily.
- When nectarines are cooked they tend to become sweeter and softer.
- To bake a nectarine, just slice it in half and place it cut-side up. Brush the exposed surface with lemon juice and sprinkle with granulated sugar or drizzle a small amount of honey on top. Bake at 325°F for about 20-25 minutes.
- Broil nectarines by slicing in half and sprinkling them with brown sugar, which will caramelize in about 5-8 minutes.
- Nectarines poach very well in any fruit juice.

ORANGES

- Leave the fruit at room temperature if it has been refrigerated for at least 30 minutes before juicing.
- To loosen the juice in citrus fruits, put pressure on the fruit and roll the fruit on a hard surface a few times.

The white portion just under the peel is somewhat bitter and should not be used in dishes.

- The white material under the peel is easily removed when exposed by either immersing the citrus in very hot water for 5-6 minutes or by placing the fruit in boiling water for 3 minutes.
- You will obtain more juice from citrus fruits if you pierce the skin with a skewer a few times and microwave the fruit for about 10 seconds on high.
- If you require a very sweet orange flavor, use the blossom end of the orange only.

To prepare an "orange fizz" for the kids just add $1/4$ teaspoon of baking soda to orange juice.

- The best juice orange is the Jaffa with Valencia coming in second.
- If you are going to garnish with slices of citrus fruit, try cutting grooves in the peel with a "canelle" knife.
- Orange peel can be removed (without the white pith) and dried in a microwave then frozen for future use.
- If you are using frozen citrus juice concentrates to prepare juice for dishes, remember that the nutritional content, especially vitamin C will be gone in about 5-7 days. Once reconstituted frozen juice does not have a long life.

PAPAYAS

- When papaya has not fully ripened, it can still be prepared as you would most vegetables.
- Papaya seeds have a peppery flavor and can be added to salad dressings when crushed.

Never use papaya in a gelatin since the fruit contains an enzyme that breaks down gelatin.

- Papaya makes an excellent meat tenderizer. However, the more ripe the papaya the less meat tenderizing qualities and the less "papain" levels.

- Papaya will ripen at room temperature in about 3-5 days.
- The shells make excellent holders for dip or as a fruit cup.
- Papaya can be baked like squash by cutting it lengthwise, scooping out the seeds and sprinkling a small amount of sugar on top. Bake at 325°F for 20-25 minutes depending on the level of ripeness.

PEACHES

- To broil peaches, just slice them in half, brush the exposed halves with orange juice and broil for 5-7 minutes or until tender.
- Peach halves lend themselves very well to poaching in any fruit juice.

Peach Melba

The dish was first prepared by Chef Georges Auguste Escoffier in the late 1890's and named after the Australian opera singer Nellie Melba. The dish was originally created at the Ritz-Carlton Hotel in London with special peaches obtained from the Montreal suburb of Paris.

- Be sure and skin the peaches before poaching them.
- The peaches are poached in vanilla-flavored syrup and then cooled in the refrigerator before placing them on vanilla ice cream.
- They can them be coated with raspberry sauce and a sprinkling of fresh raspberries.

PEAR

- To sauté pears, just peel and slice them and sauté in fruit juice or stock with cinnamon for 2-4 minutes or until tender.

Dry Poaching

To dry-poach a pear, pre-heat a deep pan and fill it with kosher salt to 450°F for 1 hour. Place a wooden skewer into the top of the pear and bury it in the hot salt, allowing only a small portion of the wooden skewer to be exposed. Bake the pear for 15 minutes until the pear softens, then remove it, remove any salt that is clinging and cool it before serving it.

- If you add sugar to the poaching water it will help keep the pears in shape.
- Make sure that the pears are at room temperature when you start to poach them.

PLUMS

- When poaching plums, leave them whole with the skins on and just prick the skin with a fork. The skin will help the plum retain its shape.
- They can be poached in sugar and water or wine for 4-8 minutes or until they are the firmness you desire.

PRUNES

- If you want to plump up prunes, just measure the fruit and combine it with an equal amount of water in a saucepan. Only simmer the prunes, if you boil them, they will fall apart very easily. You should only have to cook them for about 8-10 minutes at the most.

RAISINS

- Raisins will not stick to a food chopper if you soak them in ice cold water for 10 minutes.
- If you have a problem with raisins sticking together in the package, just place the package in the microwave for a few seconds and they will separate.
- To plump raisins, just place them in a small bowl with a few drops of water, then cover and bake in a pre-heated 325°F for 7 minutes.

If you are going to add raisins to cookies, cakes or other baked goods, it would be best to toss them with a small amount of the same flour you are using in the recipe. This will keep the raisins from falling to the bottom during the baking process.

- Try stewing raisins and prunes together for a real treat.

RHUBARB

Rhubarb was originally grown in monasteries throughout Europe and used for medicinal purposes for hundreds of years. In the mid-1800's the stalks were sold in London fruit markets and it was mentioned as an ingredient for pies in 1855. Sweetened, stewed rhubarb also became a favorite dessert. The plant was called "pie plant" at one time. Strawberry-rhubarb pie is an American invention, however, it was found to be too sweet by many a chef.

- To bake rhubarb, place the cut up stalks (leaves are poisonous) in a glass or ceramic baking dish and sprinkle with granulated sugar. Cover the dish and bake for about 30 minutes at 300°F.
- Rhubarb tastes sweeter after it is cooked. Best to cook it first before sweetening it with sugar or honey.

When cooking rhubarb, never use aluminum or cast iron cookware. The chemicals in rhubarb will react with the metal.

- To stew rhubarb, place the cut up rhubarb in a large saucepan with just enough water to cover. Bring to a boil then lower the heat to simmer and cook gently until tender.
- After rhubarb has cooked, sweeten to taste and cook for about 5 minutes more to be sure that all the sugar has been dissolved.
- To sweeten rhubarb, it usually takes about ¹/₂ cup of granulated sugar per pound of rhubarb.
- Stewed rhubarb is excellent cold and if served cold it would be best to taste it just before serving to be sure the sweetness is correct.
- The total time to stew rhubarb is 6-8 minutes.

Rhubarb Pie

- Use 4 cups of chopped rhubarb, not too small pieces. Never use the leaves they are poisonous.
- Add 1-1¹/₃ cups of honey, 7 tablespoons of all-purpose flour, 4 tablespoons of angelica and ¹/₂ teaspoon of salt.
- Use a double crust. Dot the bottom crust with unsalted butter.
- Bake for 10 minutes at 450°F then reduce the heat to 350°F for 50 minutes.

FRUIT SAUCES

Fruit sauces go well with a large variety of foods, from desserts to meat dishes. When you make a fruit sauce; it would be wise to choose the best quality fruits you can find. The resulting sauce will be more appetizing and flavorful.

Apricot and Lemon Sauce Recipe

20 fresh ripe apricots, pitted and sliced
1^1/$_2$ cups pure water
1 cup granulated sugar
2^1/$_2$ Tablespoons of lemon juice (fresh if possible)
^{2}/$_3$ teaspoon real vanilla extract

Using a large saucepan, add the apricots, water and sugar to a boil, then simmer for 15 minutes. Remove from the heat and allow the mixture to cool for 5 minutes before placing the mixture in a blender to puree. Allow the mixture to cool, then beat in the lemon juice and the pure vanilla.

CHAPTER 4

GENERAL COOKING SECRETS

GENERAL COOKING METHODS

BARBECUING

- Best not to use "real" charcoal to barbecue with. Fat dripping on the coals produces a chemical that gets on the meat.
- If you do get a flare-up, place lettuce leaves on top of the coals to cool them and not put them out.
- Never cook foods next to each other, leave about 1" between foods.
- If you are in a hurry, partially pre-cook foods that take a long time to cook, such as chicken breasts.
- Make sure you spray the grill before you start the fire so that the food will not stick.

Barbecue Sauces

- The base for most barbecue sauces include dark brown sugar, lemon juice, pepper, Worcestershire sauce or soy sauce, salt and garlic.
- When barbecuing the sauce should not be placed on the food during the first $^3/_4$ of the cooking time or the sauce may burn and produce a bitter taste.

BOILING

- Always place vegetables into the water after the water begins to boil.

   Allow the water to boil for 2 minutes to release a percentage of the oxygen. This will help retain some of the nutrients longer. Excess oxygen will reduce the potency of a number of nutrients and vitamins.

BRASING

- Braising may be done either on the range or in the oven. This method is preferred for certain foods since the heat surrounds the pot.
- A heavy pot with a lid that closes tight is recommended.
- The liquid used for braising is always used as either all or part of the sauce.

- Braising (browning) is almost always the initial step in the cooking process of any meat on which, a brown crust is desired.
- Pan-frying is the typical method of braising.

- If braising is called for in a vegetable recipe, it usually refers to cooking them in a small amount of liquid at a low temperature without browning the vegetables first.
- When braising, the food is never completely covered by the liquid.
- Braising can be used for many cuts of meat. The meat is first browned in a very small amount of oil or butter. The pan is then covered as tightly as possible while the meat continues to cook.
- If you oven braise, you can do it at 325°F and it will braise more evenly.

Sprinkling a small amount of flour on the meat during cooking will help it to brown.

- Make sure that there is only a very small amount of liquid or the steam generated will poach the meat.
- The liquid in the pot should only be simmering, not boiling.
- Occasionally blot the top of the meat with paper towel to eliminate excess moisture for the best results.

BROILING

- Broiling is done in a broiler in the bottom of the oven. Grilling is done on a grill, usually outside. High-heat cooking method used for tender cuts of meat.
- Lower heat is used for large, thick meats.

- Meats are sometimes dipped in oil to reduce sticking and to keep them moist.

Always place meats under the broiler as dry as possible.

- Meat and fish will brown more evenly if they are at room temperature instead of directly from the refrigerator.
- Always heat the broiler and the pan before placing any meat into the pan.

- Higher heat for thinner cuts and for meat that are to be cooked rare.
- Fat around meat may have the tendency to catch fire if it gets too hot or if it is too close to the flame or element.
- The distance from the top of the meat and the flame given in the recipe needs to be adhered to.
- If the meat you are cooking is thin, it should be cooked close to the flame or element so that it will cook faster and retain its moisture.
- If you are going to baste the meat, be sure and use a warm solution. If the solution is cool or cold, it will slow down the cooking time.
- A thin basting solution can be placed in a spray bottle.
- To reduce the risk of flare-ups. Place a few slices of bread on the bottom of the pan to soak up the excess fat drippings.

- If you want your steaks to be rare or medium rare, then they need to be cooked close to the heat source.
- Chicken breasts or thick cuts of meat are cooked away from the heat source.
- Only turn meats once when broiling.

BROILER TEMPERATURES

Cut of Meat	Thickness	Minutes per side		
		Rare	Medium	Well Done
Beef (all steaks)	1 in.	5 min.	6 min.	7 min.
	1 1/2 in.	9 min.	10 min	12 min.
	2 in.	16 min.	18 min.	20 min.
Lamb (loin, rib or chops)	1 in.	N/A	6 min.	7 min.
	1 1/2 in.	N/A	9 min.	11 min.
	2 in.	N/A	15 min.	17 min.
Pork (ham shoulder slice)				
Raw	1 in.			10 min.
Pre-Cooked				5 min.

CLAY POTS

- Place the complete pot in warm water for 15-20 minutes before using. A cold pot may crack.
- Never pre-heat the oven when using a clay pot. The temperature must rise gradually to protect the pot.
- When you remove the pot from the oven, never set it on a cold or even cool surface. Place the pot on a rack or folded kitchen towels.
- Never attempt to use a clay pot on the stovetop or any direct heat source or it will crack.

CONVECTION OVEN

- If you are going to use a convection oven, reduce the recommended temperature for a recipe by 25°-75°F.
- It is not necessary to pre-heat a convection oven. They heat up very quickly and evenly surround the food with heat.

- When baking in a convection oven, lower the temperature by 50-75°F to be safe or the baked goods may burn or over brown.

How a convection oven works

The standard oven and convection oven work very similar to each other. The notable difference in the convection oven is that it has a fan that increases the distribution of the heat molecules providing heat to all areas more evenly and faster. Because of the fan and the efficiency of the heat circulation, a lower temperature is usually required.

CROCK-POTS

- Never use a crock-pot to re-heat leftovers. The bacterial count will be higher and the food needs time at a higher temperature to kill them.
- Vegetables should be placed in crock-pots just before serving depending on their thickness.
- All foods should be at refrigerator or room temperature before placing them into a crock-pot.
- Never put partially or frozen foods in a crock-pot.
- Make sure that the cooker is $^1/_2$ to $^2/_3$ full or the food will not absorb enough heat to penetrate fully.
- The food must be covered with a liquid to generate sufficient steam.
- The original lid should be used and be tight-fitting.
- If possible allow the cooker to remain at a high setting for the first hour
- Make sure that the manufacturers recommended temperatures for foods be followed.

FRYING

- Never use "all-purpose oil" for frying.
- Peanut oil is good for frying but not for baked goods.
- Frying oil should never be re-used. Oil breaks down as it is heated and is not healthy.
- One of the best oils for frying is canola, which has a smoke point of 525°F.

- Dry foods thoroughly before placing them into a fryer.
- If you are going to use shortening to fry with, heat the shortening slowly. Shortening will scorch easily.
- Never crowd a deep-fat fryer for the best results.
- Always start shortening at 225°F and keep it there until all melted before raising the temperature.
- Never allow even a hint of soap scum to remain in the fryer or it will affect the results.
- If you coat the inside of the fryer with a very thin coating of white vinegar before you place the oil in, the foods will be less greasy.
- To test the fat to see if it too old, just drop a small piece of bread in. If the bread develops dark specs the oil is bad.
- Frying oil should never exceed 380°F.

- To slow the deterioration of the oil between batches, it would be best to reduce the temperature of the fat to 250°F until you are ready to use the oil again.

A low frying temperature results in a high fat product.

- Always allow the temperature to return to the normal frying temperature when frying a number of batches.
- Frying oil will darken prematurely if your frying pan is the slightest bit dirty.
- Too many food particles accumulating in the fryer can cause problems with discoloring the food.
- Never use brass or copper utensils in the fryer or they will react with the oil creating foam.
- If the fryer starts smoking while you are cooking it is probably because excess food has built up or the fat is too old.

- Never salt foods to be fried until you are ready to serve them or the salt will draw liquid out of the food.

GRILLING

- Normally done on an open grill over charcoal, gas or electric element. Cooking is regulated by moving the food to a hotter or cooler location on the grill.

HIGH-ALTITUDE COOKING

- When cooking above 3,500 feet, the atmospheric pressure gets lower and this will affect cooking and baking temperatures.
- When baking cakes or cookies at temperatures over 3,500 feet, you will need to increase the temperature 25°F and add 1 tablespoon of flour to your recipe, then continue adding 1 tablespoon of flour for every 1,500 feet.
- If you are using leavening and 1 teaspoon is needed at sea level, then use ²/₃ teaspoon at 3,500 feet, ¹/₂ teaspoon at 5,000 feet and ¹/₄ teaspoon at 6,500 feet.
- Boiled foods will take longer to cook the higher the altitude.
- Additional liquid may be needed for certain recipes the higher the altitude.
- All meats will take longer to cook at high altitudes.
- Legumes will take longer to cook and may require extra liquid.

Yeast breads will not need an adjustment at higher altitudes. Allow the dough to rise twice for the best results.

- Egg whites should only be beaten to soft-peak stage and not beaten until stiff over 3,500 feet.
- When deep fat frying it will be necessary to decrease the temperature 3°F for every 1,000 feet above sea level.
- Water will boil at 198°F instead of 212°F at 7,500 feet above sea level.

Boiling Point vs. Altitude

- As the altitude increases, the atmospheric pressure decreases placing less pressure on water that is trying to boil. When this occurs it makes it easier for the water to boil and the water molecules are released more easily. Water will boil at a lower temperature at the 5,000-foot elevation. For every 1,000 feet water, will boil at approximately 2° F. less than at sea level.

ALTITUDE (feet)	FAHRENHEIT	CELSIUS
0	212°	100°
1,000	210°	99°
2,000	208°	98°
3,000	207°	97°
4,000	205°	96°
5,000	203°	95°
10,000	194°	90°

MICROWAVE- COOKING

- Shorter cooking times will retain nutrients.
- Foods need to be turned unless the microwave has a moveable turntable or the food will have "cold spots."
- Use a special dish if you wish to brown food that is specifically designed for browning. The dish should be pre-heated for the best results.

When cooking meats with bones, remember that the microwave will send more energy to the bone than the meat and the meat may not cook evenly.

- If you are baking a dish, it will rise higher in a microwave.
- If a food is frozen it will take longer to cook in a microwave, since it does not work well on frozen water.
- High fat content meats will cook more rapidly than lean meats.
- Meats should be slightly undercooked since they will continue cooking after they are removed.

PAN-FRYING

- Best to use fat with a high smoke point, such as canola.
- Never use fat that has been heated, it may have deteriorated too much.
- Always place the presentation side in first since it will probably look the best after cooking.
- Small bubbles will appear on the side of the pan when the food is finished cooking.
- Make sure that you use a heavy pan, which normally conducts heat better than thin ones, which may develop hot spots.

Similar to sautéing with the exception that more oil is used and the cooking time is usually longer.

- Used for larger cuts of meats.
- Pan-fried foods should only be turned once.
- The level of fat used should come halfway up the sides of the meat or fish.
- Don't use a thick batter on a thin food or it will hide the flavor.
- Season all food before you place it in the pan.
- The pieces are not tossed up like when you sauté.
- Pan-frying is usually done over low heat.
- Pan-fried foods are often completed in the oven for the best results.
- If you desire a very crisp coating, complete the cooking in the oven after cooking the first side.

POACHING (general)

- The best temperature for poaching is 160°-180°F.
- The cooking is done in a small amount of liquid. The liquid should be very hot but not boiling.
- Mostly used to cook more delicate foods such as eggs (out of the shell) and fish.
- Partially poaching certain meats will eliminate the harsh flavors before they are cooked using some other method.
- Poaching will also firm up meats.

PRESSURE COOKING (general)

- Make sure that your pressure cooker has a 6-quart capacity or more for greater efficiency.
- Never fill the pressure cooker more than 65% full if you are cooking a food that has a high liquid content.
- Recommended highly for soups, stews and chili. Beans will not have to be soaked, which saves a great deal of time.

ROASTING

- The cut of meat to be roasted should be large enough so that it will retain enough moisture through this dry-cooking method.
- For the best flavor, purchase a roast with the bone in it to increase the flavor and to act as a heat conductor shortening the cooking time.
- Allow a roast to remain out of the refrigerator for about 1-2 hours before cooking.

Always start a roast in a pre-heated oven to help retain the juices.

- Give the roast a massage with olive oil to help retain the moisture.

- Place the roast on fresh celery stalks to allow fat to drip to the bottom and to allow the heat to circulate around the roast more efficiently.

- Never use any seasoning that contains salt on a roast or it may draw moisture from the meat.
- If you marinated the roast, the olive oil massage is even more important to help retain the moisture.

- Placing vegetable juice in the bottom of the pan will provide more flavor than using water.
- Use a roasting pan that has a very heavy lid, the heavier the better to keep the steam in so that it will re-circulate into the cooking liquid.
- Searing a roast contributes to drying out the roast and is not recommended by most chefs.

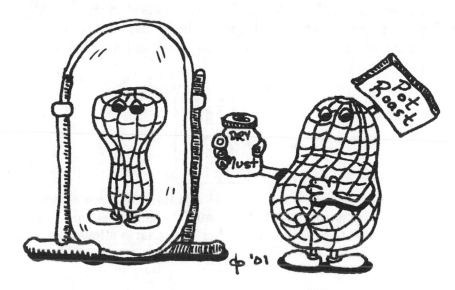

If the roast has high fat content and thick fat covering, just sprinkle the surface with a small amount of dry mustard to neutralize the fattiness.

- If the roast has a fat layer or if you are barding it, cook the roast fat-side up to naturally baste the roast.
- If you would like a nice brown coating on the roast, brush the outside lightly with white vermouth, about 15 minutes before the roast has completed cooking. If you have covered the roast remove the covering.
- If you slow-cook a roast, it will retain more moisture and will not shrink as much; however, it will not be browned very well.
- A fast method of cooking a pot roast is to tightly wrap the roast in heavy, weight aluminum foil after sprinkling 2 packages of dry onion mix over the roast. Cook in a pre-heated 300°F oven for 3 hours. Vegetables can be added to the pot after 2 hours of cooking time has elapsed.

- If you want a nicely browned roast, retain the moisture and not have too much shrinkage, then place the roast in a very hot oven for the first 20-25 minutes then reduce the heat back to the recommended setting.
- If the roast does not have a fat layer on top, then the roast should be turned once or twice and basted with the juices for the best results.
- To deep brown the roast, just raise the oven temperature toward the end of the cooking time. The juices that have been released will be available to brown.
- Try not to bast with too much liquid. The addition of additional liquid may have the tendency to create too much steam and the roast will not brown properly.

Allow the roast to rest for about 15 minutes after you remove it from the oven. The juices tend to go toward the center during cooking and will return close to the surface after the roast is allowed to rest.

- While the roast is resting, cover the roast with tin foil.

SAUTÉING

The meaning of sauté is "to jump" in French referring to the fact that the food is tossed in the sauté pan while it has been cooking.

- Heat the pan and the fat before adding any food.
- The food should be at room temperature. If the food is cold it may stick to the pan.
- Any dense foods such as carrots should be parboiled before being sautéed.
- Use a straight-sided sauté pan for large items. Sloping side pans are best for smaller items.

Before sautéing meats, always dredge the meat in a light coating of flour to hold the meat together and provide a protective coating.

- Before browning meat, sprinkle a small amount of sugar on the meat to help it brown.
- Salting food that is being sautéed will affect the browning.

- Never use salted butter when sautéing. The salt may separate and impart a bad taste to the food.
- Only use a small amount of oil and heat the oil to a high temperature.

Never overcrowd the pan when sautéing. Always choose a pan that will accommodate the full amount of food in a single layer. If the pan is too large, the juices will burn.

- Remove any excess fat with a bulb baster.
- Never cover a pan when sautéing or the food will become mushy from the steam and may prevent caramelizing.

SMOKING MEATS

- Make sure that the wood you are using is clean and has no glue or nails in it.
- If you are using a gas grill, be sure to use pre-soaked wood chips in the smoker box or at least wrap them in aluminum foil with holes so that your grill does not fill up with ash.
- If you are using a smoker, the wood may be placed directly in the box.
- If you would like a different smoked flavor, try using an old wine or whiskey barrel.
- Depending on the thickness of the meat, smoking can take up to 20 hours.
- The best temperature for smoking is between 200°-220°F and the internal temperature of most meat should be 165°-170°F.
- Higher temperatures will not allow the smoke time to infiltrate the meat adequately.
- The smoke imparts the flavor you are looking for.
- Slow cooking also has the ability to tenderize the meat.
- Using a good quality thermometer is a must.
- Make sure that the meat is totally surrounded by the smoke.

Types of Wood

Alder
This wood has a soft flavor that is used primarily to smoke fish and poultry.

Almond
Has a nutty, somewhat sweet flavor and is used on all types of meat.

Black Walnut
Has a heavier flavor than most wood and works best when added to other types of wood. Sometimes it may give foods a bitter flavor.

Fruit Wood
The most popular; are cherry or apple tree wood.

Grapevine
Never use with poultry or lamb unless you desire a real hearty flavor.

Hickory
Best with beef or lamb, but tends to impart a somewhat strong flavor and may overpower the flavor of the meat.

Maple
Best used for ham and poultry and is similar to fruit wood.

Mesquite
Provides a strong flavor but burns very quickly. Works great on meats that only have to be cooked for a short period of time.

Oak
Best used on beef or lamb, providing flavor but not overpowering the meat.

Pecan
Imparts a delicate flavor and burns cooler than most other wood.

STANDARD OVEN

- Best to use an oven thermometer and check your oven temperature at least every 6 months.
- Ovens can be as much as 25°-75°F off depending on the age of the oven and how often it is used.
- Debris and oven cleaning solution may leave a residue that causes temperature changes.
- If you find that the oven temperature is off, you can either make the adjustment in the recipe baking time or have the oven serviced.
- If food spills in the oven, cleanup will be easy if you pour salt on the spill as soon as possible.
- Place foods on the rack recommended at all times.

STEAMING

- Steaming cooks vegetables in a short period of time and retains a high percentage of the nutrients. Start with the more solid vegetables such as carrots then add the softer ones to the steamer afterwards.

The following are approximate steaming times for the more common vegetables

Artichokes	6-10 minutes
Green Beans	45 minutes
Beets	45 minutes
Broccoli with stalk	25 minutes
Brussels Sprouts	20 minutes
Cabbage	15 minutes
Carrots	25 minutes
Cauliflower	12 minutes
Celery	20 minutes
Corn on Cob	15 minutes
Green Peas	20-40 minutes
Green Peppers	5 minutes
Onions	20-30 minutes
Potatoes (all)	35 minutes
Tomatoes	15 minutes

WOK COOKING

- Only 1 tablespoon of oil is needed for four servings.
- All ingredients should be prepared before you start cooking, since the wok will cook very fast.
- The oil should be drizzled around the upper surface and allowed to fall down the sides for the best results.
- The food should be moved around continually during the cooking.

The wok should be pre-heated before placing food in to reduce sticking

- Never wok more than $1/2$ pound at a time for the best results.

- Before cooking beef, pork or chicken, partially freeze the meat for 1 hour so that it will be easier to thinly slice uniform pieces.
- Placing the meat in marinade for a few minutes will make the meat more flavorful and help to tenderize it.
- Make sure that all vegetables and meats have been cut into small uniform pieces.
- When thicker vegetables are used they should be added first to soften.

GENERAL COOKING TEMPERATURES

FOOD	DEGREES FAHRENHEIT
Ground Beef, Pork, Lamb	160
Beef, Lamb, Veal	
Rare	140
Medium Rare	145
Medium	160
Medium-Well	165
Well-Done	170
Pork	
Medium	160
Well-Done	170
Precooked	140
Poultry	
Ground Meat	165
Whole Birds	185
Parts	175
Stuffing (alone or in bird)	170
Egg Dishes	165
Leftovers	170

THERMOMETERS

DEEP-FAT/CANDY

- The bulb should be fully immersed in the candy or food and should never be allowed to touch the bottom of the cooking container.
- To check the accuracy of the thermometer, place it in boiling water for 3-4 minutes. The temperature should read 212°F or 100° C.

FREEZER/REFRIGERATOR

- These thermometers read from –20° to 80°F.
- Frozen foods should always be stored at 0°F or below to slow nutrient loss and maintain the quality of the food.

MEAT

- Insert the thermometer into the center or thickest part of the meat, making sure that it is not resting on a bone.

OVEN

- It is wise to check your oven temperature accuracy at least once a month.
- If the oven temperature is not accurate it can affect the results of the food being prepared, especially baked goods.
- When checking the temperature, the thermometer should be placed in the middle of the center rack of the oven.

CHAPTER 5

BEEF COOKING SECRETS

BEEF COOKING SECRETS

The Spanish brought the first cattle to Florida in 1550. The first slaughter-house was established in Boston in 1662. Cattle were not very popular because of their size and difficulty of caring for them. Pork was still the desired meat of that day. One of the first restaurants to serve beef was the Tunn Tavern in Philadelphia and called the dish "beef-steak." The Philly beef steak sandwich was invented.

U. S. GOVERNMENT MEAT GRADES

BEEF	Fat Calories	VEAL	LAMB	PORK
Prime	50%	Prime	Prime	U.S. No. 1
Choice	39%	Choice	Choice	U.S. No. 2
Good	30%	Good	Good	U.S. No. 3
Standard		Standard	Utility	U.S. No. 4
Commercial		Utility	Cull	Utility

MAJOR CUTS OF BEEF

There are eight major cuts of beef butchered in the United States, they are called; shank, flank, brisket, chuck, round, rib, plate and loin. The eight cuts are given a number of additional names, which will be more recognizable to the consumer. These include names such as; sirloin, porterhouse, top round, eye of the round, New York, T-bone, etc. These explain the way the eight major cuts are actually cut up. The tenderness of beef will depend on the location of the cut and the method of cutting. Some cuts are tougher than other cuts: these include, pot roasts (chuck roasts), which are cut from the neck area of the cow and will be the least expensive.

Brisket Cuts

- The brisket is cut from behind a cow's front leg or may be cut from the leg itself. Normally a tough cut of beef, it needs to be cooked in liquid for about 2-3 hours. If you wish to get the best results when preparing a brisket, rotate the roast $1/4$ turn every 25 minutes. The brisket is fully cooked when you see the fat just starting to roll off. However, if the fat can easily be removed with your fingers the brisket is over done.

Chuck Cuts (Roasts)

- These are the toughest cuts and should be cooked in a small amount of liquid and they may need to be tenderized.

Flank and Plate Cuts (Skirt)

- Most of the time if USDA Good grade is purchased, they will need tenderizing. Prime and Choice are much better choices for these cuts. They are usually cut in strips and used for stir, frying. London broil is made from flank steak. Best if marinated.

Loin Cuts (Tenderloin)

- Cut from behind the ribs, they are the most tender. They include filet, Spencer, porterhouse, and New York steaks. A New York steak is a sirloin steak that has been cut about 1" thick and was popularized in New York City.

Rib Cuts (Ribs)

- Markets may label these as baby back ribs, rib steaks, rib roasts, or just back ribs. For the best results, they should be prepared by grilling or placed in the oven and cooked slowly. The taste of ribs can be improved; by adding a sauce or using a marinade.

Round Cuts (Rump)

- Most of these will be tender and can be cooked a number of different ways. They include; top round, eye of the round, and bottom round. They can be pot roasted or spit barbecued.

RECOMMENDED WINES WITH BEEF

BEEF STEW . . . . .Burgundy, Pinot Noir
CHILI & BEANS . . . . .Zinfandel
CORNED BEEF . . . . .Merlot, Zinfandel
STEAK . . . . .Cabernet Sauvignon, Beaujolais
HAMBURGER . . . . .Zinfandel
MEAT LOAF . . . . .Zinfandel
RIBS . . . . .Beaujolais
ROAST BEEF . . . . .Pommard, Cabernet Sauvignon

COOKING BEEF

- Beef is mainly composed of protein (in the form of muscle tissue), fat and water. If you remove the fat, beef is actually about 60% water. Beef muscle fibers are supported by small bands of connective tissue: either collagen or elastin. The cuts of meat from a muscle that gets a lot of exercise has more connective tissue, resulting in a tougher cut of meat. Since the connective tissue is in these areas usually have a fat layer surrounding the connective tissue, melting it away with heat and liquid (such as stew) allows the meat to become tender. This tenderizing process actually turns the collagen into gelatin.

- The other type of connective tissue, elastin, can only be broken down by slicing the meat into small strips or pounding the beef with a tenderizing hammer. Another method of tenderizing beef is to marinate the beef in an acidic solution, which softens the collagen. Marinating for too long a period may, however, cause the meat to lose moisture when it is cooked and lose juices. When any cut of cooked beef cools, the meat may become tough since the collagen, which has turned to liquid, turns back into a solid.

Barding

- Barding is adding a layer of fat to cover meat and keep the lean meat from drying out.
- You can use some of the fat that has been removed from the meat or the fat can be from another source, such as pork.
- Bacon fat is commonly used as a substitute but should be boiled for 5-7 minutes to lower the salt content before placing the strips on a roast.

- The added fat should be removed about 10-15 minutes before the meat is fully cooked so that the surface of the meat can brown.
- The strips of fat are just placed flat on the meat and then tied on with butcher string.

Beef Stew

- The less tender the cut of beef used, the longer it will take to cook it and make it tender.
- Large beef bones should be saved to provide a great flavor for stews.
- White fat around the beef indicates a more, tender cut. Yellow fat indicates a tougher cut.
- Irish stew uses mutton or lamb to replace beef.
- Plan on 1-2 cups of stew per person.
- Beef chuck is the most common meat for stew and has an excellent flavor.
- Stews should be thick, not watery.

- The liquids should only be partially covering the food.
- Before adding the stew beef, roll the pieces in all-purpose flour that has been seasoned with your favorite seasonings. After lightly breading the beef pieces, place them in the refrigerator for 45 minutes so that the breading will adhere better.
- Best to place the pieces of meat into a frying pan with about $1/4$ inch of oil and brown the meat before placing the meat into the stew pot. The meat will not brown nicely in a stew pot.
- Always remove all visible fat from the meat. Chuck has enough fat laced throughout the meat to add flavor.
- The seasonings for old-fashioned beef stew: 1 teaspoon of Worcestershire sauce, 1 clove of garlic, 1 medium onion, 1 bay leaf (added last 10 minutes only), 1 tablespoon of salt, $1/2$ teaspoon of black pepper (freshly ground), 1 teaspoon of sugar, $1/2$ teaspoon paprika and a dash of ground cloves.
- If you don't have a pot big enough to brown the stew meat in one layer, brown the meat in small batches.

- Never add hot water when additional water is needed, always add cold water to stew. Studies show that adding hot water makes the meat tough.
- If you are going to use basil as a spice in beef stew do not put it in the stew until 10 minutes before the stew is finished cooking. Basil flavor is lost easily.

Thickening should only be done toward the end of the cooking time.

- To easily thicken beef stew, just mix 2 tablespoons of potato starch in 3 tablespoons of water then add slowly to the stew, stirring continually. This should be done for every cup of liquid in the stew for a thick, rich stew.
- Stew can be sweetened up with the addition of carrots.
- Cornstarch is commonly used as a stew thickener. Blend the cornstarch with some of the stock to make a thin paste consistency then add back to the stew.
- Bread crumbs, are also a common thickener for stew.
- Use 3-4 wine corks to tenderize beef in the stew. Wine corks contain a chemical that is released in hot liquid that has the ability to tenderize beef. Best to discard the corks before serving.

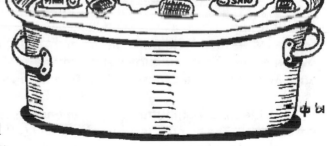

- Adding ¹/₂ cup of strong tea will also help tenderize beef.
- Cut up carrots, potatoes, onions or other vegetables should be added during the last 20-30 minutes of cooking time.
- Try not to boil the stew, just slowly simmer it for the best results.
- Remove fat from the stew by placing a few ice cubes in a piece of cheesecloth and swirling around for about 1 minute. Fat is attracted to ice cubes.
- Before adding a dried herb to stew, crush them to release more flavors.

- If you over-salt the stew, add a piece or two of raw potato and swirl around for a minute or two then discard.
- The meat should be fork tender before being served.

Beef Tartar

Originated in Baltic Russia by the Tartar and Mongolian warriors who liked to eat raw meat. The warriors tenderized the meat by placing the meat under their saddles while riding into battle. After the battle they would eat the meat, which was now nice and tender.

- Steak tartare is usually served as an appetizer in most restaurants.
- It is prepared from fresh chopped beef, onions, egg yolk, parsley and usually capers then formed into a flat pancake shape.
- In some restaurants it is a very thin slice of filet mignon that has been seasoned with onion and spices.

Hamburger

The first hamburger as we know it today was introduced in the United States by German immigrants in the mid 1800's and was called a "hamburger steak." The "hamburger steak" made its significant public appearance at the Louisiana Exposition in 1904 and has been a hit ever since.

In 1921 the first "hamburger stand" opened in Wichita, Kansas and the craze began. The stand was a roadside stand called White Castles, which popularized the hamburger, as we know it today. During the 1930's hamburgers were called "Wimpy burgers" due to the popularity of the Popeye comic strip. In England the hamburger is still called a "Wimpie."

- If the meat is ground twice through the butcher's meat grinder the meat will be more dry. When coarsely ground, the meat will more moist and will not lose as much fat.
- To keep your hamburger patties uniform in size, just scoop up the meat with an ice cream scoop.

- Chuck meat (about 30% fat) is the typical hamburger meat sold in super-markets. It will be more flavorful since the area of the cow that it is cut from is a more exercised area.
- When thawing hamburger meat, try and slow thaw it in the refrigerator. Microwave thawing is faster but removes too much moisture from the meat.
- The best onions on a burger are red; Bermuda or Italian.
- Low-fat burgers will usually have about a 15% fat content. These burgers will have poor flavor unless seasoned.
- Ground cherries give hamburger a great flavor.
- Supermarket and restaurant hamburger meat must be cooked medium-well or well done in all instances to avoid bacterial contamination problems.

- If you would like your burger medium or rare just buy a steak and sear it on both side and grind the steak up into hamburger meat then prepare. This will kill any possible bacteria that may be present.
- Ground sirloin steak (about 15% fat if labeled extra lean) will make the burgers with the lowest fat content, but you will need to add bread, crumbs or 1 stiffly beaten egg white for each pound of meat to obtain some moisture.
- Round steak (about 22% fat if labeled lean) also makes an excellent burger. Have the butcher trim all the visible fat from the steak and grind it twice.
- When preparing patties from standard burger meat, make them a little larger to make up for shrinkage due to the higher fat content.

If you mix hamburger meat too much, the burgers will be very heavy. Over-mixing is a mistake most people make when making hamburgers.

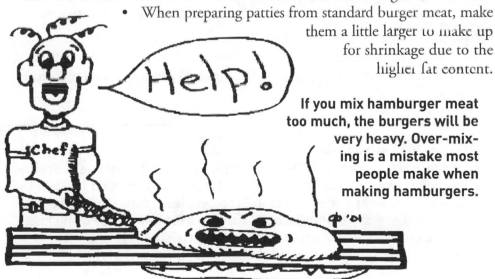

- For a great flavor, add a few tablespoons of V-8 juice to the burgers while mixing.
- For a great taste and to reduce the amount of fat and meat, try using some ground potatoes or soy meal.
- Try placing a small button mushroom in the center of the hamburger for a surprise treat.
- Don't squeeze the meat too hard when forming the burger or it will be too dense and take a long time to cook.
- For a different treat shape the burger in a roll and place them into hot dog buns.
- A cheesy burger can be made by placing a small amount of American cheese in the middle of the burger.
- To make your burgers cook up crispy, just sprinkle a small amount of cornstarch on top just before you place them on the grill.
- Always start burgers on a very hot grill for the best results and don't overcook or they will dry out.

Try not to press down hard on the burgers while they are cooking or it will remove too much of the juices. This is a common practice since people are in a hurry and believe that this will speed up the cooking time. It will, but you get a dry burger.

- When you first place hamburgers on a grill, it is best to sear them on each side and then turn then a number of times (without pressing down) for the best results. This will result in a nicely, browned crust and a juicy interior.

Hot Dogs

Hot dogs originated in Germany in the typical hot dog form, however, the sausage was invented in 900BC. The Germans called the hot dog a "dachshund dog." The hot dog as we know it today was first sold in 1880 by Charles Feltman at Coney Island in Brooklyn, New York. The name "hot dog" was coined at a Giants baseball game in 1901 when they didn't know how to spell "dachshund" and yelled "get them while they re hot." The first major sales operation was called Nathan's Hot Dogs at Coney Island.

- To boil hot dogs, place them into a pot of boiling water, allow the water to return to boiling then remove from the heat, cover and stand for 5-7 minutes depending on the thickness of the hot dog.
- To broil hot dogs, make a slit down the full length of the hot dog (do not slice in half) and spray the inside lightly with oil then place under the broiler for a few minutes until cooked. The hot dogs may be turned if desired.
- To microwave, place the hot dog in a bun and wrap completely in a piece of paper towel and cook on high for 60 seconds for 1 hot dog. Multiple dogs will take 30-40 second per dog of cooking time.

Jerky

- Jerky can be made in a smoker for the best flavor.
- The best cut of meat is a sirloin tip roast, which is very lean and has very little fat.
- The roast should be sliced across the grain and into $1/4$ inch strips.
- Jerky is best prepared at a low temperature using very little smoke. The temperature should be under 150°F for the best results.
- Electric smokers work very well when preparing jerky.

Kidneys

- Lighter colored kidneys are from younger animals and will be more flavorful.
- Kidneys should be cooked the same day they are purchased.
- All visible fat should be removed as well as the outer skin.
- Darker colored kidneys are from older animals and should be soaked in cold salted tap water for 45 minutes to eliminate any strong smell.

Larding

- Larding is the process of inserting strips of fat in the flesh of lean meats to make them more juicey.
- The fat that is inserted will melt during the cooking process and is usually pork.

Special pork fat known as "lardons" are sold by butchers for this purpose.

- The lardons can be soaked in marinades, wines or any flavorful liquid that will enhance the meat.
- Kitchen supply stores sell a "larding needle" to help you accomplish this task.
- Lardons are always inserted across the grain of the meat.

Liver

- When choosing liver, it should have a clean odor and not a strong one that might indicate that it is too old.
- Liver should be cooked and not kept even refrigerated for more than 1 day.
- The younger the liver the better since the older the cow the more contaminants may be found in the liver. Young beef or calf's liver is best.
- Liver is one of the highest cholesterol foods you can consume.
- Pork liver is only use in pates or sausages.
- Calf's liver will be a pinkish-brown color, while standard beef liver is more reddish-brown.

- Before cooking, liver should be wiped off with a damp-cloth and then remove the outer membrane and veins.
- Tomato juice can be used to tenderize liver. Just soak the liver in the juice for 2 hours in the refrigerator.

Soaking liver in milk for about 1 hour in the refrigerator will improve the flavor.

- Before cooking calf's liver, remove the thin skin and tubes.
- To prepare chopped liver, just cook the liver first for 5-8 minutes before grinding.

- Liver should be cooked no more than medium-well. If you overcook liver it will become dried out and tough.
- Liver is best broiled since it is a fast method cooking and will not dry the meat out.
- Slow cooking liver will dry it out and make it tough.
- Calf's liver can be sautéed with excellent results.

- Liver should be served slightly pink inside unless your guests request otherwise.
- Grilled onions go great with liver.

London Broil

- Flank steak is used for London broil. Occasionally, round or chuck steak is used.
- Most supermarkets label round steak as London broil.
- Make sure that all the fat and connective tissue is removed.
- The steak should be marinated for 1-2 hours in the refrigerator.
- Marinade consists of 1 pint of olive or corn oil, 2 ounces of fresh lemon juice, 2 teaspoons of table salt, $1^1/_2$ teaspoons of freshly crushed black pepper and 1 teaspoon of thyme.

London broil will be juicier if allowed to rest after broiling for about 2 minutes. This allows the juices to go back near the surface.

- London broil will be more, tender and flavorful if served medium-rare.

Marinating Beef

- Marinades are composed of oil, an acid and a flavoring.
- Excessive marinating will cause most meat to lose moisture when being cooked. The shorter the time in the marinade, the better.
- Since marinades contain acid, the best dishes to use are glass and ceramic containers.
- Be sure that the marinade completely covers the meat.
- Turn the meat occasionally for the best results.
- Always refrigerate meats while they are being marinated.
- Large cuts of meat or roasts can be marinated for prolonged periods, but not more than 3-4 days.
- Never baste meats or any food with the leftover marinade sauce unless you boil it to protect against bacterial contamination.
- Most meat that has been marinated will turn brown very quickly when cooked because of the high acid content of the marinade.

- Large plastic bags are commonly used to marinate large pieces of meat to conserve the amount of marinade required.
- Most thick cuts of beef require 1-2 days in the marinade and regular turning to completely marinade beef.
- The higher the acid, content the shorter the period needed to marinade.

When marinating food in the refrigerator allow it to stand at room temperature before cooking.

- Strips of papaya or pineapple can be spread over the surface of a piece of meat and will tenderize it under refrigeration in about 3 hours. Dry the meat thoroughly before cooking but never rinse the meat under water.
- Kiwi contains a chemical that will tenderize beef.

Meatballs

- To form meatballs, roll out the meat into a long log about 2" thick and cut even pieces the size of the meatballs you desire, then roll in the palms of your hands.
- Always dampen your hands frequently while rolling meatballs.
- A small piece of cheese or herbs in the center of the meatball provides excellent flavor.

Placing a small button mushroom in the center of a meatball will really surprise the family or guests.

- Meatballs can actually become tough if they are compacted too densely. Use mild pressure when rolling the meatballs.

Meatloaf

- Low fat ground meat is healthiest for meatloaf but lacks flavor.
- Ground round is usually the choice of chefs. However, many chefs prefer ground chuck, which is 22-30% fat for the flavor.
- If you would like a lower fat ground round have the butcher grind the meat twice, however, if he only grinds the meat once the meat will be more coarse and the meatloaf will be more moist and tender.
- Ground sirloin is too dry and too low in fat.

- When adding breadcrumbs, be sure they are moist not dry to obtain the best results.
- To reduce the amount of meat, just use a grated potato as a partial replacement.
- Finely diced and sautéed onions and celery add a great touch to meatloaf.
- To enhance the flavor, replace whatever liquid you are using with red wine or a dark beer.
- To prevent meatloaf from sticking to the bottom of the pan place 2-3 fresh celery stalks under the meatloaf. Greasing the pan or spraying it with spray oil helps as well.
- After placing meatloaf in a pan press down on the meatloaf to eliminate excess air.
- The top of the meatloaf will not crack if kept moist with occasional dampening with water or placing tomato sauce on top.
- Never place aluminum foil on top of tomato sauce or it will eat away the aluminum and put excess aluminum in the meatloaf, which is not very healthy.
- For every pound of meatloaf use $1/4$ cup of tomato juice or if you are adventurous use bloody may mix.
- One cup of grated cheddar cheese can be added to the mix.
- Meatloaf can be mixed in a large plastic bag to avoid the mess.

- As the meatloaf cooks, it is best to remove the excess drippings with a bulb-baster.

If you want a real, crusty brown meatloaf, just place the meatloaf into a 9 X 5 X 3-inch pan that has been sprayed with vegetable spray, then turn it upside down in small roasting pan and bake as you would normally.

- Bread slices under the meatloaf will soak up excess fat drippings.
- A 2-pound meatloaf will take about 1 hour 20 minutes to cook at 325°F.
- Add grated cheddar cheese to the top of the meatloaf 10 minutes before it is done.

- Try icing the entire meatloaf after it is finished cooking with hot mashed potatoes.

Use a meat thermometer to tell if the meatloaf is fully cooked. The internal temperature should be 165°F. Any higher and it will be too dry.

- Allow the steam to dissipate for about 10 minutes before slicing the meatloaf and it won't fall apart.
- The doneness test for meatloaf is when it can be pulled from the sides and the liquids are clear with just a hint of pink.
- Frost your meatloaf with mashed potatoes mixed with cheese, then place the meatloaf back in the oven to bake for a few minutes.

Prime Rib

- Prime rib; can be ordered by the rib. One rib will usually feed two people.
- Ask for the prime rib to be cut from the loin end not the shoulder end.
- Best to brown the prime rib at a high temperature first (400°F), then lower the temperature. It takes about 45 minutes to brown a 5-pound prime rib roast.
- After browning the temperature can be lowered to 350°F for 40-50 minutes depending on the doneness desired.
- Prime rib roast needs to rest for 20-25 minutes in a warm location covered

with aluminum foil to allow the juices to release.

Ribs

- If you are going to smoke beef ribs they should be cooked on low heat and slowly or they may not be tender.
- If you are going to use a rub on smoked ribs it should be sweet or savory.

Old Fashioned Rib Barbecue Sauce

³/₄ cup chicken stock
3 tablespoons of extra virgin olive oil (cold pressed)
1 teaspoon canola oil
¹/₃ cup dark brown sugar
4 cloves of finely chopped garlic
¹/₄ cup seasoned tomato sauce or ketchup
2 tablespoons of quality mustard
2-3 tablespoons of soy sauce
1 tablespoon cayenne (red) pepper (optional)

The olive and canola oil should be heated in a small pan on medium heat. When the mixture heats up, add the garlic and sauté for about 4 minutes being careful not to allow it to burn. Mix the remaining ingredients gradually and simmer for about 15 minutes, which will allow the flavors to mix and the sauce to thicken.

- If you are using prime or choice grade ribs, then the boiling may not be necessary.

- Another method of tenderizing spareribs, without the loss of flavor by boiling them, is to slow cook them in a 300°F oven for 2 hours.
- You can also use a roasting pan and place the ribs, ribs down in the pan. Then place in a 300°F oven for about 1 hour, coat the ribs with your favorite sauce and bake for an additional 45 minutes while basting and turning the ribs at regular intervals. Then allow the ribs to bake for an additional 45 minutes or

until tender.

One of the key secrets to making tender spareribs is to place them in a pot and cover with boiling water, then simmer for 30 minutes before baking or barbecuing.

- Ribs can be placed in the oven for about 30 minutes at 250°F to allow some of the fat to cook off if they are very fatty.
- Baby back ribs can be made in a roasting pan on a rack cooked at 400°F for about 1¼ hours.

Roasts

- Chuck roasts will be the toughest roast and should be cooked in a small amount of liquid. Try and buy "choice" chuck if possible.
- Round roasts will be tender and be cooked any number of ways.
- Briskets are tough and usually take 2-3 hours in a liquid to tenderize them.
- Best to start with a prime-grade, untrimmed brisket.

A medium well done roast is more easily digested than a rare to medium-rare roast.

- If the surface of a roast becomes dark after 2-3 days under refrigeration, smell it, it should still be good, but you need to use it immediately.
- When storing a roast, always place it back into its own juices.
- The presence of a high fat layer on a roast means that the animal did not exercise much and the meat will be more, tender.
- Never rapid thaw a roast or you will lose too much moisture.
- Roasts can be aged to improve the flavor if you have purchased "good" grade beef instead of "choice" or "prime."
- To age a roast, just place it in the refrigerator on a broiling rack (with paper towels under it) so that air can circulate around it. The roast should be unwrapped and in the back of the refrigerator for 3 days before you cook it.
- To easily remove fat from a fatty roast, refrigerate the roast after it has been partially cooked. The fat solidifies and is more easily removed.

- A roast should be left at room temperature for a short period of time before placing it in the oven. Roasts will cook more evenly if they are somewhat warm to start instead of cold.

When cooking a roast with a bone in it, it will not take as long to cook. If the bone goes through the meat, it will conduct heat to the center.

- Start a roast in a pre-heated over to help retain the juices.
- If you prefer moisture in the pan, try using de-fatted broth or V-8 juice. Tomato juice works well and acts as a meat tenderizer.
- If you want the fat to baste the roast, then cook it fat side up. If you want to reduce the fat, either remove it or place the fat side on the bottom of the pan.

If your roast has high fat content, sprinkle the top with dry mustard to reduce the excess fat from entering the roast.

- Basting a roast with a de-fatted broth will keep the roast moist without the added fat.
- A thin layer of vegetable oil rubbed on the roast will help to seal in the juices.
- If you want to give your roast a nice brown finish, just rub the roast with flour before placing it in the oven.
- By placing fresh celery stalks under the roast, the roast will not stick to the pan. This will also elevate the roast and allow the hot air to circulate around the roast.

- Never use a seasoning that has salt until the roast is almost finished cooking or it will draw moisture from the roast.
- To darken the roast and give it a nice dark brown coating, brush white vermouth on the surface 15 minutes before the roast has finished cooking.
- If you want the entire roast to brown evenly, then turning it is a must. Once or twice should be sufficient to produce the results desired.

- If you do baste, use a solution that is already heated otherwise it may create steam and steam the roast.
- Roasting a roast at a higher temperature will provide you with a roast that has a variety of doneness from well done ends to medium rare interiors.

To retain more juices, start a roast at a high temperature then reduce the temperature after about 20 minutes.

- If you roast in a covered pan, lower the temperature by 25°F.
- If you must cook a frozen roast increase the cooking time by about 50%.
- Do not slow-cook a roast or it may dry it out. Cooking roasts in the oven provides a dry heat cooking method, which tends to dry out the meat. Large cuts of meat do well and hold their moisture better than small cuts.

- When a roast is finished cooking, leave the roast rest for 10 minutes and allow the moisture that has gone to the center to dissipate back to the edges of the roast before slicing. Keep the roast covered while it is resting either with the roasting lid or a piece of aluminum foil (providing it does not have tomato sauce on top).
- While the roast is resting the roast will still cook slightly and increase the internal temperature about 5-8°F.
- Remove a roast when it is about 10° below the required temperature and it will continue cooking while it is resting for 10-15 minutes. The roast should be at the correct temperature when you get ready to serve it.
- A roast will shrink due to water loss. The cells lose their ability to retain water the more the meat is cooked.

Rib Roast

- If you want the most tender and flavorful rib roast, ask your butcher to cut the rib roast from the "small end." This is between the 9th and 12th ribs or ask for the "first-cut."
- Have the butcher remove the short ribs and the shinbone to make carving the roast easier.
- Another trick is to have the butcher loosen the ribs and then tie the roast back together for you.

Pot Roast

- The best cut of meat for pot roast is the first-cut or flat-cut brisket. This cut will have just the right amount of fat for a good pot roast.
- Always slice pot roast across the grain to avoid shredding the meat.

Steak

If you are worried about E. coli contamination of your steak and you would like to prepare a raw steak dish, just rubbed crushed garlic on the surface of the meat. Garlic is a powerful antibiotic herb that can kill E. coli as well as many other bacteria.

- A rare steak contains very little blood, if any at all. The red liquid is usually composed of myoglobin (red muscle pigment) and water.
- The more firm a steak becomes the more it has been cooked.
- Steaks should be served on hot plates since when the steak is cooked the collagen turns to gelatin. When the steak cooks it reverses and become tougher.
- Never use onion salt, garlic salt or any other salt on a steak until it is almost done or it will draw moisture out of the steak.
- Aging steaks cause the enzymes in the meat to soften the connective tissue and the meat to become more tender. Temperature must be kept between 34° and 38°F.
- A slow, moist heat cooking will tenderize a tough steak.

If the fat on a steak is white, the steak will be more tender than if the fat is yellow. Yellow indicates grass-fed, white indicates corn-fed.

- Prime steaks are hard to find and the majority go to restaurants. They are higher in fat content.
- Most meat now sold in supermarkets is graded "good." Try and find "choice" when possible.
- Bacterial contamination is possible and a steak needs to be seared on each side to be safe to eat. Rare is not a problem if this is done.
- The meat closest to the bone absorbs more flavor and is the most flavorful part of the steak.
- The government ink stamp on a steak is harmless.
- If the steaks are frozen, many chefs suggest that you do not thaw the steak, but to just rub the surface of the steak with oil and then increase your cooking time.
- All flat bones are associated with tender cuts of meat. Round bones are associated with tougher cuts.

To seal in the juices of a steak, just lightly flour it instead of searing it.

- Ideally a steak should be between 1-3" thick. If it is less than 1" it will be very dry and usually tough. These thin steaks have to be pan-fried. If over 3" the surface is usually overcooked and the interior undercooked.

Best not to use pepper on a steak too early during cooking since pepper becomes bitter when it is scorched.

- Never wash meats or water may seep into the meat. If you feel that the meat must be cleaned first, use a clean damp washrag.
- Pounding steak with a meat mallet will tenderize steak by mashing the connective tissue making it more palatable.
- Most tender cuts of meat should be cooked using a dry-heat method. These methods include frying, broiling or roasting.
- Steaks can be tenderized by placing the steak in a glass dish with sides and cover the steak with beer and refrigerate for 3 hours. Discard the beer, dry the steak well and cook.
- Searing a steak does not keep the juices in as previously thought, especially if you use any salt on it.
- Searing will, however, cook the juices making a tasty brown coating on the surface of the steak.

- Never turn a steak with a fork always use tongs. Poking holes in a steak release the juices and is worse than salting steaks when you first start to cook them.
- Steaks should only be turned once; continual turning does not do any good. If you do sear the steak that turn should be sufficient.

When broiling or frying a steak, be sure that the steak is at room temperature when starting for the best results.

- If you want to flambé a steak, just bring it to the table in the pan and pour 2 tablespoons of brandy (warm brandy) over the steak and ignite it with a long match. Pour the sauce over the steak for a great flavor.
- When barbecuing a steak, be sure that you do not use "real" charcoal. The fat dripping on the charcoal forces a carcinogen into the steak and it is the equivalent of smoking 15 cigarettes.

- Steaks should not rest after they are cooked, they should be served immediately.

Swiss Steak

- The best Swiss steak is made from bottom round.
- Best to use a very heavy skillet with a tight-fitting lid.
- Chefs will pound flour into the steak with the side of a meat cleaver until almost all the flour has been absorbed by the meat. For 2 pounds of steak, they use 4-5 tablespoons of flour.
- After the flour is pounded in, the meat should be allowed to rest for 10 minutes.
- The flour in the Swiss steak will provide body and thicken the sauce as the steak cooks.

Skirt Steak

- Cut from the pad of muscle that runs from the ribs to the loin.
- Be sure that the butcher has removed the silvery membrane.
- Usually sold in pieces that are about 12 ounces each.
- Use high-moisture meat that should be allowed to reach room temperature before you cook the steak.
- Cook over high heat to sear then cook very quickly.
- The steak should be allowed rest for 5 minutes before serving to allow the juices to return to the surface.
- Slice the steak on the bias to allow for a larger, thinner slice.

Sweetbreads

- The best quality will be from young animals. Calves sweetbreads (thymus gland) are more, tender since they are from young animals.
- Calves sweetbreads will be white.
- Sweetbreads tend to become more reddish as the animal ages.
- Best to use the same day they are purchased since they only have a refrigerator life of 1 day.

Cooking Sweetbreads

- Soak the sweetbreads in a solution of 1 quart of cold tap water mixed with 3 tablespoons of pure lemon juice for 1 hour to draw out residual blood.
- If you are concerned about the sweetbread retaining their shape when cooked, slice into strips and place on a flat plate or cookie sheet, then place a very heavy weight on top and refrigerate for 2-3 hours before you cook them.
- Blanch for 5 minutes; then place into a bowl of cold water, which will firm them up.
- After they have been firmed and cooled, remove the outer membrane and connective tissue.
- Best when grilled or sautéed.

Veal

- Be sure that the fat on veal is very white and not yellow.
- Veal is very delicate meat and should be cooked similar to chicken.
- Cook veal within 1-2 days after purchase for the best flavor.
- Veal is best when cooked using a moist-cooking method and should be cooked slowly.
- Veal is low fat meat and if you cook a veal roast it would be best if it were barded. Your butcher can do this for you if you have never done it before.
- Ground veal is rarely used in meat loaf or hamburger since it requires added fat.
- Veal will easily turn tough if overcooked. Since many dishes call for thin slices of veal such as veal scaloppini it is easy to overcook veal.
- The best seasonings for veal are sage, thyme, tarragon and basil.
- Veal should never be aged.

Veal Breast

- Breast of veal is the least expensive cut and is best stuffed and cooked very slowly.
- The breast is cooked, stuffed for 20-25 minutes per pound at 350°F to an internal temperature of 170°F.

Veal Chop

- Because veal is so lean, the only cut that is good for grilling is a veal chop that is cut about 1½ thick.
- Veal chops should be grilled about 4 inches from the heat.

  Veal chops should never be placed under the broiler.

- Veal chops can be sautéed in just a few minutes and if not watched will be overdone very quickly.

Veal Cutlets

- Breaded veal cutlets should be sautéed in a small amount of olive oil with 1 teaspoon of canola oil added for the best results.
- Sautéing cutlets are the only recommended method of cooking by almost all chefs.
- Clarified butter may also be used in place of the oil with excellent results.
- Use a kitchen mallet to flatten out the veal. Pounding too hard will tear the meat, so do a gentle pounding.
- Place the breaded cutlets into the refrigerator for 45 minutes to help the breading adhere better when they are cooked.

Veal Parmigiana

- Pound the veal until it is in very thin slices.
- The veal should be dipped in a mixture of egg and milk, then immediately into fresh breadcrumbs and sautéed in clarified butter or olive oil until it has browned.
- The dish is usually topped with a thin slice of mozzarella cheese and tomato sauce with a hint of garlic.
- Bake at 400°F only until the cheese melts or it will dry out the veal.

Veal Roast

- Chefs tend to rub butter on the roast and them sprinkle paprika on top to give the roast a nice brown color.
- Allow the roast to sit still in a warm environment, covered for about 30 minutes before attempting to slice it or it will fall apart.

You can also rub oil on the outside instead of butter to help keep the moisture in and to allow the spices to adhere to the surface.

- Many chefs cover a veal roast with a layer of fat since it is so lean and may cook somewhat dry.
- Bacon, which has not been smoked or salt pork is used by many chefs to cover a veal roast.
- Boneless veal roasts are also frequently rolled in breadcrumbs to protect the delicate skin before being placed in the roasting pan. The best method is to place the breadcrumbs on a piece of wax paper and hold the edges with one hand, while you roll the roast back and forth with the other hand.

Veal Scaloppini

- The best pot; recommended by chefs to prepare veal scaloppini is an enamel frying pan and a good heavy one.
- High heat and speed are very important.

A small amount of sugar in the coating will hasten the browning and will not sweeten it.

- The easiest method is to buy the veal scaloppini from the butcher already cut.
- If you are going to cut your own scaloppini, be sure that the veal has been placed in the freezer until it is very firm. Cut against the grain and if the grain changes, turn the meat as you are cutting it.
- Blanching the veal will keep the meat firm and will not fall apart.

CHAPTER 6

COOKING LAMB, PORK & GAME MEATS

COOKING LAMB

Lamb is one of the leaner meats with an excellent taste and texture. Most lamb sold in the United States comes from animals that are about 1 year old. New Zealand supplies 12% of all lamb sold in the U.S. New Zealand does not allow their lamb to be fed hormones. Most cuts of lamb are smaller than beef cuts, which make them more tender. Overcooking will, however, cause some cuts of lamb to become tough. Mutton is produced from lamb that is only 3-12 months old. Lamb is produced from lambs that are at least 2 years old. Prime lamb is only sold to restaurants. Lamb should never be aged.

Chops

- The blade-end chops have a higher fat content than loin-end chops. However, the loin-end chops are more tender.
- A thin layer of fat is desirable on lamb chops.
- The darker the meat, the stronger the taste and the older the animal.
- Cuts of lamb that have the bone in will be more flavorful.
- Should be served hot or cold, never just warm for the best flavor.
- The rack will cook in about 30 minutes at 450°F.
- If the stock is to be used add a clove or two of garlic then caramelize and use on rack.
- The normal serving size is two chops.
- Rack of lamb is usually roasted medium or medium-rare.

Irish Lamb Stew

- Follow your recipe with a few variations if you wish. Place a clove inside one of the small onions.

   If you add one cup of black coffee to lamb stew it will improve the flavor and darken the meat.

- Make a sachet (use cheesecloth, tied) containing garlic, thyme, parsley, one bay leaf and whole black peppercorns.
- Place the meat, onion with the clove and the sachet in the water and boil. Use just enough water to cover the meat.
- Add any other vegetables your recipe calls for.
- Remove the onion with the clove and the sachet before serving and discard.
- To maintain good flavor, cook the vegetables before adding them to the stew.

Leg of Lamb

- If the leg is too heavy, than it is from an older lamb and will have too strong a taste.
- Ask the butcher to remove the large piece of pelvis and tailbone.
- A supermarket butcher will rarely take the time to remove the bone for you.
- The "fell" is a thin parchment-like membrane that covers the fat and is usually removed before cooking.

   Young spring lamb legs weigh 4-7 pounds, winter leg can weigh up to 9 pounds; the more the leg weighs the older the lamb.

- The color of the fat just under the fell will tell the age of the animal. For the more tender meat the fat should be clear to creamy white. The more yellow the fat, the older the animal and the stronger tasting the meat will be.

   If the leg of lamb has a strong lamb odor that you would like to eliminate before cooking, just boil 2 gallons of water and after it begins to boil, add 2¹/₂ cups of white vinegar. Pour the mixture over the lamb and allow it to stand for 4 minutes before draining and roasting.

- The best way to grill leg of lamb is butterflied.
- Leg of lamb is cooked for 24 minutes per pound for a nice medium at 325°F to an internal temperature of 153°F.
- If you are going to grill leg of lamb, it should be covered and cooked over indirect heat in a covered grill.
- The leg of lamb should be allowed to stand in a warm location for 20-30 minutes before serving.

Rack of Lamb

- Each rack should have 8 ribs.
- Score the membrane and remove it as well as the fat from the ribs. This leaves the ribs "naked" and without any fat. This process is called "Frenching."
- Only a thin layer of fat should be left on the eye of the chop.
- Rack should be placed fat side up in roasting pan that is just large enough to hold it.
- Bones that are left over from racking should be placed on the bottom of the pan under the roast.

A rack of lamb needs to stand before being carved more than any other type of meat.

- Allow the rack to remain in a warm location for 15 minutes before carving.
- The rack should only be served medium and never any more done than that.
- Rack of lamb should be cooked for 12 minutes per pound at 400°F until the internal temperature is 145°F.
- Make sure that the butcher removes the central backbone (chine bone) for you.

Shish Kebob

- The lamb should be prepared the day before by cutting it up into cubes and placing it in a marinade overnight.
- Portions should be 6 ounces per person.
- Place the lamb cubes on the skewers and grill or broil separately from the vegetables.
- The most common vegetables are mushrooms, onions, tomato and green pepper.
- Broil or barbecue the vegetables separate and place them between the lamb cubes just before serving.
- When the vegetables are placed on the skewers and cooked at the same time, the steam from the released liquid makes the lamb too moist.

COOKING PORK

Wild pigs originally crossed the Bering Straight and may have originated in Africa. Explorers reported having seen wild pigs in Mexico in
1522 but the first actual domesticated pigs were brought from Spain
to Tampa, Florida in 1539 by Hernando deSoto. Salting and smoking
were the early methods of preserving pork. The old adage "living high
on the hog" referred to someone who was eating the best cut of meat
on the pig.

Bacon

In most countries of the world, bacon is not considered to be a breakfast food and will rarely ever appear on a breakfast menu. A "rasher"
or portion of bacon is a term that originated in England in the 16th
century and is still used to day to denote a "side of bacon." The pagans
regarded bacon as a sacred food and a symbol of prosperity and
offered bacon as an offering to the Gods.

- Bacon is derived from the fatty pork belly meat, which has been cured and smoked.
- Canadian bacon is prepared from the boneless loin, which only has a thin layer of fat.
- If you need to separate bacon slices in a hurry, just microwave for 20-30 seconds on high.
- Always select bacon with the lowest amount of visible fat.
- Once a package of bacon is opened, it will only stay fresh for one week.
- To separate bacon more easily, just allow it to remain at room temperature for 20 minutes.
- Unopened bacon can be stored for only 1 week past the expiration date on the package.
- Bacon does not freeze well.
- Never purchase bacon if it looks slimy.
- Salt pork bacon is from the belly and is only cured in a coarse salt. It is usually found in beans for added flavor.

To reduce splattering, try soaking the bacon in ice water for 2-4 minutes and dry very well before frying.

- Sprinkling the bacon with a small amount of flour also helps reduce splattering.
- To reduce shrinkage, try starting the bacon in a cold pan.
- Use a skewer to make small holes in the bacon before separating the slices and the bacon will not curl up when cooked.
- Raw bacon can be easily cut with a scissors if you need small pieces.

- Bacon is processed in brine, which causes more grease to be released resulting in excess splattering.
- Lower heat settings when cooking bacon will reduce splattering.
- Bacon should be placed in a room temperature skillet (no oil) and heated slowly for the best results.
- Turn bacon as it is cooking and never overcrowd the pan.
- Bacon can be baked in a 400°F oven on a rack for 10 minutes.
- When frying bacon, it is best to drain off the fat once or twice.
- Removing some of the fat as the bacon cooks makes a crispier bacon strip.

- Cooked bacon strip will last 3-5 days in the refrigerator if wrapped tightly.
- Placed cooked bacon strips on a piece of paper towel in a cookie sheet in a 200°F oven after it warms, then turn the oven off.

Ham (Leg of Pork)

- The ham bone is excellent for soups.
- The flavor of a ham can be improved by heating even if it doesn't require it on the label.

If you purchase a "country ham," it will have been smoked and aged through a special curing process. Unfortunately this process tends to make these hams relatively salty. These hams may need to be skinned, soaked for a period and simmered.

- If you need to store the ham, check the wrapper for specific instructions.
- Many canned hams go through a special sterilization process and can be stored at room temperature for a prolonged period.
- Honey-baked hams will have the best flavor if allowed to warm to room temperature before being served.
- When you purchase a cured ham, be sure that it has the U.S. inspection seal on it. This assures you that the meat was cooked properly.
- If you ask a butcher (real nice), they will remove the bone from the ham for you.
- To remove a canned ham, just immerse it in hot tap water for 2 minutes to loosen the gel.

- The rind can easily be removed if you slice it lengthwise straight down the center before baking. The ham should be cooked slit-side down and the rind removed as soon as the ham is removed from the oven while the rind is still hot.

- When using ham for soups, use a number of small pieces instead of large chunks to intensify the flavor.

If you are going to glaze a ham, it is best to remove about ¹/₄ inch of the fat before glazing.

- To caramelize, the exterior of a ham use light brown sugar.
- A glaze can be made by combining 1 cup of brown sugar, ³/₄ cup of unsweetened pineapple juice and 1 teaspoon of dried mustard.
- If you would like to glaze a ham use 2 tablespoons of Dijon mustard with ¹/₂ cup of honey.
- If ham slices are too salty place them in a container of low fat milk for 20 minutes, rinse and dry before cooking.

- If you think that you have a ham that is too salty, just cook it for half the cooking time, then remove it from the oven and pour a small bottle or can of ginger ale over it. This will de-salt it about 30%.
- If you want to de-salt a ham further rub salt on the outside of the ham after pouring the ginger ale on and it will dram more salt water out of the ham and de-salt it about 60%.
- Pre-cooked ham slices dry out very easily and only need to be browned on each side.
- If you cook ham slices too fast, they may become tough.

Pork Chops

Pork is no longer the high fat meat that it was before the 1980's. New feeding methods have resulted in lower fat content in many of the more popular cuts. Preparation methods can also help reduce the fat content. In most cuts sold, pork will have a lower overall fat and cholesterol content than beef. Pork should never be aged at home unless you have special a refrigeration unit.

- Cook loin pork chops in a greased skillet adding a small amount of water to the pan, then cover and cook for about 30-40 minutes or until tender. The water will create just enough steam to keep the chops moist.

- When purchasing raw pork, be sure that the meat is a nice pale pink color. The darker the meat the older the animal.
- Check the color of the fat, it should be white on pork and beef, which indicates more tender meat. If the fat is yellow, the meat may be somewhat tough.
- Just to be safe, even though there is rarely a health problem with rare pork, cook it to an internal temperature of 155°-165°F.
- Pork chops should be purchased that are about 1" thick to maintain the juices when they are cooked.
- If you prefer thin pork chops, cook then with the lid on the pan for a short period of time since they dry out very quickly.
- Pork chops that are to be stuffed should be at least 1½" thick and should be rib or loin chops.
- Always cut the pork chops to be stuffed from the fat side and make the slit almost to the bone. After you stuff the chop, use small metal skewers to close the opening while they are cooking.
- Pork should never be left at room temperature for more than 1 hour before being refrigerated.

The juices should be clear when the pork chop is done.

- When cooking pork chops the excess fat should be removed.
- Pork chops do well on the grill, but be sure they are at least 1" thick for the best results.
- For a juicier pork chop allow them to stand for 10 minutes after they are cooked. Keep them warm and covered and they will be juicy all the way through.

Pork Loin

- When boiling a pork loin, allow it to remain in the water until it cools. This will result is a juicier more, tender loin.

If possible, try and find a pork loin that is graded "US No. 1." This is prime pork and the best for a loin.

- Cooks for 20 minutes per pound at 350°F to an internal temperature of 160°F to be safe.

Prosciutto

- Italian ham that been specially seasoned and salt-cured making it safe to eat without cooking.
- Make sure that the fat is very white and not yellow.
- If the ham is labeled "prosciutto cotto" it means that it has been cooked. If it is labeled "prosciutto crudo" it means that is has been cured.
- When you use prosciutto in dishes add it during the final 5 minutes of cooking time or it will become tough.
- Should be sliced paper-thin.

Ribs

- Bake on a rack in a shallow baking pan with your favorite seasonings at 325°F for about 1¹/₂-hours or until tender. Do not use high heat or they will dry out.
- Ribs do very well on the grill. Be sure and cover the grill for the best results.
- When grilling, be sure and remove any visible fat to avoid flare-ups.
- Cooks at 30 minutes per pound at 350°F until well done.
- Ribs can be cooked in the oven for about 30 minutes to cook off some of the fat before placing them on the grill.
- If you are going to smoke pork ribs, be sure and use a covering of yellow mustard, which will hold the spices in place and compliment them.
- Using mustard on smoked ribs will produce a crust that will not have the mustard flavor.

Pulled Pork

Pulled pork originated In North Carolina in the early 1800's when settlers brought pigs and allowed them to run wild. Since cattle were in short supply and there was an abundance of pigs, the pigs became the "meat of the south." The term "pulled pork" was a term used during that period to denote ham that was smoked over a low fire to the point when it could easily be "pulled" apart by hand.

- A pork shoulder is placed in a smoker and cooked until the internal temperature is 170°F. However, never cook the ham more than 190°F for the best results.
- The collagen in pork when smoked breaks down and allows the connective tissue (collagen) to turn into a simple sugar making the meat taste sweet.
- A good pork shoulder should weigh in at 12-15 pounds.
- Pork shoulders are sold either as a Boston butt or picnic variety. If you prefer less bone, choose the Boston butt. However, they will both weigh in at about 7 pounds.

Whole Hog

- One whole hog will feed about 50 people if no other meat is to be served.
- You will need a good home smoker to cook the hog.
- The pig should weigh 80-100 pounds and be skinned and trimmed.
- Try to purchase as lean a hog as you can. Hogs are notorious for starting grease fires if they are too fatty.
- Have the butcher butterfly the hog for you so that you can cook it flat.
- It takes about 10 hours to cook a hog. Be sure that the internal temperature reaches 170°F to be safe.
- The hog should be cooked skin side up for 5-8 hours before turning over, then cook for 2 hours before turning over again and cooking to 170°F.
- The hog should be basted every 45 minutes for the best results.

GAME MEATS

The meat from game animals, such as deer, wild turkey, ostrich, etc. has a stronger flavor than most people will enjoy. If the flavor is not to your liking, there a number of seasonings and chef's tricks that can be done to prepare the meat and make it more acceptable to your individual taste.

- All game birds should be trussed and the cavity sealed since they do not have enough fat on them.
- Small game birds cool very quickly and must be served as soon as they are done cooking.

Alligator

- The American alligator got its name from the Greek "krokodilus" meaning "worm of the pebbles," since alligators like to lie on pebbles near a river to absorb the heat.
- The tail meat is the choicest meat and sought after.
- The tail meat is best when prepared in a stew.

Bear

- The meat is very gamy and should be marinated.
- A strongly seasoned sauce is usually preferred to add flavor.
- Restaurants that serve bear meat usually serve it in a stew.

Buffalo/Beefalo

In the 1800's the Great Plains hunters who were too far from a watering hole would drink the liquid in a buffalo's stomach and called it "buffalo cider." Indians made jerky from buffalo strips and called it "pemmican." The strips were preserved in pouches made from buffalo hides and berries and fat were added to improve the nutritional content.

- Prepared the same as beef, but is lower in cholesterol and fat content.
- Buffalo roasts have a lower level of fat than beef roasts and should be cooked at a lower temperature of 275°F instead of 325°F.

Duck

The most popular and tastiest duck in the United States is the canvas-back duck. The first record of the name being used was by Thomas Jefferson in 1782. The duck enjoys wild celery, which is the reason the flavor is so good. Ducks from the Northeast are the most sought after. European chefs will import the ducks for their best clients.

- Duck or goose should be refrigerated for no more than 1-2 days before being cooked if it is purchased fresh.
- For the best results, purchase a duck that is 4½ -5 pounds.
- Pressed duck is prepared by removing the legs and breast then placing the remaining parts in a special press which removes the juices while the breast is cooking. The juices are used over the breast and are mixed with cognac, butter and wine.
- A frozen duckling can be used if the government inspection stamp is on the package.
- Wild duck and goose will have less fat that a farm raised fowl.
- Best not to stuff a duck or goose since the stuffing will become soggy due to the excess fat being released during cooking.
- The older the duck, the tougher.
- A farm raised duck will have more meat than a wild one.
- Defrost a frozen duckling on the bottom shelf of the refrigerator overnight.

Never re-heat, roast duck from the refrigerator; always allow it to return to room temperature.

- Rinse the fowl in cold salted water several times.
- The wings on ducks usually get overcooked unless you wrap them in aluminum foil.
- For a nice brown skin color, try brushing the skin with a mixture of 1 tablespoon of honey or Karo syrup mixed with 1 teaspoon of gravy flavoring about 2-3 minutes before the bird is finished cooking.
- To glaze the duck, brush with a mixture of fresh orange juice and current jelly.
- Use a skewer to prick the skin (not through to the flesh) numerous times to allow excess fat to be released while cooking.

If you are going to pluck a duck, make sure that the water is 155°F and the feathers will come out easier.

- Remove any excess fat from the inside of the fowl.

- Fat is normally added to roast duckling in your recipe because the fat is lost very quickly when you heat duck. The fat is placed in the bottom of the pan and has a boiling point of 360°F, while water boils at 212°F. If the fat was not in the pan, the water would create a steam vapor and surround the duck in a covered pan. The duck would be steam-cooked and not very tasty and prevent the fat under the duck skin from oozing out as it does in dry air.
- Use a meat thermometer to bring the fowl up to 160-165°F.

Peking Duck

In 1873 a Yankee Clipper ship arrived in New York with 4 white Peking ducks. There was 1 drake (male duck) and 3 females. These four ducks were the start of all the Peking ducks in the United States and were the start of an industry. The ducks first took up residence in Connecticut and were then transplanted to eastern Long Island and called the "Long Island duckling" in restaurants.

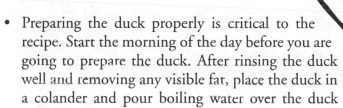

- Preparing the duck properly is critical to the recipe. Start the morning of the day before you are going to prepare the duck. After rinsing the duck well and removing any visible fat, place the duck in a colander and pour boiling water over the duck until the skin turns white. Gently pat the skin dry and rub the inside with sherry and kosher salt, then place the duck (uncovered) on a wire rack in the refrigerator for 10-12 hours.

Before you go to bed that same night, brush the breast with 1 tablespoon of honey and refrigerate it overnight.

- After the duck has cooked and you are ready to season the duck, be sure and prick the skin just before seasoning is placed on to allow the seasoning to seep into the duck. A metal skewer usually works well.

Smoked Duck

- The fat needs to liquefy and leave the meat to have a good product.
- Ducks should be smoked breast side up so that the fat will drain from the breast meat.
- Piercing the skin will help release the fat after it liquefies. The skin on a duck is tough and the fat cannot penetrate it easily.
- Placing the duck in a brine bath overnight will tenderize the meat and make the fat more, easier to release.

Brine Recipe

1¹/₂ cups of iodine-free salt
1 gallon of water
¹/₂ cup of white vinegar
3 tablespoons of brown sugar
1 tablespoon of pickling spice
1 teaspoon of fresh black pepper
1 teaspoon of allspice
1 teaspoon of garlic powder (not salt)
1 teaspoon of tarragon

The salt and brown sugar should be dissolved in the water. Add the vinegar and spices. Then bring to a full boil and allow it to cool before adding the duck.

Duck can also be steamed first before smoking. This works best if the duck is cut into pieces. A whole duck will take about 6 hours to smoke at 200°F.

Goose

- To reduce fat, cook the duck or goose breast side down on high heat (500°F) for 20-30 minutes.
- If you are plucking a goose, make sure that the water is 135°F and the feathers will come out easier.
- Goose will be tastier if roasted.

Goose will have more small bones than duck and meat may have to be removed before serving.

- Best to carve a goose in the kitchen to avoid embarrassment. This is one of the hardest birds to carve due to all the small bones.
- If salt is added to the water when cooking goose, the juices will not ooze out from the skin allowing the goose to remain juicy and tender.
- Wild geese will be much leaner than farm-raised geese.
- Allow about 1¹/₂ pounds of raw meat per person.
- Goose should be cooked to an internal temperature of 180°F.

Foie Gras

Foie gras was considered a delicacy by the Egyptians. The Perigord region of France is best known for producing the best foie gras and was first prepared in the 1700's for King Louis XV.

- Prepared from goose liver, however, duck liver may work just as well.
- Before using the liver should be soaked overnight in milk or a quality port wine.
- Marinate the livers in Madiera with the recommended seasonings before preparing.
- The livers should be baked for the best results.
- Serve chilled.
- When purchasing foie gras, the best is called "foie gras natural." The next best quality is called "pate de foie gras."

Emu/Ostrich

Ostrich eggs were popular in the 1800's but are not sold in the United States at present. The average egg weighs in at 3^1/$_2$ pounds and will make an omelet that would feed 8-10 people. Ostrich brains were considered to be a delicacy and frequently consumed by Nero.

- If you encounter a gamy flavor it can be eliminated if cooked in ginger ale.
- Most emu and ostrich do not normally have a gamy flavor.
- For the best flavor when eating emu steaks, they should be cooked medium-rare.
- When emu is cooked above 160°F, it has the tendency to become tough. The meat also dries out very easily.
- Many chefs serve emu with a fresh fruit puree in better restaurants.

Both emu and ostrich meat are very lean and make excellent hamburgers and meatloaf

- The meat is low in cholesterol.
- Both animals are allowed to grow "free range" without the use of hormones.

Frogs' Legs

There are two frogs that are mainly used for food in the United States; the American bullfrog and the northern leopard frog. Florida and Louisiana are the two main states that supply these frogs to American restaurants.

- The most common marinade for frogs' legs is prepared from 1 cup of white vinegar, 1 chopped onion and 3-4 crushed cloves of fresh garlic.
- Frogs' legs should be marinated for 3-4 hours before being placed in a batter and fried.
- The typical batter is composed of 1 well beaten large egg, 1 cup of all-purpose flour, $^1/_2$ cup of milk, $^1/_4$ teaspoon of cayenne pepper (if desired) and sea salt.
- Make sure that you place the frog legs on a piece of paper towel and dry them well before placing them into the batter.
- Fry the legs in corn oil at 375°F just until they are brown.

Grouse

- The recommended method of preparing grouse is to split them down the back and flatten the breastbone.
- Grouse can be broiled for 15-20 minutes after generously brushing with butter.
- One grouse per person is recommended.

Guinea Hen

- The hens at supermarkets will weigh 2-2$^1/_2$ pounds.
- To protect the delicate breast meat, guinea hens should be barded and then roasted.
- Most people prefer them well done.

Partridge Family

- Partridge are now being raised on farms in the United States.
- They have tender, delicate meat and weigh 1-1$^1/_2$ pounds each. Older birds can weigh as much as 3 pounds.
- Partridge are best braised and stewed.
- Young partridges can be roasted if barded.

Pheasant

George Washington was responsible for pheasants coming to America. He imported the birds from England in 1789 for his Mt. Vernon estate and they proliferated from there. By 1832, there were enough of the birds to have recipes appearing in cookbooks.

- The flavor of pheasant is similar to chicken, but a bit more gamier.
- Older birds should be braised and when roasted the breast meat should be barded.
- The bird will be fully cooked when the juices run pale pink.
- One 3-pound pheasant will feed 2 people.
- You can roast the bird at 375°F for about 45 minutes.

Quail

- Quail usually run about ¹/₂ pound each and care needs to be taken not to over cook them or they become very dry.
- Gently braising or sautéing is the recommended method of cooking, however, they do well if roasted or grilled but can easily be overcooked.
- It takes 2 quail to feed one person, 3 if they are very hungry or have a big appetite.
- Wild rice is the side dish of choice with quail by most chefs.

Rabbit (Hares)

Rabbits were worshipped by the Aztec Indians and they were considered a God, while the North American Indians ate them and considered them a delicacy. Rabbits have never been a big favorite in the United States with the general public ever since they were made into the "Easter bunny." Children could not possibly eat the Easter bunny; however, we still manage to consume about 50 million pounds of bunnies every year.

Rabbits

- Rabbits have special scent glands that need to be removed before cooking. The glands are located on either side of the spine, just under the forelegs and between the shoulders and in the back.

  Do not damage the scent glands when you remove them or the fluid will ruin the meat in that area.

- Rabbit can be cooked the same as chicken.
- Rabbit meat does not contain hormones since they grow very quickly; farmers don't have to give them hormones like they do chickens.
- Rabbit is more tender and flavorful than most meat.
- The best rabbits for quick cooking should be under 2 months old.

Hares (Jackrabbit and Snowshoe rabbit)

- Hares should be under 1 year old for the best flavor. The hind legs are the best eating.
- A young hare should be barded with pork fat and slowly roasted for the best results.
- Older hares should be stewed in stews and casseroles and de-boned.

RATTLESNAKE

- The head should be removed and buried one foot down in the ground.
- After removing the skin and intestines, wash the meat very well several times in cold salted water.
- The meat can be cut into pieces and batter-dipped and fried similar to fried chicken.
- Rattlesnake meat is usually used in stews.

Grilled Rattlesnake

- After the head and skin are removed, cut the snake meat into 2-inch chunks and parboil them for 30 minutes in a water broth with salt, ground black pepper and your favorite herbs.
- The basting solution usually consists of 1 cup of lemon juice, $^1/_2$ cup of honey, 2 tablespoons of soy sauce, 2 tablespoons of red wine vinegar, chopped chili pepper (optional), 1 clove of chopped garlic and white pepper.

VENISON

Freshly killed deer cannot be sold to restaurants unless the deer has been inspected by United States Government meat inspectors.

- To remove the gaminess from venison, just cook it in a small amount of ginger ale.
- The gamy flavor is usually caused by fat. If the fat is removed, this should solve the problem.
- Venison is best when aged at 38°F for about 1-2 weeks.

The meat of older animals will improve when marinated in buttermilk in the refrigerator overnight.

- Venison and elk are lean cuts of meat and if prepared properly, should be very tasty and tender. Moose tends to be much fatter.

- Venison has the tendency to dry out very easily, so be cautious and not over-cook it.

Roast Venison

- About a 3 pound roast is average.
- Venison should be marinated in a solution of $2^1/_2$ cups of de-fatted beef bouillon, $1^1/_2$ cups of red wine, 4 cloves of crushed garlic, $^1/_2$ teaspoon of basil, 6-10 peppercorns and 1 bay leaf.
- Marinate the venison for 2-3 days under refrigeration making sure that the venison remains covered with liquid at all times.
- Remove the venison from the marinade, dry well and then coat with a mixture of $^1/_2$ cup of all-purpose flour, 2-3 tablespoons of kosher salt, $^1/_4$ teaspoon of thyme, $^1/_2$ teaspoon of paprika, $^1/_4$ teaspoon of marjoram and pepper to taste.
- The marinade that the veal was in should be brought to a boil for 2-3 minutes if it will be used to baste the venison roast.
- The coated meat should be braised in very hot oil and then placed into a baking pan and cooked at 350°F for 3 hours.

COOKING SNAILS (ESCARGOT)

- Snails that are used to prepare escargot are specially grown for that purpose and are not your common garden variety. They are now grown in the United States. However, the American variety are somewhat smaller than the European cousins.
- Gourmet markets normally sell canned snails along with shells that can be used to place them in
- The best brands of snails are Ugma and Ile de France.
- Snails are available canned, but when the can is opened they should be placed in a bowl and soaked in cool water for a few minutes.
- Fresh snails should be purchased the day they are to be prepared. They will store in the refrigerator for 4-6 hours.

- Fresh snails should be purchased in their shell and soaked in warm water for about 8-10 minutes.

- Discard any snails that have not emerged to see what is going on.
- If you want to use the shells from the snails, just place them in a pot with 2 tablespoons of baking soda and 1 tablespoon of table salt and bring to a rapid boil. Reduce the heat and simmer for 30-45 minutes. Drain and rinse very well before use.
- The shells can be cleaned or purchase shells from the market (much easier).
- Drain the snails well then use a snail fork to remove them from their shell and cut off their heads and tails.
- After rinsing, place the snails in another bowl with lightly salted cool water and 1 clove of crushed garlic. Cover the bowl and refrigerate for use the next day. They must be used the next day or discard them.
- If you see any of the green gall, discard it.

- The snails should be poached in either water or wine depending on the dish for about 1-2 hours. They should be fork tender at that time.

Place the poached snails in re-fatted chicken broth and allow them to cool to room temperature before adding them to a recipe.

CHAPTER 7

FOWL COOKING

COOKING & PREPARING CHICKEN

The chicken as we know it today was originally bred from the wild red jungle fowl and was first domesticated about 2000 BC in India. The chicken appeared in English recipes about 2500 BC. Columbus brought the first chickens to the America's in 1493.

BAKED

- Always bake chicken on medium heat, since a high heat setting will result in a drier, stringier piece of chicken or turkey.
- Only bake chicken to 180°F. Any higher or lower and the fowl will be either underdone or dried out.

Chefs submerge chicken parts in buttermilk in the refrigerator for 2-3 hours to improve the taste.

- To keep the breast moist, try placing some bacon strips on top of the breast, alternating directions to hold them in place.
- Use low-salt soy sauce to brown the chicken parts, just brush it on 30 minutes before the chicken is finished cooking.
- If you remove the white hard tendon running lengthwise in the chicken breast, it will reduce shrinkage when the breast is cooked.

Since the majority of the fat content in both chicken and turkey is found in the skin, removing the skin is recommended in almost all instances when preparing the fowl. The quality of the fowl you are purchasing is important and freshness is one of the most important factors, which will make the dish more flavorful and appealing. If you can purchase a bird that is fresh and has never been frozen, you will probably notice the difference in taste. A kosher chicken will even taste better and will be a cleaner bird.

BARBECUED (GRILLING)

- Only purchase Grade A chicken for barbecuing.
- If you plan on grilling a turkey, the temperature needs to be kept at 325°F or slightly higher until the internal temperature reaches 165°F.
- A 14-pound turkey will take 2-3 hours rotating on a grill at 325°F.

- Best to partially cook the chicken or turkey in the oven or microwave before barbecuing to save time.

   When barbecuing a whole chicken, be sure and wrap the wings in aluminum foil to protect them from burning.

- Be sure that chicken is at room temperature when you start to grill.
- Chicken will not stick on the grill if you rub mayonnaise on the chicken before barbecuing. The heat will burn it off and it will not flavor the meat.
- Make sure that you grease the barbecue rack before placing the chicken on it. The collagen in the chicken skin turns into a sticky gelatin and the chicken will stick to the rack. If you pre-bake the chicken this will not occur.
- When spit-barbecuing a chicken, it is best to remove the breast bone so that the chicken will cook more evenly.
- After searing, use a cooler fire to complete the cooking for moist chicken.

- For excellent results, sear the chicken skin-side down. Then turn the chicken over and grill on a covered grill until the meat looks opaque.

- White meat pieces will cook faster than dark meat pieces and should be placed on the grill 15 minutes after the dark meat pieces have started cooking.

- When you cut into the chicken, the juices should run yellow, with just a slight hint of pink.

BOILED

- If you are going to use chicken or turkey in a casserole or pot pie, just boil the chicken until it is about $3/4$ cooked, allow it to remain in its own liquid for about one hour under refrigeration before using in the dish.
- Partial boiling for dishes produces a juicier piece of chicken.
- Can be basted with wine. Use a quality red or white wine. Sherry is highly recommended. Baste every 10-12 minutes for the best results.

BREADED CHICKEN

- Most breading recipes for chicken call for an egg-milk-water mixture (egg wash).
- Be sure to strain the mixture before using it to avoid large parts of the egg white in the wash.
- Straining the egg wash will also make the coating even.
- To avoid having lumps of flour and bread crumbs on your fingers, which make breading more difficult, just designate one hand as "wet" and the other hand as "dry."
- The "wet" hand will handle the chicken pieces that are not coated and dip the pieces in the milk and then place the pieces in the flour.
- The "dry" hand will then sprinkle flour over the top of the piece coating it and removes it from the flour and places it in the egg wash and remove it with the "wet" hand.
- The above method is how chefs prepare large quantities of chicken pieces without getting lumps on their fingers or leaving clumps on the chicken pieces.

BROILED

- To reduce flare-ups, just wipe the surface of the chicken with paper towel and remove all visible excess fat.
- Chicken breasts should be placed on the pan as far from the burners as possible to avoid burning the tops.
- The breast meat should be white with no hint of pink.
- If you would like the skin to be crisp, just be sure and wipe the skin with a dry kitchen towel and do not place any salt on the skin.
- To obtain a nice brown glaze, just sprinkle some sugar through a sieve over the surface of the chicken during the last 1-2 minutes of cooking time.
- Glazing the skin will not produce a sweet skin, just a beautiful brown sheen.

FRIED

- To bread fried chicken, dip the pieces in evaporated milk with a small amount of well-beaten egg before placing the pieces in the breading with the spices.
- If you soak the chicken pieces in milk for 1 hour before you bread the chicken it will be more, tender.
- Use a paper bag to place your breading ingredients in after they have been mixed.

If you want real crispy fried chicken, make the breading from equal parts of all-purpose flour and cornstarch instead of just flour.

- Before starting, soak the chicken pieces in cold, salted water for about 1 hour, using one pint of water to 1 tablespoon of table salt. This will remove any blood residue and some bacteria.
- After breading the chicken, place the pieces in the refrigerator for 45 minutes to set the breading and it won't fall off.

- Chicken parts can be par-boiled for 3-5 minutes before you fry them to speed up the process.
- Light meat fries faster than dark meat and should be fried in separate baskets.
- Fry chicken at 365°F for the best results, which should take about 15-20 minutes for the pieces to become brown.

- Fried chicken can be placed into the oven at 350°F after it has browned in the fryer to dry the coating and make the chicken even crispier.

LIVER

- The center should be barely pink when cooked.
- Chicken liver is overcooked if brown inside and too dry to use.
- When making pate, push a skewer into the center and if it comes out hot the pate is done cooking.
- Calf liver is cooked very quickly for about 1 minute on each side on high heat or it will dry out.

POACHED

- The chicken should be started in a cold broth or water.
- If you place the chicken into a pot of hot water, the broth will be cloudy.
- Bring the poaching water to a simmer. A 3-4 pound chicken will cook in 40 minutes.
- Poaching should be done in an uncovered pot.

ROASTED

A roaster chicken is between is between 2-6 months old when slaughtered and a fryer or broiler is only 6-8 weeks old.

- A free range chicken will be tastier if roasted.
- Roasting chickens have more fat than broilers.
- Roasters should weigh at least 3 pounds.

- After cleaning the chicken inside and out, rub "chef's salt" on the inside and allow the chicken to remain at room temperature for 20 minutes.
- Place all the vegetables plus one garlic clove in the bottom of the roasting pan and then the chicken is placed breast side up on top of the vegetables.
- Place very thin lemon slices under the skin to tenderize the chicken if you use an old bird.
- Heat about 5 tablespoons of corn oil almost to the smoke point and pour it over the top of the chickens before roasting.

- The roasting should be done in a 350°F oven for 1-1¹/₂ hours and only baste once after 1 hour of cooking time.

  When basting, try adding a small amount of ground turmeric to the basting solution providing it has an oil base and the chicken will have a great deep rich brown skin.

- For a great self-basting treat, just saturate a piece of cheesecloth with olive oil and place it over the breast of the bird. When the cheesecloth is removed after the bird is cooked the breast meat will be moist and the bird will have a brown skin.

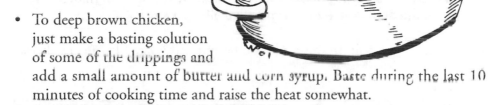

- To deep brown chicken, just make a basting solution of some of the drippings and add a small amount of butter and corn syrup. Baste during the last 10 minutes of cooking time and raise the heat somewhat.

- The thermometer should read 185°F when finished cooking.

SAUTÉING

- Best to sauté chicken in unsalted butter, extra virgin olive oil or bacon fat.
- The choice of fat should relate to the dish.
- It requires 2-3 tablespoons of fat to sauté a whole chicken.
- Always sauté over medium to high heat.

Sauté skin-side down and serve the chicken skin-side up.

- Chicken browns well over medium heat because of the time it takes to cook it.
- If the skin sticks to the pan, allow a little more time and it should release by itself as soon as more of the fat renders down.

Breaded

- If you are going to sauté breaded chicken, be sure and have $1/8$ inch of oil in the pan.
- Breaded chicken should be sautéed over medium heat, never high heat.
- If the breading is browning too fast, reduce the heat.

If you use clarified butter, there will never be brown specks of milk solids clinging to the breading. Extra virgin olive oil works great as well.

- Try breading with half, fresh bread crumbs and half, grated Parmesan cheese.

SMOKED

Chicken

- Make sure you start with a plump bird weighing about 4-5 pounds.
- One chicken will feed 2-3 people.
- The smoker should be set at 180°F and the internal temperature of the chicken should be 165°F when cooked.
- If the internal temperature goes over 165°F, the bird will be too well done.
- Placing beer inside the bird adds a great flavor.
- If you use a rub it should include sage, thyme and bay leaves.
- Make sure the juices run clear when the bird is done cooking.

Turkey

- A 12-14 pound turkey will take 6-8 hours to smoke. However, the flavor is worth the wait.
- A smoked turkey will be more juicy than an oven-roasted turkey.

SPECIAL DISHES

Buffalo Wings

This dish was first served in Buffalo, New York at the Anchor Bar in 1964. The dish was fried chicken wings with a hot barbecue sauce. In 1977 Buffalo, New York declared "Chicken Wing Day" on July 29th to commemorate the occasion.

- When preparing buffalo wings, be sure and separate the wing from the joint.
- The tip is then cut off the wings and the wings fried in peanut oil.
- In many bars, the complete wings are fried to reduce the work of removing the wing.

Chicken a la King

The first mention in print of Chicken a la King was in 1912. The dish was originally served at the Brighton Beach Hotel in New York in 1898 and was prepared for the owners Mr. and Mrs. E. Clark King III. His chef was named George Greenwald. One year later, the dish was being served at the famous Delmonico's Restaurant in New York City.

- The original recipe called for sherry and blanched toasted almonds to be added just before serving.
- After you prepare the sauce, be sure and temper the eggs with a small amount of the sauce before adding the eggs.
- Onions, mushrooms and green peppers were the vegetables of choice.
- The original recipe called for 4 pounds of butter, which may be replaced with olive oil if you are using a high butter recipe.

Chicken Breast Parmesan

- Use clarified butter in the recipe.
- Make sure you coat the breast on each side, flour and seasoning first then the egg mixture.

- Grate fresh Parmesan cheese.
- Do not use the leftover flour or egg mixture.

Chicken Cordon Bleu

- Always remove the skin from the chicken breast.
- The breasts must be pounded out to increase their surface.
- The pounding helps to make the thickness of the breast uniform so that the cooking time will be accurate for both halves.
- The temperature of the shortening is very important and to test the oil, just drop one or two breadcrumbs into the oil. If the breadcrumbs immediately rise to the surface in the center of a small amount of white foam, the oil is ready.
- After placing the cheese and slice of ham and folding the breast together, be sure and shape the pieces into a nice oval and freeze them for 2 hours so that they will retain their shape when cooked.

Chicken Fricassee

- One of the oldest chicken dishes ever recorded in a cookbook.
- Use a heavy-bottomed pan.
- The chicken pieces should be lightly browned in a combination of hot fat and butter.
- Remove the chicken from the pan before browning the onions.
- Onions are very important and the oil should be heated in the pan before adding the onions to lightly brown. The caramelized onions gives the fricassee its characteristic flavor.
- After browning the onions, return the chicken to the pan.
- When you are separating the whites from the yolks, it is critical not to leave any hint of white on the yolk or it will harden and the sauce will have lumps.

Chicken Kiev

This dish was invented by the Frenchman Nicolas Appert in 1801. The name Chicken Kiev was used in New York City by a restaurant who served the dish to Russian immigrants. In Europe the name was Chicken Supreme, but was eventually changed to Chicken Kiev.

- Make sure that when inserting the butter, it is frozen as solid as possible.
- The chicken breast must be flattened evenly to allow for even cooking.
- The chicken needs to be fried until crisp.

The chicken should be very cold when the butter is inserted.

- If you leave the wing bone on, it provides a little handle and makes a nice touch.
- Some chefs will flavor the butter with garlic and herbs. Soften the butter at room temperature, blend the herbs and then freeze the butter before using.

Chicken Tetrazzini

- This dish was named after an Italian opera singer Luisa Tetrazzini who died in 1940. She was so popular in the United States around the turn of the century that the dish was named after her by the owner of a San Francisco restaurant and was first mentioned in print in 1951.
- The roux for the dish is prepared with 4 tablespoons of all-purpose flour and 4 tablespoons of butter.
- After the roux is prepared, add 2 cups of heavy cream and 1 cup of de-fatted chicken broth.
- Best to remove from the heat and add 3 cups of cooked chicken that has been cut into cubes.
- Butter a glass casserole dish and place ³/₄ pounds of cooked spaghetti in and pour in the chicken mixture.
- Most chefs sprinkle breadcrumbs or Parmesan cheese on top.

Sweet & Sour Chicken

- Many butchers will sell you chicken already cut in cubes. This will save a lot of time.
- The first step is to sprinkle the pieces with a small amount of soy sauce mixed with 1 tablespoon of white vinegar to give the chicken an oriental flavor.

Prepare the flour and seasoning mixture that your recipe calls for and dip the chicken pieces in one at a time (not all at once).

- After you fry the pieces, discard the oil (do not re-use it).
- If your sweet and sour sauce is not thick enough, use cornstarch to thicken it. Be sure and mix the cornstarch with cold water before adding it to the sauce. Only add the cornstarch drop by drop until the desired thickness is achieved.
- If you prepare the ingredients before you are ready to prepare the dish, never mix them until you are ready to make the dish.
- When preparing this dish, prepare the vegetables, sauce and chicken sepa-

rately and combine them in a casserole before placing them into a 350°-375°F oven for 45-60 minutes.

STEWING

- Never allow stewing chicken to come to a full boil. You will lose the flavor of the base in the chicken.
- Stewing should always be done on top of the stove or in the oven.
- Somewhat fatty chickens are best for stewing. Fat hens are the best and usually weigh about 4-5 pounds.
- If you are preparing a cream sauce, be sure and cook the chicken in unsalted butter.

WHOLE CHICKEN

- If you are going to stuff a chicken, figure $^3/_4$ cups of stuffing per pound.
- The chicken will be cooked through when the leg feels loose.
- A 3-4 pound stewing chicken will take 1-2 hours to cook.

Rock Cornish Game Hens

- These mini-chickens are about enough food for one person if they are not too hungry.

- It will take about 1 cup of stuffing to stuff the little bird.
- Serve adequate side dishes.

If you stuff the bird, the aluminum foil should be opened up 10 min-

utes before the bird has finished cooking to release the moisture built up from the stuffing.

- To obtain a delicate flavor, pour a mixture of 1 tablespoon of fruit-flavored brandy (not a sweet cordial) over the bird.
- Small game birds do not brown well in the oven due to the short cooking time.

Game hens should be browned on each side in a pan on top of the stove over a very high heat.

- Oven roasting only takes about 30 minutes.
- Before you grill, cut off the last two sections of the wings or fold them under the bird.

COOKING TURKEY (in cooking bag)

- Turkeys should be cooked breast-side down for the first hour on a "V" rack so that it will baste the breast naturally. Turn the bird and continue cooking for the balance of the time.
- Allow turkeys to rest for 20 minutes after cooking so that the steam dissipates out of the white meat and it won't fall apart when sliced.
- Turkey should be cooked at 325°F for the best results.
- The internal temperature of a cooked turkey should be 180°F.
- Turkeys should only be stuffed just before being placed into the oven, never before.

Stuffing Tips

- All ingredients that will be used for stuffing must be cooked before using them in the stuffing.
- Cool all the ingredients before combining.
- Never leave stuffing at room temperature for more than 1 hour.
- Stuffing causes the bird to cook longer and may dry out the meat.
- Over-mixing bread stuffing causes the stuffing to become too pasty.
- All ingredients should be lightly tossed for the best results.
- If you do stuff the bird just before placing in the oven, be sure and do not overstuff or force stuffing in. Never pack it in.

Turkey (no cooking bag)

- The outside of the turkey should be brushed with vegetable oil before placing it into the oven.
- Make sure that the oven is pre-heated.
- If the turkey starts to brown too early, just cover it with an aluminum foil tent.
- Brush the breast skin with white vermouth 20 minutes before the bird has completed cooking for a rich brown, crispy skin.

CAPON

In ancient Rome, it was against the law to eat any type of fowl except a hen that was not intentionally fattened. A Roman surgeon found a way around the problem (since roosters were more flavorful and in demand) by castrating the roosters and calling them "capon." A capon can weigh in from 6-8 pounds and has a better texture and flavor than a hen. The capon was declared to be within the Roman law.

CHAPTER 8

HOW TO COOK FISH & SHELLFISH

COOKING FISH & SHELLFISH

The best advise when it comes to purchasing fish and shellfish is to know your market fish department and be sure that the fish and shellfish are from safe fishing grounds. The problem with contaminants being found in both fish and shellfish is reaching serious levels. Many fish and shellfish are now being grown in aquafarms that have control of what the fish are consuming. Choosing fresh seafood is important and the best book for in-depth information is the "21st Century Reference Guide to Cooking Secrets & Helpful Household Hints" by Dr. Myles H. Bader.

FISH

- Preparing a fish with its head and tail on will allow more of the juices to remain in the meat and produce a juicier, more moist dish. Make sure, however, that the fish has been scaled and gutted.
- Lean fish should be cooked with liquid or basted and fatty fish should be cooked dry.
- When freezing all fresh fish, they should be frozen in water.

Creole Blackened Fish

Creole cooking is based on French soups and stews. It is a combination of different foods from a variety of cultures. Creoles were originally of French and Spanish heritage and established New Orleans in 1692. The unique flavors are a blend of Spanish, American Indian, African and local cuisine of that era and called Cajun cooking.

- Never fry if the fish has been previously frozen due to the high water content.
- The fish is heavily coated with special Creole spices and fried in a very, very hot cast iron skillet.
- The outside of the fish needs to become black and very crunchy.

De-Boning Fillet

- An easy trick used by chefs to de-bone fillet is to use a vegetable peeler and just lightly run it over the fillet allowing the tiny bones to catch in between the blade. Then they just give a slight twist and the bones come out.

Game fish

- Game fish should not be frozen for more than 1 month for the best results when preparing them.

  When freezing game fish, be sure and remove the gills or the fish will be bitter.

- All scales must be removed before freezing.
- The head can be left on if desired.
- If the fish is over 2 pounds, place a double sheet of aluminum foil or plastic wrap inside, which will make a big difference when de-frosting the fish.
- The fish should be wrapped in plastic wrap, then aluminum foil. After it is frozen, pack the fish in freezer paper.
- To de-frost the game fish, place it into a sink of cold water and allow it to remain until it has reached the temperature of the water and is thawed and flexible.

COOKING METHODS

Baking Fish (general information)

- Pre-heat the oven to 425°F.
- Rinse the fish well under cold running water and pat dry with paper towel.
- If you are going to bake a whole fish, make sure that you dry the inside as well.
- Spray a shallow baking dish with vegetable spray or lightly grease it.
- The fish should be placed in the dish skin-side down.

- It is really not necessary to add fat or any liquid when baking fish.
- The fish should remain moist as long as it is not over-baked.
- The fish should be measured at its thickest point and should be baked 6-10 minutes per inch of thickness.

Add 5 minutes to the total cooking time if the fish is being baked in a sauce or if you wrapped it in foil.

Broiling Fish (general information)

- The best cuts of fish to broil are fillets and steaks that are ¼ to 1½-inches thick.

- The fish should be rinsed well under running cold water and dried on paper towel.
- Pre-heat the broiler pan.
- It is not necessary to add any additional oil or butter.
- The broiler pan should be sprayed with vegetable oil before placing the fish on.

If you are broiling a whole fish, be sure and slash the skin on both sides a few times to avoid curling.

- The fish should be seasoned on both sides.

- The fish will retain good moisture if you don't overcook it, which is easy to do under a broiler.
- Lean fish such as bass and pike should be basted to prevent drying out.
- Turn the whole fish only once; halfway through the broiling.
- Fillets do not have to be turned and should be skin-side down.
- The pan should be placed 4-5 inches from the heat source.
- Broil for 6-10 minutes per inch of thickness or until the flash is opaque.
- If you are going to broil frozen fish, double the cooking time and turn the fish halfway through the cooking time.

Frying Fish (general information)

- Basically, all you need is peanut oil and a crispy coating.
- The typical batter contains beer, flour and eggs.
- The fish can also be coated with just cornmeal and flour.
- The seasonings that are added are up to your taste.
- The three-container method is normally used. The first contains flour; the second contains egg that has been whisked with milk and the third with your special blend of seasoned flour.
- Press the fish into the flour. Shake off well then into the milk mixture and very gently into the seasoned flour.
- When battering a frying fish, the batter should be cold to prevent too much oil from being soaked up into the fish.
- The oil should be 350°-360°F.

Grilling Fish (general information)

- Make sure that the fish is rinsed well under cold water.
- Best to marinade the fish for 1-2 hours under refrigeration.
- One of the best marinades is a combination of olive oil, cloves, chili peppers (mild), orange and lime juices. Salt and pepper to taste.

Grilling should be done over direct high heat for 6-10 minutes per inch of thickness.

- Grilling times are dependent on the thickness, type of fire source (wood, charcoal, gas or electric), the distance the fish is from the heat source and whether the grill is open or closed.
- Make sure that the fish is cooked until the insides are opaque.
- The fish should only be turned once for the best results.
- Covered grilling imparts a great smoky flavor to the fish.

Microwave Fish Cooking (general information)

- All fish needs to be defrosted before placing in the microwave.
- Generally to microwave a fish takes 3-6 minutes per pound in a 600-700 watt oven on high power.
- The skin side should be placed down and a few slashes made into the skin to avoid curling.
- Thicker pieces of fish should be placed along the outer edges so that will cook more evenly.

- Use a microwave-safe dish that has a lid.
- Do not use plastic wrap in the microwave since it may give off fumes that will alter the taste of the food.

Never salt fish when microwave cooking or the salt on top of the fish may cause the fish to cook unevenly.

- The fish should not be totally opaque since it will continue cooking for a few minutes after you remove it. Allow it to sit for about 5 minutes, covered, before serving.

Poaching Seafood (general information)

- This entails cooking the fish in gently simmering liquid, usually lightly salted lemon water, fish or vegetable stock or a mild wine.
- Do not poach tuna, swordfish or shark.
- Poaching should never overpower the flavor of the fish, but should compliment it.

The fish should first be rinsed well under cold water and wrapped in cheese-cloth leaving enough room so that the ends can be twisted and knotted.

- The skin can be removed before serving if you wish.
- When preparing fish in this manner, the ends can be used as handles if you have to raise or lower the fish.

- Use a deep pan and place your liquid in the bottom. Then bring it to a boil, reduce the heat to a slight simmer and add the fish in single layers with enough liquid to cover the fish by about 1 inch.
- The fish should be cooked gently for 6-12 minutes per inch of thickness or until it is opaque all the way through.
- Fish do not have to be turned when poaching.

- Poaching liquid can be served as a broth if you wish.
- Poaching liquid can also be frozen and used as the liquid of choice when poaching again.

Sautéing (general information)

- This method is best for thinner fillets or very small whole fish if they are 1" thick or less.
- If you can't fit the whole fish in a 10" skillet, forget about pan-frying the fish.

- Rinse the fish or fillet under cold water and pat dry with paper towel.
- If you would like to seal in the juices, lightly flour the fish before placing it in the pan or heavy-duty skillet, which is preferred.
- Sauté in 1-2 tablespoons of butter (clarified is OK) and 1-2 tablespoons of vegetable oil. Do not use olive oil unless you are using clarified butter.
- Heat over medium-high heat, then add fish to the heated oil and be sure not to crowd the fish. They need their space or they will get soggy.
- Fry for about 6-12 minutes per inch of thickness or until the flesh is opaque.

The fish should be turned over halfway through the cooking time.

- If the fish is very thick or you are frying a whole fish, reduce the heat to medium and cook for a few minutes longer.
- Make sure that you place the fish on paper towel to remove the excess oil before placing on a platter to serve.

Spices Recommended for Seafood

- Basil, bay leaves, dill, oregano, paprika, black & white pepper, tarragon, thyme, rosemary, sage, marjoram, chervil, fennel, ginger and garlic.
- Commercial pepper and lemon blends are excellent on fish.

GARLIC & DILL BUTTER

$1/4$ pound unsalted butter or clarified butter
1 small garlic clove, crushed and minced
1 teaspoon dill
1 teaspoon fresh lemon juice
Salt & pepper to taste

Steaming Seafood

- Most types of fish can be steamed, especially if you want to avoid fat.
- Whole fish to fillets can be steamed and especially shellfish steam well and provide a tasty broth that can be used to pour back over the shellfish.
- Steaming can be accomplished using a regular steamer or placing a cake rack in a roasting pan. Water or stock can be placed in and the liquid brought to a simmer. The fish or shellfish should be rinsed well under cold water and placed on the steaming rack.

Be sure that the fish is resting above the liquid and does not touch the liquid. Seasonings may be placed on top of the fish and the pot closed tightly.

- It takes about 6-12 minutes per inch thickness or until the flash is just opaque.
- Tuna does not steam well.

Smoked Fish

- Fish can be cold smoked at temperatures as low as 80°F. However, it takes 3-4 days.
- Hot smoking is the recommended method of smoking fish at temperatures up to 200°F for 1-2 hours.
- A brine solution is recommended before smoking the fish. The brine can be prepared with $2^1/2$ tablespoons of salt, without iodine, per cup of water. Tap water should be allowed to remain static for 1 hour before using it to allow the chlorine to dissipate in the air. Best to use bottled water.

- A percentage of the water may be replaced with a quality white wine if you prefer.
- The fish only has to remain in the brine for 15 minutes per $^1/_2$ inch of thickness.
- It requires about 1 quart of brine per pound of fish.
- Seasonings can be added to the brine if so desired.
- Any fish can be smoked. However, salmon and trout are the best.
- Fat fish tends to absorb more of the smoked flavor into the fat.
- Any wood can be used, but the best are fruit woods and alder.
- Salmon is best smoked with alder.
- Mesquite is not recommended for smoking since it does not last long enough.
- Ideally, if your smoker can maintain a smoking temperature of 150°F for the first 1-2 hours it will allow the fish to have a better flavor. The heat should then be turned up to 200°F for the balance of the cooking time.
- The internal temperature should be 160°-165°F when cooked.

COMMON FORMS OF SUPERMARKET FISH

Whole Fish

- Complete with entrails, needs to be sold shortly after it is caught.

Drawn Fish

- Whole fish with only the entrails removed.

Dressed Fish

- Totally cleaned up with entrails removed and ready to party or cook.

Fish Fillets/Steaks

- Large pieces of fish with the bones removed. When both sides are removed, they are sometimes called butterfly fillets.

Cured Fish

- These are usually sold as smoked, pickled, or salted fish. If the fish is sold as "cold smoked," it was only partially dried and will have a very short shelf life. If the label reads "hot smoked," the fish was not fully cooked and should be kept frozen until used.

Dried Fish

- Fish that has been processed using dry heat, then salted to preserve it.

Salted Fish

- These fish are used mainly for pickling in a brine solution.

LEAN FISH

Light-colored flesh usually indicates a low fat fish. Darker flesh fishes are usually high-fat fishes.

- Lean fish have a fat content of 2-3%, most of which is in the liver.
- Cooking tends to neutralize most of the contaminants, especially if the skin is removed.
- Low fat fish cannot be barbecued with good results.
- Low fat fish can be baked if you baste the fish every few minutes.
- If the fish is to be cooked whole and has a nice looking skin that will present well, leave the skin on one side and serve it skin up. The fish can then be turned over and consumed.
- Low-fat fish is best cooked using moist heat such as poaching, stewing or sometimes steaming works well.

Wrapping low fat fish in aluminum foil helps retain the moisture when baking.

- The fins and tail can easily be removed with a kitchen scissors on most low-fat fish.
- If you poach low fat fish, be sure and keep the fish in a single layer. Never place them on top of each other.
- Never steam or poach fish over boiling water, only allow the water to simmer. Boiling water can break the fish apart.
- When steaming, be sure that the fish is on a rack and above the water at least 2 inches.
- If you add 1 tablespoon of lemon juice to the water when steaming, the fish will retain its white color.
- If you pan fry in butter or oil, these fish do well since they cook in a few minutes.
- When baking low fat fish, it is best to bake them quickly at 450°F to retain the moisture.

- The fish should be covered when baking and baked for 8-10 minutes for each 1" thickness in the dish.

When poaching any fish, a small amount of wine or lemon juice should be added to the water to preserve the flavor at the beginning of the cooking.

- Lean fish should be breaded or covered with a light coating of oil or sauce to help retain moisture during baking.
- Should be served immediately after cooking. These fish should not be kept warm in an oven or they will dry out.
- Allow 10 minutes per inch of whole fish when poaching, oven frying, braising or simmering.
- When poaching fish, wine can be added at the beginning of the cooking. Recommended wines are a dry white wine or vermouth.
- If the fillet is somewhat yellow around the edges, do not buy it. It is too old.
- Smell the gills before you buy fresh fish. If the gills have an off-odor, don't buy the fish.
- Slimy fish is a sign of early decay.

Cooking a low fat fish with its head and tail on will result in a more moist and flavorful fish.

Bass, Black

- Best when fried, grilled, poached or broiled.
- The tastiest black bass are under 3 pounds.

Bass, Largemouth and Smallmouth

- Best when baked, poached, fried or grilled. Tends to keep a nice firm texture when grilled.

Bass, Striped

- A flaky, firm textured fish.
- Mild flavored fish, but one that is very distinctive making it prized by connoisseurs.
- Sold as fillets, steaks, chunks and whole.
- Can be baked, broiled, pan-fried or poached.

Blackfish

- Excellent for chowders and stews.
- They have very firm white meat.
- Tastes similar to sea bass with a mild taste.
- Commonly substituted for cod in recipes.
- Can be baked, broiled or sautéed.

Blowfish

- Best breaded and pan-fried. Figure 4-6 per person.

Flounder

Flounder is the only fish that is born with normal eyes, one on each side of the head then. When they are ¹/₂ inch long, both eyes migrate to one side. In the winter flounder, the eyes are both on the right side of the body. For the summer flounder, the eyes migrate to the left side. When both eyes are on one side, it allows the fish to sit on the bottom of the ocean with both eyes searching for prey.

- Best pan-fried, broiled or sautéed.
- The whole fish can be steamed with good results.
- The sand dab is related to the flounder and has a delicate, sweet flavor.

Grouper

- Grouper is best baked, broiled or fried. Excellent fish for chowder.
- Usually sold as fillets and steaks.
- Great for stews and soups.
- The skin is tough and should be removed before cooking.

Haddock

- Best when stuffed, poached or baked.
- Can be substituted for cod. However, the flesh will be slightly softer.
- Smoked haddock is known as finnan haddie.

Hake (Whiting)

These fish are often called "frostfish" since they swim offshore into cold winter waters with the tides and freeze before they could reach the warmer ocean currents they were heading for. The frozen fish or "frostfish" would then become frozen and wash back up on the shore and were harvested by people and eaten by waiting seagull.

- Tend to be softer and more moist than cod, which hake is commonly compared to.
- Whole dressed fish as well as fillets are usually available in supermarkets and fish markets.
- The fish is best poached, steamed, baked or pan-fried.
- Small whiting are usually floured and fried whole.

After the fish is cooked, the bones are easy to remove.

- Very versatile and inexpensive fish.

Halibut

- Usually prepared as steaks, fillets or poached.
- Can be sautéed similar to salmon with good results.
- White-flesh halibut can be substituted for sole in most recipes.

John Dory

- Use a delicate sauce and just lightly sauté or broil.

Mahi Mahi

- Best filleted, poached, grilled or baked.
- Usually sold as fillets and steaks.

The skin should be attached to hold the meat together while it is cooking.

- The flesh is sweet and dense.

Monkfish

- Skinless monkfish tails are available in specialty markets and are popular in seafood restaurants.
- The meat has different colors, but is white when cooked.
- The meat has delicate, firm meat.
- Known as the "poor man's lobster."
- Can be cooked by baking, steaming or pan-frying.
- Poaching is the favorite method of preparation of most chefs.
- Broiling may cause monkfish to lose too much moisture and get tough and dried out very quickly.
- Very popular for soups and stews.

Mullet

- Should be smoked or grilled.
- The meat has distinct areas of light and dark meat.
- The dark meat has a stronger flavor and is more oily.
- The light meat is milder and sweeter.

Ocean Perch (Rockfish)

- Best if steamed, baked, broiled or fried.
- Usually sold whole, dressed or as fillets.
- Sold mostly in the form of fillets.
- Has mild, firm white flesh.

Orange Roughy

- Best pan-fried, grilled, baked or poached; but can be cooked by almost any method with excellent results.
- Usually sold as frozen fillets.
- The flesh is sweet and tastes similar to a flounder.
- Easily substituted for haddock or halibut in recipes.

Pollack

- Used primarily for fish sticks and imitation crabmeat.

  Absorbs seasonings well and retains them, which is why Pollack is so popular for making imitation seafood products.

- Used to make surimi.
- Can be baked or broiled.

Pike

- Best if stuffed, roasted, grilled or poached.
- Very difficult fish to fillet because of an intricate bone structure.
- The flesh is dry and is best baked with a sauce.
- Probably one of the leanest fish you can buy.

Red Snapper

- The red snapper is found in the Gulf of Mexico and is prized as one of the best-tasting fish in the world.
- Red Snapper produces the sweetest, moist fillets of any fish.
- Excellent in chowders or fish stews. Good baked or broiled.
- Make sure you purchase it with the skin on to see the red color or it may not be a real red snapper.

Salt Cod

When an English explorer was sailing in 1602, he saw so many cod in the waters of Nova Scotia that he named the area of land "Cape Cod." The area was later developed into the center of the fishing industry in New England.

• Salt cod should be soaked in cold tap water for 18-24 hours under refrigeration in a glass bowl; then all bones and skin should be removed before cooking.

The more you cook salt cod, the tougher it becomes; then loses most of its flavor. It should be moist and tender.

• Poaching for about 15 minutes is all that is needed.
• Commonly used in fish sticks.
• Excellent when added to soups or chowders.

Scrod (young cod)

• Has a firm texture and is low fat.
• Related to the haddock and considered a delicacy.
• Sold whole, dressed and filleted.
• Actually a scrod is a young cod.

Shark

• Steaks are best and can be grilled.
• Never a bone problem.
• Has tough skin instead of scales.
• Can be easily grilled.
• If you notice a somewhat ammonia odor, just soak the flesh in salted water with a small amount of lemon juice for 2 hours before preparing.
• The odor of ammonia means that the shark was not properly processed when it was caught. If you do notice this smell, it would be best not to buy the fish.

Skate

- Best sautéed, poached or steamed. However, poaching is usually the cooking method of choice by most chefs.
- Skate has very tough skin and no scales.
- The body of the fish is never eaten, only the triangular wings.
- Best to purchase skinned and filleted.
- Looks a little like crabmeat.

Tastes better if aged for a few days in the refrigerator.

- The wings are removed after they are caught and iced immediately.
- Their flesh has a sweet, mild flavor similar to shellfish.

Sole

- Best steamed, poached or baked.
- If you see spots on fillets, especially sole, the fish was probably handled roughly. This can affect the flavor of the fish. Best not to purchase damaged fillets.
- If you would like a firmer texture in fillet of sole, just soak the fillet in a bowl with 1 quart of cold water and 2 tablespoons of white vinegar.
- Sole does not have to be turned. However, never turned more than once if you do turn it.
- Most common fillet sold in supermarkets.

Sunfish

- Best deep-fried, pan-fried or broiled.

Tilefish

Called the "Clown of the Sea" because it has a very colorful appearance. The tilefish body has a multitude of colors such as green, rose, yellow, silver and golden spots. The fish also has a yellow mask around the eyes. The colors fade very quickly after the fish is caught.

- Has a firm texture and mild flavor.
- Can be poached, baked, broiled and deep-fried.
- Excellent in chowders and stews.
- Very popular fish in oriental cooking.

- Has a sweet, clean taste.
- Used frequently in sushi and sashimi.

Turbot

- Best poached, grilled, steamed, baked or broiled.
- Similar to halibut and flounder; a flatfish.
- Usually sold as fillets.

Walleyed Pike

- Best pan-fried, grilled, baked or broiled.
- Considered one of the best freshwater eating fishes.
- Sold as dressed, whole or filleted.

Yellowtail Snapper

- Best if sautéed, broiled or grilled.

MODERATE-FAT FISH

- The fat content of most moderate-fat is around 6-7%.
- When pan-frying fish, it is best to use canola or peanut oil since they both have very high smoke points.
- If you are going to deep fat fry fish, the best oils to use are either corn or sunflower oil.

Margarine is not recommended for pan-frying.

- When barbecuing or broiling, fillets should be at least 1" thick to retain enough moisture. If they are too thick, the outside will cook before the inside is done.
- Make sure that the eyes are bulging and sunken into the head when choosing fish.
- Cod, carp and bass may have a higher amount of contaminants since they are bottom feeders.

If fish is kept for more than 24 hours, the gills need to be removed.

- If you marinate fish, it should always be done under refrigeration since moderate-fat fish decompose easily at temperatures over 60°F.
- Partially thawing in low fat milk will improve the flavor of frozen fish.
- Many oils can be used to fry fish, providing you add some canola oil to them to raise their smoke points.
- The barbecue grill should be 4-6 inches from the coals for fish.
- Butter can be used to pan-fry fish if you add some canola to the butter so that it will not smoke.
- If you are breading the fish, do not bread until just before you are ready to cook the fish or the fish may become soggy instead of crispy.
- The skins should be left on the fish when barbecuing. This helps keep the fish in shape and it won't fall apart.
- When deep-frying, make sure that the fish has a good coating or is well battered to stop it from falling apart.
- Always use a three-container method when frying fish. The first should contain all-purpose flour, the second egg that has been whisked with milk and the third with seasoned flour or cornmeal.
- To keep the tail of a fresh fish that you are going to cook whole from curling up, just trim the tail even then cut a slit up the center for about 1".
- A hot fire is recommended for grilling moderate-fat fish; then cook the fish in a short period of time.

- Can be barbecued with good results if wrapped in aluminum foil.
- Can be broiled or barbecued with fairly good results.
- Can be easily pan-fried in butter or oil with excellent results.
- Best if they are cooked partially frozen. Thawing causes too much moisture loss.
- When steaming in the microwave, wrap the fish in moistened paper towel and cook on high for 2-3 minutes on each side.
- Fish steaks about 1" thick take about 10 minutes to poach or simmer.
- The temperature should be between 360° and 375°F and not more than 3" deep. When the cold fish is put in. the temperature will drop to the desired 325°F.
- High heat will make the fish tough.

- Can be kept in a warm oven for about 15 minutes before serving.
- Fish is fully cooked when the internal temperature reaches 140°F.

Anchovy

One of the favorite dishes of the ancient Romans was called "garum," which was a sauce prepared from fermented anchovies. Anchovies deteriorate very quickly and have to be heavily salted to preserve them when caught, which is why they are so salty.

- If you soak anchovies in cold tap water for about 10 minutes it will reduce the saltiness.
- If you are not going to use them immediately store them in the refrigerator covered with olive oil.
- Best to discard the oil that the anchovies are packed in. The oil is too fishy and salty for most recipes.
- Hors d'oeuvres can be made by mixing anchovies and cream cheese.

Always use the best brand of anchovies for your recipe. Lower priced anchovies are usually poor quality and have a bad taste.

- Fresh anchovies are served in France but are rarely seen in the United States since they only have a shelf life of 48 hours.
- Never store anchovies in their original tin once they are opened.
- Anchovies need to be stored in a good grade of olive oil if they are not used up when you open the tin.
- Usually pan-fried or grilled.
- Anchovy paste is prepared by grinding up anchovy fillets into paste then blend in salt and a small amount of sugar to mellow it out.

Bass, Stripped

- Excellent stuffed, baked or grilled. Can be used raw in sashimi.

Black Sea Bass

- Best grilled, broiled and can be served raw in capriccio with a lemon, soy sauce.
- Marketed mostly in the Northeast.
- Usually sold whole.

Barracuda

- Best broiled, poached or fried.

  Great barracuda is toxic and should not be eaten.

- The Pacific barracuda has an excellent flavor and can be substituted for mahi mahi in recipes.
- The only barracuda that is edible is the Pacific Barracuda; all the other species are too toxic.
- Sold whole, dressed and filleted.
- Commonly used on soups and fish stews.

Buffalofish

- Best to just split open, clean out and fry in butter and a small amount of canola oil. The flesh is sweet and firm.
- Buffalo fish and catfish are great on the barbecue.

Carp

- The first fish ever to be aqaufarmed hundreds of years ago in China. Very popular in Chinese cuisine. Carp were brought to the United States from Germany in 1876.
- Best to pan fry.
- Can be poached with good results.
- Difficult fish to skin and de-bone.
- Best to purchase fillets.
- Try and purchase carp that has been aquafarmed.

Catfish

- Catfish were named for their 8 "barbels" or whiskers. Over 2,000 species of catfish have been identified to date. The catfish was first mentioned as a "catfish" in 1612. Small Mississippi catfish are called "mad toms" and are only used as bait fish.
- Best if baked, broiled, deep-fried or poached.
- Catfish should never smell fishy when cooked.

  If you like catfish, choose ones that have been aquafarmed for the best quality. Mississippi aquafarmed 70% of all catfish sold in the United States.

- The skin is very tough and can be hard to remove.
- Best to purchase catfish fillets.
- When buying catfish, make sure that the flesh is not spongy or dry.
- If the catfish has a strong "fishy" smell, don't buy it.
- When buying frozen catfish, be sure that the package has no partial thawing.
- If you purchase catfish that has been skinned, be sure that the meat is white with no sign of blood sores.
- Catfish must be cooked or refrigerated immediately after purchasing.
- Frozen catfish cannot be kept for more than 6 months.

Never refreeze catfish.

- Catfish should be cooked to an internal temperature of 140°F.
- Catfish has almost no connective tissue and cooks very quickly.

Baked Catfish Recipe

1 cup milk	*1 tsp. salt*
Bread crumbs	*Olive oil*
Butter	*Pepper (to taste)*
Paprika (to taste)	*1 quality catfish*

Make sure that the catfish is fresh, then wash it and dry it well. Cut into small pieces, then dip the pieces in milk that has the salt added and then into the bread-crumbs. Use a baking pan with a small amount of olive oil in the bottom. Sprinkle a small amount of pepper and paprika over the fish then place 4-5 small dollops of butter on top of the fish and bake at 400°F for about 20-25 minutes or until brown. Be careful not to over bake. Catfish bakes very quickly.

Dogfish (cape shark)

Dogfish got their name because they travel in schools and feed in groups or packs similar to a pack of hunting dogs or hounds.

- Good fish to serve to children because of the absence of bones.
- Excellent deep-fried.
- Steaks can be prepared by broiling or placed on the grill.
- Excellent in chowders and stews.

Porgy (Scup)

- Best if steamed, baked or grilled.
- Usually cooked whole.
- Must be scaled and dressed before cooking.
- Large ones can be filleted.
- The meat should be removed from the backbone before serving.

Smelt

- Best if fried and eaten whole.
- The soft bones of the smelt are edible.
- If you do want to bone it, it should be done after you cook it.

Swordfish

Swordfish received its name from the Roman gladiators. Its Roman name is "Xiphias gladius," which is from the Latin "short sword" that was carried by the Roman legions called a "gladius."

- Best grilled, baked or broiled.
- Very rich, tasting fish that has been over-fished.

Testing is showing that the fish may contain high levels of mercury and should only be consumed in moderation.

- Usually sold in boneless loins, steaks or chunks.
- Very popular for shish kebobs.
- Swordfish steaks are a popular fish restaurant favorite.
- Has a firm texture and mild taste.

Sea Trout

- Sea trout are best baked or broiled.

Trout (Brook)

- Best pan-fried, poached or baked.

Trout (Rainbow)

- Best pan-fried, smoked, steamed or poached.
- The only rainbow trout sold in supermarkets are aquafarmed.
- They have a mild, sweet flesh.
- The larger the trout, the higher the fat content will be.
- Trout can be substituted for salmon in recipes.

Tuna (Albacore)

- Best baked, broiled or grilled.
- Sold as dressed, fillets, steaks and canned.
- The only tuna that can be sold as "white" or "white-meat" tuna.
- All other species are called "light-meat" or "dark-meat" tuna.
- This is the best quality and the most flavorful tuna.

Capriccio

- To prepare capriccio, place a piece of plastic wrap on your counter, then brush it lightly with extra virgin olive oil.
- Use a 3-ounce piece of raw tuna and place it on the plastic wrap then fold the wrap completely around and seal up as best as possible.
- Using the flat side of a cleaver, pound the fish on both sides about 2-3 times until the tuna is flat and very thin.
- Serve raw.

Tuna (Bonito)

- Should be baked, broiled or grilled.
- Will be less expensive than other tuna.
- Tuna has less flavor than most other tuna.
- When it is canned, it will not be called tuna.
- Sold as whole, steaks, fillets and can be found canned.

Tuna (Bluefin)

- The ancient people of the Mediterranean and Black Sea areas traded tuna for goods and it became such an important trading commodity that it has been found on coins dating back to 400BC. The image of tuna was also found on coins from Carthage, Cadiz and Gibraltar.
- Commonly used in sushi; also can be grilled, broiled or poached.
- Steaks should be 1" thick and will take 10-12 minutes to cook on a pre-heated grill.
- Usually sold in steaks and slices.

Can be eaten well done or even medium-rare.

- Commonly called "Tonno" tuna.

Tuna (Yellowfin)

- Best poached, grilled or broiled.
- 95% of all tuna consumed is canned.
- Tuna resembles beef, when it is raw.
- The flesh is reddish but turns almost white when cooked.
- Should be marinated in the refrigerator for 15-45 minutes before grilling.

HIGH-FAT FISH

- Have a fat content of as high as 8-12%. Eels can go as high as 30% fat.
- High-fat fish are excellent for barbecuing.
- Use tweezers to remove bones
- Can easily be barbecued or broiled with excellent results.

Too high fat to provide good results if pan-fried.

- After pan-frying high-fat fish, be sure and place the fish on paper towel to remove the excess fat.
- High-fat fishes that are at least 1" thick can be turned once. Thin cuts are never turned.
- When you bake fish in aluminum foil add a sprig of dill to the fish.
- If you feel that the fish needs to be tenderized, soak the fish in 5 parts of white vinegar to 1 part of water for about 6-8 hours.
- The skin on an eel must be removed before it can be cooked.

Bluefish

Bluefish were so popular in New England in the 17th century that by 1800, they were almost extinct. However, the fish made a comeback and by 1825, they were back in abundance. Bluefish cannot be purchased on the West Coast since the fish is only caught of the Northern Coast since it deteriorates very quickly even under refrigeration.

- Best to marinade in acidic medium, then broil or bake.
- Bluefish do not freeze well.
- Should be prepared and consumed shortly after they are caught or they may have a very strong flavor.

Bluefish have a thin dark strip of flesh running down their middle that should be removed before cooking or it will affect the flavor. If left in, the fish will have a very strong fishy flavor and smell.

- Sold as fillets, dressed or whole.
- Smaller fish are safer to eat and have less contamination.
- These fish need to be kept iced from the time they are caught until they are prepared for cooking due to their high fat content.
- Can be baked, pan-fried, broiled or grilled.

Butterfish

- Butterfly, then broil or bake.
- Sold whole or drawn.
- Very small fish that is usually cooked whole.
- If butterfish is sold as fillets, it is probably sablefish and not really butterfish.

Herring

In European history, there was the Battle of the Herring in 1429, which was actually fought over the herring fishing grounds between England and France.

- Best if smoked, pickled in sour cream, baked or grilled.
- Used mainly for appetizers.
- Bismarck herring are fillets that have been pickled in vinegar, sugar, onions and salt.
- Rollmops are herring fillets that are rolled around onions or pickle slices and preserved in vinegar and spices.
- Schmalz herring have been preserved in brine.
- Maatjes herring is young herring fillets that are skinned and cured in sugar, vinegar and spices. Will have a reddish color.
- Kippered herring is high fat mature herring that are split, salted and cod-smoked. Frequently found on the British breakfast table.

Mackerel

- Fishermen will tell you that mackerel can predict the weather. Just before a storm, mackerel will bite at anything. The best time to catch mackerel is just before a big storm when the barometer is falling. The old term "mackerel sky" refers to storm cloud formations that look like the mackerel coloration.

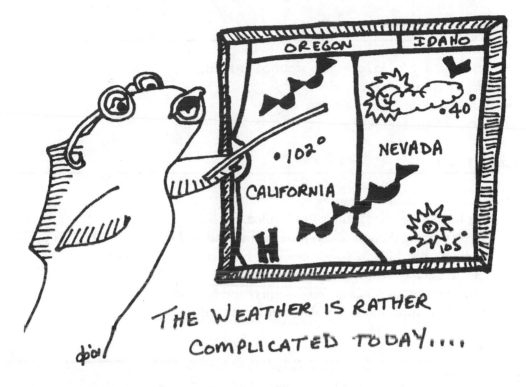

THE WEATHER IS RATHER COMPLICATED TODAY....

- Mackerel is best cooked in an acid medium for the best flavor. Citrus juices are one of the best marinades for mackerel.
- Very oily fish that is related to tuna.
- The outer layers of meat are red and the inner layers are lighter.
- Light, mild-flavored meat.
- Very perishable and needs to be purchased fresh and used that day.
- Sold as whole fish, skin-on fillets and steaks.

Mackerel must be kept well iced from the moment it is caught to the time it is being prepared for cooking.

- Has one of the highest levels of omega-3 fatty acids of any fish.
- Can be pan-fried, baked or broiled.

Pompano

- Best sautéed, baked, broiled or grilled.

   Expensive fish due to over-fishing in Florida.

- Has oily, firm white meat.

Sablefish (Black Cod)

- Best bakcd, broiled, poached, steamed or fried.
- Has a rich, mild taste.
- Usually sold in fillets or steaks.
- May be found smoked.

Salmon

- Commonly used in mousses.
- Best baked, poached, sautéed or broiled.
- When filleting salmon always start at the head and cut around the gills until the fillet knife hits the backbone. Use the backbone as a guide.
- Sold smoked in many countries.
- Usually found in supermarkets as fillets and steaks.
- One of the most moist and flavorful of all fish.

Lox

- Most people believe that lox is "smoked salmon." Lox is actually raw salmon that has been salt-cured for 2 months, then soaked in water to reduce the salt content.

Salmon, Smoked

- The best cuts to smoke are fillets and steaks.
- Salmon fillets have the ability to absorb more smoke flavor, but also have a tendency to fall apart too easily.
- The piece of fish should be wrapped in aluminum foil and folded tightly into the shape of the fish you are using, otherwise the foil may block some of the smoke.

Sardine

Napoleon was responsible for being the first person to can sardines in the early 1800's for his troops. The first U.S. cannery opened in Maine in 1873.

- Best grilled fresh or pan fry.
- Sardines are actually canned herring
- Large sardines can be purchased as steaks or fillets.
- The best quality sardines come from Maine. Look for the word "Maine" on the can for the highest quality.

Shad

In New England, the shad run to the rivers in the spring is about the exact same time as the blossoming of the "shad bush." American Indians celebrated "shadtime" in the spring and used the fish mainly for fertilizer.

- Best smoked, broiled, baked, or sautéed.
- Popular for its roe, which can be pan-fried or sautéed and usually accompanies scrambled eggs.
- Very bony fish with sweet flesh.
- Best to purchase fillets unless you are really good at de-boning.

The female shad is more desirable than the male because it is larger and fatter.

- Shad are normally caught during the spawning migration; they contain large amounts of roe.
- Commonly found pickled or smoked at specialty markets.
- The largest member of the herring family.

Sturgeon

- Best sautéed, baked or fried.
- The roe makes excellent caviar.

Trout (Lake)

- Best pan-fried, poached or steamed.

Weakfish

- Best if stuffed and baked if cooking the whole fish.
- Small fish are usually baked or broiled.

This fish got its name because when it is caught, the mouth tends to break easily.

- Usually sold whole, dressed or filleted.
- Can be substituted for striped bass in recipes.
- Weakfish is actually a sea trout.
- The meat is white and sweet.

Whitebait

- Best if floured and deep-fried.

Whitefish

- Best if broiled, baked or grilled.
- Related to trout.
- Whitefish is best barbecued.
- Has sweet, very moist delicate flesh.
- Usually sold smoked in delicatessens.
- The skin should be left on fillets to hold the fish together.

SPECIAL FISH DISHES

Capriccio

- Place a thinly sliced piece of smoked salmon (lox) on a small serving plate; then place a piece of plastic wrap over the plate. Brush the plastic wrap with a small amount of oil; then using the back of a spoon, press the salmon toward the edge of the plate. Place another plate of the same size on top of the first one with the serving side up and press down very firmly giving the plate a twist. Clean up the rough edges and place the rest of the accoutrements on or around the salmon.
- Raw tuna can also be used to prepare capriccio, but needs to be pounded with the flat side of a meat cleaver to stretch it out.
- The tuna is usually served on a bed of very thinly sliced tomatoes sprinkled with fresh basil leaves then sprinkled with olive oil, lemon juice and freshly ground pepper.

Fillet of Sole

- If you are going to use frozen fillets, it is best if they are submerged in room temperature water to de-frost.
- If frozen fillets are wrapped in plastic wrap, start de-frosting them while they are still in the plastic wrap and remove later.
- If you are lucky enough to purchase real "Dover" sole, have the butcher fillet it for you.

  Dover sole is the only sole that will remain firm after cooking.

- If you are going to sauté the fillet and are going to baste it, do not touch the fillet with the spoon you are using.

Flounder fillets

- Always sprinkle a small amount of lemon juice on flounder fillets to provide a bit of flavor and to keep the flesh firm.

  Make sure that all the exposed parts of the fillet are well, floured or the oil will seep in between the fish and the coating and remove the coating.

- Always run the egg mixture through a sieve before using it.
- Before frying, place the fillets on a tray covered with wax paper for about 10 minutes and gently turn once. This will help the coating adhere better.

Poached Salmon

- Pull any pin bones out of the salmon with a pair of needle nosed pliers.
- Remove all small bones before poaching.
- Poaching takes 7 minutes per inch.
- Poaching can be done in white wine and water; the liquid should be brought to a simmer before adding the salmon.
- The poaching liquid can provide you with a flavorful fat free sauce.
- Salmon is frequently poached in a "court bouillon." This is a combination of vegetable broth and white wine.

FISH SUBSTITUTIONS BY TEXTURE & FLAVOR

- Many fish can be interchanged in recipes if their texture and flavor are similar with excellent results.

Type of Texture	Mild Flavor	Moderate Flavor	Full Flavor
DELICATE	Cod Flounder Haddock Hake Pollack Skate Dover Sole	Black Cod Butterfish Lake Perch Whitefish	Atlantic Mackerel Bluefish
MODERATE	Rockfish Tilapia Walleye Pike Orange Roughy	Tuna Mullet Ocean Perch Shad Smelt Trout	Canned Salmon Sardines Herring King Mackerel Smoked Fish Spanish Mackerel
FIRM	Blackfish Grouper Halibut Monkfish Ocean Catfish Porgy Sea Bass Tilefish	Amberjack Catfish Mahi-Mahi Pompano Shark Stripped Bass Sturgeon	Marlin Salmon Swordfish Tuna

If you see a seafood product with "USG INSPECTED" on the label, report it to authorities, this is not a legal designation. The label should read "Packed Under Federal Inspection" or (PUFI). This means that it was packed in the presence of, or at least inspected by, a Federal Inspector.

METHODS OF AQUA-FARMING

Offshore Farming

- Deep water farming, which involves the use of boats in specific waters.

Onshore Farming

- Shallow water farming done close to shore.
- Boats are not needed.

Tank Farming

- Fish are bred in large metal, cement or fiberglass tanks onshore.
- Very efficient method of farming under strict controls.

Pond Farming

- The most popular method of fish farming.
- Man-made ponds are used to grow a number of popular fish such as catfish and trout.
- The ponds can be drained and are linked to a system of dikes for harvesting.

Tray Farming

- Provides a permanent structure for mollusks to adhere to.
- The trays are set underwater in areas where there is relatively calm year round.
- Used mainly for mollusks, clams and oysters.

CHAPTER 9

SUSHI PREPARATION & SECRETS

SUSHI

- Sushi bars seem to be popping up everywhere these days. The following information should help to enlighten you to some of the more popular sushi that is available.

General Information

- Rolling sushi is an art. If you roll a sushi and it doesn't turn out right, eat it and try again.

Rice will not stick to nori (eatable seaweed wrapper for sushi).

- Rice should be somewhat sticky when used to prepare sushi.
- If the roll does not stick together you probably did not use enough vinegar in the rice.
- If the roll is too thick or does not hold together, you probably used too much rice.
- The rice should be spread on the nori to within $5/8^{th}$ inch of the outer edge.
- The rice should never cover the nori completely.
- The nori should be seen under the rice.
- Cucumber needs to be quartered and the seeds removed.
- The length of the thin cucumber slices should be half the width of the nori.
- Thick-skinned black avocados are best.
- Make sure that you place a piece of plastic wrap between the nori and the bamboo mat.
- Never wash a bamboo mat that is used to prepare sushi since it will warp when it dries.
- Peel the plastic mat back with the mat as you roll.
- When you get finished, wrap the roll in the plastic wrap and place the roll in the refrigerator.

Unwrap the rolls and slice before serving, not before, for the best results.

TYPES OF SUSHI

Anago (sea eel)

- Always boil a sea eel before preparing, then grill it.
- Normally served in a special mixture of sugar, soy sauce and eel stock.
- No dipping sauce is needed because of the stock.

Buzuguri

- This is simply chunk-style octopus.

California Roll

- Best for beginning sushi eaters.
- Contain cooked crabmeat, avocado and cucumber.
- The biggest mistake when preparing California Roll is that of using too much rice.
- The nori should always be placed on a sheet of plastic wrap, preferably on top of a bamboo mat.
- Cut the roll into 6-8 pieces per roll.

California Roll

Spread 1 cup of cooked white rice on a sheet of nori, allowing about 1" of nori uncovered at one side. Do not pack the rice; just leave it loose. Make sure that the rice is less than $1/4$ inch thick. The nori should be easily seen through the rice. Place thin avocado slices on top of the rice; only one thick slice near the edge of the rice; the edge opposite the uncovered nori. Split a piece of imitation crab lengthwise into two pieces. Place the two pieces, end to end on top of the avocado. Then add several strips of cucumber next to the crab and on top of the avocado. It is too messy to roll if the avocado is placed on last.

Ebi (boiled shrimp)

- Have a very sweet, fresh taste.
- Jumbo shrimp are used and boiled in salted water, shelled and spread into a butterfly shape.
- The shell of the tails; are always left attached.
- Usually served with wasabi and soy sauce.

Gari (sliced ginger)

- Used to freshen the palate between sushi dishes.
- Ginger root is pickled in salt and sweet vinegar. Make sure the gari you purchase is firm with a smooth skin.

Gunkan

- Called "boat-style" sushi.
- Prepared by wrapping a band of seaweed around a pad of rice and pressed down so that the ingredients can lie on top.
- Popular method of serving fish roe and other small ingredients.

Hamachi (yellowtail)

- This is a variety of yellowtail, which is a common name for amberjack.
- It is a light, yellow color and has a rich, smooth somewhat smoky taste.
- Most sushi chefs consider the tail and the cheek of the fish the best parts and save these parts for their best customers.

Hiro Special

- Contains cucumber, cream cheese, crab, avocado, salmon and tuna.

- The sushi is wrapped in reverse style with the rice on the outside.

Ikura (salmon roe)

- Red shiny ball-like sushi.
- Ikuri was derived from the Russian word "ikra" for roe or caviar.

Called red caviar in American restaurants.

- Never served raw because of potential parasites.

Kani (crab)

- Always served cooked.
- Excellent choice for sushi beginners.
- Usually wrapped in seaweed and served in California Rolls.
- This is real crabmeat and not imitation.
- Kanikama is the name for imitation crabmeat, which is used in some sushi.

Kyuri

- Cucumber that has been wrapped in seaweed.

Maguro (tuna)

- This is the popular sushi in sushi bars in America.
- Has a fresh, clan taste.
- Lean cuts of yellowfin or bluefin tuna are usually used.

Maki-zushi (rolled sushi)

- Made by wrapping rice, fish and other ingredients into long seaweed rolls, then slicing it into small pieces.
- There are two types: hosomaki, which is a slender roll and cut into 6 pieces and temaki, which is a hand roll eaten in 2-3 bites and looks like an ice cream cone.
- Usually served with soy sauce and gari.

Makisu

- Used for preparing rolled sushi.
- It is a mat made from bamboo sticks and tied together with cotton string.
- This is a must if you are going to make rolled sushi.

Masago

- Small orange flying fish eggs.
- This is a delicacy in Japan at sushi bars.
- Often used as a garnish on the outside of hand rolls.
- It is somewhat salty and firm.

Nigiri-zushi (pressed by the hand)

- Slice of cooked or raw fish, which lies across a pad of rice.
- All ingredients are gently pressed together.
- Fish roe may be used and a strip of seaweed wrapped around to hold it together.
- Usually served with soy sauce to dip it in.

Sake (salmon)

- Very popular sushi and easily recognized by its bright orange color.

  Never served raw in sushi bars.

- It is lightly smoked first or cured in salt and sugar for a few days.

Sashimi (raw fish)

- Raw fish that is dipped in soy sauce.
- Selected from the purest waters and only prepared by special sushi chefs, which assures the highest quality fish.
- Usually eaten at the beginning of the meal.

Sonosan Roll

- Combination of cheese, cucumber, avocado and tuna.

Sushi

- A combination of vinegar-flavored rice with fish.
- Served in many forms and is eaten with chopsticks or your hands.

Suzuki (sea bass)

- Japanese fish with shiny white flesh and mild flavor.
- Sometimes it is served as sashimi.

Tako (octopus)

- Octopus that has burgundy tentacles.
- The legs are more commonly eaten than the body.
- Always boiled before serving to tenderize the flesh.
- The meat has a chewy, subtle flavor.

Tekka Maki (gambling parlors in Japan)

- Raw tuna and rice roll.
- Popular snack at the gaming tables.

Unagi (freshwater eel)

- Tastes similar to marine eel in color and taste.
- Usually grilled before being boiled, then glazed with a soy sauce, mixed with sugar and eel broth.
- Normally eaten without a dipping sauce.

Uni (sea urchin)

- Considered a delicacy.
- The gonads of the sea urchin and has a soft texture.
- Has a subtle nut-like flavor.
- Favorite food among the advanced sushi eater only.

Wasabi (horseradish)

- Spicy, green horseradish spread with a very pungent taste.
- Used to bring out the flavor of sushi.

CHAPTER 10

SHELLFISH

SHELLFISH

- Certain shellfish such as abalone, oysters and lobsters can be tenderized (if they need to be) by immersing them in a solution of 5 parts of white vinegar and 1 part of water for 8 hours.

    Be sure that you purchase shellfish that have been aqua farmed or from an area that has been recognized as safe.

- Presently, about 34% of all shellfish beds in the United States have been officially closed because of pollution. All coastal waters worldwide are in jeopardy of also being closed to fishing.
- One of the world's best known seaports, Boston Harbor, is so polluted that fishermen are advised not to fish there anymore. Mutant fish are being caught in Boston Harbor with tumors and bacterial infections.
- The sewage problem is so bad in the Gulf States of Louisiana and Florida, that 67% of the oyster beds have been closed to fishing. In Europe about 90% of the sewage is still dumped into coastal waters.

ABALONE

- Abalone must be cooked 12-24 hours after they have been caught. After 24 hours, they tend to release a chemical that turns the meat bitter.
- Cut abalone into the thinnest slices possible, then pound those slices even thinner using a meat-tenderizing hammer.
- If abalone is not tenderized, it will be very tough.
- When cooking abalone, cook only 20-30 seconds on each side for the best results.
- If you make small slashes about 1" apart along the entire piece, you will avoid curling.

Never buy abalone if the foot does not move when touched. If the foot doesn't move, it is dead.

- The smaller abalone will be more tender.
- The most popular form is abalone steak.
- If you overcook abalone, you will ruin it.
- If you can't get abalone for a recipe, you can substitute squid. The taste and texture are very similar.
- Abalone may go by a number of names such as "ormer" in England, "awabi" in Japan, "muttonfish" in Australia and "paua" in New Zealand.

CLAMS

Long Island, New York was originally known as the "Island of Shells" because of the vast number of shells found there. Purple beads were made from clamshells and were used by the local Indians for decoration and for trading purposes. The shells were called "wampum."

- Hard-shelled clams are the tastiest clams. The soft-shelled geoduck clam is not as tasty.

The best shellfish are aquacultured and have fewer, if any contaminants.

- To open clams, use a bottle top opener.
- Saltwater clams must be cleaned as soon as they are caught or they will not be edible.
- Clams have firm texture and full flavor when used in a dish.

- Clams are a good source of vitamin B_{12}, iron, iodine and many other trace minerals.
- Save the clam juice for sauces or add back if serving raw clams.

- To open shellfish, just rinse them in cold water and place them into a plastic bag in the refrigerator for about 30 minutes.
- Soak the clams in clean seawater (not fresh water) for about 20 minutes; then remove all debris or sand. The water should be changed every 4-5 minutes.
- To open clams, squeeze the clam while forcing a sturdy knife blade between the shells and slide the knife flush against the top shell to sever the adductor muscle.

- When making clam chowder always add the clams during the last 15-20 minutes of cooking time or the clams will be tough or soggy.
- Shellfish should be cooked in heavily salted water to draw out the sea salt.
- If the clam is healthy, the shell should remain closed during cooking, but should relax and open after they are boiled.
- The best clam for steaming is soft-shell clams. They will be the most succulent and tender.

Clam Fritter

These deep-fried clam treats were first prepared at Woodman's Restaurant in Essex, Massachusets for the July 4th holiday in 1916. At that time, they were called "fannie daddies" or "boat steerers" in New England.

- Most recipes use 2 large egg yolks, beaten well, $^1\!/_2$ cup of milk, 1 cup of all-purpose flour, 1 tablespoon of fresh lemon juice and salt and pepper to taste.
- Make sure that the above is mixed well, then add 2 stiffly beaten egg whites and 1 pint of fresh clams.

- Make sure that the clam mixture is chilled for 2-3 hours before frying to allow the batter to adhere really well.
- This is one food that you do not want to crowd the fryer. Fry small batches for the best results.

CRABS

There are more than 4,000 species of crab in the world. Their sizes range from the tiniest pea crab, which weighs a few ounces to the Tasmanian crab, weighing in at a whopping 30 pounds and is big enough to feed a good-size group. The West Coast Dungeness crab has the sweetest meat and weighs in at 1-5 pounds. The largest of the restaurant crabs are the Alaskan king crab.

- Crabs and lobsters will have their claws broken off and sold. They have the ability to regenerate a new claw.

Crab is second only to lobster in having the sweetest meat of any crustacean.

- Spices and herbs for the "crab boil" are usually sold in packages in any supermarket or fish market that sells crabs.
- Crabmeat is graded in three categories: Jumbo lump (backfin), flake and claw meat.
- *Flake* refers to smaller bits of meat from the body.
- *Claw meat* is small pieces from the claw and is usually brownish.
- Crabs should be active when purchased.

If canned crabmeat has a metallic taste, just soak it in ice water for 5-8 minutes, then drain and blot dry with paper towels.

- Try not to salt the cooking water too heavily or it will not be able to be used for a sauce.
- Before boiling crabs, place them into warm, salted water for 30 minutes to stabilize them or they will shed their claws when dropped into boiling water.
- Crab and lobster claws should be tied or a strong rubber band placed on them to protect the chef.

- Crabs are usually cooked in a "crab boil," which is a combination of the water the crabs are cooked in and herbs.
- If you arc steaming crab, only steam for 7-10 minutes.
- Hard-shelled crabs can be simmered for 10-15 minutes in salted water (use ¹/₂ cup of salt per gallon of water).

- If crab shells are orange after they are cooked, they may not have a good flavor. Crab shells should be red after cooking.
- Crabmeat has delicate texture and mild flavor when used in a dish.

Blue Crab

- Has blue claws making it easy to recognize.
- Has a hard shell, spring through fall.

    The lump meat is the best and is usually sold in large pieces of white meat. It may also be called "backfin."

- Serve 2-3 crabs for each person.

Dungeness Crab

This crab was named for a town in Washington where it was first harvested. The only Dungeness crabs that can be harvested must be at least 6¹/₄ inches long and are harvested usually only in the winter months.

- Can be killed by immersing it in boiling water for 2-3 minutes.
- The meat can then be removed and used for sautéing or stews.
- Can be purchased live, frozen, whole or canned.

King Crab

- Averages about 10 pounds.
- Very little is marketed fresh.
- Usually sold as crab legs, claws and clusters (shoulder sections).

Snow Crab

- Half the size of a king crab.
- Has very sweet, delicate flavor and is very tender.
- Has better flavor than king crab and is one of the most sought after by chefs for dishes.

Stone Crab

- Almost all edible meat is in its claws.
- The claws are usually removed and cooked as soon as they are caught and frozen on the boat.

How to dress a soft-shell crab

If you ask your butcher, they will almost always dress the crab for you. However, if you have to do it yourself, rinse it thoroughly; then cut off the eyes with a knife or kitchen scissors. Press the area where the eyes were to expose the bile sac and pull the sac out. Turn the crab on its back, lift up and remove the apron, which is a rough triangle of soft-shell. Lift up the flaps at each side near the legs and remove the spongy gills. Rinse the crab well and pat dry with paper towel. The entire crab is edible including the soft-shell.

CRAYFISH (crawdads))

Originally, the crayfish were called "mudbugs" since they lived in the mud of freshwater bayous. These small crustaceans have only become related to Cajun cooking in the last 40 years. Before that, they were only considered as bait for the local fisherman. Since the price of lobster was so high, Cajun cooks started using the crayfish to replace the lobster. The crayfish are raised commercially in aqaufarms in Louisiana. The flavor is better than lobster and more delicate than even shrimp.

- Crayfish should always be cooked live. Drop them into boiling water for about 7 minutes.
- The stomach and intestinal vein should be removed before cooking. They are removed by pulling the middle tail fin.
- The flavorful juices in crayfish may be sucked out from the head after eating the meat in the tail.
- Crayfish are only steamed for 4-8 minutes.
- They are usually found in markets at about 5 inches long.
- Most are aquafarmed in the Southern United States.
- Crayfish have moderate texture and mild flavor when used in a dish.

LANGOSTINOS

- Crustacian that is mainly caught in the Gulf of Mexico and is a cross between a shrimp and a lobster.
- Langostinos are usually sold as "rock shrimp."
- Used mainly in soups and stews.
- Can be cooked the same as lobster.
- Usually sold cooked or frozen.

LOBSTER

The best eating lobster is the Maine lobster, which usually is sold up to about 3 pounds. However, there have been a number caught that have weighed in up to 10 pounds. The quality of the meat is about the same regardless of size. Lobsters grow by molting and shed their outer shell. This process can take up to 12 days until the new shell becomes hard. While this is occurring, the lobster is very vulnerable to predators. In 1935, a 42-pound lobster was caught off Virginia, which is the world's record.

Because of this vulnerability, the male lobster molts in the dark, which occurs during the new moon. The female lobster, however, molts during the light of the full moon so that she will be noticed by male lobsters and get a new mate.

- Lobster meat is the sweetest meat of any shellfish.
- Rock lobsters have less flavor than a Maine lobster.
- When making Lobster Newburg, it is OK to purchase the less expensive lobsters such as the spiny lobster.
- The size of the lobster does not determine how tender or flavorful the lobster meat will be. Large lobsters will taste just as good as small lobsters.
- Finer small, toothed lobster claws will have sweeter meat.
- Lobsters will turn red due to the "chitin" in the external skeleton.
- Lobsters will stay alive for 1 week if you wrap the lobster in newspapers that have been dampened in cold water. Wrap the lobster and place in the refrigerator.
- The second a lobster dies, they cannot be cooked since a digestive enzyme is released into the meat making it bitter.
- Rock lobsters have no claws; therefore only the tail is marketed.
- A 1-pound lobster only yields about $1/4$ pound of meat.
- Lobsters can remain alive for a long period by extracting oxygen from the water that will cling to their gills.
- Store lobster in a 50°F environment and place, wet seaweed around them to keep them moist.
- Lobster has moderate texture and mild flavor when used in a dish.
- Lobsters should be moving when purchased or at least the tail should curl under when touched.

- To avoid the lobster tail from curling up when they are being cooked, just place a bamboo skewer through the back of the tail and out the front. When the skewer is removed the tail will remain straight.
- If a moving lobster bothers you, place the lobster in the freezer for 10 minutes to dull its senses and it will only have a reflex action for about 20 seconds.

Placing a live lobster into boiling water before cutting the spinal cord may produce tough meat. To put the lobster out of its misery, just thrust a knife between the head and the abdomen to sever the spinal cord.

- Restaurants place lobsters in a bowl full of beer before cooking them to get them drunk before placing them into a pot of boiling water.

- To steam a 1-pound lobster, it should take 10 minutes.
- To steam a 2-pound lobster, it should take 18 minutes.
- Some of the better restaurants now microwave lobsters to retain their flavor and moisture.

To microwave a lobster, you will need to place the lobster into a large microwave-safe plastic bag and knot it loosely. A 1¹/₂ pound lobster should take about 5-6 minutes on high if the oven is at least 600 watts. If using a lower wattage microwave, allow 8 minutes, but be sure that the lobster is fully cooked.

- An 8-ounce lobster tail can be grilled in 10-12 minutes.
- A 2 pound lobster can be broiled in about 14 minutes. Keep the lobster about 5" from the heat source.
- Lobsters contain a high percentage of glycogen in their muscle, which converts to glucose when heated, making the meat sweeter than fish.

Boiling Lobsters

- Use a large kettle or pot and fill it ³/₄ full of salted water.
- Allow 2¹/₂ quarts of water per lobster.

Bring the water to a boil and place the live lobsters in one at a time, head first.

- Allow the water to return to a boil then simmer for an additional 15 –20 minutes depending how many lobsters are in the pot.
- For a 1 to 1¹/₄ pound lobster it takes 15 minutes.
- Add about 3 minutes for each additional pound.

- After removing lobster meat from the shell, use the shells and return them to the liquid that the lobster was cooked in to prepare a great shellfish stock.
- When you first start to break a cooked lobster apart, be sure and place a towel around it so that the juices will not spray all over.

To retain flavor in lobster when added to a dish, be sure and add the cut-up lobster just before serving.

- Cracked pieces of lobster shell should be added to any sauce for the lobsters. Strain the shell out before serving. The sauce will have a richer lobster flavor.
- Make sure that the "tomalley" is green when the tail is separated from the body.
- The "tomalley" can be eaten and is often used to flavor lobster dishes or sauces that accompany lobster.
- The tomalley can be mixed with melted butter and served with the lobster. This commonly done in Europe.
- If you order a female lobster, you may get a portion of the roe or coral. The roe is usually red before cooking and turns dark green if it has been heated. This is considered a delicacy in many countries.
- The coral (roe) can be mixed with melted butter similar to the "emerald" or tomalley and served as an appetizer.
- Lobsters have a sac or stomach right behind the head, which is not edible and usually very sandy.

Lobster Newburg

This dish was first prepared at Delmonico's Restaurant in New York City in 1876 by Chef Charles Ranhofer. The recipe for lobster Newberg was given to him by a sea captain named Ben Wenberg and the dish was originally named "lobster a la Wenberg." Wenberg had a disagreement with the restaurant and his name was removed but only changing the first 3 letters from Wenberg to Newberg.

- The lobster meat should be sliced and sautéed in unsalted butter with cayenne or a dash of Tobasco added.

- The sauce is prepared from 1 cup of heavy cream and 2 tablespoons of sherry, which should be boiled to eliminate the alcohol but allowing the flavor to remain.
- The sauce should be thickened with 3 well beaten, large egg yolks.
- This dish is usually prepared with a large amount of butter in most restaurants.
- Margarine does not work in this recipe.

Lobster Thermidor

- To save time, you can boil the lobster a day ahead of time and cube the lobster meat.
- Place the cubed meat in a plastic container and pour sherry over the meat and refrigerate overnight (no more).
- Never use commercial breadcrumbs for this dish. Use day old bread broken into pea-sized pieces. Do not press the bread so that it becomes solid.
- Unsalted butter will make a big difference.

MUSSELS

- Mussels should only be purchased from reputable fish markets that purchase their mussels from aquafarms. The level of contamination in mussels has been found to be too high in most areas off the coasts of the United States.
- Mussels are steamed for 4-8 minutes.
- Mussels can be served on the half-shell or in the whole shell.
- Mussels can be steamed in wine or water with 2 ounces of lemon juice added to provide a mild acid base.
- Mussels spawn usually in May and it would be best not to purchase them during this period.
- Mussels may have barnacles that can easily be removed with a clam knife.
- Mussels are rarely ever served raw and are almost always served steamed in their cooking juices.
- The liquid in a mussel when it is shucked should be clear. If it is cloudy, discard the mussel.
- Mussels are cooked when their shell opens. Never force the shell open.
- Live mussels and oysters can be stored in the refrigerator covered with a damp towel for 2-3 days only and in a single layer.

Once you remove a mussel's beard, it will die.

- The liquid from cooking the mussels should be strained through a fine sieve and placed back in the pot. Combine the liquid with 1-2 teaspoons of flour and salt and pepper; then use as a dip for the mussels or pour it over them.
- Mussels have delicate texture and full flavor when used in a dish.

OYSTERS

An adult female oyster lays 100 million eggs during a single season, however, only less than 1% ever mature. The most famous oyster restaurant in the world is the Grand Central Oyster Bar in Manhattan, which was built in 1913 under Grand Central Terminal. They use over 283,000 oysters per year in pan-roasts and stews, 600 of which are prepared every day and 1,700,000 oysters are served raw every year.

"Diamond Jim" Brady ate 3-4 dozen oysters every day. However, the record was recorded in 1972 by Bobby Melacon who consumed 188 oysters in 1 hour at the Louisiana State Oyster Festival.

- Oysters should have a somewhat sweet smell when shucked.
- Littleneck oysters are small but are the most tender when eaten raw and best for steaming.
- Insert a sturdy knife into an oyster and twist to break the hinge.
- Shellfish are not recommended for a low-salt diet.
- Shellfish can be opened by placing them on a cookie sheet in the freezer for 15 minutes. This relaxes the muscle.

When shellfish is kept on ice, they may open their shell but will close the shell when tapped. If they don't close their shell when tapped, they are probably sick.

- If shellfish do not open their shells after being cooked, they should be discarded. Never force the shell open.

- Oysters can now be eaten all year, even in months that do not have an "R" in them. However, they will be less flavorful.
- If an oyster shell is cracked or broken, throw them away.
- Gulf Coast oysters should never be eaten raw because of the high level of contaminants in the Gulf.
- Shucked oysters can be frozen for 3 months if stored in their juices, but only 2 days in the refrigerator.
- If you are poaching oysters, only poach them until the edges start to curl otherwise they will be tough

Oysters will be easy to remove from the shell if you soak them in unflavored club soda for 5-10 minutes.

- Oysters can be grilled by placing the deep half of their shell down on the grill and placing a small amount of flavored butter on top; then some bread crumbs. Only cook until they are just barely bubbling.
- Oysters have delicate texture and full flavor when used in a dish.

Oyster Fritters

- Blend together the ¹/₄ cup of all-purpose flour, 2 beaten egg yolks (substitute OK), 2 tablespoons of room temperature softened unsalted butter and salt and pepper to taste.
- Make sure that you add about ³/₄ cup of strained oyster liquid from 2-3 dozen oysters.
- Always allow the mixture to remain standing for 2 hours before adding 4 stiffly beaten egg whites to it.
- The oysters are dipped in the batter and placed into the refrigerator for 30 minutes to allow the batter to adhere better before frying.

Oysters Rockefeller

Oysters Rockefeller was first prepared by Jules Alciatore in 1899 at Antoine's Restaurant in New Orleans. It is a spiced full flavored baked oyster dish that is served on the half shell. Jules needed a replacement for snails which were in short supply and invented a new dish. The sauce that was prepared for the oysters was so rich that he named the dish after John D. Rockefeller, one of the richest men in America at that time.

- Use the large half of the shell and allow the oysters to remain in that half shell with its juices.
- Mix together in a mortar and pestle some fresh chives, chervil, tarragon leaves, stale breadcrumbs, Tabasco sauce and clarified butter.
- Make sure that all items are well blended to allow all the flavors to mix.
- Add 2-3 drops of absinthe or anise cordial and ½ ounce of white wine to the mixture.
- Use a fine sieve and push the mixture through.
- Only place one spoonful or a little less on top of each oyster.
- The oysters should be placed on a bed of crushed rock salt and the baked until just brown and served immediately.

SCALLOPS

The scallop shell was worn by the apostle St. James as his personal emblem. When he was put to death by sword at the order of Herod Agrippa I (44AD), it became a badge for the pilgrims who visited his shrine in Compostela, Spain during the Middle Ages.

- Scallops should be purchased moist and never dry.
- Scallops are always shucked as soon as they are caught otherwise they die very quickly.
- Only the adductor muscle that is used to open and shut their shell is used for food.
- The largest scallop is the Sea Scallop.
- The Bay Scallop is an intermediate size.
- The Calico Scallop is the smallest scallop. Always try and find the Bay Scallop, which is the most delicate and excellent eating.
- Calico Scallops are easy to recognize since they are pale white and look like a marshmallow.
- If you are going to sauté scallops, make sure that you dry them well before sautéing them.
- Scallops should be cooked quickly and should be done within 1-3 minutes.

Overcooking scallops will toughen them and cause them to lose most of their moisture and flavor.

- If possible, ask for the shells and use them to serve the scallops in.
- Sometimes it may be possible to find scallops still in their shell with a small amount of roe. The roe is a delicacy and is excellent.
- Scallops that are old will have a smell similar to sulfur.
- Have a mild, sweet flavor, making them popular for many dishes.
- Scallops have been served raw after being soaked in lime juice; however, this does not protect you against any parasites. Best to cook them.
- Never overpower scallops with seasonings since they have a natural sweetness and mild flavor.
- Scallop recipes utilize mild ingredients that compliment them, and do not overpower the scallops with fancy ingredients.
- Never place scallops in a pan to fry them until the oil is hot. The less time they are cooked the better.
- Imitation scallops may occasionally be found in supermarkets and are made from surimi (fish fillets). These products must be labeled as "imitation."

SHRIMP (Prawns)

Since shrimp have high water content, one pound of shrimp will reduce down to ³/₄ pound or less after cooking. Prawns are the largest member of the shrimp family and has pincer claws. Scampi are another member of the shrimp family. Shrimp are usually white after being cooked. However, if they feed on algae, they may be brown and have a stronger flavor to the iodine content in algae.

- Shrimp can be stored longer if the heads are removed.
- The head contains most of the digestive system and all of the vital organs.
- If shrimp starts to smell like ammonia and does not a fresh non-fishy smell, throw them away.
- The term "green shrimp" refers to raw shrimp that are still in their shell.
- Shrimp has moderate texture and mild flavor when used in a dish.
- Shrimp should be defrosted in the refrigerator or in ice cold water.
- Never thaw shrimp in a microwave or in a warm location.
- Flavor is lost if shrimp are frozen after they have been shelled.
- Thawed shrimp will only last for 2 days at the most.
- Shrimp cannot be re-frozen; most are sold frozen or thawed.

Most shrimp is actually frozen right on the shrimp boat since it deteriorates very quickly. Best to purchase frozen shrimp and use as needed from the freezer since it thaws very fast.

- If you are concerned about an off-flavor from canned shrimp, just place the unopened can in a pan of ice water for 1-2 hours before opening.
- To improve the flavor and texture of shrimp, it is best to place them into a brine solution before cooking them.
- To prepare brine solution, mix together 1-cup table salt, $1/2$ cup sugar and 2 cups of boiling water. After the mixture is dissolved, place it in a bowl full of ice and allow it to cool. The shrimp can then be left in the refrigerator for about 2-2$1/2$ hours before it should be rinsed well and cooked.

De-veining Shrimp

- De-vein shrimp using an ice pick down the back to remove the black intestinal tube. If you leave the tube, then the shrimp must be cooked since there may be bacteria in the tube.
- Shrimp can also be de-veined and split opened easily using a kitchen scissors and cutting along the back toward the tail after the head has been removed. The skeleton and intestinal tract can then be removed.
- If the intestinal tube is not removed and cooked, the shrimp may be gritty due to sand granules.
- Raw shrimp are easier to de-vein before cooking.

- One pound of raw shrimp in their shells will cook up to about $1/2$ pound.

Cooking Shrimp

- Cook shrimp in its shell whenever possible for better flavor.
- Use 3 tablespoons of salt to 1 quart and allow the water to boil before adding the shrimp. After adding the shrimp, cover and cook.

Shrimp should be cooled down before cooking. Just place them into the freezer for 10-15 minutes and they will cook up tender.

- If you prefer to cook shrimp that has already been shelled, cook the shells in water for 10-12 minutes then use the water to cook the shrimp in for better flavor.
- Jumbo shrimp cook in salted, rapidly boiling water in 7-8 minutes.
- Large shrimp cook in about 5-7 minutes.
- Medium shrimp cook in 3-4 minutes.
- The flavor of shrimp is often ruined by overcooking.
- As soon as you have cooked shrimp, place them into a bowl of cold water to stop the cooking or they will continue cooking.
- Never leave shrimp in the cooking liquid or they will be ruined.
- Simmering unshelled shrimp in beer provides an excellent flavor.
- High heat will cause shrimp to become rubbery and tough.

Fried Shrimp

- Beer batter makes the best fried shrimp. The yeast in the beer provides a leavening effect on the batter.
- The batter should be made ahead of time and allowed to rest before being used.

If using batter, be sure that it is at room temperature for the best results.

- Do not fry more than 4-5 shrimp at a time so that the oil does not cool.
- The oil should be at 375°F.
- As the shrimp are fried, place them in a pre-heated 250°F oven on a baking sheet that has been lined with paper towels. Turn the oven off before you place the baking sheet in.

Serving Shrimp

- Large and jumbo shrimp that are served in a stemmed glass should be served with an oyster fork and picked up with the fork, dipped in the sauce and a small bite taken, they dipped again.
- When shrimp are served on a platter, then it is permissible to pick up the shrimp with your fingers to dip and eat.

Shrimp Cocktail Sauce

1 pint of quality ketchup
$1^1/_4$ cups of chili sauce (not too hot)
$^1/_2$ cup prepared horseradish (drained well)
2 ounces of fresh lemon juice
1 tablespoon of Worcestershire sauce

Shrimp in Dill Sauce

- The boiled shrimp will not dry out or become rubbery if you keep it at room temperature in a bowl of tepid water.
- By adding a small amount of lemon juice to the dill sauce, it will strengthen the flavor of the dill.
- Use a high quality sour cream or add a small amount of sugar to improve the flavor.
- Sprinkle the top of the dish with a small amount of the dill.
- Don't overcook the sauce. It should be removed from the heat as soon as it starts to cook. A small amount of chicken broth can be added to improve the thickness of the sauce if needed.

COMMERCIAL SIZES OF SHRIMP

- Shrimp are sold in a variety of sizes and are classified on the package. Their size will determine the number of shrimp in the package. The following is the classification system used for shrimp.

SIZE	PER PACKAGE/Lb.	SIZE	PER PACKAGE/Lb.
Extra Colossal	under 10	Medium Large	36-40
Colossal	under 15	Medium	41-50
Extra Jumbo	16-20	Small	51-60
Jumbo	1-25	Extra Small	61-70
Extra Large	26-30	Tiny (Bay Shrimp)	over 70
Large	31-35		

OCTOPUS

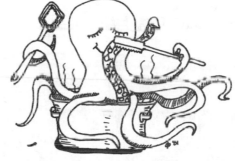

- Octopus has a hard beak that is found in the center of the tentacles and should be discarded.
- Octopus is cleaned and prepared the same as squid except it has a tough skin that needs to be removed.
- Best to choose an octopus under 2 pounds since it will more tender than the larger ones.
- Octopus takes longer to cook and is relatively tough if not cooked just right.
- If the skin does not come off an octopus easily, it will be necessary to parboil it for a few minutes to loosen it.
- Most octopus are caught on the West Coast or imported.
- Octopus is usually sold frozen and already cleaned. If sold thawed, it has probably been frozen and should not be re-frozen.

Octopus has firm texture and moderate flavor when used in a dish.

SQUID

- Squid becomes tough very quickly and should only be cooked for no more than 3 minutes.
- Squid may be marketed as "calamari."
- Squid is commonly stuffed since it has a hollow body cavity.
- Squid is very tender and has a mild flavor.
- Make sure that squid is well breaded and placed in the refrigerator for 30 minutes to allow the breading to set before deep frying.
- If adding squid to a dish it should be added toward the end of the cooking cycle when there is about 15 minutes left.
- Squid is usually sold either whole or dressed.
- Only the hollow body and tentacles are eaten, the rest of the squid is discarded and does not have a very good flavor.

When the head is pulled out the internal organs will usually be attached making it easy to remove and discard.

- Remove the plastic-like "quill" from the body and discard.
- The tentacles are usually chopped into small pieces, fried or added to soups or stew.
- Squid has firm texture and mild flavor when used in a dish.

CHAPTER 11

COOKING WITH CHEESE

COOKING WITH CHEESE

Cheese was discovered by accident when an Arab nomad filled one of his saddlebags with milk to have a source of nutrition while crossing the desert. When he rested at an oasis and wanted a drink, he found that the milk had partially turned into curds and whey, since the saddlebag was made from the stomach of a goat and contained the enzyme "renin." Cheese was first produced in the Middle East and the actual process of cheese making was known to the ancient Sumerians 4,000 years before the birth of Christ. Cheese was first produced commercially by the Romans.

- The cheese industry has perfected methods of changing a good quality nutritious product into a chemical smorgasbord, which is why chefs will mainly use white cheeses. White cheeses are for the most part, natural cheeses without the addition of chemicals and additives.

- These chemicals are used to give cheese their sharp taste, color them, make them smell more appealing or just to change their texture. The public needs to be more aware of the type of cheese they purchase and try not to buy cheeses with added chemicals. If the label says "all-natural," you still need to see the wording "no preservatives or coloring agents."

Cooking with Cheese Facts

- When melting cheese, the temperature cannot be too high for too long a period of time. When this occurs, the protein is separated from the fat and the cheese becomes tough and rubbery. If this does occur, it cannot be reversed and the cheese is ruined.

- Remember to keep the heat on low and best to use a double boiler. If you are going to melt cheese, don't try and melt large pieces.
- Cheese should be cut into a number of small chunks before you attempt to melt it.
- Cheese should be added last to most recipes.

Grating cheese will make it easier to melt and this method is recognized as the best method for making sauces. Certain exceptions are ricotta, Camembert and Brie, which have higher water content and lower fat content. These are not as good for certain dishes.

- The wax coating on cheeses will protect it. If there is an exposed edge, try covering it with butter to keep the area moist and fresh.
- To keep cheese longer without mold forming, place a piece of paper towel that has been dampened with white vinegar in the bottom of a plastic container that has a good seal before adding the cheese. Also, add 5-6 small sugar cubes for any mold that does get in.
- Soft cheeses can be grated using a metal colander and a potato masher.
- Cheeses that have dried out may still be used for dishes that require grated cheese.
- White or yellow cheddar cheeses contain about 70% fat, of which 40% is saturated.
- If cheese becomes moldy, just remove the mold and cut back ½" inch past any mold to make sure the "feelers" sent out by the mold are gone.

Cheese should never be served on any kind of metal platter, since the cheese contains chemicals that will react with most metals and alter the flavor of the cheese.

- When chefs use hard cheeses for dishes, they always allow the cheese to remain at room temperature for 30-45 minutes before using the cheese.
- All cheese should be served at room temperature.
- Very soft cheese should be left in their wrapper until you are ready to serve them.
- Hard cheese and semi-soft cheeses lose 30-40% of its flavor when cold.
- If you are going to grate a hard cheese, then it should be cold since it will be easier to grate and will warm up quickly and regain its flavor.
- When using a food processor or blender to grate or chop cheeses, it would be best to spray the blades and interior surfaces with a non-stick spray.
- Thin slices of hard cheese can be obtained by using a wide vegetable peeler.

- Using a hand grater usually works better than most food processors when grating cheese. Since the cheese is relatively soft, it is a fast job anyway.
- Purchasing grated cheeses are handy but a bit more expensive.
- Cheeses that have a soft creamy texture should not be purchased if they are too thick. They tend to be overripe around the edges. Best to purchase them when they are about 1-1½" thick at the most.
- If you use lemon juice in a cheese recipe, always add it and mix well before adding the mixture to a cream base.
- Cheese sauces can be kept smooth with the addition of starches such as flour, cornstarch, potato starch or tapioca.
- To crumble blue cheese, place it in a plastic bag and crush with your hand.
- Low fat and non-fat cheeses are not recommended for most dishes since they do not melt very well. Use low heat if you are going to use them and be patient.
- If cheese becomes stringy or rubbery, just cut the cheese into small pieces and place it in the blender with a small amount of cream and blend until smooth.

When re-heating a dish that contains cheese, which will easily separate or become tough, try re-heating the dish in a hot water bath.

- One-quarter pound of semi-soft or hard cheese will measure up to 1 cup after being grated.
- Because of their high moisture content, ¼ pound of soft cheese only measures up to about ½ cup.
- Cheese should be served before a sweet dessert to cleanse the taste buds so that you can enjoy the dessert.
- When making fondue, the best cheese is Gruyere.

CHEESE RIPENING CLASSIFICATIONS

Unripened

- Normally consumed shortly after manufacture; and are the more common cheeses such as cottage cheese, which is a high-moisture soft cheese.
- Examples of unripened, low-moisture cheeses include gjetost and mysost.

Soft

- Cured from the outside or rind of the cheese toward the center. The process entails using specific molds or cultures of bacteria, which are allowed to grow on the surface of the cheese creating the specific characteristics flavors, body and texture of that cheese.
- These cheeses usually contain more moisture than the semi-soft ripened cheeses.

Semi-soft

- When cheese ripens from the inside as well as the exterior, curing continues as long as the temperature is warm.
- These cheeses have higher moisture content than firm-ripened cheeses.

Firm

- These cheeses are ripened by utilizing a bacterial culture which continues as long as the temperature is favorable.
- Firm cheeses have lower moisture content than softer cheese varieties and usually requires a longer curing period.

Very hard

- Cheeses are cured utilizing a bacterial culture and specific enzymes. They are slow-cured, have a higher salt content and are very low in moisture.

Blue-vein

- Cured with the aide of mold bacteria and specific mold cultures that grow throughout the inside of the cheese. This produces the familiar appearance and unique flavor.

COOKING WITH COMMON RECIPE CHEESES

Beer Cheese

- This is a smooth, soft cheese that has been compared to Limburger but is somewhat milder

Bel Paese

- Originated in Italy. It is a semi-soft cheese with a mild flavor. Usually eaten for dessert with fruit.

Blue (bleu)

- Is easily identified by its white and blue streaks. Blue cheese crumbles easily and has a somewhat soft texture.
- It is sold in various shapes; the most common of which is a block.
- The Maytag blue cheese is one of the finest in the world and is produced from the freshest unpasteurized milk obtainable from only two Holstein herds located near Newton, Iowa. The moisture content is higher than that of most other blue cheeses making it very easy to spread and creamy and the cheese is aged in a special manmade cave that was dug into the side of a hill. The cheese is a somewhat sharp, yet mellow to the taste. It can be ordered by calling (515) 792-1133.

Brick

- A somewhat soft, yellow cheeses with a medium-soft texture; commonly available in brick form.

Brie

- The cheese is produced with an edible white outer coating.
- It has a mild flavor with a creamy white texture.
- Brie and Camembert are both sprayed with special mold to form a very thin, white, flexible rind. These cheeses ripen from the outside in and turn creamier with a more intense flavor as time passes.
- These cheeses are normally found in boxes which when opened, may smell a little musty but should never have an ammonia smell.
- Ideally, the cheese should be somewhat springy when prodded and never have a hard core.

- These cheeses will continue to ripen when refrigerated for 1-2 days and should be consumed within 3-5 days after purchase for the best taste.
- If the cheese appears "runny," then has been over-aged and may be bitter. Other cheeses in this category include Limburger, Coulommiers, and Liederkranz.

Goat Brie cheese should be allowed to warm to room temperature before being served.

- Kerry Ingredients, a cheese manufacturing company, has developed a new form of Brie cheese that can be deep-fried and retain its shape, which in the past has not been possible. The new Brie is composed of Brie, cheddar and mozzarella cheeses and can be extruded into a number of shapes that will interest the consumer.
- The finest Brie cheeses that reach perfection in taste and texture are made in France and are always made from unpasteurized milk.
- The United States will not allow this "surface-ripened" cheese to be imported unless it is made from pasteurized milk, aged for 60 days, or stored in such a manner that the flavor would be adversely affected during shipping. Natural Brie if aged for 60 days would lose its flavor and become overripe.
- The Brie that we do buy does not have the flavor or quality of French Brie and has a lower fat content by about 10%.
- Brie without the rind can be easily melted when added to hot dishes, especially pasta.

Boursault

- French cheese that is soft and has a creamy texture.
- It is a delicate, mild cheese usually served at desert with wine.

Camembert

- Soft, somewhat yellow inside, with a thin dull white coating which is edible.
- Ripens in about 4-8 weeks and was reputed to be Napoleon's favorite cheese.

Cheddar

- The natural color of cheddar is white not yellow. The yellow color is produced by dyes since yellow cheese is more salable.

- It has mild to very sharp taste and has a fairly firm texture. Sold in numerous shapes and sliced.
- One of the first things to look for when purchasing cheddar cheese is uniform color. If the cheese has white spots or streaks, it has not ripened evenly or is starting to develop mold.

If yellow cheddar has white spots or streaks, it has not ripened evenly and should not be purchased.

- To smoke cheese, choose a cheddar or Swiss and slice the cheese into 1" pieces; then smoke at 60°F for about 2-3 hours.
- The texture should always be relatively smooth. However, it is not uncommon to purchase cheddar that is grainy and crumbly.
- If the cheddar has a rind, be sure that the rind is not cracked or bulging. This may mean that the cheese will be bitter due to poor manufacturing practices.
- Cheddar will continue to age in the refrigerator for months and should be stored in a container with a vinegar dampened paper towel underneath.
- When preparing a cheddar cheese dressing, the dressing should be allowed to remain in the refrigerator for 1 hour before serving; then allowed to remain at room temperature for 20 minutes after removing it from the refrigerator.

Cheshire

- A hard cheese with a mellow and rich flavor similar to cheddar.

Colby

- Usually sold as a light, yellow cheese and has a somewhat mild flavor.
- The texture is similar to that of cheddar. Normally sold in wedges cut from a large round and originated in Wisconsin.

Coldpack

- Sold as both fresh and aged.
- Contains whey solids and usually has a somewhat mild flavor.
- Soft, easy to spread cheese; sold in a variety of colors using artificial colorings and flavorings.

Cream Cheese

Cream cheese was invented in 1872 by a Wisconsin dairyman while attempting to duplicate neufchatel cheese from France. James Kraft developed a method of pasteurizing cream cheese in 1912 and produced Philadelphia Cream Cheese. Cream cheese was first popularized in New York in the 1920's. Cream cheese was produced by the Breakstone Dairy Company of Downsville, New York and was an instant hit with the Jewish community to be used on bagels.

- Usually made with light cream or whole milk before the cream has been skimmed off and is 90% fat.
- Some cream cheese is made with propylene glycol alginate. This chemical is not one of the more healthy chemicals and should be avoided.
- Sold in a semi-soft form and usually white; however, colorings may be added.

Edam

- Commonly sold in a large ball-shape with a red wax coating.
- The interior is a creamy-yellow orange color and the cheese has a light nut-like flavor.
- The consistency is semi-soft and has a lower milk-fat content than a Gouda cheese.
- Should be an additive-free cheese.

Feta

- A small curd cheese usually produced from goat's milk. The taste is somewhat salty and sharp.

Farmer's Cheese (pot cheese)

- A close relative to cottage cheese and is usually pressed into a block shape.
- Sold mostly in a delicatessen.

Fontina

- One of the finest semi-soft cheeses from Italy. It has a mild, somewhat nutty flavor with a light brown rind. It is usually a fondue cheese.
- The flavor is similar to Swiss cheese.
- Excellent for grilled cheese sandwiches and melts easily in omelets.

Gjetost

- Relatively mellow cheese that is sold in cubes or rectangles.
- Usually found in a pleasant golden color and made from whey or fresh goat's milk.
- The consistency is semi-soft.

Gorgonzola

- Mold plays a big role in the coloring of this cheese and it is called the Italian blue cheese.
- It is always found with blue-green stripes and has a soft texture with an off-white exterior. The flavor is tangy and somewhat peppery and the cheese tends to crumble easily.
- It is usually made with whey or goat's milk.
- Use very sparingly in salads since it has a strong flavor.

Gouda

- Usually sold in a ball shape with a red wax coating.
- The insides are a semi-soft, creamy yellow, with a nut-like flavor.
- The cheese contains irregular or round-shaped holes.

Gruyere

- Similar to Swiss cheese, but with a higher nutrient content.
- Usually sold with mold inhibitors added, check the label.

Limburger

- Smooth, creamy, semi-soft aged cheese.
- It is a stronger smelling cheese than we have become used to and has been relegated to being produced by only one plant in the United States in Monroe, Wisconsin; the Chalet Cheese Company. This company produces about a million pounds per year using 32 very hard working cows.

Limburger is "real" cheese, while most of the processed cheeses in the market are only 45 percent real cheese then fortified with whey powder and lactose.

- Limburger will continue to age after it is purchased and will actually develop more flavor. It will remain fresh for 5-6 months and should be stored in a well-sealed glass container.

Mascarpone

- Called a "triple-cream" cheese and is usually prepared from low-fat fresh cream.
- Must be made from cows that eat special grass that contains herbs and flowers.
- Easy to spread and often used to replace butter on bread.

Mozzarella

Mozzarella was accidentally invented when someone dropped cheese curds into a pail of very hot water in a cheese factory near Naples, Italy. The first mozzarella cheese was produced from water buffalo milk and was not pasteurized. Buffalo mozzarella is still produced in Italy.

- Produced from part-skim or whole milk and has a firm texture.
- Favorite pizza cheese.
- Sold in rounds, shredded, or slices.
- Preservative are sometimes added to keep the moisture content low.
- The best mozzarella is called buffalo milk mozzarella.
- The rubbery mozzarella found in supermarkets is not the best quality mozzarella cheese.

Muenster

- Usually sold in wedges or blocks and has more moisture than brick cheese.
- The insides are a creamy-white with a yellowish exterior and possibly small holes.

- The flavor is mild and the texture is semi-soft.
- The American variety is unsalted.
- The Italian variety is purchased in water and is more firm. Both have about 45% milk fat.

Myost

- Sold in pie-shaped wedges or cubes and has a buttery consistency.
- The color is usually a light brown and has a sweet caramel flavor.

Neufchatel

- Has a soft texture and a mild acidic flavor.
- The fat content is lower than cream cheese due to a lower milk-fat content.

Parmesan

Italy produces 2,850,000 wheels of Parmesan cheese annually. Parmesan cheese is easier for the body to digest than milk and has the lowest cholesterol level of any cheese.

- Usually sold grated; however, will have a better flavor if it is purchased in bulk and then grated as needed.
- In bulk, it is a creamy-white cheese with a hard granular texture.
- The moisture content is lower than Romano and is usually produced from partially skimmed milk.
- Use a rotary hand grater for easily grating Parmesan cheese.
- Grated Parmesan cheese may be used to thicken sauces providing you use low heat or it will turn stringy.

Pasteurized Processed Cheese

- Usually a blend of various cheeses with varying degrees of consistency.
- The flavor is relatively mild and is frequently used for cheeseburgers since it has a low melting point.
- Processed cheeses are not recommended for high quality dishes since only 50-60% of the cheese is "real" cheese in most packages.
- Processed cheeses contain too many preservatives and additives that may alter the flavor of a dish.
- Processed cheeses do melt fairly well since most of them contain emulsifiers to keep the ingredients in suspension.

Pasteurized Processed Cheese Food

- Similar to the standard processed cheeses except that milk or whey are usually added. They have lower fat content, have a milder flavor and are softer.
- Moisture is added to lower the fat content per ounce.

Port Du Salut

- Mellow, robust, creamy yellow cheese with a buttery texture and has small holes.
- Usually sold in wheels.

Provolone

- Produced from bleached milk; it has an off-white interior with a somewhat yellowish exterior.
- The texture is relatively smooth and the cheese is unsalted with a mild flavor.

Quark

- This is a soft unripened cheese, which has the texture of sour cream.
- The flavor is richer than low-fat yogurt.
- Sold in non-fat and low-fat varieties.
- Commonly used to prepare cheesecakes.

Ricotta

- Actually produced from whey and not really a cheese.
- Usually produced from whole or skim milk with a somewhat nut-like flavor.
- Looks like cottage cheese.
- If you can find Italian ricotta cheese, you will never purchase ricotta cheese made in America unless it is freshly produced.

Romano

- Has a sharp flavor with a dark green exterior.
- Sold mostly in wedges or grated and is made with whole cow's or goat's milk.
- Yellow-white; cheese with a greenish-black exterior.

Rouquefort

- Mold is introduced to create marbling and blue veins throughout the cheese.
- It has a white interior and is usually produced from sheep's milk.
- The flavor is somewhat peppery and the texture is always crumbly.
- When preparing Roquefort dressing, be sure and whisk in the extra virgin olive oil in a steady stream until the mixture is thick, then stir in the cheese last.
- Sold mostly in wedges or packaged already crumbled.

Stilton

- Similar to Roquefort, it has a white interior with blue mold streaks. However, it is normally produced from cow's milk and has a crumbly texture.
- When eating Stilton cheese, the best method is to scoop out the center, pour a small amount of sherry or port in and allow it to soak into the cheese before serving.
- It is usually sold in logs or wedges.

Swiss

- The interior is a light yellow and the cheese has a somewhat sweet, nutty flavor.
- The texture is firm and the holes may vary in size.
- It is usually sold in rectangular form or sliced. Produced using bleached milk, which gives it its yellow color.
- One ounce = 105 calories, somewhat high due to the fat content of the bleached whole milk.

When cooking with Swiss or mozzarella cheeses, which are very susceptible to becoming stringy, just add a small amount of lemon juice or wine to the recipe to eliminate the problem.

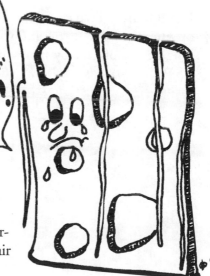

- When Swiss cheese is curing, special microorganisms produce gas that causes pockets of air to form and remain after the cheese ripens.

- The holes should, however, be relatively the same in size and not oversized or irregular sized holes, especially large ones.
- The border of the holes should also have a moist, shiny look about them. If the rind is grayish looking, it should not be purchased.
- The flavor of Swiss cheese will become stronger when wrapped in plastic wrap and refrigerated.
- Cut wedges should last for about 1-2 months.

Tilsit

- The insides are usually a light, yellow color and the cheese is semi-soft.
- It is produced from raw milk and takes about 5 months to ripen.
- The fat content runs about 40%.

Cottage Cheese

Cottage cheese originated in the United States and is made from skimmed milk either plain-cured, or plain-cured with cream. It is always sold in a soft texture with different size curds. If the label says, "curd by acidification," it will be a synthetic product. Cottage cheese only retains 25-50% of the calcium from the milk due to the method of processing. The higher the water content of cheeses, such as cottage cheese, the sooner they will go bad. Cottage cheese will only last until the expiration date unless it is stored upside down after opening. This will increase its life up to 10 days past the expiration date.

- If you want to keep cottage cheese fresh, another method is to add 1 teaspoon of vinegar to the carton and stir it in well. This will really keep it fresh for a long period of time by increasing the acidity.

TYPES OF COTTAGE CHEESE

Creamed

- Creamed cottage cheese contains 4.2% fat or 9.5 grams per cup.
- It is not a low-fat product.

Low-Fat

- This is produced using either 1% or 2% milk.
- Low-fat cottage cheese may soon be produced using the new .5% milk, which will lower the fat content a little more.
- The 2% low-fat is really not low-fat at all; it is just reduced-fat..

Uncreamed

- Can be used in recipes calling for cottage cheese.
- Usually sold as low-fat and possibly even salt-free.

SUBSTITUTING CHEESES

CHEESE	SUBSTITUTE
Brie	Camembert
Edam	Cheddar
Farmer's Cheese	Creamed Cottage Cheese (drain well)
Feta	Muenster
Blue	Roquefort
Monterey Jack	Mozzarella
Swiss	Monterey Jack
Ricotta	Cottage Cheese

- Cheeses that have a strong ammonia smell are not worth cooking with and best discarded.

Roquefort, Danish blue, Italian Gorgonzola and English Stilton should never be placed on a platter with each other and covered or they will all go bad. The different molds will literally kill each other and ruin the flavor.

CHEESE PREPARATIONS & DISHES

Cheese Balls

- When preparing cheese balls, make sure that you wet your hands with enough cold water to make your palms cool before you start to handle the balls.
- If you have a problem coating the balls with the nuts, refrigerate the balls for 1-2 hours, then roll them between your palms that have been dampened with hot water so that the surface of the balls start to melt. The coating is sure to stick.
- Cheese balls will last for 1 week under refrigeration or can be frozen for 1 month.

Welsh Rarebit

- The unsalted butter should be melted in the top of the double boiler over the direct heat then add the cheese.
- The cheese secret is to just barely melt the cheese in the butter before placing the top back on the bottom of the double boiler with the water boiling.
- If you are using $^{1}/_{2}$ cup of beer, combine the beer and the eggs before pouring the mixture into the melted cheese.
- The mixture should be cooked until the desired thickness is obtained.
- Club soda can be substituted for the beer if you wish.
- The carbonation from either the beer or club soda is what is really needed.
- If you really want to have a great dish, use champagne.

CHAPTER 12

COOKING WITH DAIRY PRODUCTS

BUTTER

Butter is graded by taste, body, texture, aroma and color. Grade AA butter is the best with a grading of 93-points, Grade A butter at 92 points and Grade B at 90 points. Grades AA and A must be made from fresh sweet cream. Unsalted butter may be called sweet butter by some manufacturers. The amount of salt in salted butter may vary from manufacturer to manufacturer. There are fewer preservatives in unsalted butter and it will not last too long.

- Butter should be allowed to soften at room temperature and never softened in a pan or microwave or it will lose 40% of its flavor and aroma.
- All butter in the United States is made from cow's milk.
- Use unsalted butter unless a recipe calls for salted. Salted butter can upset the salt balance in a recipe since salted butter can have different levels of salt depending on the brand. Varieties can vary from 1% to 3% salt.

Refrigerated butter only retains its flavor for 3 weeks. Fresh butter is recommended if you desire a buttery flavor.

- Always use "Grade AA" butter for all sauces and dishes that you would like a butter flavor. Lower grades have an off-flavor and aroma.

I'M THE BEST!

- Butter smokes at only 260°F, which is why it is advisable to add a small amount of vegetable oil to raise the smoke-point.
- Salted butter may have the tendency to burn certain foods when quick-frying. Unsalted butter does not have the problem.
- If you beat butter after it has softened, it will go farther and have fewer calories per serving.

Beurre Blanc

- Sauce that is prepared by whipping a large quantity of raw butter into a small amount of a reduction of white wine and vinegar.
- The butter melts and forms an emulsion with the reduction.
- Can be prepared very quickly by adding the cold butter all at once and stirring vigorously using a moderate-high heat.
- The sauce will not separate easily because the butter keeps it cool enough and stops it from separating.
- Shallots are added for sweetness and to reduce the harshness of the vinegar.
- If you increase the amount of shallots and wine, it will produce a smoother flavor, thus reducing the astringency.
- Remove from the heat as soon as all the butter has melted.
- If the sauce is overheated, it will start to break down.

Ingredients for Most Beurre Blanc Recipes

4 ounces of quality dry white wine
$^1/_3$ cup of white wine vinegar
2 ounces of shallots
$^1/_2$ cup of heavy cream
$^3/_4$ pound of cold unsalted butter
$^1/_4$ teaspoon salt

By adding cream to the recipe, it will become more stable and somewhat thicker.

Black Butter

- Black butter is prepared the same as brown butter, except it is heated a little bit more and has a few drops of apple cider vinegar added and possibly a few capers. Care is necessary so that the vinegar will not cause splattering.

Brown Butter

- Basically, this is an unsalted butter that has been heated until it is light brown and has a somewhat nutty aroma. It is prepared just before serving the dish and usually used on vegetables and fish dishes. The butter is easily burned and should not sit after it is prepared since it may deteriorate very quickly.
- Unsalted butter will only last for 2 weeks in the refrigerator.
- If you forgot to soften butter to room temperature, just grate the butter and it will soften very quickly.
- If the recipe call for brown butter, all you do is use unsalted butter and brown it in a pan; but be careful not to burn it.

Clarified Butter (drawn butter)

This type of butter is preferred; the best butter for dipping since it does not revert back into a solid as fast as regular butter at room temperature. It is preferred for dipping lobster and crab meats tableside. It has a high smoke point and can be used to sauté without adding canola oil to raise the smokepoint.

- Clarified butter is made by melting unsalted butter in a heavy saucepan on moderate heat. Skimming the foam off as it develops and then pouring out (or ladle off) the clear butter leaving a white milky liquid on the bottom.
- Clarified butter retains its buttery flavor better than butter. Clarified butter has had the protein removed.

Compound Butter

- A compound butter is just a butter that has added ingredients and flavorings.
- It is usually prepared from unsalted butter. However, unless you prefer a sweet, slightly sour taste, you might prefer using salted butter for most recipe variations.
- Basically, the butter is softened and beaten to add air and create a degree of fluffiness before adding any ingredients.

When preparing a compound butter, it would be best to start with the highest quality butter available.

- Many pasta dishes are served using a flavored compound butter instead of a sauce.

- Never soften the butter to be used in preparing compound butter in a microwave or on the stove. Remember, butter loses 40% of its flavor and aroma if it is not softened at room temperature.
- Before any ingredients are added to flavor the butter, it should be beaten until it is soft, light and fluffy.
- Never use a blender or the compound butter will not have the desired texture.

Drawn Butter (clarified butter)

- When you see drawn butter used on a menu, it means that it is clarified butter with the sediment drawn off. It is a very clear butter that has a refrigerator life of about 2 weeks.

Ghee

- Butter that has been melted to separate the milk solids from the surface liquids.
- Ghee ends up to be clarified butter that keeps better than standard clarified butter.
- Ghee can be substituted in most recipes for clarified butter.
- Ghee is similar to clarified butter and is made using real butter.
- Ghee has a big advantage over butter in that you can cook and especially sauté with it without it breaking down and burning too easily. Therefore, you are able to treat ghee similar to oil.
- The smoke point of ghee is around 375° F. (190.6° C.), which is still lower than most oils but it is still much better than plain butter.
- Ghee tends to impart a great flavor to many sautéed foods, which is not possible with standard butter.

To prepare ghee, just place some butter in a saucepan on high heat and heat until all the water evaporates. Butter is approximately 19% water. Continue cooking at the lowest heat point until the milk solids start to coagulate and caramelize (turn a light brown). The excellent flavor is released into the ghee when the milk solids turn brown. The milk solids are easily skimmed off and removed and you are left with the ghee. Strain the final mixture through a few pieces of cheesecloth to remove any remaining milk solids.

- If you want to give popcorn a new taste treat, just use ghee instead of the oil you are presently using. There will be no heavy oil taste and the popcorn will have a new light buttery flavor.

Meuniere Butter

- Brown butter is seasoned with a small amount of lemon juice and used as a sauce over fish.
- Care needs to be taken when adding the lemon juice into the hot brown roux to avoid splattering.
- Most chefs tend to lightly sprinkle the lemon juice on top of the fish before pouring the sauce over the fish.

Whipped Butter

- Whipped butter should not be used in a recipe unless it is called for due to the high concentration of air.
- Whipped butter is not recommended for use in desserts, pastries and confections since the air pumped into it changes the volume and makes it difficult to measure accurately.

CREAM

- When cream has begun to sour, just stir in $1/8$ teaspoon of baking soda to neutralize the acid.
- Chefs make a horseradish sauce for roast beef and prime rib by adding 2 tablespoons of horseradish to 1 cup of heavy cream, then partially whipping it.
- Use only fresh confectioner's sugar when making whipped cream if you decide to add sugar at all.

When cream is poured over acidic fruits, it has the tendency to curdle. Just add a small amount of baking soda to the cream before you pour it.

- The higher the fat content of the cream, the less chance of curdling.
- Adding cream to a highly acidic food such as tomatoes will cause curdling unless you reduce the cream by cooking it over medium heat to decrease the volume by about $1/2$. Add the reduced cream back into the mixture to make up the balance the recipe calls for.
- Evaporated milk can be substituted for heavy cream only in baked goods, cream soups, custards and cream-based sauces.
- Sour cream can be made from heavy cream by just adding 4 drops of lemon juice concentrate into $3/4$ cup of heavy cream. Allow the mixture to remain at room temperature for 20 minutes before refrigerating it.

Never add sour cream to a dish if the dish is hot or it will separate, wait until the dish has cooled.

- White sauces that are made with milk and cream burn easily and it is better to use a stock.
- Cream can be used to make a design for presentation. This process is called "feathering" when a number of drops of cream are placed in a pattern and a toothpick is then lightly touches the cream droplet and moves it slightly just touching the next droplet.

CRÈME FRAICHE

Cream that can be used in soups and sauces without curdling, which is why it is popular over desserts such as hot cobbler.

- To prepare a quick crème fraiche, just mix together equal quantities of sour cream and heavy cream. The mixture is then covered and allowed to remain at room temperature for about 2 hours or until it thickens, then refrigerate.
- Works well in soups and sauces since it does not curdle very easily, even if it is boiled.
- After the crème fraiche has thickened, a variety of seasonings can be added depending on the dish it is to be added to.
- Buttermilk can be substituted for heavy cream if you would like to reduce the calories.
- To prepare crème fraiche, just mix 1 cup of whipping cream and 2 tablespoons of buttermilk in glass bowl and allow it to remain at room temperature for 10-24 hours or until it is very thick. Mix the crème fraiche well, then refrigerate. It lasts for 8-10 days.

CUSTARD

- Evaporated milk should not be used in custards. Large amounts of lactose (milk sugar) can affect the thickening.
- Granulated table sugar should not be used when preparing custard.
- Sugar may also cause the temperature to become higher than desired and may cause a reduction in volume.
- Acids, such as lemon juice, will reduce the thickening of custards and cause the starch granules to disintegrate.
- If want to add an acid food or liquid, it should be added toward the end of the cooking time.

One of the most popular sweet sauces is a custard sauce, which can be made in a number of great flavors such as chocolate, vanilla, raspberry, mint, blueberry, apricot and lemon

- If you are going to prepare a lemon custard pie filling, be sure and add the lemon juice while the filling is still hot and toward the end of the cooking time.

- After placing custard in the oven, never open the oven door or the retained heat will be lost and the center will not be cooked.
- The formula for a very delicate custard is one large egg or two large egg yolks per cup of cream or milk.
- Custards can be thickened by adding 1 large egg for every cup of milk used.
- You can substitute 2 egg yolks for 1 egg when preparing custard to make it richer and higher in cholesterol and fat.

Only beat custard slightly. If the surface becomes foamy, the custard will have air pockets on top that pop and leave little holes.

- Never allow even the smallest amount of egg white in custard that calls for the yolk only. The white solidifies at a lower temperature and will cause the custard to have lumps.
- When preparing custard, eggs are sometimes a problem if not handled properly. The eggs should be beat first with sugar and set aside.

- The milk or cream must then be scalded until small bubbles, form around the edges of the pot. Pour a small amount of the hot liquid into the eggs mixing thoroughly, slightly cooking the eggs. Add the egg mixture into the hot milk and heat on low heat until it starts to thicken.
- Custard must be stirred continually to prevent the bottom burning.
- Chefs always use a wooden spoon when stirring custard since some of the eggs, minerals may react with certain types of metal spoons. When stirring,

always stir in a figure eight pattern to cover the complete bottom.
- Custards must be slow-cooked to prevent them from separating or curdling.
- Never cook custard on high heat.
- When custards are baked in the oven, they will hold their shape well.
- Baked custards are occasionally baked in a water bath of about 1¹/₂ inches to assure that the mixture will set properly and will not separate.
- Best to use a water bath with terrycloth towel lining that is about one inch larger than the custard pan. This will protect the custard and prevent over-cooking.
- After you remove the custard from the water bath, it should be refrigerated immediately. If you leave the custard in the water bath it will continue to cook.
- Custard will coagulate at 175° to 185°F.

If baked custard starts weeping, then the custard has been baked too long.

- One of the best methods of preparing custard is to use a double boiler with water that is very hot but not boiling.
- If the heat gets too high, the milk will curdle and the eggs separate.
- When preparing custards in a double boiler you will need to stir constantly so that the eggs will evenly distribute in the custard.
- If custard starts to curdle, just place the mixture in a blender on low and mix for a few seconds, then place it back into the pot and mix.
- When mixing creamy custard, allow at least 10-12 minutes of stir time and don't be in a hurry.
- Custard is fully cooked and should be creamy when a candy thermometer reaches 170°F.
- Bake at 350°F for 20-25 minutes if placed in small dishes or 40-50 minutes in large dishes.

- The custard should then be strained into a bowl to remove any solidified egg or film that had formed.

- When using whole eggs, be sure and strain the custard through a fine sieve to assure that it will be smooth.
- Custard can only be kept refrigerated for 2-3 days.
- Cool custard to room temperature by placing it in a bowl with a larger bowl underneath filled with ice water.
- Place plastic wrap directly on the surface of the custard and refrigerate to slightly thicken. This will stop a film from forming on the surface.
- Custard hardens as it cools after it has cooked.
- Insert a skewer into the center of the custard and if it comes out clean then the custard is fully cooked.

Crème Anglaise

- Always use a double boiler and never allow the water to go over 212°F.
- Temperatures over boiling will ruin this starch-free custard.
- Make sure you cover the warm crème anglaise with plastic wrap directly on the surface to stop any skin from forming.
- If you dot the top with butter, this will also stop the skin from forming.

Crème Brulee (burnt cream)

The dish originated in England in the mid 1600's when a chef was preparing custard and burned custard that he had sprinkled with sugar. He served it as "burnt cream." The name crème brulee; was given to the dish by Thomas Jefferson who brought the dish to the United States in the 19th century.

- Basically it is cold custard that is sprinkled with sugar, which is then caramelized and gives it a brittle topping.
- Can be lightened with half-and-half.
- Baked in a water bath, then chilled in the refrigerator.
- Place the dish under the broiler just before serving and sprinkle sugar on top allowing it to melt and caramelize.
- Should be served immediately or the sugar will weep.

Flan (crème caramel)

- Baked in a ramekin, called a "flan ring" that is lined with caramelized sugar.
- The special custard is baked, chilled then inverted onto a plate.
- The caramel oozes from the top creating its own sauce.
- Grand Marnier is a great addition.

ICE CREAM

One of the first ice cream machines in the United States was owned by George Washington. The machine was called the "Cream Machine for Making Ice." Thomas Jefferson threw egg yolks in to make it richer and called it "French-style ice cream." Ice cream was, however, popularized by James and Dolly Madison who served it regularly at the White House.

- Follow the manufacturer's directions to the letter when preparing homemade ice cream in an ice cream maker.

To avoid ice crystals from forming when you are freezing the ice cream, place a piece of plastic wrap on top of the ice cream.

- It takes 3-4 hours in the freezer to set ice cream after it is made to allow it to obtain its optimum flavor and smooth texture.
- To avoid the crystals forming, you can also add 1 packet of unflavored gelatin for each 6 cups of liquid used in the recipe. Allow the gelatin to soften in $1/2$ cup of the liquid you are using, then heat the gelatin until it melts before adding the balance of the liquid recommended in the recipe.
- When using an ice cream maker, you should crank slowly at first to be sure that all the ingredients are at the same temperature.
- When ice cream in an ice cream maker starts to thicken, crank faster to keep the crystals small and add air into the mixture.
- To obtain a creamier texture, prepare and chill the ice cream mixture a day before you are going to make it. The mixture will freeze faster as well.
- The more room you give the mixture to expand, the lighter the texture will be. Only fill the canister $2/3$ full for the best results.

To improve the texture of ice cream, just allow the ice cream to age at 32°-40°F for 5-10 hours before placing the ice cream in the freezer.

- Most ice cream makers require 1 cup of rock salt to 6 cups of ice.
- Best to add a small amount of salt to your ice cream recipe. Salt has the ability to bring out the flavors in certain ingredients.
- If the ice cream is allowed to freeze too fast, it will develop larger ice crystals. Have the ice cream mixture between 27°-35°F when you place it in the ice cream maker.
- If the ice cream comes out gritty, you may have added too much milk in the recipe.

MILK

- When a skin is formed on the top of cooking milk, it is caused by the protein coagulating and calcium that is released from the evaporation of water. Stirring and placing a top on the pot should stop this from happening.
- To scald milk for a recipe, just heat it to 198°F, just below the boiling point. Best to use a double boiler.
- If you are using pasteurized milk, it is not really necessary to scald milk for recipes other than dough.

When using milk to make dough, it is best to scald the milk, which alters the milk protein so that it interacts better with the flour protein.

- Milk needs to be cooked after scalding and before adding to the batter or it will damage the yeast.
- Use very fresh milk for the best recipe results. Stale milk tends to scorch too easily.
- If you need to cook a dish that requires vinegar, which is a mild acid and will curdle milk, just add a teaspoon of cornstarch to the cold milk before adding the vinegar.
- Yogurt or milk can be used to replace oil in low fat dressings.
- Milk can be scalded in the microwave on high for 2- $2\frac{1}{2}$ minutes per cup.

Buttermilk

- If you have an old recipe and it calls for buttermilk, you had better purchase it directly from a dairy. The supermarket buttermilk is made from a culture of skim milk.
- Buttermilk can replace 2% milk in most recipes.

Condensed Milk (sweetened)

- Condensed milk cannot be substituted for evaporated milk in recipes.
- Milk that has had 60% of the water removed and a sweetener added.
- Will not remain fresh if left in the can.
- To prepare caramel from condensed milk, just put the milk into a double boiler and cook over water that is just simmering (never boiling) for about 1¹/₂ hours or until smooth or the consistency you prefer.
- May be stored at room temperature for 6 months.

Evaporated Milk

- Evaporated milk can be sweetened by adding 3 tablespoons of sugar per can.
- Evaporated milk can be slightly frozen and used for whipped ice cream topping.
- Can be purchased in low fat, nonfat or whole.
- Can be stored at room temperature for 6 months.
- Goat's milk is now available in evaporated milk.

Add evaporated milk to custards to increase the richness.

- If evaporated milk is partially frozen, it can be whipped and used as dessert toppings. If you add 1 tablespoon of lemon juice for every cup of milk, it will help to stabilize the topping.
- Whipped milk will retain its consistency for about 40 minutes if refrigerated.
- Condensed milk cannot be substituted for evaporated milk.

Milkshake

- To make a malted milkshake, just place 1 teaspoon of unflavored powdered malt into the blender with the rest of the milkshake ingredients.

The thickness of the shake will depend, more on the quantity of the milk than the ice cream.

- If you want a "really" thick shake, then use half-and-half instead of milk.
- Any flavor syrup will flavor it.

SOUR CREAM

- Always allow sour cream to warm to room temperature before adding it to any recipe for the best results.
- Never add sour cream to hot soup or sauce until just before you are ready to serve it.

Sour cream should never be added to any liquid that will be brought to a boil after it is added.

- Do not remove the liquid that forms on the top of sour cream after you have removed a portion from the container. The liquid is "whey" and is a good protein to stir back in.

TAPIOCA

- A starch that has been extracted from the cassava root and can be used as a thickener or consumed as a pudding.
- Pearl tapioca is used to prepare puddings and needs to be soaked for several hours to soften the starch before it can be cooked.
- Pearl tapioca is sold as a pudding mix.
- Quick-cooking tapioca is sold in granular form and used as a thickener for soups and stews; does not require a lengthy presoaking.
- Tapioca flour in found in health food stores and is an excellent thickener for glazes, soups, stews, fruit fillings, etc.
- Tapioca flour does not breakdown when frozen or reheated like cornstarch.
- When using tapioca flour to thicken, always prepare a thick paste first and then gradually add it to the food.

Never add tapioca flour paste to a liquid that will be boiled after adding the flour or it may become stringy.

- If you add too much tapioca thickening to a dish, it may become somewhat gelatinous.
- If you have a problem finding tapioca flour, just place some quick-cooking tapioca in a food processor or blender and powder it.

WHIPPED CREAM

- When whipping cream, be sure that all the bowls and utensils are as cold as possible for the best results.
- Make sure that any bowl you use when whipping cream is very deep and narrow so that there is enough room for expansion when a high volume is created.
- If you can't chill the bowl, try and use a metal bowl placed over another bowl filled with ice cubes.
- Chocolate whipped cream; can be made by adding 1-2 tablespoons of cocoa powder when adding the confectioner's sugar. If you use sweetened cocoa powder, delete the sugar.
- If you are going to use whipped cream for cake icing, you will need to add gelatin to the cream. Mix 1 teaspoon of gelatin with 3 tablespoons of tap water and allow it to set for about 4-5 minutes. Slowly add the gelatin mixture to the cream just as the peaks are forming and continually mix, then use the cream to ice the cake immediately
- When using an electric mixer to make whipped cream, always start out on a low setting first then increase the speed.
- Allow the cream to develop soft high peaks before you add the sugar or any flavoring for the best results. The sugar will slow the development of the peaks.

Whipping cream will turn to butter if you whip it for too long a period. If this occurs, just add additional cream until it reverses.

- Heavy whipping cream can be used for hot sauces in most instances without the problem of curdling.
- Light cream can be whipped if all the utensils are ice cold and by adding 1 tablespoon of unflavored gelatin that has been dissolved in 1 tablespoon of hot water to 2 cups of light cream. Refrigerate for 2 hours after mixing.
- To make coffee-flavored whipped cream, just add 1 teaspoon of quality instant coffee and 2 tablespoon of sugar to 2 cups of whipped cream.
- For lemon-flavored whipped cream, add 1 tablespoon of lemon juice and 2 tablespoons of sugar.
- Cooling the cream in the freezer before whipping works very well to speed up the process. Be careful not to allow it to freeze.
- To make cinnamon whipped cream, just add 2 tablespoons of sugar, $1/2$ teaspoon of cinnamon and 1 teaspoon of pure vanilla extract to the whipped cream.

CHAPTER 13

PREPARING EGGS AND EGG DISHES

BOILING

- If an egg cracks when it is being boiled, just remove it, leave it wet, then pour a generous amount of salt on the crack. Wrap the egg in aluminum foil, twirl the ends and continue cooking it.
- A soft-boiled egg must be cooked for $3^1/_2$ minutes to kill bacteria if it is present.
- Boiled eggs will slice easily if you use wax-free dental floss.
- Soft-boiled eggs should take about 2-4 minutes.
- Never freeze hard boiled eggs, they become tough.
- The yolks and the white can be frozen separately for a short period of time. The white, however, may get rubbery.

Rub fresh lemon on the shell before placing the egg into the boiling water and it should not crack.

- Add salt to the cooking water to toughen the shell and make it easier to remove.
- Add a small amount of vinegar to the water to prevent the shell from cracking and soften the shell.
- Cool the egg before trying to slice it or it will fall apart too easily.
- Never place hard boiled eggs in a bowl of cool water after you peel then or they will absorb water.
- To tell if an egg is hard boiled, just spin it. If it wobbles, it is not hard boiled.

- Add a drop or two of vegetable, coloring to the water and you can easily tell the hard, boiled ones from the fresh ones.
- Roll hard, boiled eggs in your hands while crushing the shell, then place a tablespoon between the shell and the white and circle it around.

DEVILED EGGS

- To keep the yolk centered so that you will have a centered hollow to place the filling in, just stir the eggs while they are boiling.
- Using older eggs will make them easier to peel since the acidity level in the shell gets lower with age.
- Allow the eggs to remain in the hot water for 10-15 minutes instead of completely cooking them will provide you with a more tender white.
- Cool the eggs immediately when they have finished cooking or the yolk may get a greenish tint from the chemicals that have been released.

If you place the carton of eggs to be used for deviled eggs on its side the night before, the yolks will remain centered while they are cooking.

- If you cut a slice from the wide end of the egg, the egg will stand upright. Then you slice ¹/₄ down from the top just enough to be able to remove the yolk.
- If you salt the water, it will solidify any leaking white and help to seal the shell.

EGGNOG

Eggnog originated in England with the upper class who could afford eggs, milk and brandy. The drink was originally called "egg flip." The drink was popularized in the Southern United States and bourbon replaced the brandy. Mexican eggnog added cinnamon and rum, which became popular in the United States.

- If you want to lighten the texture and sweeten supermarket eggnog, just fold in 2-3 stiffly beaten egg whites.
- Non-fat evaporated milk and egg whites can be used when preparing home-made eggnog. For every whole egg called for in the recipe, you can substitute 2 egg whites. The non-fat evaporated milk is substituted equally for whole milk.
- If you would like a lighter homemade eggnog that is not as thick, just separate the egg whites and beat them until they are stiff and add them to the mixture just before you are going to serve it.

Homemade eggnog will not last more than 1-2 days even under refrigeration.

- Try substituting eggnog for whole milk in other baked goods recipes.
- In Spain, red Spanish wine is used. In America, we normally use bourbon and in other countries it is made with rum.

EGG SUBSTITUTES

- Check the recipe before using egg substitutes to replace whole eggs. If the recipe doesn't say its OK, don't use them.
- Some egg substitute products contain MSG.
- Egg substitutes without MSG can be used for Caesar salad.

FRIED

- Fried eggs can be shaped if fried into a cookie cutter. Make sure your spray the cookie cutter with oil to make the egg easy to remove.
- If you like a white film over the eggs when cooking sunny-side up, just add a few drops of water to the pan just before the eggs are done and cover the pan for a few seconds.
- Best to use a heavy pan since they conduct heat better.
- Add a small amount of flour to the pan and the fat won't splatter.

Fry eggs at a low temperature and they will be more tender and have a smooth yolk.

- When you microwave eggs, the yolk will cook first because the microwave tends to cook the fat first.
- Make sure that butter is very hot before adding the egg, then reduce the heat.
- A small powdering of cornstarch added to the pan before adding the eggs will prevent splattering.
- Salted butter may cause eggs to stick to the pan. Best to use unsalted.

OMELET

- Eggs should be at room temperature for the greatest volume.
- If you warm the eggs under hot tap water for 4 minutes, the omelet will be more tender. Cold eggs tend to produce a tougher omelet.

- Add a small amount of water instead of milk to create steam and fluff up the omelet.
- Never mix the omelet in an aluminum bowl or they may blacken.
- Do not mix the eggs until they are frothy.
- Use $1/2$ teaspoon of baking soda to every 3 eggs to increase the volume.

Make sure that the butter is very hot before adding the omelet to the pan.

- Ingredients should be warm before adding them to an omelet either inside or on top.
- An omelet pan with sloping sides is a must for shaping the omelet.
- Use a well-seasoned pan or one with a quality non-stick surface.
- When preparing an omelet, you can replace the egg yolks with an equal amount of egg substitute.
- Eggs should be 3-5 days old for omelets.
- Never make an omelet with more than 3 eggs.
- If you have a stainless steel omelet pan, never wash it, just scrub it with kosher salt and wipe it out.
- If you would like a nice brown coating on top of the omelet, just brush the top with melted butter before you turn it.
- Slide the omelet out of the pan onto the plate to keep it in one piece.

POACHED

- Never salt the water you are placing poached eggs in or they will break up.
- The fresher the eggs the better. The whites will remain firmer and keep the yolk in shape.
- Eggs are less likely to stick in a heavy non-stick pan and the results are better.
- Make sure that you bring the water to a boil and then to a simmer before adding the eggs.

Add $1^1/2$ teaspoons of vinegar to 1 quart of water before adding the egg and it will cause the egg to remain firm and keep their white color.

- Always drain poached eggs well before serving; they should not be served with any water in the dish.
- Poaching should take 3 minutes for a soft yolk, and 5 minutes for the yolk to still be soft and the white hard. After 5 minutes,s they will be almost hard-boiled.

- Trim off ragged edges before serving for a better presentation.

QUAIL EGGS

- Opening quail eggs can be easy if you notice that the egg has a pointed end and a flat end. At the flat end, take a paring knife and very easily press the tip of the blade into the shell and crack the shell while you turn it. Continue to make a circle around the egg and lift off the top, and then pour out the contents.

RAW IN RECIPES

- Never pour raw eggs into any hot mixture; it may cause curdling.
- When beating raw eggs, always use a copper bowl. Copper tends to absorb the heat friction from the beating and stops the formation of air pockets. It will also release ions that help the protein to become stiffer. Cream of tartar will not be needed if you use a copper bowl.
- If you use a stainless steel bowl to mix raw eggs, add a pinch of cream of tartar to help the protein stiffen up and increase the volume.

Allow raw eggs to go to room temperature for 1 hour before beating them.

- Never over-beat or the whites will look dry and curdled.
- If you do over-beat egg white, just add one more egg white and beat.
- Add a small amount of sugar and the whites will remain stiffer for a longer period.
- Over-beating will cause the peaks to be fragile.
- White strands should be strained out before using the egg. They will form lumps and affect the quality of the dish.
- Never break raw eggs into a mixing dish. Always break eggs separately into individual bowls in case one of them is bad.
- When adding eggs or egg yolks to a hot mixture, it is best to add some of the hot mixture into the eggs or yolks slowly and stir well before adding to the balance of the mixture. This will make it easier to blend the egg yolks into the mixture.
- Eggs will separate easier when cold. Best to separate from the refrigerator.
- Sauces or Caesar salad that call for raw eggs may be a problem since salmonella may be present in the egg. Best to use pasteurized liquid eggs.

SCRAMBLED

- If you want to increase the volume, use a bowl with a small rounded bottom.
- Pre-heating the pan will reduce the possibility of sticking.
- A small heavy pan with a non-stick coating and a plastic spatula is the choice of most chefs.
- If you want creamy fine egg curds, prepare the scrambled eggs in the top of a double boiler.

If you are going to use a standard pan and a non-stick spray, the pan should be warmed before spraying with a non-stick spray. Be sure and remove the pan from the heat before spraying. Warming the frying pan first expands the metal and makes the non-stick spray more efficient.

- Allow 3 eggs per person unless other ingredients are added, then 2 eggs will be fine.
- When making more than one batch of eggs, wipe the pan with paper towel dipped in salt to clean the pan so that the eggs won't stick.
- Cook the eggs over medium-heat and start in a cool pan for the best results.
- Add 1 teaspoon of water per egg if you would like lighter eggs.
- Scrambled eggs hold the heat and will continue cooking after they are removed from the heat. Best to remove them just before they are done cooking.
- Do not allow the eggs to brown. Stir continually.
- Overcooked scrambled eggs may turn greenish due to the chemicals being released from the yolk and uniting with other chemicals.
- If you use butter, it would be best to add a small amount of canola oil to raise the smoke point.

To make a fluffier dish, add ¼ teaspoon of cornstarch per egg before you beat them.

- To prepare light and fluffy scrambled eggs, just add a small amount of club soda to the eggs.
- The longer it takes to scramble an egg the better it will turn out.

SHIRRED EGGS (baked)

- Made in small individual glass dishes called "ramekins."
- The oven should be pre-heated to 350°F.
- Always butter the ramekin and place 1 large egg, 1 teaspoon of salted butter and 1 tablespoon of half-and-half.

- The ramekin is placed into a pan with 2-inch sides and boiling water is added to about halfway up the sides. Bake the egg for 14 minutes or until it is fully set.

YOLKS

- If you are using egg whites and want to save the yolks, just place them into a bowl of water in the refrigerator. They will last for 2 days only.
- Egg yolks will coagulate at 144° to 158°F.

SPECIALTY EGG DISHES

Eggs Benedict

Invented by a Boston restaurant owner named Benedict, whose chef left him and went to work in New York around 1905 in a classier restaurant. His chef made the dish famous serving it in New York. A later story credits the origination of the dish to Delmonico's Restaurant in New York when a patron of theirs complained that there was nothing new on the menu. The chef made the dish and named it after the patron, Mr. and Mrs. LeGrand Benedict.

- Make sure that the water in the bottom of the double boiler never stops simmering and is never allowed to boil.
- When melting the butter, never allow it to bubble or boil or you will lose flavor.
- When you slowly incorporate the melted unsalted butter into the egg yolks, beat in a circular motion.
- Do not substitute any other bread, English muffins only.
- Read the secrets regarding making poached eggs.
- The round shape of Canadian bacon and its low-fat content compared to standard bacon has been used for many years as the meat of choice.
- The sauce is always a hollandaise.

Soufflés

- The most popular soufflé is chocolate with vanilla sauce.
- Cold soufflé is usually called a mousse and is served cold.
- Be sure there is not even the slightest trace of egg yolk in the egg white or it will ruin the soufflé.
- A copper bowl should be used to help stabilize the foam.

- Be careful not to add sugar too soon or it will reduce the volume and take longer to produce the desired foam.
- When adding cheese, be sure that it is only grated cheese not melted cheese. The egg whites will not blend well with melted cheese.
- Sugar should be added just when the soft peaks form as the beaters are lifted.
- Make sure that all utensils used are very clean; the slightest hint of oil or dirt will ruin the egg whites.
- The egg whites must be at room temperature or it will take too long to beat them.

- Never microwave an egg that is to be used in a soufflé. The eggs will not puff-up enough.
- Lightly butter a soufflé dish. They can also be lightly powdered with Parmesan cheese.
- Just before baking a soufflé, try running a knife around the inside edge completely around the soufflé. This will cause the soufflé to have a high cap, which makes for a great presentation.
- Always use a "soufflé dish" when preparing a soufflé. These dishes have straight sides so that the soufflé can expand upwards.
- Make sure that the egg whites and the base mixture, is allowed to remain at room temperature for 30-40 minutes before preparation.
- Always use more egg whites than yolks for a lighter soufflé.

Never allow the egg whites to stand after they have been beaten or they will lose volume. Add to mixture immediately.

- Try not to over-beat the egg whites or they will be dry and possibly collapse easily.
- Add a small amount of the egg whites to the base and mix well before adding the balance to temper the base; this is a very important step.

The height of the soufflé will depend on the number of air bubbles that were trapped in the egg white. The bubbles expand from the heat. However, to be sure that it rises properly, you need to eliminate any large air pockets by giving the soufflé a hard tap on the counter before placing it in the oven.

- Never open the oven door when baking a soufflé or it may collapse.

- Soufflés are commonly served somewhat underdone with a creamy center to which a sauce has been added.
- Soufflé must be served as soon as it is removed from the oven and should be allowed to remain in the original dish or it will collapse and the air will escape.
- The sauce is usually added at the table when the top is punctured.

- To caramelize the top of a soufflé, just sprinkle confectioner's sugar on top as soon as it is removed from the oven. This will take the place of a sauce and the center should not be left creamy.

CHAPTER 14

COOKING WITH OILS

COOKING WITH OILS

Smoke, flash & fire points of oils

- The smoke point of oil is the point at which the oil starts deteriorating. All oils have different smoke points. Flavor would be a determining factor in using oil with a lower smoke point. The smoke point is the point at which the oil is starting to convert a percentage of the oil into trans-fatty acids. The flash point is the point that the oil starts to show a small amount of flame emanating from the surface of the oil. This usually occurs at about 600° F. and should tell you that the oil has reached a dangerous level. The fire point is about 700° F., which is the point that you had better have a fire extinguisher ready and remember **never to use water** on a grease fire. The fire needs to be smothered to extinguish it.

SMOKE POINTS OF FATS AND OILS

FAT	SMOKE POINT
Canola Oil	525° F.
Safflower Oil	510° F.
Soybean Oil	495° F.
Corn Oil	475° F.
Peanut Oil	440° F.
Sesame Oil	420° F.
Animal Lard	400° F.
Vegetable Shortening	375° F.
Unclarified Butter	250° F.

COMBINING OILS

- The most common combination of oils is for canola oil to be added to butter and olive oil to raise the smoke point so that they will last longer before breaking down and smoking.
- A number of herbs can be combined with oil for excellent flavors. These include garlic, cayenne peppers, fennel, bay leaf, rosemary, oregano, cloves and citrus peelings.
- After the herb is added to oil, the oil must be heated to 240°F to be sure and kill and bacterial organism that may be present especially botulism.

FRYING AND BAKING OILS

- The following are some of the more common oils that are used for frying and baking.
- Oils will vary as to the type of fats they are composed of, color, aroma, nutrients, and smoke points. Oils may be categorized in many different ways, such as; how refined the oil is, the plant or animal it was extracted from, the method of extraction (cold or hot), smoke point, consistency and color.

Almond Oil

- Unrefined almond oil is commonly used in many dishes and is commonly substituted for butter. It adds an amber color to foods and has a mild sweet flavor.

- Refined almond oil is produced by crushing almonds and heating them until a thick, golden-colored paste is produced. The paste is then squeezed to produce the oil. This extensive processing makes almond oil one of the more expensive oils.

Some people who are allergic to aspirin may be allergic to almonds and almond oil.

- The French almond oil is the highest quality.

Avocado Oil

- A light, nutty tasting fruit oil that is usually only used on salads.
- The oil does contain a small amount of saturated fat, but is mostly monounsaturated.
- The smoke point is too low to be considered for cooking and frying.

Canola Oil

- Produced from the rapeseed plant, which is a relative of the mustard family.
- It is normally found in the refined state and has a very high smoke point making it one of the best all-around oils.
- This is the best oil for frying since it does not breakdown as easily as most other oils.
- The oil is high in monounsaturated fat and low in saturated fat. It is also one of the lowest priced oils.
- Canola oil is one of the few oils that contain omega-3 fatty acids. The name canola was derived from the word Canada and oil.

Coconut Oil

- This oil is very high in saturated fat and may be capable of raising cholesterol levels.
- Normally, not sold for home cooking uses. Ist is present in numerous products, especially baked goods, candy and margarine.
- The oil has the ability to extend the shelf life of foods and it would be best to read labels to see if the product contains coconut oil or as it is sometimes called "tropical oil."

Corn Oil

- One of the most common oils that is manufactured in large quantities and extracted from the corn germ, a by-product that is obtained from cereal and corn syrup producers.
- The oil is a light yellow color and has a mild flavor, which does not overpower recipes.
- Corn oil excellent for baking, pastries, and most recipes that call for vegetable oil.
- A darker corn oil is sold that is extracted from the whole corn kernel and has a stronger aroma, similar to that of popcorn.
- Other types of corn oil include unrefined, expeller-pressed oil that has a strong aroma and not recommended for delicate dishes since it will overpower the flavors. This type of oil, however, is good for baking, in sauces and dressings. These oils cannot be used for frying since it tends to foam and boil over easily.
- A highly refined corn oil can be used for frying and has a relatively high smoke point. Corn oil is about 87% polyunsaturated fat and contains about 60% of the essential fatty acid, linoleic acid.

Corn oil contains more vitamin E than most other oils after processing. Processing of oils normally either reduces or destroys the vitamin E content.

Cottonseed Oil

- This oil is normally not sold to the general public since it may be easily contaminated. The oil is heavily used in many products such as shortening, baked goods, margarine and dressings.
- It was one of the most popular oils in the United States until the 1940's when more efficient processing methods were invented.

Flaxseed Oil

- One of the best sources of the essential fatty acid, omega-3.
- Has a strong golden color and the flavor is not overpowering.
- The oil mixes well with most foods and imparts a pleasant flavor.
- Health food restaurants tend to use the oil in salad dressings, cole slaw, dips, marinades and sauces for vegetarian dishes.

- Best not to cook oil since it tends to lose its flavor and aroma. The essential fatty acids, such as the omega-3 and omega-6 fatty acids are more active in this oil if it is not heated.

Grape-seed Oil

- A light colored oil that is produced from grape seeds.
- The majority of the oil sold in the United States is imported from Europe; however, the United States is starting to produce larger amounts of the oil.
- Grape seed oil has a very high smoke point and can be used for frying and in dishes that need to be cooked at high temperatures.
- Excellent: for stir-fried foods.

Hazelnut or Filbert Oil

- It is strong, full-flavored oil with a roasted nutty aroma.

  This oil has been used in France for hundreds of years and is one of the more popular oils.

- The unrefined hazelnut oil is difficult to refine, hard to find in the United States and very expensive.
- It is used by European chefs when preparing special hot sauces and for breading. The refined oils is produced by crushing the nuts, then heating them before squeezing out the oil.

Olive Oil

Olive oil has a high level of vitamin E since it is cold processed and will stay longer at room temperature than any other oil before going rancid. The oil can last up to one year; however, the flavor will mellow over time.

- Olive oil is high in monounsaturated fat (77%) and is gluten-free.
- Extra virgin, cold processed olive oil from Italy is the choice of most gourmet executive chefs worldwide.
- One tablespoon of olive oil contains 8% of your daily requirement of vitamin E.
- Greece is one of the largest producers of olive oil with an annual output of 300,000 tons.
- The oil produced is of the highest quality, which is the low acid, extra virgin variety.
- Most of the Mediterranean countries produce olive oil of such poor quality that it must be refined to produce an acceptable flavored product. Look for oil from Greece or California that states "cold-pressed, extra virgin, pure organic."
- The color of the best extra virgin olive oil should be emerald green. If the oil is a deep green then it is young oil and has not had time to mellow with aging and lose a percentage of its flavor.
- The difference in color and taste of olive oil is very subjective and some people prefer the green while others prefer the golden yellow oil.
- The green olive oil has more flavor and is frequently used on salads.
- The green oil tends to lose some of its spicy flavor when heated.

Palm Oil

- This is one of the highest saturated fat oils and may raise cholesterol levels.
- May also be listed on the list of ingredients as a "tropical oil" and is frequently found in baked goods with coconut oil.
- This oil is one of the most popular oils used for making soap.
- The oil is extracted from the pulp of the oil palm plant.
- Palm oil is normally a solid at room temperature due to its high degree of saturated fat.

Peanut Oil

- Peanut oil is one of the more popular oils and one of the easiest to extract oil from since peanuts are about 50% fat.
- They tend to maintain their nutty flavor in recipes and especially stir-fried foods.

Many chefs tend to mix the oil with unrefined sesame oil, which will compliment each others flavors and aromas.

- Peanut oil has a high smoke point and is a common oil for most cooking purposes, especially frying. However, 90% of peanut oil is saturated fat, which is higher than almost every other vegetable or nut oil. Also, peanut oil is low in vitamin E, trace minerals and essential fatty acids.
- Peanut oil is produced from pressed, steam-cooked peanuts and will not absorb or transfer flavors to other foods.

Safflower Oil

- A popular all-purpose oil that is relatively inexpensive and has a mild flavor.
- Since the oil lacks flavor, it can be used in almost any dish that requires liquid oil without the risk of flavoring the dish.
- Unrefined safflower oil is best used cold in dressings, salads and sauces. The oil is high (80%) in essential fatty acids, especially linoleic acid.
- The oil is difficult to extract because of a very hard husk and hydraulic presses are required to extract the oil.
- The lower-priced safflower oil is usually extracted with the use of chemical solvents. However, the method of extraction is not required to be placed on the label, which means that you don't know whether you are purchasing a high quality product or not.
- Safflower oil is second only to canola in its vitamin E content.
- The refined oil has a high smoke point and is good for frying.
- Cold-pressed is the best oil to use in salads or dishes that are not heated.

Sesame Oil

- Sesame oil can be purchased in two distinct varieties; the type that is produced from roasting the bean, which is the dark oil and the lighter oil that is recommended for use in salads and dishes that are not cooked.
- The more popular of the two is the dark variety, which is commonly used in many Chinese dishes producing a nutty flavor.
- The lighter oil is produced from pressed, raw sesame seeds and is considerably milder and used when you desire just a hint of the sesame flavor.

It only takes a few drops of sesame oil to add flavor to vegetables, soups, or salad dressings.

- One of the major advantages is that sesame oil is very stable and does not turn rancid easily even in hot, humid climates. It is considered one of the more healthful oils and is high in polyunsaturated fats and especially essential fatty acids.

Soybean Oil

- Unrefined soy oil is one of the more difficult oils to extract, which makes the oil somewhat expensive.
- The oil is used in baking and contains an excellent amount of lecithin, which is an emulsifier.
- The oil is also high in essential fatty acids and polyunsaturated fats.
- Unrefined soy oil tends to become rancid rather easily and should be used shortly after purchase and should be stored in the refrigerator.
- The highly refined soy oil is lower in price and used extensively in the baking industry.
- Almost 80% of all oil that is used for baking are soy oil. If you see "vegetable oil" on the label it is probably soy oil. Good source of omega-3 fatty acids.

Sunflower Oil

- Most sunflower oil is produced by a cold-pressed method, which only mulches the sunflower seeds then presses the mulch to obtain the oil.
- Heat and chemicals are not used, thereby producing healthy, high nutrient oil.

New Zealand is one of the major producers of sunflower oil.

- Russia produces as much as 80% of their usable oil from the sunflower.
- It has a low smoke point and not recommended for high temperature cooking or frying.

Walnut Oil

- This is another expensive oil when purchased in the unrefined state.
- The finest grades of this oil are produced in the Perigord and Burgundy provinces of France.
- To produce unrefined walnut oil, the nuts are dried and cold-pressed.

The oil is high in polyunsaturated fat and has a pleasant nutty flavor.

- Walnut oil tends to become somewhat bitter when heated and is best used cold in salads.
- Refined walnut oil is produced by crushing the nutmeats and heating them to produce a paste. The paste is then squeezed to extract the oil.

NOTE:

- When oil is processed, the breakdown process is started and rancidity occurs at a slow pace. However, it can increase at a faster pace if the oil is left under the light in a market in a clear container. It is best to purchase oil in dark containers or tins and store in the refrigerator if the oil will not be used up within 30 days.

SALAD OILS

- The best salad oil is "cold pressed" extra virgin olive oil.
- Olive oil will stay longer than any other oil.
- To make a creamy salad oil, just slowly pour the olive oil into a running blender that contains the other ingredients or spices.

CHAPTER 15

BAKING LIKE A BAKER

BASIC INGREDIENTS — TYPES OF FLOUR

All-Purpose Flour

- This flour is a blend of hard and soft wheat flour. It has a balanced protein/starch content which makes it an excellent choice for breads, rolls, and pastries.
- All-purpose flour may be used for cakes when cake flour is unavailable but is not highly recommended.
- Pre-sifted, all-purpose flour has been milled to a fine texture, is aerated, and is best for biscuits, waffles, and pancakes. Contains 12% protein.

Bleached Flour

- White flour with a higher gluten-producing potential than other flours.
- Used mainly to make most bread.
- National brands such as Pillsbury and Gold Medal are not recommended for yeast bread due to high protein content.

Bran Flour

- Whole wheat flour that is mixed with all-purpose, white flour; tends to produce a dry effect on baked products.

Bread Flour

- Hard-wheat, white flour with high gluten content used to make breads.
- Best for making yeast breads, pizza and pasta.
- Has a high protein content.

Bromated Flour

- White flour in which bromate is added to the flour to increase the usefulness of the gluten.
- Bromated flour makes the dough knead more easily and may be used in commercial bread making plants.

Browned Flour

- This is really just heated white flour that turns brown adding color to your recipe.

Brown Rice Flour

- Contains rice bran as well as the germ and has a nutty flavor. Commonly substituted for wheat flour.

Cake Flour

- Very fine white flour, made entirely of soft wheat flour and is best for baking cakes.
- Tends to produce a soft-textured, moist cake. Also excellent for soft cookies.
- Has a lower protein content than most other flours.

Corn Flour

- Usually very starchy flour used in sauces as a thickener with a slightly sweet flavor.

Cottonseed Flour

- High protein flour used in baked goods to increase the protein content.

Durham Flour (semolina)

- White flour that has the highest protein content of any flour and has the sability to produce the most gluten.
- Used mostly in pastas.

Farina Flour

- Made from hard wheat flour with no Durham wheat added.

Gluten Flour

- Very strong white flour that has twice the strength of standard bread flour.
- Used as an additive flour with other flours.

Instant Flour

- White flour that pours and blends easily with liquids and is used mainly in sauces, gravies, and stews.
- Rarely used for baking due to its fine, powdery texture.
- Has lower protein content.
- Wondra is one of the better brands.

Oat Flour

- Milled from oats and primarily used to prepare porridge, some breads and cookies.

Pastry Flour

- The gluten content is between cake flour and all-purpose white flour.
- Best for light pastries and biscuits.

Potato Flour

- Provides a thickening texture and used mainly for stews, soups, and sauces.

Rice Flour

- Excellent for making delicately textured cakes.
- If you add a small amount of Parmesan cheese to your recipe, it will provide a great taste and will not affect the growth of the yeast.

Self-Rising Flour

- Soft-wheat; white flour that should not be used in yeast-leavened baked goods. Contains a leavening agent that tends to cause deterioration.
- The flour should be used within 1-2 months of purchase.
- Best for quick breads, biscuits and muffins.

Semolina

- White flour with a yellow tint made from Durham wheat.
- Used mainly in commercial pasta and bread.
- Has a high protein content.
- When using semolina flour, try adding a small amount of olive oil to your recipe to improve the flavor and increase the volume.

Soy Flour

- Produced from raw soybeans, which are lightly toasted.
- Soy flour has a somewhat sweet flavor and tends to retain its freshness longer than most baked goods.

Tapioca Flour

- Made from cassava root and used as a thickener in gravy and sauces.

White Rice Flour

- This type of flour will absorb more liquid and may need additional liquid added as well as increasing the mixing time.

Whole Wheat Flour

- Reconstituted flour made from the white flour with the addition of the bran and endosperm.
- Wheat flour is sometimes sold as graham flour and has small specks of brown.
- 100% whole wheat flour is more difficult to digest than white flour. It tends to cause flatulence and intestinal upsets in susceptible individuals.

BISCUITS/ROLLS

Biscuits

- Baking powder must be very fresh for good results.
- Buttermilk will make the biscuits slightly tart.

- When greasing a biscuit pan, try not to use too much oil or butter or it will cause the biscuits to over-brown.

Cream will make a light, buttery biscuit.

- If you dip your biscuit cutter in flour, the dough won't stick to it.
- For soft biscuits, brush them with milk or melted unsalted butter then place the biscuits into the pan touching each other.
- Sift all dry ingredients together. This is the key to a light, fluffy biscuit.
- Shortening is preferred over other fats or butter if you want the biscuits to be light and not heavy. Shortening is a more refined product.
- To make biscuits that will easily be broken in half, just roll the dough out to about a ¼ inch thickness and then fold it over before cutting the biscuits.

If you are going to use frozen biscuits, heat them frozen at 350°F for 15-20 minutes. Frozen biscuits should not be kept for more than 2-3 months.

- Replace the yeast with 1 teaspoon of baking soda and 1 teaspoon of powdered vitamin C and you won't have to wait for the dough to rise.

Never overwork dough; if you are gentle you will have lighter biscuits.

- One baker told us that when he mixes biscuit dough, he only uses 20 turns and just the tips of his fingers and the heels of his hand.
- To remove muffins or biscuits from a sectioned pan, place the pan on a damp towel for about 30 seconds.
- To make biscuits that split open easily, just roll out the dough to ¼ inches thick and then fold it over before you cut it.
- To glaze the tops of rolls, just beat 1 egg white lightly with 1 tablespoon of milk and brush on the tops before baking.
- For flaky biscuits, be sure that the fat used is cold.
- The more you handle biscuit dough, the tougher the biscuits. Roll out as many as possible from the first rolling.
- For flaky biscuits, cut chilled butter into the flour before adding any other ingredients.
- To prepare soft fluffy biscuits, place them very close together on the baking sheet.
- If you prefer crustier biscuits, place them about 1" apart.
- When he used the term "turn," he meant to push the dough away from yourself, lightly touching the dough that is closest to you with the heels of your palms and then pushing away until the heels of your palms are at the other end of the dough. Then you need to gather the dough with your fingertips from either side, place it in front of you and start pushing it away again, twenty times.

- Bake at 425°-450°F for the best results.
- Baking time is usually 20-30 minutes, but they need to be checked regularly after 20 minutes.

- For a nice brown top, add a small amount of sugar to the recipe.

Sweet Rolls

- Make sure that you do not mix the yeast and egg into the milk before it cools to around lukewarm.
- The yeast must not be subjected to liquid that is too hot or it will impair the yeast's ability to rise and may also partially cook the egg.
- Warm honey can be brushed on the top of rolls to provide a nice glaze.
- Try brushing the rolls with melted butter while they are still hot. This will enable the butter to seep into the rolls and make it unnecessary to serve butter with the rolls.
- Another trick is to remove the rolls and brush the bottom with butter then return them to the pan before buttering the top.
- Make sure that you only fill the muffin tin ¹/₂ full to allow for expansion.

Method for Proofing (still active) Yeast

Dissolve 1 tablespoon of sugar into 1 cup of warm water (95°F) and add the yeast. The yeast should start bubbling after 5-7 minutes; if it doesn't bubble, it is no good (dead yeasties).

BLINTZES

Blintzes originated with the Jews of Russia and were first mentioned in an English cookbook in the late 1800's. Blintzes are a very thin pancake that is stuffed with a variety of ingredients depending on the occasion or holiday.

- The normal blintz batter is made from 3 beaten large eggs, $^3/_4$ cup of matzo meal, $^1/_2$ teaspoon of table salt and $1^1/_2$ cups of tap water.
- Frying pans used for blitzes should be heavy and in the size of the blintz. The pans should only be used for blintzes and kept seasoned and never washed.
- Blintzes are only browned on one side in a very slight layer of oil. Most chefs use a brush to just brush oil on the pan before adding the batter.
- The blintzes are folded over three sides, then rolled into shape.
- The most common filling is a mixture of cottage cheese, sugar and sour cream.
- After the blintz has been filled they are placed back into the pan and lightly browned so that the filling is warmed before serving.
- Some chefs bake blintzes. However, frying seems to be the more desired method of cooking.

BREAD

The science of bread making and how proteins in flour interact with water and leavening agents produce a loaf of bread is interesting and educational for the professional baker. I have chosen to leave out this information and just provide the pertinent facts regarding the tricks and secrets used by bakers to produce the finest loaf of bread.

Baking Pans

- If you substitute a baking pan that is shallower than the pan the recipe calls for, it would be best to reduce the baking time by 25%.
- If you substitute a baking pan that is deeper than the pan recommended in the recipe, then increase the baking time by 25%.
- If you use a glass baking dish, reduce the temperature in the oven by 25°F.

Batter Breads

- Batter breads are always beaten and never kneaded.

Cornbread

- To make a crispy crust, pre-heat the pan before you place the cornbread batter into it. The pan should be oiled and allowed to be in a 400°F oven for about 8 minutes before adding the batter.
- Use a cast iron skillet or glass baking dish for the best results.
- The skillet is best and the fat that you use needs to be heated on the range until it just starts to smoke. Remove the skillet and spread the batter in evenly then place the skillet in the oven and bake for 30 minutes or until well browned.
- If you would like to sweeten up cornbread, just add 2 tablespoons of brown sugar and 2 pinches of ground nutmeg to the dry ingredients.
- Cornmeal batter should be mixed until it is smooth for the best results

If you would like to avoid a lumpy batter, just add the liquid in two stages. Cornmeal does not absorb water very well so take it slow and easy.

- White cornmeal is best for biscuits.
- If you use coarse stone-ground cornmeal, the bread will have a gritty texture, which some people like.
- The fine yellow cornmeal will give the bread a softer texture.

Raisin Bread

- Adding raisins to bread slows down the staling, which is why raisin bread will last twice as long as regular bread at room temperature.

Rye Breads

- When baking rye bread, do not place any containers with water to create steam; the steam will ruin the bread.
- Rye flour is low-gluten flour that will rise better if you use twice the amount of yeast called for in the recipe.

Quick Breads

- Combine the wet and dry ingredients until till barely moistened.
- Too much mixing and the bread will be tough.
- When adding raisins or dried fruit, be sure and toss them in the same flour you are making the bread with.

- If frozen, they should be thawed at room temperature. If they were frozen in aluminum foil, then heat the bread in a 400°F oven.
- Quick bread should not be kept frozen for more than 2-4 months.
- The baking powder or baking soda must be very fresh.
- Allow the bread to cool for 5 minutes before removing it from the baking pan, then set it on a wire rack to cool.

Sourdough Breads

The Egyptians invented sourdough bread around 2000BC, not a baker on the wharf in San Francisco. However, the best flavored sourdough bread is produced in San Francisco.

- Make sure that no metal comes into contact with the sourdough starter. This can cause a chemical reaction that will kill the starter. If this happens, a black, blue or pink liquid will come to the surface.
- Always use the least-processed flour. King Arthur or quality organic, unbleached flour is best.
- Clay or crock containers may also have metal in them and should not be used.
- Pressure in starters may build up and they need to be covered with loose-fitting lids.
- Starter should always be separated into two batches: one to use now and the other to store as a "back-up."
- If you use a sourdough starter instead of a mix, the bread will have a more open texture.
- Starter that is being used should be refrigerated overnight.

Sourdough starter is really "wild yeast" that lives in a batter of flour and water. Starters were as valuable as gold in the early days, guarded and treasured.

Prospectors actually slept with the starter on cold nights so it would not die from freezing. A 240-year old sourdough starter can be obtained by calling 1 (800) 827-6836.

- The "back-up" starter should be fed about every 2 months.
- Your main starter should be stored in a 3-4 quart container to allow you to build up enough "starter" to use for baking.
- Never use chlorinated water when making sourdough bread. The chlorine can injure the starter.
- Always use a clear container for starter (not glass) so that you can easily see the bubbles when the starter needs to be fed.
- Transfer the starter to a clean container every 2 months.
- If you would like to prepare bread with a sourdough flavor, just replace the milk or water with yogurt.

Yeast Breads

The basic formula for "enriched," white bread was invented by Dr. Clive M. McCay at Cornell University in 1934. The formula was one tablespoon of soy flour, one tablespoon of dry whole milk and one tea-spoon of wheat germ to one cup of white flour. The formula added additional protein, calcium and B vitamins and did change the taste of the bread. It was called the "Triple-Rich Formula."

- Always add yeast to water, never water to yeast or you will kill a lot of the yeast.

Active dry yeast is a domesticated relative of the old "wild yeast." This type of yeast has been grown to produce predictable results when it comes to flavor and speed of growth.

- A wet measuring spoon is never placed into a baking powder box.
- If you store dry yeast in the refrigerator, it will slow down their metabolic process and it will stay fresh longer. Be sure and warm it up to room temperature before using.

- On humid or very hot days, most yeast dough rises faster and may be hard to knead due to a loss of elasticity.

If you want to increase the shelf life of your bread, try adding some raisin juice concentrate to the recipe as part of the liquid. Professional bakers use this trick instead of adding preservatives.

- If you want to slow the rising, just place the dough ball in a cool location.

Whole Wheat Breads

- Whole-wheat bread will not rise as high as white bread due to its higher volume from lack of refining.
- When mixing whole-wheat bread dough, add 1 tablespoon of lemon juice as you are mixing it and the dough will rise faster.
- When making whole-wheat bread, it will be more moist if you slowly add the flour to the water and mix gently.
- Whole-wheat absorbs water more slowly than other flours.

Use of Eggs

- Whole eggs have the ability to provide a degree of leavening and hold the bread together.
- Egg whites also have leavening ability as well as lightening and strengthening, the bread.
- Yolks have very little leavening ability.
- Egg yolk is the more efficient emulsifier keeping ingredients, such as fat and water, in suspension.
- Egg yolks provide a creamier, smooth texture.
- Egg yolks will help bread stay fresher for a longer period of time.
- Egg whites are a drying agent and can be used if needed.

When working the dough, you need to punch down and manipulate the dough a few times to break up any pockets of yeast that have gotten friendly and are sticking together. Yeast will tend to congregate in the center and does not get enough oxygen to multiply to the degree required. Make sure that you lightly oil your hands before starting.

- When starting to work, all ingredients for baking should be at room temperature.

Use of Liquids

- Water from boiled potatoes can be used to replace water in a bread recipe. The bread will remain fresher for a longer period of time.
- Hard water should not be used for baking since it may cause the gluten to become tough.

- Using water that is too soft results in sticky dough. Low mineral water is best to tighten the gluten.
- Low-rising bread is usually cause by old yeast. If it is a high-riser you have added too much yeast or water.
- If you use milk in your recipe, the bread will have a finer texture than if you use water.
- If you use buttermilk in place of milk, reduce the amount of baking powder by 2 teaspoons and replace it with $1/2$ teaspoon of baking soda for every cup of buttermilk used to replace the milk with.
- Always combine the wet and dry ingredients separately.
- When beer is added to the dough, it will give the bread a smooth crust.
- A vegetable or meat broth added to the dough will provide you with a lighter, crispier crust.
- Nonfat dry milk has the ability to provide more moisture and flavor and can increase efficiency of the yeast growth.
- If you run out of yeast you can substitute 1 teaspoon of baking soda mixed with 1 teaspoon of powdered vitamin C.
- Adding a small amount of powdered vitamin C to your recipe will make the gluten development more efficient.
- To speed up dough rising, just place the pan on top of a heating pad on medium.
- Using honey in the dough will slow down the coagulation of protein allowing the dough to increase in volume making the loaf fluffier.
- To help your bread rise and provide better texture, add 1 tablespoon of cider vinegar for every $2^1/2$ cups of flour.

As a rule of thumb, count the number of cups of flour in your recipe. It takes 1 teaspoon of baking powder per cup of flour. If the recipe contains a cup or more of decorative ingredients, it would be best to add an additional $1/2$ teaspoon per cup of flour.

- If you make the loaves tight, it will result in even loaves of the same shape.
- Instant flour will dissolve more readily than regular flour. Instant flour will not form lumps.
- Kneading very well is important to distribute the yeast and other ingredients throughout the dough.

Sifting flour is important to return the flour to its original fluffiness. Flour tends to compact down during shipping. If you don't want to sift the flour, just shake the bag and fluff it with a spoon really well to aerate the flour back to its original fluffiness before you measure it out.

Use of Salt

- The best salt to use is sea salt, which contains a variety of different salts and chemicals and may impart a somewhat sweeter taste to your bread.
- Adding salt to yeast dough makes the gluten in the dough stronger; however, it also increases the mixing time.
- If bread has a crumbly texture, try adding a small amount of salt.
- Professional bakers prefer to knead the dough first, then work in the salt resulting in a shorter kneading time.
- Salt is added to strengthen the dough just before the rising and shaping.
- Be careful not to use too much salt or it will affect the growth of the yeast.
- Sea salt in the dough makes the crust crispier and slows down the growth of the yeast.
- Celery salt or garlic salt can replace salt in most bread recipes with and provide a different flavor.
- Only use non-iodized salt (sea salt). The iodine will slow down the yeast activity during the first fermentation.

GENERAL BAKING INFORMATION

If you use a dough hook in a heavy-duty mixer, add 4-5 ice cubes to the dough to keep it cool so that the gluten will absorb more water and produce higher quality gluten and a lighter loaf of bread.

- Too much cinnamon or citrus fruit will actually stop the yeast activity completely.
- When adding yeast to water,s the water must be below 140°F.
- When the recipe calls for you to grease and flour the pan, the best method is to grease the pan with oil and then sprinkle the flour in and move the pan around to allow the flour to distribute evenly. However, chefs recommend that you use $^1/_2$ cup of room temperature shortening mixed with $^1/_2$ cup of vegetable oil and $^1/_2$ cup of flour. Blend all the ingredients well then grease the pan.

- When you are allowing the dough to rise, be sure that there are no drafts or the bacteria will catch cold and not rise evenly or to slowly.
- To make sugar-free bread, just replace the sugar with 1 teaspoon of malt for each package of yeast used.
- Yeast breads are leavened with yeast and are always kneaded to stretch the gluten in the flour. Use room temperature ingredients for the best results.
- If the recipe stays to grease a pan, grease the whole pan including the sides.
- To slow down the rising time, just add one extra cube of yeast to the batter. This won't change the taste just slow it down 45 minutes to 1 hour.
- When working with sticky dough, just spray a small amount of oil on your hands.
- If you knead too much flour into the dough, just sprinkle the dough with warm tap water.

Brewer's yeast cannot be substituted for baker's yeast. Brewer's yeast has been heat-treated and kills the live bacteria.

- A small gully is cut into the tops of some yeast breads before baking. This allows gasses to escape while the loaf is baking and prevents the top from becoming ragged.
- High wheat flour is recommended for pizza, rolls and buns since they are best when they have a chewy texture.
- Other flours need to be added to rye flour when baking rye bread. Rye flour is not capable of developing adequate gluten bonds to hold the bread together.

- Never place bread pans next to each other for the best results.
- Bread crust will not become too hard if you place a safe container of water in the oven while the bread is baking. This will provide just enough moisture from the steam to keep the crust soft.
- If you want the loaf to have an arch, then fill the bread pan ³/₄ full.
- If you want the loaf to have a flat top, just fill the bread pan ¹/₂ full.
- Never use the microwave to cause the dough to rise faster. It will rise faster but it will affect the flavor. If you do use the microwave then use only a 10% power setting.
- If dough does not rise well, it may be too cool for the yeast to be active enough. The temperature must be between 76°F and 85°F.
- Unbleached flour is the bakers choice for most baking projects.
- Breads should be baked at 400°F to allow the expanding gasses to sufficiently increase the dough volume before the protein has a chance to coagulate.
- If the bread you are baking has a high sugar content, it should be baked at 325°-375°F or the sugar will burn instead of caramelizing and turn black instead of brown.
- When baking bread, always pre-heat the oven since dough rises best in the first 15 minutes.
- If bread has started browning too fast, cover the bread with a loose tent of aluminum foil.

If your recipe calls for you to create steam in the oven, place a large roasting pan on the base of the oven and throw an ice-cube tray full of ice cubes in. This will cause enough steam to last for 8-10 minutes providing you with the original "hearth loaves" our grandmother made.

- Always check the oven 10-15 minutes before the cooking time is up in case your oven temperature is not accurate.

If you are getting coarse, crumbly loaves, the liquid in your recipe may be too low. If using dry, whole grain, then be sure and soak the grains first.

- Excess yeast will cause the bread to go stale quicker.
- When freezing bread, be sure and use freezer paper or freezer bags, not plastic wrap or aluminum foil.

BREAD-MAKING, SOLVING PROBLEMS

THE CRUST IS TOO THICK

- Used too much flour in the dough
- Did not allow sufficient time to rise
- The oven temperature was too low

THE DOUGH DOES NOT RISE

- You may have used old yeast
- The dough was too stiff
- The water may have been too cold or too hot and killed the yeast
- You poured the water on top of the yeast
- The location you placed the yeast to rise was too cold

THE BREAD WAS TOO CHEWY

- Too high-protein flour was used
- Too little fat added
- Fat added at wrong time

THERE IS A CRACK ON THE SIDE OF THE LOAF

- The oven may have been too hot
- Not enough time was allowed for rising
- The loaf was not shaped correctly

THE BREAD FALLS IN THE OVEN

- Usually happens when the dough rises too much and gets too light

THE BREAD DOES NOT BROWN ON BOTH SIDES

- Did not use dull pans; the pans were too shiny and reflected the heat
- Overcrowding in the oven

THE TOPS OF THE LOAVES ARE CRACKED

- The bread cooled too rapidly and was in a poor location
- The dough may have been too stiff
- The dough was not mixed enough

THE BREAD CRUMBLED EASILY

- The dough was not mixed well
- Too much flour was used
- The location that was used for rising was too warm
- The dough was allowed to rise for too long a period
- The oven temperature was too low

THE BREAD HAS A DOUGHY BOTTOM

- The loaves were not removed from the pan and placed on racks after they were baked

THE BREAD IS TOO HEAVY AND DENSE

- Too much flour was used
- Not enough time was allowed for rising
- A heavier flour was used other than all-purpose unbleached flour

THE BREAD IS SOGGY INSIDE AND HAS A COARSE GRAIN

- Not enough time was allowed for rising

THE BREAD IS TOO DRY AND HAS A COARSE GRAIN

- Too much flour was used
- The dough was not kneaded long enough
- The rising period was too long
- The oven temperature was too low

THE BREAD CONTAINS DARK STREAKS

- The kneading or mixing was uneven
- Your bowl was greased too heavily
- The dough was not covered properly while it was rising

THE BREAD CRUST WAS TOO DARK

- Too much protein in the dough
- The sugar content was too high

THE BREAD HAS HOLES IN IT

- The air was not completely squeezed out of the dough when shaped
- The dough rose for too long a period before being baked

THE BREAD SMELLS AND HAS A YEAST TASTE

- The dough was allowed to rise for too long a period
- The rising location was too warm

THE BREAD HAS A SOUR TASTE

- The dough rose too quickly
- The dough was allowed to rise for too long a period before baking
- Too much yeast

THE BREAD HAD AN AIR SPACE UNDER THE CRUST

- Was not slashed or vented
- The oven temperature was too high
- Bread needed to be on a lower shelf

THE BREAD HAS A TEXTURE SIMILAR TO CAKE

- Did not rise for the correct period
- Too much sugar was added
- Too much salt added
- The fat was added at the wrong time
- The oven temperature was too high

THE BREAD GOT STALE TOO FAST

-
    - Inadequate sugar or honey in recipe
    - The dough rose too fast
    - Too much yeast used

BREADING

- Produce a lighter coating when breading a food for frying, try adding ½ teaspoon of baking powder per ½ cup of flour in your batter.
- When using eggs in breading, be sure that they are at room temperature for the best results.
- Always place all food in the refrigerator for 45 minutes after it is breaded and the breading will stay on. Always allow the food to return to room temperature before cooking.
- Never over-beat the eggs or there will be too much air and the breading will not stay on.
- The smaller the breadcrumbs the better. Large breadcrumbs do not adhere well.
- Homemade breadcrumbs are coarser and will adhere better.
- Make sure that the food is dried well with paper towel before placing it in the flour.
- Sometimes milk is used in place of egg; however, it does not have the adhering power of egg.
- Many cereals can be used to bread foods. Be sure that they are unsweetened such as rice or corn flakes.
- To make breadcrumbs, just place toasted bread in to the blender; add any seasonings and blend to the texture you desire.
- Crackers can be placed into the blender for a few seconds and used as a breading.

BREAD MACHINES

- Most bread machines are timed for the use of dry yeast. Compressed fresh yeast should never be used.
- Dry yeast needs to be stored in an airtight container since it absorbs water easily.
- If you replace whole-wheat flour with ¼ cup of gluten flour it will give the bread better texture.

The flour to liquid ratio should be 2½-3 cups of flour to 1¼ cups of liquid. In the summer (due to higher humidity), however, you will need a little more flour and in the winter use a little less.

- The machine can be opened to check the dough as it is being kneaded, but don't touch the dough.

When using a machine with a delayed cycle, never place fresh ingredients in such as eggs, milk or cheese. Bacteria may have a field day and give everyone food poisoning.

- Always soften butter at room temperature before adding it to the recipe.
- If you use too little yeast, the bread will not rise properly.
- If you use too much yeast, the bread will rise and then collapse.
- Time the completion of the bread to about 1-hour before you will be eating it.
- If the bread is undercooked and somewhat gummy on the inside, the bread did not rise sufficiently

The ratio of salt to flour in bread is ½ teaspoon of table salt for each cup of flour used. Some recipes call for less salt, but it would be best to use the ½ to 1 ratio.

- The dough should be pliable around the blades. If it's chunky, then it is too dry and additional liquid is necessary.

- For a great nice sweet loaf, just double the amount of yeast; cut back on the salt, use $1/8$ teaspoon of vitamin C powder and use the longest cycle on your machine or remove the dough and form it by hand before baking it in the oven.
- If your bread machine does not have a cooling off cycle, be sure and remove the loaf as soon as it finishes baking.
- High-protein flour will produce high-rising bread.
- Whole grain flours will produce denser, heavier breads.
- If the bread rises, then collapses in the middle, you have used too much liquid.

Salt is used in bread for flavor and bread can be made without salt if you are on a salt-free diet. Remember, however, that salt inhibits yeast and the dough will rise more quickly if you don't use any salt.

- In most cases, bread machine dough is better than hand kneaded dough.
- Use special instant yeast for sourdough or for sweet breads.
- Most bakers who use bread machines prefer instant yeast, either regular instant or instant gold for most all-purpose baking needs.
- If you add raisins or nuts to the machine, it would be wise to add 1-2 teaspoons of additional flour. This helps the dough "open up" more easily.
- Never use rapid-rise yeast in a bread machine.
- Normally 1-2 teaspoons of sugar is added to a 1-pound bread.
- Any kind of sugar can be used in bread machines. That includes corn syrup, molasses, honey and all other syrups.

The best flour for bread machines is King Arthur's unbleached, all-purpose, high-protein flour.

- A one-pound bread machine can handle 2-3 cups of flour.
- A $1^1/_2$ pound bread machine can handle 3-4 cups of flour.
- Almost all bread recipes can be made in a bread machine.
- Whole-wheat flour may not be the greatest flour nutritionally as once thought. The additional fiber tends to cause a percentage of the nutrients obtained from the whole wheat to be flushed out of the body.
- Whole wheat is fine for additional fiber and texture.

BRIOCHE

- Quality bread flour should be used or King Arthur's all-purpose flour. By using this flour, you will have a more tender brioche.
- The fresher the yeast the better. Fresh yeast will cause the dough to rise faster. Never use rapid-rise yeast.
- Test the yeast to be sure that it is active.
- Never allow dough used for brioche to rise in an area where the temperature is over 80°F.
- Only allow the dough to rise to the level desired or it will weaken the dough structure and the brioche may fall apart.
- Be careful not to deflate the dough before it is chilled or the butter will leak out.
- If the butter does leak out, chill the dough for 1 hour in the refrigerator, then knead the butter back in.
- If you plan on freezing the unbaked dough, add 25% more yeast to assure that the yeast will be active when it is thawed out.

BROWNIES

Brownies first appeared in print in the 1897 Sears Roebuck and Co. catalog.

- Brownie mixes are high in moisture and do well in the microwave.
- The old-fashioned formula for brownies calls for 2 cups of granulated sugar, $1/2$ cup of all-purpose flour and $1/2$ cup of cocoa.
- To the above was added 4 beaten large eggs, $1/2$ pound of melted butter at room temperature, 2 teaspoons of pure vanilla and 1 cup of nuts.
- Everything was mixed together and placed in a pre-heated 300°F oven for 45 minutes.

BUNS, CINNAMON

- If you use raisins, be sure and soak them before adding them to recipe; will add moisture and reduce the formation of mold forming.
- Best to add an egg yolk to act as an emulsifier.
- If you use evaporated milk, it will improve the overall flavor and increase the sweetness.
- Cinnamon has the ability to improve yeast activity.

CAKES

Until about 1870, cakes were all baked in bread pans and looked likes loaves of bread. When more modern ovens and leavening agents became available, cakes made a change and were baked more like the cakes we know today.

Angel Food

Angel food cake was first made by the Pennsylvania Dutch in the late 1700's. By the 1870's, the cake was well known and was mainly used to use up the leftover egg whites from other baking projects.

- If your angel food cake shrinks or falls, the egg whites were beaten too long.
- Angel food and sponge cakes need to be cooled upside down to release the steam.
- Angel food cakes can also be placed upside down on an ice cube tray to cool it.
- If angel food cake is tough, you over mixed the batter.
- These types of cakes are also called foam cakes.
- Angel food cake needs to be baked on the bottom shelf and at 325°F to retain their moisture.

To improve the flavor of angel food cake, just add 1 teaspoon of almond extract to the batter.

- If the angel food cake is frozen and is frosted or filled, unwrap it and allow it to thaw in the refrigerator.
- Frozen angel food cake that is wrapped in aluminum can be thawed at 300°F for 15-20 minutes.
- If your angel or sponge food cake has poor volume, you may not have beaten the egg whites long enough. Only beat until the peaks stand straight up.
- Be careful not to over mix the batter on angel or sponge food cakes when you add the flour. The batter should just be smooth.

Cutting a Tiered Cake

- The top should be removed if it is a wedding cake and wrapped well and frozen for the 1st anniversary party.
- The cutting should begin with the 2nd layer, then the 3rd and the 4th.

Chiffon Cake

- The original name for chiffon cake was "chiffon pumpkin pie" and was first mentioned in 1929 and served at the Beverly Hills Woman's Clubs "fashions for foods" event.
- The leavening of chiffon cakes is accomplished by using beaten eggs and a small amount of baking powder and using oil instead of shortening. Since they contain a large amount of beaten eggs folded into the batter they develop their "spongy" quality.
- If your chiffon cake has yellow streaks, you have added the yolks and the oil directly into the dry ingredients, instead of mixing it in a "well" in the center of the dry ingredients.
- Chiffon pies should be thawed in the refrigerator.

If your chiffon cake has a layer, you have either over-beaten or under-beaten the egg whites. Only beat them until they become stiff and look moist and glossy.

- Citrus fruit can be blended with custard, then set in gelatin and lightened with beaten egg whites.
- A crunchy nut crust is excellent on a chiffon pie.

Fat-type Cakes

- These include sheet, layer, cupcakes and pound cake. The formula for a fat-type cake must be precise to obtain the best results. The oven temperature is an important factor and should be checked for accuracy. The common problem of shrinkage with the cake pulling away from the sides of the pan is usually due to using too much liquid, shortening or too hot an oven. Cakes must cling to the sides of the pan for support as they bake. The best cake pans for fat-type cakes are made of iron with a dull (not shiny) finish. Dull finishes tend to transmit heat more efficiently and faster.
- Always use cake flour for cake not all-purpose flour. Cake flour consists of all soft flour and makes a lighter, more moist cake. All-purpose flour is a blend of hard and soft flours.

Never substitute a granulated sugar for a powdered sugar.

- Pre-heat the oven for about 10 minutes before placing a cake in.
- Baking powder is only fresh for about 6 months.

- There should always be more sugar than flour in the recipe.
- Whatever liquid is being used plus the eggs should more than equal the sugar.
- The volume of the eggs should always be more than the total shortening.
- If your recipe calls for 1 cup of shortening, you can replace it with 1 cup of applesauce to lower the fat.

Never use oil in a cake recipe, it does not distribute evenly and causes baked goods to become grainy.

- If your layer cake has a coarse texture or is heavy and solid, you probably did not beat the sugar and shortening long enough.
- Butter cannot be substituted easily for other fats since it contains 16% water. If you do want to substitute it you have to multiply by 1.25 to make up for the water.
- You can make your cake even lighter and more moist by mixing 2 tablespoons of cornstarch in 1 cup of cake flour. Use this mixture in place of all cake flour.

- Over-beating the egg whites will sometimes cause a dry layer cake.
- Over-beating in general will cause excessive gluten to develop resulting in a poor textured cake.
- Never use baking powder in a chocolate cake. Chocolate has a high acid content and baking soda is recommended.

Recipes usually call for baking soda when they contain acidic ingredients. Baking soda will neutralize the acid. Some ingredients that call for baking soda to be added are buttermilk, molasses, sour milk, sour cream, yogurt, etc.

- If you have air bubbles in your batter, hold the pan about 5" off the floor and drop it. It may take 2-3 times to get out all the bubbles.
- The reason flour must be sifted is that flour tends to compact during storage or it is somewhat lumpy, Also it is best to aerate the flour to produce a lighter textured product.
- When butter or shortening is mixed with sugar it needs to be beaten for the complete time the recipe calls for or you will end up with a heavy, coarse-textured cake.
- If you don't care about cholesterol, a richer cake can be made by substituting 2 egg yolks for 1 whole egg.
- Never fill the baking pan more than ³/₄ full to leave room for expansion.
- When butter is called for in the recipe, do not melt the butter; just allow it to soften at room temperature. Never place it in the microwave or you will lose 40% of the flavor.
- Vanilla extract can be used to replace sugar. Five drops will replace ¼ cup of granulated sugar.
- If you are adding dried fruit to the cake, be sure and coat the fruit with the same flour that you are using in the cake and the fruit will remain in suspension and not fall to the bottom.
- Never use low fat margarine or whipped butter for baking.

- Bake all cakes on the center rack in the oven for the best results.
- Never open the oven during the first 15-20 minutes of baking time or the cake may collapse.

- If you use a glass baking dish, lower the temperature in the oven 25°F.
- Cakes should be baked on the center shelf to allow for even distribution of heat.

- A dry layer cake usually indicates overcooking.
- If you notice a long hole or two in your layer cake, it usually means that the batter was mixed too much. Batter should only be mixed enough to blend the ingredients.
- Allow a cake to remain in the pan for a few minutes before removing it and allow the steam to escape or it will turn to water.

Dome-top cakes are the result of adding too much flour to your batter. The batter around the edges tends to set before the batter in the center. This will also occur if there is too little baking powder or if it is not fresh.

- When placing a fresh baked cake on a platter or plate, be sure and sprinkle a thin layer of sugar on the plate first so that the cake does not stick.
- If you use parchment paper on the bottom of your cake and find it hard to remove, just brush the paper with a small amount of warm water and peel it off.
- When you cut a round cake, always start at the center and go toward the edge.

Cut a whole round cake in half then cut your slices and move the two halves back together.

- Never wrap frosted cakes in aluminum foil, always use plastic wrap.

Pound Cakes

- These are mixed first by creaming the butter and sugar together, then adding the eggs and then the dry ingredients last.
- Usually not a very sweet cake.
- Should be baked on the center rack for the best results.
- Always slice when they are cold.

Sponge Cake

Grandma's sponge cake contained no fat and tended to dry out very fast. Today's sponge cake does contain some fat, which gives it a longer shelf life. The fat comes from the addition of whole eggs. By adding the fat it also makes the sponge cake more palatable.

- Sponge cake requires timing, light-handedness and correct temperature.
- Sponge cakes should be allowed to remain in their pan for about 3-4 minutes. This will allow time for it to contract and to firm up somewhat, making it easier to remove from the pan.

If you want the finest texture, use superfine sugar. Superfine sugar can be made by processing granulated sugar into a powder.

- Best to use cake flour and no leavening.
- Make sure that the bowl you use, the beaters and egg white are 100% free of any hint of grease or the slightest spec of egg yolk.
- Don't worry about over-beating, the egg mixture needs to be very stiff.
- Once the eggs are beaten, you will not have very much time. Fold the flour into the batter and bake immediately after mixing.
- Using the correct size pan is very important.
- Never grease a pan when making sponge cake.

Shortcake

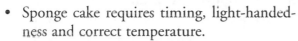

- When mixing shortcake, you can use a wire whisk since the dough is very light.
- Use a rubber or plastic spatula when folding the ingredients into the egg mixture.

SOLVING CAKE PROBLEMS

THE CAKE FELL IN THE OVEN

- Usually this is caused by not baking the cake long enough
- Used too much baking powder
- Used too much baking soda
- The egg white were beaten to a foam

THE CAKE CENTER ERUPTED

- The oven temperature was too high
- The cake pan was too small for the amount of batter
- The ingredients were not in the proper proportion

THE CAKE HAD HOLES INSIDE

- The oven temperature was too high
- There was too high a level of gluten, possibly from over-mixing

THE CAKE WAS TOO CHEWY

- Too much gluten developed
- The flour used had too high a protein content
- There was too little sugar used
- There was too little fat used
- Once the flour and liquids were added, the batter was over-mixed

THE CAKE WAS TOO CRUMBLY

- The gluten level was too low
- Used too much sugar
- Used too much fat
- The cake was not mixed enough to blend the ingredients adequately

THE CAKE WAS VERY GRAINY

- The oven temperature was not high enough
- Ingredients were not mixed properly

THE CAKE WAS TOO HEAVY

- The oven temperature was too high
- Ingredients were not mixed adequately
- Too much sugar was used
- Too much fat was used

THE FRUIT/NUTS SANK TO THE BOTTOM

- The batter was not thick enough
- The fruit or nuts were not floured before adding them

CAKE FROSTINGS (ICINGS)

Buttercream

- Prepared by creaming the sugar and fat, which may be either butter or short-ening and eggs. The eggs will provide the consistency. The level of mixing and creaming will depend on the lightness.

  Make sure you sift confectioner's sugar before adding to buttercream icing or it will not be smooth.

- Frostings made with butter can be placed on warm cakes.

Fondant Icing

- Composed of corn syrup and water, which is cooked to 240°F, then cooled off to 110°F and must be worked immediately into creamy, white, very smooth icing.

Flat Icing

- Prepared with water, icing sugar, corn syrup and a flavoring. If applying the flat icing to Danish or other pastry, be sure that it is at 100°F when applying for the best results.

General Icing Information

- Boiled icing is made by boiling syrup of sugar, water and corn syrup and adding a beaten egg while the mixture is still hot. This icing will hold peaks well when used on cakes.
- An iced cake will stay fresh longer.
- Icing has an important function, that of placing a protective coating on the cake keeping the moisture in.

- Confectioner's sugar should be sifted before using to prevent lumps from forming.
- If you are going to add a liquid to confectioner's sugar that has not been sifted, warm the liquid first to avoid lumps forming.
- If you add 1-2 tablespoons of soft unsalted butter into confectioners' sugar icing, it will keep the surface of the cake more, moist.
- The butter can be replaced in confectioner's sugar icing by using $^1/_4$ teaspoon of baking powder. The icing will remain creamy and moist.
- Icing won't get crumbly if you add a pinch of baking soda to the powdered sugar.

- To keep boiled icing from hardening, just add a small amount of white vinegar to the water while it is cooking.
- When cooked icing becomes granular, just add $^1/_4$ teaspoon of lemon juice and mix well.
- If you stir boiled icing prepared with sugar and water it will turn grainy.

- If you sprinkle a small amount of cornstarch on top of the cake, the icing won't run down the sides.
- A light-bristled brush should be used on any areas that will be iced to remove any crumbs.
- All cooked frostings cannot be placed on a cake until the cake cools.

Never ice a cake until it cools down.

- Cut layers to give you more layers that can be iced.
- Food colorings can be used to change the colors of each layer of icing.

If you are worried about the cake falling apart when you frost it, just place it in the freezer for a few minutes until it becomes more solid.

- When icing the middle layer, ice the layer and allow it to dry for a few minutes before placing the top layer on.

Royal Icing

- Prepared by mixing together icing sugar, egg whites and an acid agent until a smooth consistency is developed. Used mostly In bakeries for fake cakes since it hardens up well.

CASSEROLES

Casseroles became popular in the 1950's when certain dishes were manufactured that were easy to use for one-dish meals. Glass became the most popular material for casseroles and tuna casseroles were the most popular. Women's magazines popularized the dish so much that it became a national phenomenon.

- If you prefer a crisp topping on your casserole, don't cover it while it is baking.
- Place cheese on top of a casserole during the last 10 minutes of baking if you want a cheesy topping.

CHEESECAKE

The first mention in print of cheesecake was in 1440. There are two main varieties, the Jewish cheesecake invented by Jewish immigrants from Eastern Europe (New York cheesecake), which is prepared with a smooth cream cheese filling and the Italian cheesecake, which is prepared with a ricotta cheese filling. The most famous cheesecake is prepared by Lindy's Restaurant in New York City.

- Never substitute a different size pan for the exact size recommended.
- Make sure that you blend the ingredients in the order given in the recipe for the best results.
- If you are preparing an unbaked cheesecake, be sure and mix all the ingredients until they are very smooth before gently folding in whipped cream.
- When you are mixing the ingredients, beat at medium speed only and just until the batter is smooth.
- Over-mixing at high speeds can cause cracks to form as the cheesecake bakes.
- The cheese must be at room temperature when starting.
- Best to use a 9-inch spring-form pan and butter the sides.

- The oven should never be opened for the first 25-30 minutes or it may develop cracks or partially collapse.
- Bake for 10 minutes at 550°F then reduce the heat to 200°F and bake for about 1 hour.
- When the edges are light brown and the center is almost completely set, turn off the oven, open the door ajar and allow the center to set for about 20-30 minutes. This is another method of reducing the incidence of cracks.

To avoid cracking, just place a pan of hot water on the bottom shelf before you preheat the oven.

- Always bake cheesecake on the center rack in the oven.
- Slowly baking cheesecake will not shrink as much when cooled.
- Egg based cheesecakes should always be baked on low heat for the best results.
- If you get too much shrinkage, then the cheesecake was baked on too high a heat setting.
- Cheesecake usually takes $1^{1}/_{4}$-hours to bake.

- Cracks can be repaired with softened cream cheese or sour cream.
- The center of a cheesecake will firm up as it is cooling.
- Cheesecake should be served cool. Refrigerate overnight for the best flavor and texture.
- Always cut cheesecake with dental floss that is not waxed.
- To remove cheesecake from the pan, first make sure that they are cool, then invert them on a lightly sugared plate, then transfer them to your serving plate.
- Remember never to jar a cheesecake when it is baking or cooling.

COOKIES

Originally cookies were just small biscuits until the Dutch named them "koekie" or small cake. The name "cookie" was first used in America, while in England, "cookies" are still called biscuits.

- Cookies are made from dough that is high in sugars and fats and lower in water content than other dough.
- Use only sugar cane or beet sugar for making cookies. Blended sugars have a tendency to cause cookies to spread too much.
- Flour does not have to be sifted when making cookie batter.
- Never use a thin cookie pan. If you don't have a thick one place one on top of the other.
- Cookies with fats and a high water content will be soft.
- Careful about using too much egg white in a cookie since it may dry the cookie out too much.
- Unbaked cookie dough may be frozen for 10 months if wrapped airtight.

- To keep soft cookies soft, just place ½ apple or a slice of fresh bread in the cookie jar.
- Butter is the best shortening for making cookies.

- Using butter as the fat will cause the cookies to spread.
- A combination of shortening and butter will reduce the spread.
- The protein content will determine the color of the cookies in most instances. The more protein, the darker the color.
- Flour with a lower protein content will produce more tender cookies.
- Flour with a high protein content will produce chewy cookies.
- Sugar helps make the cookies tender and crispy.
- Corn syrup will brown at a lower temperature than standard granulated sugar. It will also make the surface of the cookie crispier.
- When brown sugar is used the cookie may absorb moisture and become softer even when allowed to stand after being baked.
- If you want consistency in the quality of your cookies then you need to use the same brand and type of flour every time you bake them.

When using a cookie cutter, rock the cutter back and forth to release the dough if it won't release easily. This will eliminate any air holes that may appear.

- Too much shortening will make a cookie crumble too easily.
- Never use margarine, whipped butter or any spread in a cookie recipe.
- If you over-stir cookie batter the cookies will be tough.
- When making oatmeal cookies, lightly toast the oatmeal on a cookie sheet at 185°F for about 10 minutes before adding it to the batter to give the cookies a nice brown color.
- Sugar cookies will remain soft if you roll them out in granulated sugar instead of flour.
- If you want crunchy cookies use 100% whole-wheat flour and use butter instead of shortening. Never use oil or the cookies will be soft.

Keep cookies soft and moist by adding 1 teaspoon of jelly to the batter (not preserves).

- The oven should be pre-heated for 30 minutes before placing cookies in.
- To make sharp edges on your cookies, dip the cutter in warm oil occasionally.
- Cold cookie dough will not stick to the rolling pin. Place the dough in the refrigerator for 20 minutes before you start.
- When working with cookie dough, always keep the dough that you are not working with covered with plastic wrap to keep it moist until you are ready for it.
- If you add a small amount of additional baking soda to your recipe to reduce acidity, add about ¼ teaspoon per cup of flour. The cookies will get darker faster and will not puff up as much.
- Using high protein flour instead of all-purpose will cause the cookies to brown more. You can also milk for part of the liquid.

If your cookies are too crumbly, just sprinkle a small amount of water on the flour before you mix in the other ingredients.

- To make a cookie with the texture of a cake, mix the shortening, eggs, sugar and liquid together, then gently fold in the flour and leavening agent. If you want a more dense cookie, just mix the ingredients slowly.

- Check cookies when they are baking at least 3-4 minutes before the recipe says that they should be done.

- Burned bottoms on cookies are very common. To eliminate the problem, just rinse the bottom of the pan under cold water after each batch or wipe the bottom with a wet towel to cool it off.

- If your cookies are not browning well, then place them on a higher shelf.

- Cookies will continue to cook if left on the pan so it is best to remove them from the oven just before they are finished cooking.
- Cookies should be cooled on an open rack not left in the pan.
- Make sure that your cookie jar has a loose fitting cover if you want the cookies to remain crisp. The air needs to be able to circulate.

Chocolate Chip Cookies

Chocolate chip cookies were invented by Ruth Wakefield in 1927 in Whitman, Massachusetts. Ruth was the manager of an inn near a popular tollgate and loved to prepare cookies. One day she added chocolate bits to her butter cookies and called them Toll House Inn cookies. Nestle offered Ruth a lifetime supply of cookies if they could publish her recipe on the back of their larger chocolate bars. Nestle started selling chocolate chip morsels in 1939 so that people would not have to chop up the chocolate bars.

- Never use margarine to make chocolate chip cookies; always use unsalted butter that has been softened at room temperature then melted in a double boiler.
- If you use cake flour, it will create steam and puff up the cookie, but the cookie will not brown as much.
- If you use shortening instead of butter, you will have less spread due to the high melting point of the shortening.
- Make sure that you use 3 times the amount of pure vanilla called for in the recipe. Do not use imitation or vanillin.

Use only superfine granulated sugar. Granulated sugar will not give the cookies as good a texture.

- If you use brown sugar, the cookie will be more moist and soft.
- If you use egg, the cookie will have more moisture for puffing.
- Add 2 tablespoons of milk to the batter and the cookies will not be as stiff and hard.

- When using milk in the recipe, be sure that batter is cold before placing the dough on the cookie sheet.
- If you don't want to use the milk, a teaspoon of sour cream will make the cookies softer.
- The best chocolate chips are semisweet Nestle Morsels. Other chips do not melt as well in cookies.
- The cookie sheet should be at room temperature when placing the cold dough on.
- Real maple syrup can replace brown sugar if you wish, but be sure it is the "real" syrup not an imitation.

TYPES OF COOKIES

Bars and Squares

- Dough is prepared into 1-pound pieces and then rolled out to the length of the cookie sheet. Place three strips on the sheet leaving some space between them.
- Flatten the strips with your fingers and shape them into equal 1-inch strips then egg wash them and bake.
- Slice when finished baking. It is important when making bar cookies to have the right size pan. If the pan is too small, the cookies will be too cake-like and when the pan is too big, the cookies tend to be too dry.

Drop Cookies

- The cookie dough is dropped onto the cookie pan by hand or with a spoon, then flattened out with a cookie die.
- If the dough is rich enough, it will spread out by itself and does not have to be pressed.

Refrigerator Cookies

- Prepare the dough in $1\frac{1}{2}$ pound pieces, place on waxed paper and roll into bars that are 18 inches long.
- Refrigerate the dough for 8-10 hours, then cut into $\frac{1}{2}$ inch strips and bake.

Rolled Cookies

- Chill a flour bag and roll the dough out on the bag in $\frac{1}{8}$-inch thick pieces. Cut into shapes and sizes that you desire with a cookie cutter and place on cookie sheet to bake.

- Make sure you dip the cookie cutter in water to stop the dough from sticking to them.

Sheet Cookies

- The cookie dough is spread out on cookie sheets, then sprinkled with raisins or nuts and baked.
- Once it is cool, it can be cut into squares or any shape you desire.

SOLVING COOKIE PROBLEMS

THE COOKIE SPREAD TOO MUCH

- Decrease the amount of butter used and increase shortening
- Substitute egg for liquid
- Use cake flour
- Reduce sugar by just a few tablespoons
- Make sure that the dough has been adequately chilled

THE COOKIE DIDN'T SPREAD ENOUGH

- Increase the butter or use all butter
- Add a small amount of additional liquid
- Add 1-2 tablespoons of granulated sugar

THE COOKIE WAS NOT TENDER ENOUGH

- Use low-protein cake flour
- Add 1-2 tablespoons of granulated sugar
- Add additional fat

THE COOKIE WAS TOO SOFT

- Use higher protein bread or unbleached flour
- Reduce sugar by 1-2 tablespoons
- Reduce fat by 1-2 tablespoons
- Add a small amount of water to flour before combining with other ingredients

THE COOKIE COLOR IS TOO LIGHT

- Substitute corn syrup for the sugar
- Substitute egg for the liquid
- Use bread flour

THE COOKIE COLOR IS TOO DARK

- Use water for the liquid
- Use cake flour or bleached all-purpose flour

CUPCAKE

- Twenty cupcakes can be made with $2\frac{1}{4}$ cups of flour.
- Make sure that you only fill the cupcake holders about $\frac{2}{3}$ full at the most to leave room for expansion.
- Allow the cupcakes to cool for about 5 minutes before attempting to remove them.
- Cupcakes should be completely cool before you ice them.
- A butter cake recipe will make great cupcakes.

CREPE

Crepe is the French word for pancake and the most famous crepe is the "crepe suzette," which was named after Madame Suzette, who was the star of a French comedy show presented at the Comedie Francasise Theatre in Paris.

- The batter is prepared from: beaten eggs, all-purpose flour, soft butter, a pinch of salt and milk.
- Serve with a sugary sauce prepared from orange juice and Grand Mariner (orange liqueur).

CROISSANTS

In 17th century Hungary, local bakers were baking at a very early hour of the morning and detected a surprise attack by Turks and warned the officials who were able to fight off the attackers. The bakers, as a reward were given the right to prepare a unique crescent-shaped pastry. The "croissants" were shaped to represent the crescent of the Turkish flag and were first prepared in Budapest, Hungary in 1686.

- Chill the dough for 20-30 minutes (no more) before starting to turn the croissants.
- The butter should be evenly dispersed as the turns are made.
- Make sure that you brush off all flour when you are rolling the dough.
- All unused dough must be kept covered to avoid drying out.
- If you are working in an air-conditioned room that is under 68°F, allow the dough to acclimate to the temperature for 15-20 minutes before you start shaping it.
- Try not to roll the croissant too tightly.

DOUGHNUTS

In the early 1800's in England a woman made what she called "fry cakes" with dough that had been leftover form other bake products. The "fry cakes" were very tasty with the exception of the soggy centers. In 1847 a young man named Hanson Gregory accidentally poked his finger through the soggy center of the fry cake and everyone liked the taste, thus the first doughnut was born. Another story is that Hanson Gregory was a sea captain and placed the fry cakes on the spokes of the ship's wheel, making the holes.

- Doughnut dough should be allowed to rest for 20 minutes before frying to allow the air in the dough to escape giving the doughnut a better texture.
- By resting the dough the doughnut will also absorb less fat.
- If you place a doughnut into boiling water for 3-5 seconds as soon as it leaves the frying vat it will be lower in fat.
- Fry doughnuts at 365°F for 50 seconds on each side and only turn once.
- Never crowd doughnuts in the fryer.
- To stop doughnuts from becoming soggy and absorb too much oil, add 1 teaspoon of white vinegar to the frying oil.

- The more egg yolk you use in a doughnut recipe, the less oil will be absorbed.
- Doughnuts may be leavened with yeast if you are making raised doughnuts or baking powder if you are making cake doughnuts.

Glazed doughnuts will lose their glaze when frozen and thawed.

- Doughnuts are about 27% fat.

DUMPLINGS

- To avoid soggy bottoms on your dumplings, just wait until the dish is bubbling hot before you place them on top. They will also be lighter and absorb less moisture.
- Try using biscuit dough to make dumplings.
- When making potato dumplings, make sure that when you place them into the boiling water to cook that they immediately rise to the top and not stick to the bottom. They should only simmer for 10 minutes.

Dumpling dough should not be mixed too much, just enough to combine all the ingredients.

- If possible, place the dumplings on top of the vegetables or meat.
- Dumplings need to be simmered for about 10 minutes uncovered, then 8-10 minutes covered. Be sure that the cover has a dome so that the steam won't make them soggy. A top with a steam release opening is best.

Hush Puppy

The name "hush puppy" was probably derived from the period just after the civil war in the late 1860's. Food was scarce and to feed their dogs people used to throw scraps of corn batter to their dogs when they barked and said: "hush puppy." The hush puppy is basically a dumpling made from cornmeal and fried.

- The basic recipe for cornmeal hush puppies is $1\frac{1}{2}$ cups of cornmeal mixed with $\frac{1}{2}$ cup of all-purpose flour. Then add 2 teaspoons of baking powder and $\frac{1}{2}$ teaspoon of salt.
- Add 1 well, beaten large egg that has been mixed with $\frac{3}{4}$ cup of milk and add 1 finely grated onion.
- The shape of the hush puppy is usually cylindrical and fat.

FRENCH TOAST

French toast was created to utilize French bread, which is prepared with no fat and therefore goes stale very quickly. Because of the short life span of the bread, the French used stale French bread to prepare a dish they called "pain perdu," which means "lost bread." The bread was soaked in a mixture of bread and milk then fried.

- The batter consists of 2 large eggs and $\frac{1}{2}$ cup of whole or non-fat milk. Whole milk makes a creamier product.
- Sourdough bread is usually preferred, but almost any bread can be used.
- The bread should be at least 2 days old, fresh bread does not work as well.
- The bread must be allowed to absorb the mixture before placing it on the skillet.
- Unsalted butter is recommended.
- Sprinkle a small amount of powdered sugar on top before serving.
- Only turn the bread once as soon as the egg sets up.

FRUITCAKE

- The color of your fruitcake may be determined by the spices and fruits used.
- If you omit nutmeg, cinnamon and use only light-colored fruits such as golden raisins and pineapple the fruitcake will be lighter.
- Fruitcake will be fully cooked when you can insert a skewer and it comes out clean.
- Fruitcake batter will rise over the edges of a pan if the pan is filled more than $\frac{2}{3}$.
- To keep the outer edges from burning, bake a fruitcake slowly and place the pan into a larger pan filled halfway with hot tap water.
- Wait until the fruitcake cools before slicing it and use a serrated blade knife.

MERINGUE

- If the weather is rainy or even damp outside, the meringue peaks will not remain upright. High humidity will kill peaks.

    Meringue recipes will work better if the eggs are 4-5 days old.

- All utensils must be very dry; egg whites do not like moisture.
- Adding 4-5 drops of lemon juice for every cup of cream also helps.
- Overcooking may cause beads to form on meringue.

Stronger peaks can be made if you add ¹/₄ teaspoon of white vinegar for every 3 egg whites while beating.

- Egg whites must be at room temperature.
- When making meringue, be sure that there is no egg yolk left with the white or it will affect the result. Remove the slightest trace with a piece of paper towel.
- Add a small amount of baking powder as you are beating them.
- Add 2-3 teaspoons of sugar for each egg used.
- Beat with a hand mixer and only until they stand up.
- Another method to reduce weeping is mix 1 teaspoon of cornstarch with any sugar used in the recipe before you mix it in with the egg whites.

The sugar should be added gradually while beating the whole time. Only add a few spoonfuls at a time.

- To make a crispy crust on your meringue, just sprinkle the top with a finely sifter confectioner's sugar before you place it in the oven.
- It is easier to separate eggs when they are cold.

- When you have to store a meringue pie, be sure to rub butter or spray vegetable oil on the plastic wrap before placing it on the meringue to avoid the plastic sticking to the meringue.
- When cutting meringue, use a knife dipped in cold water.
- If you sprinkle very fine cake crumbs on top of a hot filling before placing meringue on, it will stop any leakage from ruining the pie.
- To eliminate meringue tears (weeping) caused by condensation, just allow the meringue to cool in the oven and turn the oven off just before the pie is done. Overcooking will also cause the problem.

MUFFINS

- Substitute buttermilk for milk in a muffin recipe for the lightest muffins.
- The secret to the greatest muffins is how well you combine the ingredients.
- The oven should be pre-heated for 10-15 minutes before baking the muffins.
- Separating the eggs will make muffins lighter. Mix the yolks with other moist ingredients then beat the egg whites until they are stiff before blending them into the rest of the ingredients.
- Muffin batter should be stirred gently or it will produce tough muffins.
- Muffin batter needs to be poured into the pan immediately when you stop stirring it.
- The muffin batter should be somewhat lumpy and not smooth.

Frozen muffins should be thawed at room temperature for 1 hour or heated, unthawed at 300°F for 20 minutes.

- If you want a high-dome muffin, just grease the bottom of the tin and $1/2$ inch up the sides.
- If you add $1/2$ cup of raisins or nuts you need to increase the batter by adding 2-3 tablespoons of milk and $1/4$ teaspoon of baking powder.

- Muffins are easy to freeze and defrost well.
- To check whether the muffins are done, just insert a skewer into the muffin and if it comes out clean, the muffins are done.
- If you have a problem removing the muffins from the tin, just place them on a wet towel for 1-2 minutes or until they release easily.

English Muffin

The English muffin that is sold today was originally made by Samuel Bath Thomas who began making the muffins in 1880. Mr. Thomas used his mother's recipe that he brought with him from England to start a thriving business with a single product. The S.B. Thomas Company of New York makes the majority of the supermarket English muffins sold today.

- Use muffin rings or very clean (dishwasher clean) tuna cans.
- Only fill a muffin tin $^{1}/_{2}$ full and only turn once if using a grill.
- One of the best recipes to follow will be found in The *Joy of Cooking*, cookbook.
- Make sure that the butter has been allowed to soften at room temperature and that it is unsalted.

PANCAKES

- Club soda should be used to replace milk or water in the recipe for the lightest pancakes. Make sure that the club soda is at room temperature.
- Mix the batter gently and never over mix.
- Adding a small amount of sugar will produce a nice brown pancake.
- Placing the batter in the refrigerator and keeping it cool until it is needed will slow the development of the gluten.
- The butter or oil can be left out of the batter, providing you grease the griddle well.
- If you add one teaspoons of white wine to waffle batter it won't stick to the waffle iron. The alcohol will evaporate during cooking.
- One tablespoon of "real" maple syrup added to pancake batter would really improve the flavor.
- Different fruit juice can also be used in place of milk or water.
- When adding acidic fruit to pancakes, be sure and adjust for the acid by reducing the baking powder by $^{1}/_{2}$ teaspoon and adding $^{1}/_{2}$ teaspoon of baking soda.
- Only mix pancake-batter until the ingredients are moist. The batter may still be somewhat lumpy, which is OK.

- If any lumps of flour are left, crush them don't keep trying to mix them in.

- Pancakes should be turned as soon as air pockets appear.
- The batter should always be mixed between batches to keep it aerated.
- Pancakes need to be cooked on a griddle with the temperature of 325°F for the best results. If a drop of water bounces on the griddle it is ready. If the griddle is too hot the water will jump off the griddle.
- The griddle should be wiped off with coarse salt wrapped in cheesecloth after each batch to stop any sticking.

Never use a spatula to press pancakes down. This tends to make them heavier.

- To keep the pancakes warm, place them on a cookie sheet with foil between the batches in a pre-heated 200°F oven.

Cornstarch Pancake Recipe

1 cup granulated sugar
2 tablespoons cornstarch
2 tablespoons unsalted butter
2 teaspoons of pure vanilla
2 cups boiling water
$\frac{1}{8}$ teaspoon nutmeg

Whisk the sugar and cornstarch, then add the boiling water a little at a time, while stirring constantly. Cook the mixture for about 9 minutes then add the butter, vanilla and nutmeg. Whisk and serve.

PASTRY/DANISH

- One of the best flours for making pastry dough is King Arthur's.
- Danish pastry is 23% fat.
- If you are using your own blend of pastry flour and the pastry is coming out too tender, reduce the amount of cake flour you are using.
- Ingredients for pasty making should be chilled or cold when starting.
- Puff pastry is basically very thin strands of gluten mixed with egg and kept separated by the fat. It is actually leavened by steam created by the hot air.
- The fat in puff pastry boils and bubbles then forms air pockets.
- Never put too much pressure on the rolling pin.

Pastry should be glazed as soon as it is taken from the oven to seal the surface.

Custard Cream Fillings for Pastry

- Never use copper bowls to store custard.
- Never place your hands in the filling since they are too easy to contaminate.
- Leftover custard should be discarded and never stored.
- Add any flavoring to the custard while the custard is still warm for the best results.

Dust should never come in contact with custard.

- Cool as fast as possible to avoid contamination.
- Never place custard in day old baked goods.
- Éclair paste dough should be made with bread flour so that when it bakes it will stretch and not tear apart.
- After adding egg yolks, bring the custard back to almost a full boil, this will inactivate the enzymes in the egg yolk. These enzymes are responsible for breaking down the starch and will ultimately cause the custard to become too thin.
- After filling keep under refrigeration.
- Custards; are easily contaminated by bacteria.
- The cream can be brought to a boil if desired since it contains starch.

Pastry Dough

- Puff pastry dough is prepared from soft wheat flour, butter and water.

- Exactly when you add the salt is critical since you do not want tough gluten.
- Never use cake flour to prepare pastry dough, there is insufficient gluten development and the dough will stay together adequately when it is being rolled out.
- Wondra flour can be substituted for pastry flour, however, the protein per gram is a little lower and the crust will not be as tender.
- Special margarine can be purchased from a bakery supply house to prepare pastry with. A combination of butter and special margarine may be used for flavor if so desired.

- Baker's like to add salt to the flour instead of into the dough to distribute it more evenly, while other baker's like to add it to the liquid instead.

It is best to roll your pastry out on a sheet of waxed paper that has been lightly floured. When finished invert the dough over your pan, or filling, and peel the waxed paper off.

- Place a small amount of butter between the layers of dough before it is folded several times. The butter or fat should be placed in pats or small globs. The more you fold, the more air pockets will form and the lighter the pastry.
- To stop pastry crust from becoming soggy, brush the surface with well-beaten egg white.
- Place the dough in the refrigerator for about 15-20 minutes before baking. If you leave it in too long, the fat will harden.
- When cutting the dough be sure and use a very sharp knife and cut straight down. Never pull the knife through the dough or cut the dough at an angle.
- The dough should be allowed to rest for 10-15 minutes between rolling and folding or dough can become tough.
- If the dough is not cut straight down, the end will puff up unevenly as the pastry bakes.
- Pastry dough should look like coarse crumbs.
- When making Danish dough it must rest for 4-8 hours after it has been rolled and folded. It should be placed in a "retarder" at 35°-45°F so that it can be easily worked.

SOLVING PASTRY PROBLEMS

THE PASTRY CRUST IS NOT FLAKY

- The fat was not cut into the flour properly
- The pieces of fat were too small
- The fat was not cool enough
- The type of fat used melted too fast

THE PASTRY CRUST WAS TOO SOGGY

- The crust was not baked long enough
- The crust was baked with a filling that was too moist
- The pastry was baked with a filling at too low a temperature
- The top was not properly glazed
- The bottom did not receive adequate heat

THE PASTRY CRUST WAS TOO TOUGH

- The gluten (protein) development was too high
- The flour used was too high-protein flour
- The fat was not worked into the flour properly
- Excess water was added
- The dough was overworked

THE PASTRY CRUST LOST ITS SHAPE

- The crust was not chilled enough before placing the pastry into the oven
- The oven temperature was not high enough

THE PASTRY CRUST HAD BURNT SPOTS

- There were thin spots in the dough from poor rolling

THE PASTRY CRUST WAS TOO BROWN

- There was too much sugar used
- There was too much protein in the dough
- The oven temperature was too high
- The pastry was baked for too long a period of time

THE PASTRY CRUST WAS TOO SOFT

- The fat was worked into the dough too much
- The fat was too warm and was not chilled enough

THE PASTRY CRUST SHRANK AWAY FROM THE EDGES

- The dough was stretched too much
- Too much water was added to the recipe
- Dough was overworked
- Protein content was too high

PHYLLO (FILLO) DOUGH

- Frozen phyllo dough should be thawed in the refrigerator for at least 12-15 hours.
- Never thaw phyllo dough in a microwave.
- Clarified butter produces a crispy product.
- Never allow the phyllo dough to set or it will dry out very quickly. Prepare all ingredients before you unwrap, the dough.

- Phyllo dough should be covered with wax paper and then a very damp towel should be placed on top to assure that the dough will not dry out.
- Fresh phyllo dough is easiest to work with.
- One pound of frozen phyllo dough contains about 22 sheets. Fresh dough contains about 25 sheets and is a little thinner.
- Baker's recommend $1^1/_2$ teaspoons of clarified butter for each sheet of phyllo dough.
- Use olive oil or peanut oil; to lightly brush on the dough before you bake any savory pastries in phyllo dough.
- Egg whites can be brushed on the phyllo dough instead of the oil.

When brushing butter on phyllo dough, start with the edges and work in. The edges tend to dry out much faster.

- If phyllo dough splits or tears, just brush the area with butter and place a small piece to patch the area.
- When cutting phyllo dough, use a metal ruler and make sure that the knife is very sharp.
- Once you complete the assembly using phyllo dough, be sure and brush the exterior with butter to prevent drying.

- Phyllo should be baked at 375°F on one of the upper shelves until just golden and not brown.
- If you have to bake phyllo when it is frozen, do so without thawing for the best results and to prevent sogginess.

PIZZA

About 200 years ago in Italy, pizza dough was rolled in the shape of a leg of a man's trousers that were worn at that time and called "calzone," which means "trousers" in Italian. These were prepared either as small appetizers or large ones to feed a family and included a variety of meats and vegetables. The first pizza parlor in America was on Spring Street in Manhattan, New York and opened in May 1905. Pizza became a favorite food when service men returned home after World War II from Italy. The men had tasted pizza in Naples and wanted more.

The stylized pizzas that we have in the United States, such as Tex-Mex, Chicago, etc. did not really start until the mid1970's. The best New York pizza is prepared with a very thin crust and in a coal-fired oven that can reach 750°F giving the pizza "New York blisters." The first pizza in Chicago (deep dish) was introduced in 1943 at Pizzerio Uno

Making the Crust

- To prevent a soggy crust on a homemade pizza, just place the cheese on before the tomato sauce.
- If you add a small amount of olive oil to the dough while you are working it, it will produce a crispy crust with a soft interior.

Brushing olive oil on top of the dough before adding toppings is another pizza parlor secret in order to stop the ingredients from making the dough soggy.

- When the pizza is done, try brushing a small amount of olive oil around the outer crust to keep the crust from getting too hard.
- Some of the best pizzas in the United States sprinkle some extra virgin olive oil on top of the pizza just before placing it into the oven to keep it from becoming too crispy.
- Another trick to preventing a soggy crust is to sauté vegetables that have a high water content, such as peppers, onions and mushrooms to decrease their water content before placing them on top of the pizza.
- Pizza crust is easily cut with large kitchen scissors.

Pizza crust is best made with Gold Medal, high-gluten bread flour. The crust will be more tender and crisp.

- Never use all-purpose flour for making pizza crust or the texture will not be the same as using the Gold medal flour.
- Pizza dough should be allowed to rise for at least one hour to double in size.
- After pizza dough rises, it should be "punched" down and divided into balls, then allowed to rest for 15 minutes before being used.
- If you add a small amount of whole-wheat flour, the crust will have a nuttier taste.
- If you add semolina flour, it will produce a very crispy crust.
- If you use a food processor to mix the dough, the dough will be thoroughly kneaded when the dough forms one or two balls on the top of the blade.

Shaping Pizza Dough

- Dough should be lightly floured after it has rested for 15 minutes. The surface you are working on should be dusted with flour.
- When working the dough, use your fingertips and heel of your hand and work in a circular motion, continually flattening the dough. Flip it and continue to stretch it out until it is the size you want.
- If the dough is relaxed, it will be easier to work.
- The pan that you place the dough on should be lightly dusted with cornmeal.

Freezing Pizza Dough

- Allow the batch to rise only once, then punch it down and separate it into separate balls enough for one crust.
- Flatten the balls into discs and then wrap them separately with plastic freezer wrap or freezer bags that have had oil sprayed on the inside first. This will allow you to remove the dough without it sticking to the bag.
- Frozen pizza discs will stay fresh for 3-4 months.
- Thawing is best done by placing the disc in the refrigerator overnight.
- Frozen pizza dough should not be shaped until it is at room temperature.

Cheese for Pizza

- Mozzarella is the cheese of choice for pizza since it melts easily and does not become tough.
- Mozzarella originated in Italy and was made with the milk from water buffalo, which is where the term "buffalo mozzarella" came from.
- The best pizzas use the "real" Parmesan cheese, which is called Parmigiano-Reggiano on the rind and is grated fresh.
- Romano cheese is also used with excellent results.
- Imported provolone will add a somewhat sharper flavor.
- New England style pizza uses white cheddar as the cheese of choice.

Tomato Sauce

- It takes $1^1/_2$ cups of tomato sauce for a 12" pizza.
- The basic pizza parlor recipe for tomato sauce is one can of Italian style tomato puree, one large crushed garlic clove, one teaspoon of dried oregano, four fresh basil leaves, salt and fresh pepper to taste. This is the basic recipe but not recommended if you want the best tasting pizza.

If you want the best tasting pizza never add the spices to the tomato sauce only salt and pepper as desired. Spices should be added last on top of the ingredients after the pizza is complete. The acid in tomato sauce tends to reduce the potency of many spices, especially as the tomato sauce heats up.

Toppings

- If you use meats they are best if pre-cooked, such as salami, pepperoni, sausage, ham or hamburger.
- Tuna is an excellent topping, but should be a good quality and placed on in chunks.
- Meats that are high in fat such as sausage need pre-cooking because of their high fat content.
- Vegetables other than tomatoes should also be pre-cooked since they may not cook through if they are thick or the water content is too high.
- Grilling vegetables is recommended, however, they can be sautéed or just blanched.
- Sautéing vegetables allows you to add additional flavors, which enhance the taste of the pizza.

Baking the Pizza

- The oven should be at the highest temperature possible.
- The pizza should be placed directly on a special pizza screen, which looks similar to the screen on your screen door so that the heat can easily get to the bottom of the crust.
- If you have ordered a delivered pizza and the crust is usually soggy, just make sure that your oven has been pre-heated to 400°F before it arrives, then place it in for 5 minutes.
- Pizza will always taste better when prepared in a coal-fired or wood-burning brick oven or at least directly on the heat source, which must be at least 550°F. Home ovens usually will not go over 500°F.
- Unglazed quarry tiles can be placed on the bottom of the oven, which does help. They must be at least 1/2 inch thick or they will crack from the intense heat.
- If you are going to use the tiles, be sure that the dough is at room temperature for the best results.

The finest all-natural, handmade pizza in the United States can be found in Las Vegas, Nevada at Fasolini's Pizza Cafe. Jim and Josie Fasolini are recognized as one of the finest pizza and Italian food chefs in the world.

POPOVER

- Popovers are easily leavened using only eggs and steam.
- Make sure that you have the eggs and milk at room temperature before you start mixing a popover batter.
- Eggs will create more volume at room temperature.
- If you follow the recipe to the letter, the popovers will come out great. If you try and alter the recipe you won't like the results.
- If you prepare the batter ahead of time and refrigerate it, be sure and allow the batter to return to room temperature for 45 minutes before using it.
- Popovers should only be made in an iron popover pan for the best results. The pan should never be filled more than half full to avoid spillovers.

Most bakers recommend that if you do not have an iron popover pan you do not even attempt making them.

- Always bake popovers on the center rack of the oven and at 425°F. If glass cups are used, reduce the heat by 25°.
- Popovers may collapse if the oven door is opened during the first 20 minutes of cooking time.
- Popovers will collapse if you undercook them when they are removed from the oven.
- They should have a nice brown color when baked.

After the popovers have finished baking, puncture each one in several places with a skewer to release the steam and the insides will not be soggy.

- If you would like the insides to be somewhat crispy and very dry, just return the popovers to the oven after you have punctured then for 8 minutes but keep a close eye on them so that they do not burn.

- Popover batter should be mixed just enough to blend the ingredients even if it ends up thin it will be OK.

PRETZEL

The first pretzel; was made in 605 AD in a monastery in southern France by a Franciscan monk. The pretzel was made during lent when fat, eggs and milk were forbidden. The monk decided to prepare dough of just flour, salt and water, then twisted the dough into the shape of two arms crossed as in a "prayer." He called it a "pretiola," which is latin for "little gift." The first pretzel was then given to children as a reward for saying their prayers. The first pretzel; in the United States was introduced by Jochem Wessel in 1652 who made a pretzel and sold it to the Indians. This made settlers mad because he used "good flour" and they had to eat bran flour.

- The ingredients are 2 teaspoons of brown sugar, 1 teaspoon of fresh, dry yeast, warm water (105°-110°F), 3½ cups + 3 tablespoons of flour, ¼ teaspoons of salt and 2 tablespoons of baking soda.
- The brown sugar is mixed with ¼ cup of warm water until all the sugar is dissolved, then sprinkle yeast on top to moisten, then set aside to rest for 10 minutes.

- Sift 3$\frac{1}{2}$ cups of flour and the table salt into a separate bowl, then stir in the yeast mixture and add $\frac{3}{4}$ cup of warm water and mix into dough.

Problems occasionally occur if you are using chlorinated water, which will reduce the effectiveness of the yeast.

- Add more warm water 1-tablespoon at a time if needed. The dough should be solid, but not sticky.
- Next you need to lightly flour your work surface with the remaining 2 tablespoons of flour, then turn the dough out and knead for 4-5 minutes.
- Form the dough into a ball, then coat the inside of a medium-sized bowl with cooking spray and place the dough in the bowl covering it with a clean towel.
- Allow the dough to rest for 30 minutes, then divide it into 8 equal pieces, flatten and cut the dough into rectangles about 2X3 inches making 16 pieces.
- Next roll out each piece to form a rope about 9 inches long and shape each rope into a pretzel bow or knot. Try and keep them the same size.

If salt comes into direct contact with the yeast, it can kill the yeast.

- Next add the baking soda to 2 cups of water and bring to a boil in a large saucepan.

- Drop the pretzels into the boiling water, only two at a time for 15 seconds, turning them once. Remove the pretzels with a slotted spoon and allow them to drain.
- Preheat oven to 350°F and sprinkle pretzels with a small amount of salt or sesame seeds, then bake for 15 minutes or until brown.

QUICHE

- The biggest problem with quiche is a soggy crust. To make a crisp crust, just partially bake the pastry shell at 425°F for 15 minutes, remove it (remove lining if one was used) and brush it with egg yolk (or egg white) and return it to the oven to dry for only 2 minutes.
- Never pour the filling into the pastry shell until just before baking. This helps to prevent a soggy crust as well.

If you bake the quiche in a Pyrex dish, reduce the heat by 25°F.

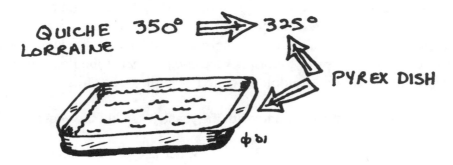

- When you think that the quiche is done, just shake the pan lightly to see if is set. The quiche should be just barely firm.
- To be sure, just insert a skewer into the center. If the skewer comes out clean, the quiche is done.
- Quiche will continue to cook for a short time after it is removed from the oven and should be removed just before it has completed cooking.
- Quiche will curdle if overcooked and become very watery.

Quiche Lorraine

- Best to use a pre-baked pie crust, since an unbaked one will probably be raw in the middle.
- Keep the filling $1/8$th from the top of the crust.
- Curdling will not occur if you only bake the quiche until you can insert a skewer into the middle and it comes out clean.

SUGARS USED IN BAKING

Granulated

Ultrafine – Best for cakes and dry mixes and is usually used to coat confectionery pans.

Very Fine – Excellent for dry mixing when producing cake mixes, puddings and gelatin desserts.

Fine or Extrafine – Standard granulated sugar we use as an all-purpose sugar in recipes and in our sugar bowls.

Medium Coarse – Used to produce crystalline syrups in candies and other sweets. Doesn't change much when heated to high temperatures.

Coarse – Used similar to medium coarse. Has the tendency not to caramelize easily.

Powdered Sugars

Confectioner's (10X) – Very fine granules, which makes a smooth textured icing.

Confectioner's (6X) – Best for cream fillings, especially in biscuits and as a topping for pies and pastries. Tends to mix well with melted fats.

Confectioner's (4X) – Normally used in the production of chewing gums and as packing for marshmallows.

Medium Coarse – Used for dusting mixtures that do not require the fine sugars. Usually used on doughnuts and related baked goods.

Invert Sugar

Produced from equal parts of two simple sugars, dextrose and levulose and is sweeter than cane sugar. Found naturally in honey and molasses.

- Has the ability to retain moisture when used in cakes, which slows down the staling of cakes.
- Will enhance smoothness in icings.
- Helps a baked product obtain a rich looking brown crust through caramelizing.

TARTS

- The crust for a custard or fruit tart should be partially baked before the filling is added or the crust will not remain a separate layer. This is called "blind baking."
- Weights may be needed to hold the crust down when blind baking. Wrapping coins in a piece of aluminum will do.
- After shaping tart dough it is best to refrigerate it for 30 minutes to reduce the risk of shrinkage.
- In Europe bakers use wide rubber bands on wither end of the rolling pin when rolling out tart dough to tell the correct height of the dough so that it is not too thick or thin.
- Unfilled shells need to be baked on the center shelf.
- After you shape the dough into a ball, place it in the refrigerator for 30 minutes to allow the dough to relax and distribute the moisture.
- Use a pastry cloth when you roll out the dough.
- Rolling the dough between two sheets of wax paper is ideal. The wax paper should still be floured.

Shells with fillings need to be baked on the bottom shelf.

- If you are making a glaze for a pear tart, the reduced pear syrup has to cool completely before any thickener is added or it will get lumpy.
- Be sure that any honey you use in a tart tastes good. Some honey does not have a good flavor.
- The shell will not become soggy if you quick-temper chocolate and brush it on the top of the bottom, crust before adding the filling.

Orange Tart

- The best orange is the Valencia orange.
- Place the orange in the microwave for a few seconds to release more just when squeezed.
- Canned mandarin oranges make an excellent substitute and work well. Make sure they are uniform in size for the best results.

For a real surprise, try using a new rasp from your local hardware store as a zester. The shards of zest look lacy and great.

- The whipped cream should be folded into the orange curd as soon as it is ready so that the gelatin will be incorporating as the cold orange curd cream begins to set up.
- Never use Seville orange zest, it is too bitter and will ruin the tart.

WAFFLES

Thomas Jefferson brought the first waffle iron to the United States from France. It was 100 years later when the waffle gained popularity and was sold by street food venders in Philadelphia and New York. Belgium waffles were first introduced at the New York World's Fair in 1964.

- If you would like crispy waffles, just add $1^1/_2$ tablespoons of additional oil to the batter.
- Never open a waffle iron to check them out until they have cooked for 1 minute.
- When waffles are cooked, the lid will rise from the expanding dough.
- Frozen waffles should be heated without thawing.
- Waffle batter will keep for several days in the refrigerator, but be sure and place the batter in a larger container since it will expand.
- Using baking soda and eggs in the batter produce a very, light waffle.
- If you want a crispier, brown surface, add 2 tablespoons of corn syrup to your recipe.

CHAPTER 16

PIE BAKING SECRETS

PIES

- The bottom of the pan can be floured if you wish. Do not leave any globs of excess flour; shake out the pan well.
- The bottom of the pan can also be sprayed with vegetable oil if you prefer not to flour it.

- You will need to protect the edges of a single crust pie after it has baked for 15 minutes.
- Double crust pies need the edges of the crust protected after 30 minutes of baking. Aluminum foil can be used.

- Pies should be removed from their cooking pan and placed on a plate for easy serving and slicing.

Slicing pies in a metal pan dulls the knife and makes it more difficult to serve.

- If the pan is prepared properly, the pie should easily slip out of the pan.
- If there is enough fat in the dough, it will not be necessary to grease the pan to make the pie slip out easily.

Apple Pies

- Different varieties of apples can be used to provide different flavors and textures.
- Slice the apples thin so that they will be able to lie close together. Thick slices create too much air space.
- Thick apple slices usually drop to the bottom creating a space between the apples and the top crust.

The best apples for pies are Granny Smith, Pippin, Cortland, Jonathan and Stayman-Winesap.

- Granny Smith apples are the most popular when preparing the pie in the winter months.
- If you spray the exposed surfaces with a solution of powdered vitamin C and water it, it will keep the surfaces from browning too soon.
- For a milder cinnamon flavor, reduce your recipe to $1/2$ to 1-teaspoon.

Cherry Pies

- If you are going to use sour cherries, use them as soon as you purchase them or freeze them. Sour cherries tend to deteriorate very quickly.
- If you don't have a cherry pitter, use an old style hairpin (if you can find one).
- The maximum amount of sugar should never exceed 1 cup.
- Butter does not go well in cherries, however, it is OK to use a crust made with butter.
- If you want to keep a nice cherry color, don't cook the cherry filling before you bake the pie.
- A small amount of almond extract is a great addition to cherries.

Chiffon Pies

- For chiffon pies, meringue is folded into the filling just before placing the cold mixture into the piecrust.

- If you place the chiffon filling into a crust that was not baked, the egg whites would get overcooked and ruin the consistency of the dish.
- The filling must be heated to a temperature of 160°-170°F to be sure that the enzyme that breaks down starch in the yolk is destroyed.

If the chiffon pie is to be eaten the next day, it is best to reduce the gelatin by ¼ of the amount recommended.

- If the custard is chilled in the refrigerator it should be stirred frequently during the first minute and the occasionally every few minutes until it starts to set up.
- If the custard becomes too stiff, it will make it difficult to fold in the whipped cream.
- To remove a chiffon pie from the pie plate, just use a hot, damp dishtowel and run it around the bottom and sides.

Chocolate Cream Pie

- Always use a heavy well-insulated pan to keep the pie filling from burning.
- Remember never beat the filling too much after it has cooled or you will cause it to have a breakdown.
- If you want to eliminate the possibility of lumps, use a 10-loop piano wire whisk to prevent lumps.
- Best to place the whipped cream of just before serving.

Cream/Custard Pies (General Information)

- When using a cream filling, coat the crust with a granulated sugar before adding the cream to eliminate a soggy crust.
- Separate whites from the yolk when the eggs are cold; it will be easier. However, allow the whites to come to room temperature before using them.
- When cutting pies with loose fillings, spray your knife with oil before cutting and the filling won't stick to the knife.
- Cream pie fillings are always added to a pre-baked piecrust.
- Topping are added after the pie has cooled.

The preferred thickener for cream pies is "regular" cornstarch not "waxy maize" cornstarch.

- Custard pies should not be frozen, with the exception of pumpkin pies.
- The reason a custard pie shrinks away from the crust is that you have cooked it too long in an oven that was too hot.
- Custard pies are usually baked in the shell for 10 minutes at 450°F; then temperature is reduced to 300°F for 40-50 minutes.
- Cream and custard pies should be stored in the refrigerator.

Four step method

1. Scald the milk and only some of the sugar in a round-bottomed pan.
2. In a separate bowl, mix the egg yolks, the rest of the sugar, thickener and any flavoring.
3. Stir in the mixture in the bowl as soon as the milk and sugar has scalded but just before they boil. Mix until it boils and remove from the heat
4. Flavorings can be added after removal from the heat.

Crumb Pie Crust/Topping

- Graham crackers can be used providing you add a small amount of sugar.
- If you are going to add nuts to the crust, additional sugar will be needed.
- Always add a pinch of salt and a small amount of vanilla to your recipe.
- The pie pan should not be greased or the crust may slip down. The rim, however, should be greased.
- For a crumb topping for an apple pie, combine $1/2$ cup of flour, $1/2$ cup of brown sugar, $1/2$ teaspoon of cinnamon and 4 tablespoons of unsalted butter. Just barely blend the ingredients and crumble over the top of the pie.

Current Pies

- If you use frozen currents, be sure they are defrosted before using them or they will not dissolve the thickener and the sugar.
- Make sure that the currents you use have no more than 4 seeds per current.

Frozen Pies

- The oven should be pre-heated to 425°F, then bake the pie for 10 minutes before lowering the temperature to 400°F and finish baking for about 40 minutes more.

Fruit Pies (General Information)

- When making a lemon pie, bakers rub a few sugar cubes over the top of a lemon then include these as part of the total sugar.
- Never substitute a granulated sugar for a powdered sugar if you run out.

Never place hot filling into a piecrust; always wait until it cools.

- Drain juices from fruit well and use with the thickener.

Always use glass, baking pans when making fruit pies or the acid will discolor the filling and the pie tin.

- If frozen, bake without thawing at 450°F for 15-20 minutes, then reduce the heat to 375°F for 20-30 minutes or until the top has browned.
- Fruit pies do not hold up well and are best eaten on the day they are prepared.
- If you are making an apple pie with eating apples instead of baking apples, be sure and add 1 tablespoon of lemon juice to the filling.
- Fruit pies should be served just slightly warm. If served too hot, the filling will be too watery.
- When using fruit for pies, make sure that the fruit is sweet enough otherwise more sugar needs to be added.
- Adding a 1-tablespoon of tapioca to the pie filling and it won't bubble over.

Another method of stopping bubbling over is to place a large tube of pasta in the center of the pie as a chimney to allow air to escape.

- Never use a microwave to bake a pie. The insides will cook long before the crust is done.
- Fruit pies can be stored at room temperature.
- Pies that are only made with berries tend to get bitter fast.
- The filling must be bubbling rapidly to be sure that the cornstarch will absorb enough liquid and thicken the fruit filling.

Fruit Pie Dough

- A method of keeping the bottom of the dough dry is to spread a thin layer of butter on the pie pan before placing the bottom crust in.
- Dough should be made the day before and allowed to rest in the refrigerator for 1-hour after it is rolled and shaped. This will prevent distortion and help the dough maintain its shape.
- It is best to decrease the amount of cornstarch used by 1 teaspoon if you are planning to eat the pie the next day. The pie will lose moisture overnight.

FRUIT PIE INGREDIENTS

Fruit	Quantity Needed	Sugar	Cornstarch
Apple	8 cups	$1/2$ cup	4 tsp.
Apricot	4 cups	$6^{1}/_{2}$ Tbsp	2 Tbsp.
Cherries	15 Tbsp.	$14^{1}/_{2}$ Tbsp.	$2^{1}/_{2}$ Tbsp.
Current	$3^{1}/_{2}$ cups	$1^{1}/_{3}$ cups	3 Tbsp.
Gooseberry	4 cups	1 cup	$2^{1}/_{4}$ Tbsp.
Peach	6 cups	$1/2$ cup	4 tsp.
Plum	4 cups	$1/2$ cup	2 Tbsp.
Rhubarb	4 cups	$2/3$ cup	4 tsp.or 2 eggs

Ice Cream Pie

- The pie shell is fully baked first, then a soft ice cream is placed in and the pie frozen.
- Toppings can be placed on at the same time that the ice cream is placed in the crust.
- Whipped cream cannot be placed on top of the ice cream until just before serving.

Key Lime Pie

Originally a special lime was used to prepare key lime pie. These limes were brought to this country from the West Indies where they had been grown since the early 1500's and were probably brought there by Columbus. The lime trees were brought to the Florida Keys in 1839 and thrived there until a hurricane destroyed almost all the orchards in 1926. The key limes were replaced with a Tahitian variety, which we still use today and still call the pie a key lime pie.

- You can use either a pastry crust or a graham cracker crust.
- Be sure that the lime juice is squeezed fresh for the best results.

Lemon Pie

- The best lemons to use for lemon pie are the Meyer lemons from California. They have the mildest lemon flavor.

Nectarine Pie

- Make sure the nectarines are ripe and sweet but not mushy.
- Spray the nectarines occasionally with a spray of powdered vitamin C and water to prevent browning.
- Never add a hot liquid to the nectarines or it will cause the cornstarch to get lumpy.

Pecan Pie

- To brown the top better, use low-protein flour (cake flour) and eliminate the sugar, then add 1 teaspoon of lemon juice to the recipe.
- Refiner's sugar and unrefined brown sugar are the best for pecan pies. It will probably be necessary to obtain these in a baker's supply shop.
- The filling dries out easily and you need to check this pie regularly.

Pumpkin Pie

- Place a layer of mini marshmallows on top of the bottom crust before pouring the filling in. As the pie bakes, the air will expand inside the marshmallows and they will rise to the top providing a beautiful layer of browned marshmallows.
- Frozen pumpkin pies should be baked without thawing at 400°F for just under 2 hours, then reduce the heat to 325°F until done.
- To be sure the pie is baked, insert a skewer into the center and if it comes out clean the pie is done.
- The cracking in the pie custard is caused by over baking.

Rhubarb Pie

- Never use rhubarb leaves, they contain a poison.
- If you don't like the tartness of rhubarb, strawberry can be added.

The combination of cherries and rhubarb makes one of the greatest pies ever baked.

- Two eggs can be added in place of the cornstarch to thicken the filling and provides custard that is excellent. The mild custard will not affect the tart flavor, which rhubarb lovers prefer.

Shoofly Pie

- Make sure that you use unsulfured molasses; the sulfured variety has a bitter taste.

Soft Pies

- Pecan, sweet potato and pumpkin pies should be made in a very deep glass pie dish with a fluted rim.
- Prepared with an unbaked crust.
- The filling normally sets during the baking process. Most filling will contain eggs, which assist in the filling setting-up properly.
- A frozen pumpkin pie will take about 15 minutes longer than a fruit pie to bake, which gives the pie longer to dry out reducing the excess moisture, which allows the filling to set better.

Thickeners

- Thickeners are not needed for apple pies.
- All other fruit pies should be thickened with a mixture of 2 tablespoons of cornstarch and 2 tablespoons of tapioca.
- Cornstarch has twice the thickening power of flour. For fruit pies NEVER use regular cornstarch, the gel obtained becomes too solid. The recommended cornstarch is "waxy maize."
- Acidic fruit pies may interfere with the thickening power of the starch used. Always add the pie filling after the thickener has set and never cook it with the acidic filling.
- The juice that was drained from the fruit should be brought to a boil and the thickener added. You can also use both the juice and the fruit together if you wish.
- After thickening with cornstarch, bring the mixture back to a boil, which will clarify the mixture and set the thickener.
- Add any sugar, salt, butter or other ingredients after the thickener has set and stir in until fully dissolved.
- Juices from pies will not run if you blend 1 egg white, beaten until stiff with 2 tablespoons of sugar and add it to the filling before baking.

Pie Washes

- To make the pie crust more appealing, many bakers use eggs, water, milk, melted butter or sweet cream brushed on depending on the appearance desired.

PIE WASHES

Cream Wash –   Just brush the crust with cream before baking the pie to give the pie a glossy top.

Egg White Wash –   Use 1 egg white mixed with 2 teaspoons of water to provide a transparent golden brown.

Egg Yolk Wash –   Use 1 egg yolk and 2 tablespoons of water to make a golden crust.

Butter Wash –   Provides a soft, rich-flavored crust.

Milk Wash –   Makes the crust softer and not as shiny.

Water Wash –   Spray a mist water on top of the loaf to make a crunchier crust.

Whole Egg Wash –   Makes loaves fancy by giving the surface a shiny bronzed surface. Use a whole egg beaten with 1 tablespoon of water gently brushed over the surface.

The Perfect Pie Crust

- Leaf lard is the best fat for preparing the flakiest piecrust. It has the largest fat crystals of any fat, which makes a flakier, lighter piecrust. Lard and shortening are 100% fat compared to butter at 80-90%. Shortening is the choice after lard.

Never use bread flour when making piecrust dough. The protein content is too high and to compensate, you would have to add more shortening to tenderize the gluten strands.

- Shortening should always be at room temperature or too much gluten will develop and the crust will be tough.
- A small amount of butter added will provide a nice flavor to the crust.
- Adding a teaspoon of white vinegar to the pie dough will produce a flakier piecrust.
- The shortening in a crust will usually provide 25-40% fat.
- If you freeze pie dough it must be thawed in the refrigerator not at room temperature.
- Pie dough that is uncooked and unrolled can be stored in the refrigerator for 3-4 days and frozen for 2-3 months.
- If you don't want to add vinegar, substitute sour cream or whipped cream for any water.

- The perfect surface for rolling out pie dough is a piece of marble with a pastry-cloth on top.
- Mealy piecrust is made by rubbing the flour and the shortening until there is a very fine distribution of the flour in the shortening.
- The coolness of a marble surface helps to keep the fat firm and not allowing the fat to be absorbed into the flour causing a loss of flakiness.
- When rolling dough and cracks develop, just remove a small piece from the edge, lightly dust it with flour and place a piece of plastic wrap over it and roll it into the dough.

All ingredients and utensils should be very cold when preparing piecrust dough. Even the flour should be placed in the freezer for a few minutes before adding it in to the recipe.

- Sea salt is recommended by bakers in place of table salt since it tends to have a slightly sweet flavor.
- Sugar can damage gluten formation, making it excellent for piecrust dough.
- When you add baking powder to your recipe, try using half the salt called for.
- A small amount of vinegar added to the ingredients when you add the liquid (if the liquid has no acidity of its own) will improve the dough and provide better elasticity and reduces the risk of shrinkage.
- If you want a buttery, great tasting crust, try using all unsalted butter to replace the shortening. The crust will not be as flaky, but the flavor will make up for it.
- Try adding the butter in large ice-cold pieces so that when the water is added it will be completely absorbed by the flour. This will develop the maximum amount of gluten.
- Cutting the butter in may not allow for enough gluten formation.

It is always best to chill the shaped crust in the pie pan/plate before baking to relax the gluten and reduce shrinking. The entire filled pie can be chilled for 15 minutes if you prefer and the crust will not pull away when it is baking.

- Pastry flour (low-protein flour) is best for piecrust. Soft wheat flour will produce a sturdy crust. However, more shortening will probably be needed. Very little gluten is needed for the perfect piecrust.
- Try using half all-purpose flour and half cake flour and you will obtain a good blend of flakiness and a tender crust.
- If you add water to pie dough, it must be ice water or at least be very cold. The water should be added to the dough until it just holds the dough together. Too much water will make the crust tough.
- Water has an important function in that it slows the gluten from developing, which allows the water to evenly distribute. This keeps the dough tender. Once you add the water, try and mix as little as possible.

When using ice water, the shortening will remain solid and reduce the development of gluten.

- Use a pizza cutter to cut strips for a lattice top.
- To stop fruit juices from making the bottom of the piecrust soggy, just brush the bottom crust with lightly beaten egg white to seal it then refrigerate the crust for 10-15 minutes before using it.
- Never stretch the dough when placing it in the pan or it will shrink.
- To make thinner dough for pie shells, just coat your rolling surface with olive oil.

Blending shortening into the flour causes it to break into many pieces, coating all pieces with flour during the process. If you incorporate half of the shortening at a time, you will create dough with many pockets of shortening. As you roll the dough you tend to flatten out those pieces of shortening, which gives you flakes or the "flaky crust" you desire.

- Make sure a ready-made piecrust is fully thawed before using it.
- To make a different top on the pie, just cut out shapes from the piecrust dough with cookie cutters and place the shapes on top instead of a full crust.
- Pie ingredients should be cold when preparing a pie.
- If you are using a single piecrust, you will need to fold the edges under and flute the edges with your fingers. Fluting is just making and indentation in the crust so that it remains in place.

Phyllo dough can be used for piecrust and will make a fat-free crust. Use two leaves for a 9-10 inch pie, sprayed with vegetable cooking spray centered in the pan, then lay two more layers at right angles to first, then two more on the bias to fill any gap to be sure that the pan is full lined. Use a piece of damp paper towel to press the phyllo into the pan. Be careful so as not to tear the phyllo.

- If your crust is too crisp and you want it to be soft, increase the shortening you are using or add milk instead of water.
- For a double-crust pie, place the pie crust on the bottom, place the filling in, then place the second crust on top of the filling and press the two crusts together by fluting them against each other.
- Never make a pie in a warm or hot kitchen, it will affect the results.
- When mixing the dough, if you use your hands, the crust will be flakier. Look at the dough while you are working with it. If you see can see small flakes of butter, the crust will be flaky; if it seems to stretch easily, it will be elastic enough so that it will not shrink.

If your dough has been refrigerated for more than 1 hour, allow it to remain at room temperature for 15 minutes before you work it.

- If the dough appears to be very fragile and breaks easily, fold it and refrigerate it for 25 minutes before working it again. The fat did not allow enough moisture into the dough.
- After the dough is mixed, roll it into a rough ball, wrap it and then refrigerate it for 45 minutes before rolling it out.
- Ceramic or Pyrex pie plates will give you the crispiest piecrust.

- Place a few slices of fresh white bread on top of your pie while it is baking and it will eliminate blistering. Remove the bread about 5 minutes before the pie has finished cooking to allow the crust to brown.
- When baking a crust for a cream pie or ice cream pie, always bake it in a pre-heated oven and on the bottom shelf. The crust should be pricked with a toothpick every 3-4 inches to allow steam to escape. Bake the crust uncovered at 450°F for about 14 minutes or until the crust has barely browned.
- To avoid a blistering piecrust, place a second pie pan on top of the crust as its bakes. This is called "double-panning."
- Glazing the top crust usually results in a tougher crust.
- Sprinkling sugar on the top crust will provide a bit of crunchiness and will not make the crust tough. It also helps to brown the crust.
- If you want a real crisp bottom on your pie, bake it on the floor of the oven for the first 25 minutes.

- If you have a problem removing pies from pans that have a graham cracker crust, just place the pan in warm water for 10-15 seconds and it will come right out.

- If your piecrust sticks to the pan, it may be due to inadequate shortening or the dough separating and the filling burning on the pan. Another good reason not to stretch the dough to fit the pan.

The Right Size Crust for the Job

- For a fluted pastry tart pan – Cut the dough circle 1" larger than the pan.
- For a single piecrust – Cut the dough circle 3" larger than the pan/plate.
- For a double-crust pie – Cut both circles 2" larger than the pan/plate.

Special Piecrusts Secrets for Lengthy Cooking Times

- These pies are made with a filling that requires a longer baking time, which could damage the normal crust.

- If the recipe calls for a dairy product, substitute water.
- A small amount of apple cider vinegar (acid) should be added to retard browning.
- Use 50% cake flour and 50% of your regular flour.
- Leave any sugar out of the recipe.
- Reduce the amount of shortening.
- Make sure that you refrigerate the dough since the cold will cause the moisture to distribute more evenly.
- Place the crust in the freezer to chill it is even better than the refrigerator and will help to retain the shape of the crust.

SOLVING PIE CRUST PROBLEMS

THE CRUST DID NOT BROWN ENOUGH

- Make sure you used a heatproof clear glass dish or dark metal pie pan
- Add additional sugar or syrup

THE CRUST BROWNED TOO MUCH

- The filling will need to be pre-cooked or at least heated before placing it in the crust
- Use a light-colored pie pan
- The edges need to be protected with aluminum foil

CHAPTER 17

PREPARING SOUPS & STEWS

SOUPS/STEWS

Croutons

- The best croutons are made from small cubes of bread that have been sautéed in butter or extra virgin olive oil with pepper flakes.
- Dust croutons with freshly grated Parmesan cheese before serving.
- Croutons should be served on the side, not on the salad.

Soups

Removing fat from soup & stews can be accomplished in a number of ways

1. Place the soup or stew in the refrigerator and allow the fat to rise, then remove it.
2. Use a separator cup for clear soups.
3. Place 3-4 ice cubes in a piece of cheesecloth and swirl around allowing the fat to attach to the cheesecloth.
4. Swirl a piece of iceberg lettuce around in the soup or stew and the fat will adhere to it.

- Depending on the density of the vegetable they should be added at different times. If you wish to add them at the same time then you may want to steam some to soften them before adding them.

- Vegetables should be sautéed before adding them to soup to retain their individual flavors and keep them firm.

- A small amount of wine will intensify the flavor of soup. Recommended is a not too dry sherry, which should be added during the last 10-15 minutes of cooking time.
- Eggshells will clarify soups. Just add 3-4 eggshells and simmer for 10-12 minutes before straining out the eggshells for clear soup.

If the soup boils while you are trying to clarify it, it will not clarify.

Cream of wheat, is used by some chefs to thicken soup.
Pasta should be pre-cooked and added to soup a few minutes before serving.
Flavors will blend better if soup is cooked with the lid on.

- Soup will have better flavor if allowed to rest in the refrigerator for 1-2 days.
- Always save leftover meat and chicken bones to provide additional flavor for soups and stews.
- If you are going to puree soup, allow the soup to cool first.
- Popcorn on top of soup is great treat for kids.
- Salt should never be added to soup that has dairy products until just before serving to prevent curdling.
- If you have lumps in your soup use a wire whisk.
- Warm bowls should be used to serve soups in.
- If soup develops lumps, just place it in the blender.

Soups & Stews

- For the best tasting soups and stews, always refrigerate the dish for 8-10 hours to allow the seasonings a chance to mingle producing a more desirable flavor.
- Try and remove as much fat as possible before thickening soup or stew for the best results.
- If you use flour to thicken the soup or stew and then add a dairy product such as milk, it won't separate as easily.

When you use cornstarch or flour to thicken soup or stew, always add any acidic ingredient after you have completed the thickening for the best results.

- Acidic vegetables and fruits need to be added to a milk-based soup. Never add a dairy product to the acid.
- Most herbs lose potency very quickly, especially when added to a hot or boiling liquid. Best to add the herbs to ward the last 20 minutes of cooking time.
- Parsley placed in a piece of cheesecloth and swirled around in soup or stew for 5-8 minutes will reduce garlicky flavor.
- If you have over-salted the soup or stew, just place two pieces of raw potato in and stir for a few minutes while simmering, and then discard the potato.
- Too much salt can be overcome by adding 1 teaspoon of white vinegar and 1 teaspoon of brown sugar.
- If you want a rich brown color to the soup or stew, just caramelize 3-4 teaspoons of sugar and add to the pot.
- Pureed okra makes an excellent thickener for soups and stews.
- For a great low fat soup or stew thickener, try using dehydrated potato flakes.
- Both salt and pepper tend to intensify the flavor of soups and stews and therefore should only be added just before serving.
- To keep the flavors in soups and stews never boil them only allow them to simmer.

There are a number of rules to remember when re-heating soups, sauces and stews

- Foods that contain fats tend to oxidize more readily and this may impart a less than desirable flavor.
- When re-heating, never place the food in an aluminum or iron pot and never add salt until the food is almost completely warmed back up.
- Soups and gravies should only be simmered for about 2 minutes.
- Creamed soups should only be re-heated at a slow simmer after it has reached a slow boil for about 2 minutes.

BISQUES

- Heavy cream soups that usually contain shellfish
- Usually made with a white base with fish puree and vegetables.
- The French sometimes thicken bisque with rice.

Shrimp Bisque

- Adding some shrimp shell to the soup will provide excellent flavor. Make sure you strain them out before serving.
- Cook the rice in the stock from the soup to pick up additional flavor.
- To add additional flavor, try adding onions or jalapenos.
- Adding pureed rice and shrimp will add body and great flavor.
- Dry sherry, adds flavor and has the ability to enhance flavors from other ingredients.

CHICKEN SOUP

- Noodles should never be added in the beginning, only toward the end of the cooking or they will get mushy.

    To prepare the best chicken soup like your grandmother made; the butcher will have to provide you with a "soup hen" not a young chicken.

- Noodles should be cooked before adding them to the soup if you want the soup to remain clear.
- Always remove as much of the fat as possible.
- Kosher salt should be used since it will not cloud the soup.
- Choose a heavy pot with a spigot on the bottom, which will allow you to drain off just the clear soup.

- Surface fat can be eliminated using a piece of paper towel or piece of white bread used as a sponge and then discarded before it breaks down.
- White pepper may be used if so desired.
- The chicken should be diced and pre-cooked, then added about 10 minutes before the soup is finished cooking allowing enough time for it to heat.
- Diced carrots and celery are frequently added toward then end of the cooking time.

When carrots are added to chicken soup; they release carotene when heated and provide the color that the old-fashioned chicken soups had.

CHOWDER

New Englanders were so upset by New Yorkers putting tomatoes in clam chowder and calling it clam chowder that they actually passed a bill in 1939 outlawing tomatoes in New England clam chowder.

- Always add clams or oysters near the end of the cooking cycle or they will become tough.
- To keep cream-based soup warm, it should be done in a double, boiler or it may get scorched.
- All chowders contain milk and potatoes.
- Prepared as thick soup, never watery. If it becomes watery, use potato flakes to thicken.
- New England chowder contains cream, potatoes, onions, clams, clam juices and salt and pepper.
- Manhattan chowder contains clams, tomatoes and an assortment of vegetables.

COLD SOUPS

- Cold soups need additional flavor since the cold tends to reduce the intensity of the flavors.

Cold soups will not be as thick as they were when they were hot and may need additional thickening if that is the way you like them.

- The most popular cold soup is vichyssoise, which is prepared from potatoes and chives.
- Cold soups should be made the day before and refrigerated to allow the flavors to mingle.
- Be sure and chill the bowls or cups before serving cold soup.

Gazpacho

- Gazpacho is cold tomato and vegetable soup.
- The major vegetables are usually tomatoes, sweet red pepper and scallions.
- The seasonings seem to vary depending on the recipe used.
- $1/4$ cup of olive oil and 3 tablespoons of fresh lime, juice are always added.
- Traditionally it is served with white onions and bread cubes on the side.

Vichyssoise

- Normally prepared from leeks, onion, potatoes and unsalted butter.
- The soup should be boiled for 40 minutes, strained through a sieve and allowed to cool in the refrigerator before serving.
- Before serving most chefs add 1 cup of heavy cream to the soup as well as a sprinkling of fresh chopped chives.

CONSOMMÉ

- Clear, concentrated soup that has excellent flavor and can be used as a soup or stock base.
- Using ground beef and leeks help to improve the flavor.
- The main ingredients are usually meat and egg white
- Best to start with a quality strong stock or broth. Weak stocks need to be reduced more so that the flavors will be stronger.

For serious consommé makers, you will need a pot with a spigot on the bottom to drain off the finished consommé without bothering the "raft" on top. After you remove the consommé from the spigot it should be strained through a sieve or china cap.

- When adding the proteins, be sure that the stock is cold so that the proteins will not cook, as soon as they hit the stock.
- Using egg whites help trap small particles and help to improve the flavor.
- Always allow the consommé to come to a simmer very slowly, don't try and rush it.
- The raft that comes to the surface is composed of proteins, usually albumin.
- Be very careful not to allow the consommé to boil or it may break up the raft and infiltrate the consommé and making a lot more work to clarify the soup.
- Consommé should simmer for about $1^1/_2$-hours without disturbing the raft.
- Be sure and remove all fat from the surface.

CREAM SOUPS

- When making cream soups, try adding a small amount of flour to the milk to make it smoother.
- Simmer the soup until there is no starchy taste.
- Always thicken the soup before adding milk.
- When adding wine to cream soups it should be added just before serving or you risk curdling the soup.
- Never add cold milk or cream to simmering soup; always warm the milk or cream first.
- Best to temper the milk or cream on low heat, with some of the soup while you are warming it.
- The best wines for cream soup are sherry or dry white wine.
- When making tomato soup always puree the tomatoes separate from the milk or cream then add the puree very slowly to the milk or cream.

If you do add a dairy product to hot soup, do not allow it to boil or the dairy products will curdle.

- If curdling does happen, just strain the soup and place it in a blender on low for a few seconds then increase to high. Only fill the blender ½ full.
- Curdling can be reduced or even eliminated by just preparing a thin paste solution of flour and water and mix it into the milk or dairy product before adding it to the acid. The most common problem occurs when making tomato soup with milk.
- Never boil soup after you add milk or cream.

TOMATO SOUP

- A small amount of sugar should be added to tomato juice or tomato paste to bring out the flavor.
- A small amount of lemon juice added to the soup just before serving will bring out the flavor.
- If you are going to thicken the soup, never sue flour always use cornstarch.

Old Fashioned Cream of Tomato Soup

14 ounce can of whole tomatoes and the liquid
1 cup plain tomato juice
³/₄ cup non-fat milk
¹/₂ pound red potatoes, peeled and diced
1 cup finely chopped red onions
1¹/₄ cup red or yellow bell pepper, diced
3 tbsp. coriander, chopped
2 cloves of garlic, peeled and crushed
¹/₄ teaspoon fresh ground black pepper
1 slice of whole wheat bread
¹/₄ teaspoon salt

Using a medium saucepan, combine the whole tomatoes, their liquid, the tomato juice, bell peppers, onions, 2 tablespoons of coriander, garlic, black pepper, salt and the potatoes. Bring the mixture to a slow boil over medium heat; then cover the pan. Reduce the heat and allow the soup to simmer for 15 minutes. Remove the pan from the heat and allow it to cool for 6 minutes then place the mixture in a food processor and puree for about 1 minute or until it is smooth. Allow the machine to run and add the milk very slowly. Return the pureed mixture to the pan and cook only until it is hot (do not boil) then serve.

VEGETABLE SOUPS (general)

- For a richer flavor, mix 1 tablespoon of butter into the soup just before serving.
- When preparing vegetable soup, only pour enough water into the pot to just cover the vegetables by two inches of water.
- Using too much water in vegetable soup tends to make the soup watery.
- Carrots will give vegetable soup a sweet flavor.
- When adding mushrooms to vegetable soup, always sauté the mushrooms separately, and then add them to the soup just before serving for the best flavor.
- Always begin with a clear tasty stock or broth. Make sure that the stock or broth is not cloudy.
- Make sure that the vegetables selected go well with each other. The average is 5-6 different vegetables.
- Be sure and slice all vegetables uniformly.
- Always cook all vegetables separately in clarified butter.
- Cook all pasta separately from all other ingredients before adding to the soup.

- Never add tomatoes to the soup until after you have removed it from the heat.
- Overcooking vegetables is a common problem with vegetable soup. Vegetables should have the same consistency as they would have when served as a side dish.

STEWS

- Stews are basically prepared from almost any combination of meats, vegetables and seasonings you enjoy. Stew should always be relatively thick and not watery.

If you have a problem with tough stew meat, you may have added hot water when water was needed instead of cold water. Studies have shown that hot water added to boiling or simmering stew may cause the meat to become tough. Cold water does not have the same effect.

- To really thicken your stew sauce, just mix 2 tablespoons of potato starch in 3 tablespoons of water and add the mixture slowly, while stirring to the stew. If you do this for every cup of liquid in the stew it will really make it thick and good.

Mulligan's Irish Stew Recipe

2 pounds of potatoes, sliced to about $^1/_2$ inch thick
3 pounds of shoulder lamb, cut into 1-inch cubes
3 stalks of celery, chopped
2 medium carrots, chopped
4 large red onions, sliced into small chunks
$^1/_4$ teaspoon thyme
2 cloves garlic
1 teaspoon freshly ground black pepper
1 teaspoons salt
6 cups of pure cold water

Irish stew is normally prepared in layers. Using a large stew pot (or preferably a large, covered casserole that can be placed directly from the oven to the table), place a layer of potatoes on the bottom of the pot; then add a layer of onions and then the lamb (or other meat). Sprinkle on the seasonings and add the garlic cloves. Place any remaining onions on top of the lamb, then the rest of the potatoes on top of the onions. Add just enough cold water (about 4-5 cups) to cover the last layer of potatoes. Slowly bring the stew to a boil, cover the pot and reduce the heat and barely simmer for 1-2 hours. Stop the cooking as soon as the meat and vegetables are just tender and not overcooked and mushy.

If the water is evaporating, add a small amount at a time as it is being lost. Pre-heat the oven to 350° F. (176.7° C.) Place the stew into the oven and check regularly to be sure that it is not boiling; only simmering.

- To tenderize the meat in stew, just add $^1/_2$ cup of strong tea. The tannic acid will tenderize beef and not add flavor to the stew.
- A small amount of quick-cooking oats added to stew; will thicken it.
- If you have over-salted the stew, just add a can of peeled tomatoes or a small amount of brown sugar.

If you place 3-4 wine corks in your stew it will tenderize the meat. Cork contains a chemical that has the ability to tenderize meats. The chemical is activated and released when placed in hot liquid. Remove the corks before serving.

- When thickening stews, if you are using flour, be sure and sprinkle the flour over the meat and do not stir for about 3 minutes. This will eliminate the floury flavor and help brown the meat.
- Never allow stews to boil, you will lose flavor.

GELATIN

- If powdered gelatin is wrapped and stored properly in a cool, dry location it will last forever.
- A 1¼-ounce envelope of powdered gelatin is capable of gelling 2 cups of liquid.
- Gelatin must be soaked in a cold liquid for about 3-5 minutes before dissolving it. This will soften and activate the granules allowing them to dissolve efficiently when heated.

Gelatin will not set up if it is allowed to boil.

- Gelatin will not set up if you add certain foods, which contain enzymes that break gelatin down such as kiwi, papaya, pineapple, figs, guava and ginger root.
- If any of the harmful enzyme-containing foods are cooked or canned, the enzyme will be destroyed and the foods can be used.
- If you are going to make different layers of colored gelatin, be sure and wait until the first layer is good and sticky before placing the next layer on.
- Make sure that you rinse molds that will be used for gelatins with very cold water or spraying the insides with vegetable oil before adding the gelatin. This will make it easier to remove the mixture.

Too much gelatin produces a rubbery textured mixture.
- To speed up the setting up, just place the gelatin mixture in a larger bowl filled with ice cubes and cold water. Stir until the desired consistency is obtained.
- The freezer will usually set it up in about 20 minutes, but don't forget about it.
- If the gelatin sets too fast, just place the mold in a larger bowl filled with WARM water, then mix until the desired consistency is obtained.

STOCKS

Stocks are the basis of many soups and sauces. There are four basic stocks: brown, white, poultry and seafood. Stocks are prepared, from a liquid that fish, meats or poultry are cooked in. The liquid is then seasoned and usually cooked for 8-10 hours to assure that the flavors are adequately incorporated into the stock. The liquid is then removed leaving the flavored residue or stock. Stocks may be frozen and used as needed.

- Kosher salt is the preferred salt that most chefs use when preparing a stock.
- Kosher salt contains no additives, which may cause the stock to become cloudy.
- Salt is important to stock but should be added after it has cooked for 10 minutes. Salt has the tendency to concentrate and ruin the stock when added too early, especially as the liquid reduces.
- Salt will help draw the albumin (a protein) from the bones to keep the stock clear.

The bones and meat from older cows will have more flavor for stock and their bones will have 8 times more gelatin than their meat. The bones are more important to making stock than the meat.

- If you prefer to purchase stock in the supermarket, it may be sold under a number of different names; these include bouillon, broth or consommés.
- An excellent poultry stock can be made using the turkey carcass from thanksgiving dinner. If you don't have the time right away, just freeze the carcass, well wrapped in freezer paper. Try to use it within 2 months for the best results.

Preparing stocks in aluminum pots should be avoided. The aluminum tends to impart a bitter taste to stocks and will stain the pot if the stock is stored in it.

- Chefs always prefer veal bones when preparing stocks since they tend to provide a more delicate flavor than beef bones. Veal bones contain more collagen and therefore have a better thickening ability.
- Stocks are usually prepared from the liquid that fish, chicken or meats are cooked in.
- There are two types of canned broth to choose from, they are, <u>ready-to-serve</u>, which has liquid added and <u>condensed</u>, which requires that you add the liquid.
- Stock should be kept frozen until needed, especially if it contains an animal product.

- Next time you prepare soup or stock, try placing a pasta basket into the pot, or just use a large pasta pot. The basket can be removed and will contain many of the ingredients you may wish to dispose of or keep.
- Always use cold water, which is usually more pure than hot water. Hot water tends to leach more impurities from water pipes and may give the stock an off-flavor.
- Make sure that all fat has been trimmed off before adding meats to the stockpot.
- Hot water added to gelatin should never be over 180° F. (82.2° C.) for the best results. If your recipe calls for an equal amount of sugar to gelatin, the cold, water step is not required since the sugar will stop the clumping. However, you still never pour hot water into gelatin, always place the gelatin into the water.

Always simmer with the pot uncovered. Condensation may affect the final result. Stock should never be boiled or it may become cloudy.

- When you simmer bones to extract the flavor, it may create foam on the surface, which is composed of a protein (albumin) and a number of impurities (mineral residues) that are released from the bone. This foam is usually bitter and needs to be completely removed. Even leaving a hint of the foam may alter the desired taste.

- If you are really in a hurry and need a stock that can easily be prepared in about 30 minutes, the following should solve your problem:

Recipe for Speedy Stock

2 cans of a low-salt broth
1 teaspoon of beef stock
1¹/₂ cans of pure water
1 medium carrot, chopped small
1 large stalk of celery, chopped
¹/₂ large onion, sliced
¹/₈ teaspoon thyme
¹/₈ teaspoon celery powder

- Place all the ingredients in a large saucepan and bring to a slow boil, then reduce the heat and simmer uncovered for about 20-30 minutes. Strain the stock through a fine sieve.
- Salt should not be added to stock during the first 10 minutes of cooking time.
- Salt helps draw the albumen (protein) from the bones, which will keep the stock clear.
- Always simmer stock with the pot uncovered. Condensation may affect the final product.
- Never boil stock or it may become cloudy.

Make sure that you do not stir stock more than 3 times during the first hour or it may become cloudy.

- The bones provide gelatin for the stock, which is important.
- Never cover stock since this may cause an increase in bacteria around the lid.

- Gelatin from the bones is important, since the stock should become completely gelled when cooled down. The stock can be spooned as needed.
- Stocks should be kept frozen until needed, especially if they contain an animal product.

- If refrigerated for storage, stock can be kept for about 6 days. For more than 6 days in the refrigerator the stock should be boiled for 8-10 minutes before using.

When dissolving dry gelatin, never pour hot water directly on the gelatin. This causes clumping and reduces the ability of the gelatin to dissolve properly. Try using a small amount of cold water until they are dissolved, then add the additional hot water.

- When the stock is finished, you should strain it once only through a fine mesh strainer before refrigerating for 2-3 hours.
- Remove the stock and skim off the fat that has risen to the top, producing an almost fat-free broth with the flavor intact.
- Canned broth should be placed into the refrigerator overnight to allow the fat to rise. Remove the fat before using for a low fat broth.
- If your gelatin develops a thick rubbery skin it is probably because it sat out in the air too long without being covered. The only other reason is that it has aged too long before being used.
- The stock is the residue leftover after the liquid has been removed and is very flavorful.

Brown Stock

- Brown stock is usually prepared from beef or veal bones, which are grilled producing a rich brown color and are included in the initial stages of preparation whenever possible.
- Veal bones are preferred for brown stock since they have better flavor.
- Brown stock can be reduced until it is syrupy or even very dark, if desired. Brown stock is usually very concentrated and very little is needed to flavor sauce. It is easy to overpower with a brown sauce and detract from the flavor of the dish. Any stock can be more concentrated the more you boil it down.
- Use a tall pot to reduce evaporation.

Brown Stock Recipe

3¹/₂ pounds beef shank (butcher will easily supply)
3 tablespoons of vegetable oil
3 red onions, sliced
4 fresh celery stalks, diced
3 medium carrots, sliced
4 sprigs of parsley, whole
8 fresh peppercorns
4 quarts pure water
2 bay leaves
1 ³/₄ teaspoons of sea salt (iodized salt is OK)
¹/₂ teaspoon ground black pepper
¹/₂ teaspoon dried thyme

Step One:

- Using a large pan with 1¹/₂ to 2 inch sides, add the vegetable oil and the beef bones that have been broken into chunks and bake in a 450° F. (232.2° C.) oven until they are brown, turning occasionally.
- This should take about 10 minutes.
- When the bones are brown add the onions, carrots and celery to the mixture and bake until the vegetables start to brown. Remove from the oven.

Step Two:

- Place the mixture into a large pot. Add one cup of boiling water to the baking pan and scrape all the residues into the water. Add this to the large pot; then add the thyme, bay leaves, peppercorns, parsley and 4 quarts of water.
- Bring the stock to a slow boil (using with cold water) over medium heat, then reduce the heat and allow the stock to simmer for 5 hours.
- Remove any fat that rises to the top for the first hour using a piece of white bread as a sponge or a thin wooden spoon. Remove from the heat and strain the mixture.
- Allow the stock to cool to room temperature. Stock will freeze for 6-8 months but will only last for a few days in the refrigerator. If any more fat rises to the top, allow it to remain until you are ready to use the stock, then remove it. The fat will protect the stock from outside contamination.

Chicken Stock

- Chicken stock is a clear liquid prepared from chicken parts and simmered with vegetables, herbs and spices.
- Always use a tall pot to reduce evaporation.
- The cooking should be started in cold water, which will improve the extraction of flavors.
- Use overripe vegetables to add flavor and utilize the soluble pectin that have developed.

Fish Stock

- Fish stock is prepared from fish bones and poached fish or shellfish.
- If you sauté the bones and vegetables first it will improve the flavor that will be released.
- The intensity of the flavor of fish stock is totally dependent on the quality of the fish not the cooking time. However, if you cook the stock for more than 20 minutes it will usually become bitter. If you want to cook it longer start with a larger amount.
- Ripe or even overripe vegetables provide more flavor to fish stock.

Steps to Clarify Stock

1. Stock needs to be strained through a piece of cheesecloth or very fine sieve.
2. For each quart of stock add 1 beaten egg and a crumpled up eggshell. Stir the egg and eggshell into the stock and bring to a slow simmer (do not stir). Foam will form on the surface as the heat rises.
3. Allow the stock to simmer for 15 minutes, remove from the heat and allow the stock to rest for 30 minutes.
4. Gently move the crusty foam aside and spoon the stock into a sieve lined with 3 layers of lightly moistened cheesecloth.

Vegetable Stock

- Vegetable stock is prepared from onions, carrots and celery, then flavored with garlic and other herbs. The formula is usually 60% onions, 20% celery and 20% carrots.

Strong-flavored vegetables are usually not used to prepare stock.

- Dark-colored bones are too deteriorated to be used in stock.

White or Veal Stock

- Originally prepared with only veal bones, providing a clear stock that contains very little flavor of its own. The stock, however, is now made with either veal, beef or poultry bones or a combination of all three.

White Stock Recipe

4 pounds of bones, broken into small chunks (meaty if possible)
1 cup red onions, chopped
2 large carrots, chopped
5 celery stalks, chopped
3 cloves of fresh crushed garlic
2 bay leaves
$1/_2$ teaspoon thyme
3 cloves
1 easpoon black peppercorns
Small bunch of parsley
Add salt to taste

Place the bones in a large stockpot and cover the bones with water to about 4 inches above the top of the bones. Cover the pot and bring to a boil, then pour off the water with foam and residues. Cover with water again to the same level and simmer for 7 hours, adding cold water as the water evaporates. Continually skim the surface to remove the foam and debris. Only stir the pot 2-3 times to make sure that the bones do not stick to the bottom of the pot.

Add the vegetables about 2 hours before the cooking time is completed then add all the seasonings 30 minutes before the end. Cover a large bowl with three layers of cheesecloth and strain the stock. Discard all the bones and vegetables. Cool the stock as rapidly as possible. The stock will keep for about 2-3 days in the refrigerator and may be frozen for 4-6 months.

NOTE:
- Most quality stock bases are not sold in markets. A 1-pound jar of base is capable of making 5 gallons of stock. However, the better brands of bases are almost all sold directly to restaurants and chefs. One of the best stock bases; is produced by the L. J. Minor Corporation, Cleveland, Ohio.

Blanching Bones for Stocks

- The bones first need to be rinsed in cold water. All blood and residues need to be removed.
- Do not use fresh bones.
- The bones should be placed in a stockpot and covered with cold water.
- Don't start the bones in hot water; it slows down the extraction.
- Bring the water to a boil and allow any impurities to rise to the surface as foam.
- Skim the surface frequently to remove the foam.
- The bones should be drained and rinsed well before being placed in the stockpot.

SOLVING STOCK PROBLEMS

THE STOCK IS LOSING TOO MUCH WATER, TOO FAST

- Use a tall, narrow pot to reduce evaporation.

THE STOCK DOES NOT HAVE ENOUGH FLAVOR

- Starting with cold water will increase the level of flavor extraction.
- Ripe or overripe vegetables will add additional flavor.
- Pectin; adds flavor and is more available and is easier to extract in older vegetables.

THE STOCK IS TOO GREASY AND CLOUDY

- The stock was probably allowed to boil and the fat emulsified.
- The foam was not removed at regular intervals.
- The stock was stirred too much causing the fat to emulsify.

GLAZES

- Glazes are actually just a stock that has been reduced to a point that it will coat the back of a spoon. They are used as flavorings in many sauces and used in moderation since they are a concentrated source of flavoring. Glazes are the original bases and are still thought of as a base.

- Even though the glaze has been reduced from a stock, it will not taste like the stock. The types of glazes are basically the same as the stock they were prepared from such as, chicken, meat or fish.

Guidelines for preparing a glaze

- The stock should be reduced over medium heat.
- The surface should be skimmed frequently to remove any debris or skin.
- When reducing by at least $1/2$ a small saucepan should be used.
- Continue reducing over low heat until the glaze is syrupy and coats the back of the spoon.
- Glazes will store well in the refrigerator for at least 3-4 weeks if not contaminated and sealed well. Glazes may also be frozen for 2-3 months.

CHAPTER 18

PERFECT GRAVIES & SAUCES

GRAVY

- Gravy differs from a sauce in that it is usually prepared from ingredients derived from the dish it will accompany.

- Add a pinch of salt to the flour and mix it in well and the flour will not lump up when liquid is added to it.
- If you would like nice brown gravy, just add 1 teaspoon of hot instant coffee. It will not flavor the gravy.
- Too much flour will ruin gravy.
- To eliminate the floury flavor in gravy, just place the flour you are going to use in a baking pan and bake at 350°F until the flour in a nice brown color.
- Gravy is best and more flavorful if you use pan-drippings, since it contains the flavor of the meat.

- Onion skins added to gravy while it is cooking will give the gravy a nice brown color. Remove before serving.
- High-fat gravy will have a better consistency if you add ¹/₄ teaspoon of baking soda to it.

- If you put too much salt in the gravy add ¼ teaspoon of brown sugar to neutralize it.
- If gravy has a high-starch content, never add baking soda or the gravy will turn black.

- A pinch or two of baking soda will keep the gravy from separating.
- One teaspoon of smooth peanut butter will remove the taste of burnt gravy without imparting the peanut butter taste to the gravy.
- Gravy will thicken as it cools and should be served medium thickness.
- Use de-fatted broth to increase the volume if you need more gravy.

Turkey Gravy

- Turkey gravy is usually prepared from the giblets or pan roasting liquid. The gravy of a stew or goulash is part of the dish itself.
- The turkey drippings in the bottom of the pan are used after the fat has been siphoned off.
- When cooking the giblets, add an onion to flavor the juices.
- The scrapings from the bottom of the roasting pan are used to flavor the gravy.
- The pan juices are usually added to the giblet stock.
- Flour is added to the proper consistency.

SAUCES

Sauces are only meant to complement the flavor or provide moisture for the dish. Sauces should never detract from the original flavor of the food. French cooking schools classify sauces in five categories: Espagnole, which is a brown, stock-based sauce; Velote, which is a light, stock-based sauce; Béchamel, which is a white sauce and usually milk-based; Hollandaise or mayonnaise, which are emulsified sauces and Vinaigrette, which is considered an oil and vinegar sauce. However, we place mayonnaise in the condiment class because it is usually always purchased as a commercial product and vinaigrette as a salad dressing.

- To thicken any sauce, you will need to increase the solids and reduce the amount of liquid. This can be accomplished by boiling away some of the liquid, however, this will reduce the amount of useable sauce and may concentrate the flavors too much.
- If the sauce is high in water content, cooling it causes the water molecules to lose energy and they relax, thus thickening the sauce.
- There are, however, a number of good substances that will thicken sauces and depending on the type of sauce you are preparing one will surely be just right for the job. These include; pureed vegetables, egg yolk, flours, gelatins, tapioca, pectin, okra, cornstarch, arrowroot, potato starch, kneaded butter, emulsified butter, cream, peanut butter, etc.

COMMON THICKENING AGENTS

Arrowroot

- Purchased as a fine powder that is derived from the root stalks of a tropical tuber. It is prepared by dissolving a small amount in water.
- These stems are mainly composed of complex carbohydrates, which has the tendency to thicken at a lower cooking temperature than most other starches.
- The advantage of arrowroot is that there is less likely the chance of burning the thickener due to its low protein content.

Cornstarch

- Produced from the endosperm of a kernel of corn and should always be dissolved in water before using for the best results.

File Powder

Originally prepared by the Choctaw Indians in Louisiana and shared with the Creoles to thicken their stews.

- Prepared from ground dried leaves of the sassafras tree.
- Best used, in gumbo, but should be added after it has been cooked to individual serving dishes.
- Never add file powder to gumbo while it is cooking or it may become stringy and ruin the gumbo.

Pectin

- When using pectin in preserves, be sure and only use the pectin specified in the recipe.
- Different brands are prepared with different ingredients that will make a difference in the final product.
- Some pectin needs acid and sugar to set, while others need acid and a small amount of sugar. Some pectin never needs acid or sugar to set.

Tapioca

- Extracted from the tropical cassava root and best used as a thickener if it is diluted with water before being added to a dish just before serving.
- The roots are finely grated, left to ferment, then pressed into cakes and baked. The baked cakes are then powdered into a pure starch.
- Tapioca is best when it is moistened, then heated and immediately used.

Vegetable puree

- A healthier method of thickening gravies and sauces. Purees may be made with any assortment of vegetables that compliment the dish it is to be used in.
- Vegetables need to be cooked first; some need to be sautéed fist then pureed in a blender or food processor.
- Use as little added liquid as possible when making purees.
- Make sure that all seeds have been removed. One tomato seed can cause bitterness.
- Once the vegetables are pureed, they should be put through a sieve or fine mesh before using.

A relatively new thickener Thick & Easy® is now available. The thickener is made from modified food starch and maltodextrim with no additives or preservatives. The product can be used to thicken any type of cold or hot food, either solids or liquids. The product can be frozen and reheated by microwave oven. The thickening activity stops after one minute and it retains its consistency. It is fully digestible, does not bind fluids, releasing 98% for consumption, while most competitive products only release 50%. For additional information call (800) 866-7757.

Textra™

- One of the better commercial thickeners is Textra™. Textra™ is a modified tapioca starch that has been designed to improve mouthfeel and texture of foods.
- It does not impart any taste to the product while providing thickening for drinks, sauces and syrups.
- It is one of the more stable thickeners and will assist particles, such as fruit pulp to remain in suspension.

ClearJel® and Rice Gel®

- There are two "jel" products that will do a great thickening job. These are ClearJel-310® and Rice Gel®.
- ClearJel-310® will thicken as soon as it is added to either water or milk and will provide a smooth, fully hydrated texture as well as being heat and acid resistant.
- Rice Gel® is produced from pre-cooked rice flour with no noticeable taste of its own. It has a high water capacity and blends well with dry foods and is non-allergenic.

Thickening a sauce

- If the food is thickened with a root starch, such as arrowroot or tapioca they can be frozen and thawed without any problem.

- The easiest method to thicken a sauce is to prepare a small amount of "paste." The paste should be prepared separate from the sauce.

- Never try and add the paste ingredients to the sauce to hasten the procedure. The paste needs to be smooth and the consistency will vary depending on the level of thickening needed. If the sauce is very thin, you will need a thick paste, etc.

- Add the paste gradually, allow the sauce to boil and stir until the desired texture is obtained. These pastes will work especially well with gravy and most other sauces.

  Thin Paste ......Use 1 tablespoon ....flour + 1 cup of liquid
  Medium Paste ...Use 2 tablespoons ...flour + 1 cup of liquid
  Thick Paste ......Use 3 tablespoons ...flour + 1 cup of liquid

- If your recipe calls for egg yolks, never add them to a sauce that is too hot. The instant change in temperature, resulting from placing the cool egg into the hot liquid is just enough of a change to curdle the egg yolk and may ruin the sauce.
- Flour will not lump if you add it to any fat that is already hot. In fact, you can add flour to any hot liquid without the flour lumping.
- Regular flour tends to turn into a form of gelatin when it comes into contact with hot water. It tends to block the water from entering. Instant flour contains smaller irregular-shaped granules that allow space for the water to enter.
- High heat will melt the butter too fast and ruin the emulsification in a saucer and cause separation. You want the butter to turn into a foamy mixture, not a liquid. Start with cold butter, which will keep the mixture cool and reduces the risk of the butter melting instead of foaming. Keep the pan moving on and off the heat if necessary while beating the butter with a whisk.
- You can also use a double boiler, which is easier for the person who is not used to making a white sauce.
- To eliminate the potential problem of adding egg yolks, just remove a small amount of the sauce and allow it to cool for a few minutes before mixing the egg yolk in. This is called tempering and the cooled sauce can then be added to the hot mixture.

- Sauces are never served hot, always warm.
- When sauce is finished cooking, it should fall from the whisk in a wide ribbon or sheet. This should take about 5 minutes of cooking.
- Most sauces and custards that are thickened with flour or cornstarch do not freeze well. The starch, amylase, which is commonly found in grain starches such as wheat flour and cornstarch tend to freeze into a very firm, spongy-texture and allows the liquid to drain out.

- If you accidentally burn your dessert sauce, don't fret just add a small amount of pure vanilla or almond extract in the sauce to cover up the burnt taste.

Egg-Based Sauces

- If your egg-based sauce separates, remove the pan from the heat and beat in two tablespoons of crushed ice to reduce the heat and place the eggs back into suspension, thus saving the emulsion.
- You can also change pans and add one tablespoons of ice water to a small amount of the sauce while slowly whisking back the balance of the separated sauce. Additional ice water can be added slowly, but only as needed.

Cornstarch, Arrowroot and Potato Starch

- Cornstarch, arrowroot and potato starch should only be used just before you are finishing the sauce, since they have twice the thickening power of flour and can only be cooked for a few minutes before losing their thickening power.

Starch Granules

- Starch granules, are a solid, which just by being there will cause a certain degree of thickening. However, the small starch granules tend to trap water molecules, thus reducing the percentage of free-flowing water that is in the sauce or soup. When you heat the starch it has the ability to expand and is capable of absorbing even more water.

Nervous Pudding

Kids call gelatin "nervous pudding" because it always shaking. Gelatin has been used as one of the primary thickeners for hundreds of years and is capable of increasing ten times its original size. Gelatin is the best water-trapping medium we have found. Care, however, must be taken when adding other ingredients to gelatin. Sugar reduces the absorption capacity of gelatin significantly and fruits such as pineapple and papaya, which contains the enzyme bromelain and papain will almost eliminate gelatin's thickening ability.

HOW TO MAKE RAW EGGS SAFE FOR A SAUCE OR DRESSING

- Since eggs may be contaminated even if they are not cracked, it would be wise to microwave the eggs to be sure that there is no contamination before you make the sauce. The procedure will not harm the eggs and they will still be in good shape for the sauce. The procedure can only be done with 2 large yolks at a time and in a 600-watt microwave oven.

The first step is to separate the egg yolks from the white and remove the cord. Then place the yolks in a small glass bowl and beat them until they are well mixed. Next, add 2 teaspoons of real lemon juice and mix thoroughly. The bowl should then be covered and placed into a microwave on high and the surface observed. When the surface starts to move allow the mixture to cook for no more than 10 seconds. Remove the bowl and whisk with a clean whisk. Return the bowl to the microwave and cook until the surface moves again and then cook another 10 seconds. Remove and whisk again using a clean whisk. Allow the bowl to sit for one minute before you use it for the sauce and it will be salmonella free.

- When melting cheese, never cook it for too long a period or at too high a temperature. When this occurs, the protein separates from the fat and the cheese gets tough and rubbery.
- Once a cheese hardens, especially in a sauce, it would be wise to discard the sauce and start over. When you melt cheese, it would be wise to grate the cheese first. The cheese will then melt in a shorter period of cooking time.
- The reason cheese tends to form lumps or strings, is that the calcium phosphate present in the cheese binds with the protein. This can be avoided if a small amount of wine, which contains tartaric acid, is added to the melting cheese. The tartaric acid prevents the calcium phosphate from linking the cheese proteins. If you prefer not to use wine, just use a small amount of lemon juice and the citric acid will accomplish the same thing.

Occasionally, sauces tend to taste a bit bitter and the reason escapes you. It may be from a tomato seed or two that ended up not being strained out. As little as one tomato seed can ruin a sauce.

Barbecue Sauce

- Barbecue sauces are prepared to provide a particular flavor to the food and is usually brushed on meat and chicken. They are not designed to tenderize the food and do not penetrate very deeply into the food. Almost all barbecue sauces contain oil, which keeps the surface of the food moist and helps avoid burning. The sauce is applied a number of times during the cooking process with a natural bristle brush or a special barbecue brush.

Grandma's Barbecue Sauce Recipe

1 cups ketchup or seasoned tomato sauce
2 tablespoons of extra virgin olive oil (cold pressed)
1 teaspoon canola oil
$^1/_2$ cup finely diced red onion
1 cloves of garlic, finely minced
$^1/_2$ cup unsulfured molasses
$^1/_4$ cup apple cider vinegar
1 teaspoon powdered cayenne pepper
1 tablespoon lemon juice
$^1/_4$ cup quality mustard
1 teaspoon soy sauce

Using a medium-sized pan, heat the olive oil with the small amount of canola oil (to raise the smoke point) over medium heat. Stir in the garlic and onion and sauté for 6-8 minutes before adding the rest of the ingredients. Mix the balance of the ingredients into the sauce, then allow it to simmer for about 15-20 minutes. The sauce may be applied either warm or cold.

Oriental Teriyaki Barbecue Sauce

$^1/_2$ cup beef or chicken stock
1 tablespoons low-salt soy sauce
2 teaspoon granulated sugar
$^1/_2$ cup dry vermouth (optional)
3 tablespoons lemon or lime juice
4 tablespoon minced ginger
$^1/_4$ teaspoon red pepper (optional)

Combine all ingredients and whisk well until blended. Lasts about 10 days in the refrigerator.

- Commercial teriyaki sauce should contain the following ingredients if the quality is superior: soy sauce, dried garlic, concentrated pear or grape sweetener, dried onion, sesame seed, garlic powder, ginger powder, onion powder and natural vegetable gum. There should be no added salt.

SPEEDY, ALMOST INSTANT SAUCES

Beef Sauce

- Whisk 1 cup of heavy cream with 2 tablespoons of mild horseradish sauce, $1^1/_2$ tablespoons of lemon juice and a small amount of salt and pepper as desired.

Chicken Sauce

- In a small saucepan on low heat, whisk 8 ounces of sour cream with one can of cream of mushroom soup, then add one cup of de-fatted chicken broth.

Fish Sauce

- Whisk together, one cup of mayonnaise with 2 tablespoons of minced sweet pickles, 1-tablespoon of minced onions and 1 tablespoon of minced stuffed green olives.

Lamb Sauce

- In a small saucepan over low heat, melt one cup of mint jelly with one cup of pure, pulp free orange juice and one tablespoon of mild prepared mustard.
- Heat and serve warm.

Low-fat Sauce

- Combine one can of quality light evaporated milk with one package of onion soup mix and one tablespoon of cornstarch in a small saucepan over low heat.
- Whisk in your favorite minced herbs or onion, remove from the heat and add one cup of non-fat sour cream.

Pork Sauce

- In a small saucepan over low heat, melt one cup of current jelly with $^1/_2$ cup of ketchup and 1 teaspoon of pineapple juice. Serve warm.

Vegetable Sauces

- Melt 6 or more ounces of Velveeta with just enough milk to make a smooth mixture, serve while it is warm.
- Slowly melt 6 or more ounces of regular or any flavored cream cheese with a small amount of milk on low heat in a small saucepan.
- Whisk one pint of heavy cream and one cup of mayonnaise and blend well.

Caramel Sauce

- The recipe usually calls for 1 cup of sugar, $\frac{1}{2}$ cup boiling water, dash of salt, $\frac{1}{2}$ teaspoon of vanilla and 1 cup of heavy cream.
- Use a heavy-bottomed saucepan.
- The sugar should always be heated over low heat and stirred constantly until it just slightly brown and melts. Any further and it may burn.
- Add the boiling water very slowly and stir until the sugar melts, then add the salt and cool slightly.
- Slowly add the heavy cream and vanilla and stir continuously.
- Use a wooden spoon or one with a plastic handle since the heat will get bad when the sugar starts to brown.
- The boiling water needs to be in a pot with a long handle. Add the water drop by drop and make sure that your hands are not over the saucepan with the sugar. A hot vapor will rise from the sugar that can burn your hands.
- If the sugar hardens, just keep stirring and it will melt again, but you may have to add a few more tablespoons of water.

Never make caramel sauce in humid weather.

- Be sure that the sugar you use is 100% free of contaminants to prevent crystallization.
- To make sure that the color is correct, drop a small amount on a white plate.
- Once the caramel is finished, don't stir it any further or it may crystallize.

De-glazing

- Place a liquid into a pan that has had meat cooked in it to dissolve cooked particles that remain after the food was removed.
- Common liquids used to de-glaze are wines, soups and stocks.
- After the liquid is added, the liquid is reduced by about $\frac{1}{2}$ to $\frac{3}{4}$ to concentrate it.

Emulsified Butter Sauces

- Too much heat destroys these sauces, melts the butter and ruins the emulsification.
- Always start with cold butter and add cold or at least cool butter at every stage of preparation.
- A double boiler is a safer pot to use to avoid too high a heat melting the butter prematurely.
- Keep the sauce warm at all times.
- Once the sauce has cooled it should be discarded.
- Butter should always be added slowly while continually whisking and creaming.

Hollandaise Sauce

Be sure and use a stainless steel bowl when preparing hollandaise sauce for the best results.

- A quick hollandaise sauce can be made in a blender by placing 3 egg yolks, 2 tablespoons of fresh lemon juice and a pinch of cayenne pepper into the blender and blend for about 10 seconds. While the blender is running very slowly add 1/4 pound of warm butter that has been melted and forced through a fine sieve. Continue to blend until the mixture has thickened.
- Make sure that you cool the reduction before the yolks are added or they will overcook.
- Always use the freshest eggs possible.
- The eggs should be beaten over heat, but don't scramble them.
- The butter should only be warm and added very slowly when you start adding them.
- If you would like a hollandaise sauce that can be prepared in 10 minutes or less, try Knorr® Hollandaise Sauce Mix. The ingredients include: modified food starch, wheat flour, non-fat dry milk, hydrolyzed vegetable protein, partially hydrogenated peanut oil, lactose, salt, fructose, onion and garlic powder, citric acid, vegetable gum, yeast extract, soup stock, spices and a natural flavor. It really is not too bad tasting, but nothing like the "made-from-scratch" original.
- To prepare a "mock" hollandaise sauce, just use 1 cup of white sauce and add 2 slightly beaten egg yolks and cook until just 2 bubbles (not 3 or 4) appear on the surface. Remove the pot from the hot burner and beat in 2 tablespoons of unsalted butter and 2 tablespoons of pure lemon juice. Voila, fake hollandaise sauce that will fool everyone but a chef.

In a classic hollandaise sauce the butter should be cold and should not be allowed to melt, just be creamy.

Mayonnaise

- Any oil can be used to prepare mayonnaise.
- Be sure that when you start the beaters and bowl are grease-free and dry.
- Many chefs actually boil their bowl and beaters in a mixture of 3 cups of water to 1 cup of white vinegar before making mayonnaise. Dry them with a fresh towel or paper towel.
- For the best oil choose an oil that is refined (such as soy or corn oil). Unrefined oil such as cold-pressed olive oil can have a negative affect on the separation of the emulsion.
- When beginning, add the oil drop by drop. This allows the emulsification to form the way that it should.
- When the mixture starts to thicken the oil can then be added in a slow, steady stream.
- Adding oil too quickly will cause the sauce to separate.

If the sauce separates while you are preparing it, just add 1 teaspoon of white vinegar to the sauce and mix it in thoroughly.

- Lemon juice can be blended in just before serving if a sharper taste is desired.
- Always serve mayonnaise at room temperature for the best flavor.
- If the mayonnaise curdles, just drip in some hot boiling water and mix continuously until it goes back into suspension.
- The starting ingredients should be at room temperature.
- Mayonnaise will remain fresh in the refrigerator for about 2 months but does not freeze well.

- A small amount of dry mustard or cayenne powder will assist in keeping the oil droplets separated.
- If your mayonnaise has a "breakdown", place the mayonnaise in a clean bowl and mix in 1-2 tablespoons of warm (not boiling) water, then pour the mayonnaise into another clean bowl and whisk the water in until the mayonnaise emulsifies again.
- When the temperature or humidity is high, the mayonnaise will be heavier and greasier than you are used to.
- Fresh mayonnaise will only remain fresh for 3 days.

Standard Mayonnaise Recipe:

1 egg yolks (large)
1 teaspoon of lemon juice
2 cup extra virgin olive oil (cold pressed)
3 teaspoon quality mustard (your favorite)
¹/₈ teaspoon crushed sea salt (if desired)
¹/₈ teaspoon freshly ground black pepper (if desired)

Combine the egg yolks, lemon juice, mustard, salt and pepper in a bowl and whisk. After they are blended, add the oil a few drops at a time, allowing the mixture to thicken and obtain a yellowish-white color. Then continue to add the balance of the oil slowly in a thin stream. If the mixture becomes too thick, add small amount of lemon juice to thin it out.

- Try diluting the egg yolks with water and lemon juice. This will make it easier to heat the eggs without the risk of curdling.
- If you add a small amount of salt to the egg yolks it will be easier to make the emulsion and it will be thicker.

Pesto

- When preparing pesto sauce place the basil leaves, garlic, pine nuts, olive oil and salt in a blender and be sure to only blend to a paste consistency. Do not allow it to become smooth and creamy.

The best pesto is prepared in a mortar and pestle, crushing and blending the ingredients the old fashioned way.

- Parmesan and Romano cheeses are added to the pesto paste as soon as it has been blended.
- A small amount of the pasta cooking water can be added to the pesto sauce just before serving if you wish to thin it out somewhat.
- In Italy a small amount of pesto is added to many different sauces, stews and soups.
- Freeze leftover pesto in ice cube trays, then remove, place in a plastic bag and freeze.

Reduction Sauces (general information)

- Make sure that the sauce is not too spicy or it will overpower the main dish.
- Wine is frequently used and should be a good quality wine for the best results.
- Make sure that as much fat as possible has been removed before adding wine.
- To prevent any curdling of cream, pour the wine into the hot pan and bring to a boil.
- Remove the sauce from the heat and then re-heat or the water lost from continual cooking over low heat can cause separation.
- If separation does occur, remove from the heat and quickly stir in one tablespoon of water.

Roux

- Made from butter and flour and is the base for many sauces.
- Use a heavy saucepan; this will reduce the chances of scorching the roux.
- As soon as you complete the roux, take the pan off the fire and allow it to cool slightly.
- Low heat is always used when preparing brown roux and cooked until it becomes a nice light brown color and has a somewhat nutty aroma.
- Medium heat is used for preparing white roux.
- Follow your recipe; there must be adequate fat to coat all the starch granules of the flour.
- White roux is not really white, but more yellow due to the butter.

Adding a Liquid to a Roux/Sauce

- Liquid can be added at this point depending on the sauce you are preparing. Make sure that you whisk continually and rapidly as you add the liquid.
- The liquid added may be hot or cool but never cold.
- Cold liquid will cause the fat to harden.
- If the liquid added is too hot it may cause splattering or cause lumps to form.
- The roux will not become the thickness you want until it almost reaches the boiling point.
- Make sure that you simmer the sauce until there is no more flour taste.
- If you melt a thin layer of butter on top, a film will not form if you are going to store it for a while before using it.

Adding Roux to a Liquid

- Cook the sauce in a heavy pot and bring to a simmer.
- Roux should be added very slowly and beat well to break up the lumps.
- Add more roux slowly and heat until the sauce has reached the consistency you desire. The thickness of the sauce will depend on the length of time it is heated and how close to boiling.
- Make sure all the starchy taste has been removed before using.

Rubs

- Dry rubs are usually prepared from a combination of herbs and spices, which are sprinkled on the meat or rubbed in.
- Wet rubs require a liquid such as oil, which is combined with spices and rubbed into the meat.
- Dry rub spices that seem to be the most popular are cayenne, chili powder, paprika and garlic to provide a somewhat hot spicy flavor to the exterior of the meat. The meat must be moist, however, to allow these spices to adhere and remain for the balance of the cooking time.
- If you want a liquid rub to enter the meat and flavor it, just add a small amount of white vinegar or lemon juice to the rub. The acid will act as a carrier and penetrate the meat.
- Best not to use salt in a rub since it will enter the meat and has the tendency to dry the meat out.
- Remember never overpower the meat with a rub.
- Never use refined white sugar in a rub since it dissolves too easily. The recommended sugar is turbinado sugar, which has a somewhat molasses flavor.

Garlic Rub

¹/₄ cup of extra virgin olive oil
4-5 cloves of fresh garlic (crushed)
1 tablespoons of fresh parsley (finely chopped)
1 teaspoon (or less) cayenne pepper

The crushed garlic, cayenne pepper and the parsley are mixed together, then the olive oil is added slowly while mixing. Store in a well-sealed glass jar.

Salad Dressings

- Salad dressing should be placed on salad just before serving. The vinegar in some dressings has the ability to wilt the lettuce if allowed to remain on too long.
- If you are preparing an oil and vinegar dressing, empty the contents of one or two ampoules of lecithin into the dressing and shake vigorously. The salad will then remain in suspension.
- Add a small amount of white wine to the vinegar before the oil is mixed in will assist in binding the dressing.

Cold salad dressings lose a high percentage of their flavor and aroma. Dressing should be served at room temperature.

- One part wine vinegar; to three parts oil is the standard ratio.
- To prepare vinaigrette, add 3 parts of virgin olive oil to 1 part of apple cider vinegar or fresh lemon or lime, juice.
- To lighten up heavy vinaigrette, just add 2 teaspoons of boiling water to the dressing after it emulsifies.
- Wine can be used to replace vinegar or lemon juice in most dressing recipes. Red wine vinegar would be an excellent choice.
- Make your salad dressing right on the salad by just adding the oil on the salad and mixing it so that the oil coats the greens, then sprinkle the vinegar and it will stick to the greens.

Sauce Béarnaise

- The most common problem is overheating. One of two problems may occur; first is if the egg protein is overheated it will coagulate forming small curds in a sauce that is supposed to be creamy. The second problem is that of the emulsion separating.
- The coagulation problem can be solved, by adding a small amount of vinegar to lower the pH.

White Sauces

There are two types of white sauces: Béchamel, which is made from whole milk or cream and Veloute, which is made from chicken or fish stock to be sure it retains a white color. In France béchamel sauce is called the "mother sauce" since all other sauces are prepared from this base. The béchamel sauce originated in 1605 by Duke Phillipe DeMornay.

- Cajun roux is cooked until the mixture of flour and fat turns black but does not burn. This is a very slow process.
- The basic white sauce begins with a "roux." Roux; is made by cooking flour and clarified butter before adding a liquid.

PREPARING THE PERFECT WHITE SAUCE:

- When you stir the liquid into the roux and lumps are formed, strain the mixture through a fine sieve before continuing.
- If the sauce is too thick, add a small amount of liquid while stirring slowly. If too thin, just simmer longer until it thickens.
- If you are preparing the white sauce and need to allow it to sit for a period of time, rub the top of the sauce lightly with the end of a stick of butter. This will result in a thin layer of melted butter on the top preventing a skin from forming.
- If a skin does form, skim it off carefully to remove it all.
- The roux should be foamy and very light in color.
- When the liquid is added it should be added all at once while whisking continually until the sauce begins to boil.
- The heat should then be reduced and the sauce simmered for 5-6 minutes. This step will eliminate the flavor of any uncooked flour.
- The liquid should be very hot before being added to the roux. If this is done then the whisking time will be reduced.

If any lumps occur when whisking the liquid into the roux the sauce needs to be strained through a very fine sieve.

- If the sauce is too thin it needs to be simmered until the consistency is right.
- If the sauce is too thick then you need to whisk in additional liquid.
- If you want a richer white sauce then beat in any number of egg yolks you desire to the taste you desire.
- If adding a hot sauce to the roux when adding egg yolks, mix a small amount of the hot sauce into the egg yolks to temper them before adding them to the roux. This will help avoid curdling.
- White sauces are best when served immediately after being prepared.

Veloute

Veloute should not be seasoned since it is used in other dishes. However, if you are not going to use it immediately, melt a small amount of butter on top to stop a film from forming.

- If you do not use cream or eggs, the sauce will freeze well for 2 weeks but will only last for one day in the refrigerator. If you do freeze the sauce with egg, the yolk will separate from the sauce when thawed. Cream in the sauce may be too thin when thawed and will require 1-2 teaspoons of arrowroot to be added.
- When wine is added to any sauce, be sure and heat the sauce long enough for the alcohol to evaporate thus leaving the flavor only.
- Mounted butter sauces gain body from both the emulsification process and air that is beaten in.

BÉCHAMEL SAUCE RECIPE

2 Tbsp. unsalted butter
3 Tbsp. all-purpose flour
2 cups hot whole milk
Pinch of freshly ground nutmeg
Salt and freshly ground black pepper

Using a heavy saucepan, melt the unsalted butter then blend in the flour using a wooden spoon. Cook the sauce over medium heat and continue stirring until the butter and flour produce foam together (about 2 minutes). Make sure the color remains a golden buttery color. Remove from heat as soon as the bubbling stops and rapidly stir in all the hot milk. Bring the sauce to a boil, while whisking continually. Simmer and stir for 2 minutes, then season to taste.

Béchamel

To improve the flavor, simmer the sauce with onion and clove. The sauce should also be brought to a boil after slowly adding the roux to obtain the desired thickness.

CHAPTER 19

COOKING WITH ALCOHOL

BEER

- When beer is used in cooking the alcohol quickly evaporates leaving the flavoring agents intact.
- Chefs always use a light beer for recipes and allow it to remain open and at room temperature for 15 minutes before using it, thus releasing a good percentage of the carbonation.
- The acid in beer will react with certain metals so it would be best not to use aluminum or iron pots.
- Glass or enameled cookware is recommended when preparing any dish that contains beer.
- Pale lager beer can be used to thin a batter.
- Lighter ales or lagers and some water can be used for steaming mussels.
- Scottish ales can be used as a substitute for chicken or beef stock.
- Beer mixes well with soy sauce if you are preparing a barbecue sauce.
- Full-bodied lagers or ales can be used in strongly flavored marinades.

Use room temperature beer for the best flavor, the colder beer gets, the less flavor it will have.

- When eating fatty foods a beer with a high acidity level such as pilsner or American pale ale will cleanse fat particles from your teeth.
- It's best not to use a malt beer in a marinade or barbecue sauce in which hot peppers or red pepper powder is used, since beer has the tendency to neutralize the hotness.
- Honey ale goes best with lamb.
- Brown ale goes best with chicken dishes.

Beer does not get better with age. In fact if you store beer for too long a period, some beer may become bitter.

- If you like the flavor of beer it can be substituted for any liquid in a recipe using equal amounts of beer.
- When boiling shrimp, beer can be used as the liquid instead of water.
- The best beer for making soup is light or dark ale.

LIQUOR

- Brandy can be used for soups, shellfish, beef, lamb, fruits and puddings.

When alcohol is added to a recipe, it will lower the boiling point until the alcohol evaporates. The boiling point of alcohol is 175°F.

- Gin has too overpowering a flavor for most dishes.
- A small amount of gin can be used in tomato sauce or sauerkraut.
- Liqueurs are sweet and go well with desserts, especially fruit salads.
- Flavored liqueurs can be poured on ice cream.
- Benedictine goes great over sponge cake.
- Rum is an excellent flavor for dessert dishes, rum cakes and fruitcakes.
- Vodka has no flavor and is usually only used in marinades.
- Whiskey is commonly used on chocolate mousse, coffee sorbet and fruitcakes.
- Whiskey can replace brandy in many recipes, especially seafood recipes.

The following will provide information regarding cooking with alcohol and how much alcohol is left after a dish is cooked. Some alcohol will dissipate, but not as much as most people may think.

Method of preparation   **% Alcohol Remaining**

Alcohol not added to boiling food until
after the food was removed from heat. 86%

Alcohol added to a flambé and ignited 75%

Alcohol used in a marinade, no heat added 70%

Alcohol stirred into baked dish and simmered. . . . .

                                15 Minutes 40%

                                30 Minutes 35%

                                60 Minutes 25%

                                2 Hours 10%

                                3 Hours 0%

Flambéing

- This is a process of flaming a dish using brandy or liqueur.

- Best to use long matches.
- Never lean over the dish.
- Make sure that the food is not on the heat when you flambé.
- Make sure there is no visible fat and that it has all been skimmed off before you attempt to flambé.
- The alcohol should burn off fast and only flame up for a few seconds.
- If you want to flame a mixed drink safely, try using a teaspoon with a small amount of the preferred liquor and hold a match under the spoon for a few seconds until some of the fumes burn off. Then ignite the liquor in the spoon and pour it over the mixed drink. Never place your face too close to the drink you are flaming, just in case there are more fumes rising. Rum flames up better than most alcoholic beverages.

Brandy works best and should be warmed first in a small saucepan before pouring it on the food.

- To reduce the alcohol taste in punch, just float a few slices of cucumber in the punch.

WINE

- Two tablespoons of fortified wine is equal to one cup of table wine. Don't overpower the recipe.
- Supermarket cooking wines; are never used by chefs since they are usually inferior products that contain preservatives and additives. Manufacturers intentionally make cooking wines undrinkable.
- Basically, never cook with any wine that you would not drink.
- Wines should never be consumed with other liquids at a meal; this includes soups, water and even vinegar-based salad dressings. The taste of the wine will be ruined.
- The alcohol content of wine is not high enough to use for flambé.
- Alcohol dissipates at 172°F and most dishes never retain the alcohol.
- Using expensive premium wine in dishes is usually a waste of money.
- Cooking sherry is just sherry with the addition of salt and additives.

Chocolate will compliment a wine and not interfere with its taste.

- If you are going to serve an expensive wine with a meal, don't cook with it, just use a close relative.
- If you use alcohol in ice cream, such as rum raisin, it will not freeze well and will always be somewhat mushy.
- Dry red wine is usually the wine of choice in marinades.
- Normally 2 tablespoons of wine would be added to soup, always toward the end of the cooking time.

- Sauces usually require 1 tablespoon of wine in most recipes.
- Stews and meats need about 1/4 cup of wine per pound.
- Cooking wine should be stored in small bottles, since the less space between the wine and the top, the longer the wine will retain its flavor and aroma.

- To replace 1 cup of wine in a recipe, use 1 cup of chicken stock plus $\frac{1}{8}$ cup of lemon juice or cider vinegar.
- Use 1 tablespoon of wine per cup of sauce or soup to flavor.

- About $\frac{1}{2}$ cup of wine is needed per quart when poaching fish.
- When cooking with wine, it should be part of the total liquid in the recipe.
- When wine is heated, it will reduce from 1 cup to $\frac{1}{4}$ cup in about 8-10 minutes.

Always add wine close to the end of the cooking period to retain the flavor and just lose the alcohol.

- If you wish to retain the alcohol, add the wine a few minutes before the dish is served.
- If you are using sherry, port or Madeira wines in soup, they should be added just before serving.

Wine has the tendency to cause curdling in recipes that contain dairy products. Make sure you blend the wine in before adding the dairy product. Don't allow the dish to cool, always keep the dish warm.

- In France it is common to poach fish in white wine.
- If you would like a unique flavored basting liquid, combine wine with melted butter.
- When adding wine to stew, it is best, added 20 minutes before you are going to serve it.

- Always taste food that you have added wine to, to be sure that the wine is not overpowering the dish.

Wine is used by many chefs to de-glaze pans.

SUBSTITUTIONS FOR ALCOHOL IN RECIPES

ALCOHOL	SUBSTITUTION
Amaretto (2 Tbsp.)	Almond extract ($\frac{1}{2}$ tsp.)
Brandy	White grape juice, apple juice
Champagne	Ginger ale
Cognac	Peach, apricot or pear juice
Crème de menthe	Oil of spearmint (small amount)
Red Wine	Red grape or cranberry juice
Grand Marinier	Unsweetened orange juice concentrate
Kahlua	Chocolate extract or instant coffee
Kirsch	Cherry syrup
Port Wine/Sweet Sherry	Orange or apple juice
Rum	White grape or apple juice
Bourbon	Orange or pineapple juice
Sweet White Wine	White grape juice + 1 Tbsp. Karo syrup

CHAPTER 20

COOKING WITH GRAINS/NUTS

COOKING WITH GRAINS

Barley

- The records on barley being grown date back 10,000 years and state that it was grown in Jericho at that time. It was grown 5,000 years ago in Japan. The Babylonians used it for making beer 3,000 years ago.

- When barley is used in soups or stews it will help thicken them by absorbing a large amount of liquid. However, barley does lose its vitamin B's to the water.

GRAIN COOKING CHART

GRAIN	QUANTITY UNCOOKED	AMOUNT OF WATER	COOKING TIME	QUANTITY OF COOKED GRAIN
AMARANTH	1 CUP	3 CUPS	5 MIN.	2 CUPS
BARLEY	1 CUP	4 CUPS	45 MIN.	4 CUPS
BROWN RICE	1 CUP	2.5 CUPS	45 MIN.	3 CUPS
BUCKWHEAT	1 CUP	4 CUPS	20 MIN.	3 CUPS
BULGUR	1 CUP	2 CUPS	15 MIN.	2.5 CUPS
CORNMEAL	1 CUP	4 CUPS	40 MIN.	4 CUPS
MILLET	1 CUP	3 CUPS	40 MIN.	3 CUPS
OAT BRAN	1 CUP	3 CUPS	2 MIN.	3 CUPS
OAT GROATS	1 CUP	2 CUPS	30 MIN.	2.5 CUPS
ROLLED OATS	1 CUP	2 CUPS	5 MIN.	4 CUPS
QUINONA	1 CUP	2 CUPS	15 MIN.	2 CUPS
RYE	1 CUP	4 CUPS	1 HOUR	2.5 CUPS
WHEAT BERRIES	1 CUP	3 CUPS	1 HOUR	2.5 CUPS
WILD RICE	1 CUP	4 CUPS	40 MIN.	3.5 CUPS

OATS

- Old fashioned oats and quick cooking oats can be interchanged in a recipe.
- Never use instant oats in a cookie or muffin recipe or it will turn them into gooey lumps.
- If oat flour is used in a baked goods recipe it must be mixed with regular flour or the baked goods may not rise properly, especially yeast breads.

RICE

Rice probably originated in China with records dating back to 2,800 BC that mentions how to plant rice. The Japanese do not like their rice to be too starchy and will rinse the rice 8-10 times or more to remove as much starch as possible. The rice is rubbed together by hand and then rinsed until the water is clear. Rice was established as a crop in the United States by Captain John Thurber in South Carolina in 1685. The rice was a present to one of Charleston's leading citizens, Henry Woodward for his garden.

- Brown rice will take twice the time to cook as white rice. It will have a nut-like flavor and a more chewy texture.

Some companies spray vitamins on rice and sell it as "enriched" rice. If you purchase enriched rice it would be best not to rinse the rice before serving it. To many rinses, will reduce the nutritional quality.

- Leftover rice usually makes excellent fried rice. Oriental restaurants commonly use leftover rice for fried rice the next day.
- To cook leftover rice, place the rice in a double boiler, very lightly sprinkle the rice with warm water and only allow the water to simmer.
- One cup of rice will equal 3 cups of cooked rice.

- Rice should be washed before cooking it to clean out the hulls.
- If you add tomatoes, tomato sauce or any highly acidic food to rice it will require additional cooking time and more liquid.

- To determine the correct amount of cooking water when cooking rice, just shake the rice to settle it then pour enough water up to the first knuckle of your index finger that has been placed gently on top of the rice. This will cover the rice with about 1" of water.

- Never add salt to water when cooking grains, it has a tendency to toughen them, especially rice.

When cooking rice, add a few drops of lemon juice to the water and the rice will remain white.

- Rice should be cooked up to a boil, then covered and simmered on low heat for 35 minutes. Turn the heat off and allow the rice to stand for another 8-10 minutes.
- If you want your rice to be dry and fluffy, just place a few folded paper towels under the lid to absorb the excess moisture and steam for the last 2-3 minutes of cooking time.
- If you add 1 tablespoon of corn oil to the cooking water, the rice will not boil over.

Steam is important to perfect rice, so be sure that the pot lid fits snug.

- Try not to remove the lid while rice is cooking or you will lose the steam.
- Rice will not stick together if you add 1 teaspoon of vegetable oil to the cooking water.

For a great, tasting rice, cook the rice in de-fatted chicken broth instead of water.

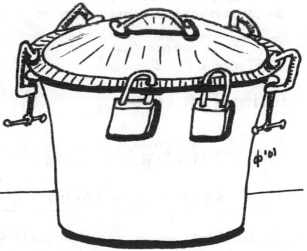

- Rice will become sticky due to excess starch being released if you stir rice while it is cooking.

- Leftover rice can be added to soups and stews but only a few minutes before you are ready to serve the dish or the rice will fall apart.
- If the rice has completed cooking and is too moist, just fluff it up with a fork and cook for a few minutes more until it reaches the moisture level you prefer.
- If rice becomes burnt, remove the good rice and place it in another pot, then place a piece of fresh white bread on top and cook for about 30 seconds to remove the burnt aroma.
- Just before serving rice, fluff the rice and release the steam allowing the grains to separate. If you use chopsticks do not fluff the rice unless it is very moist and somewhat starchy.
- To keep cooked rice at a good consistency during a meal the condensation cannot keep falling into the rice from the steam hitting the lid. Place a thin towel just under the lid before replacing the lid to capture any moisture that would fall into the rice.
- Washing rice before serving it will cause a loss of nutritional quality of the rice.

Basmati

Basmati rice is held in such high regard in India that families will store the rice for 20-30 years and only use the rice for special occasions. It is so special that it is given as a wedding present.

- Rinse the basmati rice, then simmer in a covered pot: 1-part rice to 1 ½ parts salted water for 15-20 minutes.

Glutinous Rice

- Should be soaked overnight then simmered in a covered pot in 1 part of salted water to 1 part of rice for 15 minutes.

Italian Short Grain (Arborio)

- The rice should never be rinsed and should be boiled in lots of salted water. Best to simmer 1-part rice to 2 parts salted water for 20 minutes.
- Best rice for making risotto.

Instant Rice

- Best to follow the directions on the package.

Long Grain White or Brown Rice

- Needs to be boiled in plenty of salted water. The rice can also be simmered in a covered pot. Cook 1-part of rice to 2 part of salted water without stirring. Add a small amount of oil to prevent sticking. Takes about 15-20 minutes to cook.
- Brown rice will take about 20 minutes longer to cook than white rice.

Parboiled Rice (Converted Rice)

- Same directions as long grain rice.

Wild Rice

This is basically a North American plant and not related to the rice family. Most of the commercially sold wild rice is still harvested by canoe by the original descendants of the American Indians that started harvesting it.

- Should be rinsed well and boiled in plenty of salted water. May be simmered in 1-part rice to 3 parts salted water for about 50 minutes.

RICE DISHES

Rice Pilaf

- Sauté the rice in about 2 tablespoons of unsalted butter that has been softened at room temperature on medium heat for 4-5 minutes or until just golden brown.
- Add boiling water and cook with the lid on, as you would normally prepare your rice.

Rice Pudding

- Use short-grained rice for the best rice pudding. It has a higher percentage of starch, which produces a creamier texture.
- To fluff up rice pudding and provide a great cold treat, fold whipped cream into the pudding just before serving it.

- Arborio rice is the best rice and is mixed with milk, sugar, hazelnuts and sweet dried currents.
- Rice pudding should be cooked so that it thickens slowly.
- Cream can be substituted for milk for a richer rice pudding.
- Light brown sugar can be substituted for white sugar for added flavor.
- Try adding raisins that have been soaked in rum.

Risotto

- Best not to prepare the risotto in a microwave since it will result is a less creamy dish.
- Risotto must be prepared in a very heavy pot that will not bounce around on the range. The bottom of the pot should be flat and the sides straight to allow even cooking.
- If using chicken livers make sure you do not salt them or they will become tough.
- Risotto is normally made with short-grained rice, which has a high starch content. The recommended rice in the United States is "arborio" for the best results.

- If you want to substitute broth for stock, just dilute the broth by using half the amount of liquid called for as water.
- Always sauté any ingredients that you plan on adding to the risotto and do not add them until just before you are going to serve the dish.
- The initial step should be to sauté the rice in 2 tablespoons of olive oil with $1/2$ teaspoon of canola oil added to stop any smoking of the oil for about 2 minutes or just until the rice loses its clear consistency.

- Zucchini is the only vegetable that does not have to be sautéed before adding it to the risotto since it helps the flavor.

Risotto broth must be kept hot on a simmer (not boiling). If it cooks too fast the rice may become too soft on the outside and chalky on the inside.

- When adding the hot liquid recommended in the recipe, add the hot liquid $1/2$ cup at a time, slowly and stirring continuously. Make sure that the rice has absorbed all the water before adding another $1/2$ cup.

Constant stirring will make all the difference in this dish.

- Since the high starch content is important, be sure that you do not wash the rice or the dish will not be as creamy as you would like.
- Risotto must be served as soon as it is finished cooking or it will become very thick, very quickly.
- Fresh pepper can be ground over the chicken livers for seasoning if you prefer.

NUTS/SEEDS

What is a Nutting Stone?
Native Americans in the east used a wide, flat stone with indentations the size of a mature walnut. The Indians would carve out the indentations and use the stone to break open black walnuts, which are very hard to crack open. They just placed the walnut in the groove and hit it with another stone. One stone will have 3-4 indentations.

- For a different flavor in your baked goods, just replace $1/3$ cup of finely chopped nuts to replace $1/3$ cup of flour.
- If you are purchasing pistachio nuts, be sure that the shell is open. A closed shell is an indication that the nut was not ripe.

- Many roasted nuts are actually fried in oil. Check the package to see if there is any oil listed that is different from the nut.
- To husk hazelnuts, just place then in a single layer on a cookie sheet and lightly spray them with water. Bake the nuts at 400°F for about 5 minutes and the steam produced will loosen their skins.

Nuts are much easier to chop when they are warm. A few seconds in the microwave will make your job easier.

- Make sure that you cut an "X" into the base of a chestnut to allow steam to escape or it may explode due to its high water content.
- Nut butter can be made with any nut by just placing the nuts in a food processor and processing until they are of a paste consistency. Add oil to smooth out the paste to your preferred consistency.

- If you would like to sauté nuts, just place 2 cups of nuts in 2 tablespoons of peanut oil or melted unsalted butter and cook on medium to high heat. Continue cooking while stirring occasionally until the nuts are brown.
- If you are adding almonds to a dish, try adding ¼ teaspoon of pure almond extract to the dish to enhance the flavor.
- If you are going to use fresh walnuts in the shell for a dish, try covering them with water and bring them to a boil, then remove from the heat and allow them to stand for 15-20 minutes. This will really make them easy to crack open and remove the meat.
- Chestnuts will be easy to peel if boiled for about 4 minutes first.
- To cook a chestnut until it is tender, boil for 20-30 minutes.
- Lentils are actually seeds that need no soaking before cooking and will cook slower if added to highly acidic foods such as tomatoes.

- Remove the shell of a chestnut while it is still warm. If you wait until it cools it will be more difficult.

NUT & SEED PASTES

Almond Paste

- Place 2 cups of almonds that have been blanched and toasted in a food processor or blender and process for 2-3 minutes. Add 1 teaspoon of salt; then continue processing for another 1-2 minutes.

Chestnut Paste

- Using a medium saucepan over low heat, simmer peeled chestnuts in whole milk (just enough to cover the chestnuts) for about 1 hour or until very tender. Add more milk as the milk evaporates. Drain the chestnuts and place them in a blender or food processor and blend until they are a pasty consistency.

Peanut Paste

- Combine 1 cup of roasted peanuts and 2 tablespoons of peanut oil and place in a food processor until it becomes the consistency you desire.

Sesame Paste

- Combine 1 cup of sesame seeds (or less) with $^1/_2$ teaspoon of peanut oil (more if desired) in a blender and mix until it is the consistency you desire.

Sunflower Seeds

Never add sunflower seeds to any baked goods product that contains baking soda or as it bakes it will turn blue-green. The product will be safe to eat it is just not very appealing.

- Buy unsalted sunflower seeds for recipes unless the recipe calls for salted.

Toasting (roasted) Nuts

- Toasted (roasted) nuts are not as likely to sink when added to recipes since they contain more air.
- To microwave nuts, place them on a paper plate and cook on high for 4 minutes or until they smell toasted. If you do not have a turntable be sure and turn the nuts at 2 minutes.
- Raw peanuts can be toasted by spreading them out on a cookie sheet in a single layer and baking them for 30 minutes at 350°F.
- Chestnuts can be roasted if placed on a cookie sheet in a single layer and baked at 425°F for 15-20 minutes or until tender.
- Sesame seeds can be toasted by placing the seeds on a cookie sheet and placing the sheet into a 350°F oven. Check the seeds frequently and remove as soon as they become brown.
- After you roast the nuts, allow them to cool to lukewarm then coat them with egg white and the salt will stick. Beat one egg white into a light froth and add kosher salt. Place the nuts that have been roasted into a mixing bowl and stir them with the egg and salt mixture.
- The egg white will keep the salt on the nuts.
- To toast pine nuts, just pre-heat the oven to 350°F and spread out the nuts on a cookie sheet and bake for only 3-4 minutes. Watch them carefully since they will burn very easily.

COOKING PASTA

When it comes to which sauce to serve with which pasta, the rule is: the longer the strand, the thinner the sauce should be. Noodle-shaped pastas like creamy sauces, while capellini likes a thin sauce.

- The best grade of pasta will be labeled "Amber Durham."

When pasta is used in salads it should be rinsed to remove the excess starch.

- If you need a pasta dish in a hurry, keep capellini (angels) pasta handy since it cooks up in about 3-4 minutes.
- Use plenty of water when cooking pasta.
- Pasta tends to get mushy when it has to fight for water.

It will require about 2¹/₂ cups of sauce for every pound of pasta.

- Never try and cook two varieties of pasta in the same pot of water.
- The standard pasta serving is 4 ounces of dried pasta.

- Some chef's say to never salt the pasta water or the pasta may become tough; while the next chef will say to add some rock salt to the water when you first place it in the pot.
- Experience has shown that the pasta does seem to be somewhat tougher when the salt is added, however, it may be a toss-up.
- Use cold water since there are more contaminants in hot tap water.

- The longer you cook pasta, the more nutrients are lost to the water.
- A small amount of oil in the cooking water will help keep the pasta from sticking together, however, some chefs advise not to use oil in the cooking water claiming that the sauce will not adhere as well. I have not found this to be true and still use a small amount of olive oil.
- Most pasta cooks up in 7-10 minutes and should be checked after 4-5 minutes.
- Make sure that you cool the pasta under cold tap water before tasting to see if it is done. This should be done a number of times to be sure that the pasta will be cooked just right (al dente).
- Salting the water, however, may be done 1-2 minutes before the pasta has completed cooking. Salt tends to help the sauce stick to the pasta.
- One pound of spaghetti will cook up to about 7 cups of pasta.
- One pound of pasta (elbow macaroni, etc.) should cook in 4 quarts of water. Add pasta gradually so that the boiling does not stop.
- To stop the pasta from boiling over, just rub some oil or butter about 1" down on the inside rim of the pot.
- If you are going to add pasta to a casserole reduce the cooking time by about $1/3$ since the pasta will continue being cooked after being added to the casserole.
- Place pasta in rapidly boiling water and place the lid on until the water has returned to boiling, then remove the lid.

- The water must be kept boiling after you add the pasta, if it doesn't then the pasta may get somewhat mushy.
- Stir pasta frequently to be sure that it is not sticking together or to the bottom of the pot.

- When you drain the pasta, make sure that the colander is warm. A cold colander may make the pasta stick together.
- It is not necessary to rinse pasta since this will cool the pasta and reduce the flavor.
- If pasta does stick together after sitting for a few minutes, just run it under very hot water for a few seconds.
- Serve pasta immediately when it is finished cooking. The sauce should be ready.
- Pasta and sauce should be served separately and not mixed together in most instances.
- Always serve pasta in a warmed bowl since it cools off very fast.

To test whether pasta is done cooking, just remove a piece from the water and throw it at the wall. If the pasta sticks to the wall it is finished cooking.

Pasta Dough

- Pasta dough should never be made on rainy or high humidity days or it will be hard to knead.
- The best pasta dough is made from Durham semolina flour. This flour has a high gluten content, which provides pasta with a level of resiliency and still allows the pasta to cook "al dente" and remain tender.
- The gluten content prevents starches and nutrients from being released into the cooking water.

If you are using quality pasta, foam will not appear on top of the water.

- It does not pay to purchase fresh pasta. Dried packaged quality pasta will be just as good.
- To prepare colored pasta dough:

Tomato	Use 2 tablespoons of a quality tomato paste per egg used. Add the paste to the eggs as you are beating them.
Beets	Use 1 tablespoon of cooked, pureed beets for every egg.
Saffron	Makes a rich golden color. Only add a pinch of ground saffron to the flour and blend well.
Spinach	Use frozen finely chopped spinach. Add 1/4 cup per egg used. Press-out all water before adding to the beaten eggs.

PASTA SAUCES

Alfredo

- High calorie sauce made from cream, a light cheese (either Parmesan or Romano), and garlic.

Alla panna

- Prepared with fresh cream, Marsala wine, Parmesan or Romano cheese, garlic, mushrooms, and occasionally smoked ham.

Bolognese

- Meat and tomato sauce, commonly used on spaghetti.

Carbonara

- Bacon combined with garlic, eggs, Parmesan cheese and occasionally cream.

Formaggi

- Blend of cream, garlic, Parmesan, Romano, and Swiss cheeses.

Genovese

- Hearty meat sauce that may be spiced with garlic, tomatoes, and mushrooms.

Marinara

- Somewhat spicy sauce flavored with garlic, and an herbal blend. Usually not made with meat.

The Ultimate Marinara Sauce Recipe:

3 tablespoons of extra virgin olive oil (cold pressed)
$^1/_2$ teaspoons canola oil
$^1/_2$ cup fresh carrot, finely chopped
1 cup of red onion, finely chopped
3 cloves of fresh minced garlic
3 pounds of Italian plum tomatoes (or one 6 ounce can of tomato paste)
$^1/_2$ cup Chianti (optional)
2 tablespoon fresh oregano (or 2 teaspoons powdered oregano)
3 teaspoons fresh basil
$^3/_4$ pound sliced mushrooms
Add salt and ground black pepper to flavor as desired

Heat the olive and canola oil in a medium pan on medium heat and sauté the garlic and onions for about 6-8 minutes. Add the balance of the ingredients except the mushrooms and simmer for 20 minutes. Add the salt, pepper and mushrooms and continue simmering for 7 minutes.

Neapolitan

• Made with different flavored tomato sauce herbal blend, garlic, mushrooms, and green bell peppers.

Pesto

• Made from the finest grade of extra virgin olive oil, fresh basil, garlic, a few pine nuts, and cream.

Primavera

• Sauce made from vegetables.

Puttanesca

• Made from anchovies, garlic, tomatoes, capers and black olives.

Fettuccine Alfredo

This dish was originally prepared in 1920 by Alfredo diLellio who owned the Via della Scrofa Restaurant in Rome. It was prepared for his wife who had lost her appetite after delivering a baby boy. Originally the dish was prepared with 3 kinds of flour and a large amount of butter. Fettuccine Alfredo; was brought to the United States by actors Douglas Fairbanks and Mary Pickford in 1920 after they visited the restaurant in Rome on their honeymoon. They were so impressed with the dish that they gave Alfredo a gold-plated spoon and fork with which to stir the pasta.

- A cream sauce that incorporates Parmesan cheese, cream, butter and pepper.
- Since the original richness of the butter used in Italy cannot be duplicated it is necessary to use both cream and butter.
- The Parmesan cheese must be freshly grated.

Pasta Shapes

Anellini	Shaped like small rings.
Bavettine	A narrow linguine.
Bucantini	Hollow thin strands.
Cannaroni	Very wide tubes.
Cannelloni	Hollow tubes up to 2 inches long.
Capellini	Angel hair, very thin strands.
Capelveneri	Thin medium width noodles.
Cappelletti	Shaped like small hats.
Cavatappi	Short spiral macaroni shaped.
Cavatelli	Short, shells with a rippled edge.
Conchiglie	Shaped like a conch shell.
Coralli	Tiny soup tubes.
Cresti-di-gali	Looks like a roosters comb.
Ditali	Shaped like small thimbles.
Ditalini	Small thimble shapes.
Farfalle	Shaped like a bowtie. The word means butterfly in Italian. Sold in two sizes, large and small.
Fedelini	Very fine spaghetti.
Fettucce	Flat egg noodles.
Fideo	Very thin, coiled strands.
Funghini	Pasta that are related to the mushroom family and are used in soups and stews.
Fusilli bucati	Corkscrew-shaped pasta.
Gemelli	Two stands of spaghetti twisted together.
Gnocchi	Very small rippled-edge stuffed shells.
Lasagna	Very long, broad noodles.

Linguine ....Very narrow pasta ribbons.
Lumache ....Pasta shaped like snail shells.
Macaroni ....Curved pasta, comes in many sizes with a
 hollow center.
Maccheroni ....Italian for all types of macaroni.
Mafalde ....Ripple-edged flat, broad noodles.
Magliette ....Short, curved pasta tubes.
Manicotti ....Very large stuffed tubes.
Margherite .... Narrow, flat one-sided ripple edged noodles.
Maruzze ....Pasta shaped like sea shells.
Mezzani ....Short, curved tubes.
Mostaccioli ....Tubes, about 2 inches long with a slight curve.
Occhi-di-lupo .....Very large tubes of pasta; sometimes
 referred to as "wolf's eye."
Orcchiette ....Pasta shaped like ears.
Orzo ....Pasta, the size and shape of rice.
Pappardelle ....Wide noodles with rippled sides.
Pastina ....A variety of pasta shapes used in soups.
Penne ....Tubes that are diagonally cut with ridged sides.
Perciatelli ....Thin, hollow tubes, about twice as thick as
 spaghetti.
Pezzoccheri ....Very thick buckwheat noodles.
Pulcini ....Used mainly in soups and called "little chickens."
Quadrettini ....Very small pasta squares.
Radiatore ..Resemble small radiators.
Ravioli ....Small squares of pasta stuffed with different
 ingredients.
Riccini ,,,,,,,,. Pasta shaped like ringlet curls.
Rigatoni ....Very large, grooved shaped pasta.
Riso ....Another rice-shaped pasta
Rotelli ....Small "wagon wheel" shaped pasta.
Rotini ....Very small spiral-shaped pasta.
Ruoti ....Round pasta with spokes, looks like a wagon
 wheel.
Semi de Melone ....Small, melon seed-shaped pasta.
Spaghetti ....Very long, thin strands of pasta.
Spaghettini ....Very thin spaghetti.
Tagliarini ....Pasta shaped like ribbons, usually paper-thin.
Tagliatelle ....Very long, flat egg noodles.
Tortellini ....Pasta that is supposed to resemble the Roman
 Goddess Venus' navel. "Little Twists."
Tripolini ....Very small bow ties that have rounded edges.
Tubetti ....Very tiny hollow tubes.
Vermicelli ....Italian word for worms, which they resemble.
 Also known as spaghetti
Ziti ....A very short tubular-shaped pasta.

Stuffed Pasta

- Stir stuffed pasta very gently with a wooden spoon.
- Many specialty markets have dough that is sold for stuffed pasta so that you don't have to make the dough.
- Be sure that the stuffed pasta is well sealed before placing them into boiling water.
- If you add 1 teaspoon of whole milk to the pasta dough it will make the dough more pliable and reduce the chances of the pasta breaking open.
- All stuffing should be prc-cooked.
- The stuffing should be cool when you are stuffing pasta. The pasta should be firm and not mushy before placing the pasta into the boiling water.
- Keep the pieces all the same size so that they will cook in the same amount of time.
- Almost any food can be used for stuffing.

MACARONI & CHEESE

The word "macaroni" actually came from the exclamation made by the Italians when they saw the price of pasta the Germans were trying to sell them in the 1700's. The Italians were upset at the price and said "ma caroni," which meant "but its too dear" so the Germans reduced the prices.

Macaroni was brought to the Unites States by Thomas Jefferson. When Jefferson was the ambassador to France he developed a liking for macaroni. When he returned from France he brought a machine back that made pasta. He is credited with making the first macaroni and cheese dish.

- Use small elbow macaroni for the best results.

- The butter should be melted in a saucepan, but be sure that you let it soften at room temperature.
- Your recipe should call for about $1/4$ cup of unsalted butter.

- Whatever cheese you prefer, always remember to shred it before adding it for a topping or in a recipe.
- After the butter has softened, add the ¼ cup of flour, salt and pepper to taste.
- Most recipes call for 2½ cups of milk. Low fat or nonfat milk can be used but will detract from the original richness.

The milk should be added to the butter, flour mixture very slowly, while stirring continually.

- Continue heating until the mixture starts to thicken, then remove from the heat and stir in 2 cups of shredded yellow cheddar cheese just until it melts.
- At this point add the cooked macaroni and place into a casserole dish and crumble bread slices (about 3-4) on top before sprinkling on ¼ cup of shredded yellow cheddar.
- Bake the dish for 30 minutes at 375°F until it bubbles.
- Make sure that you add a small amount of olive oil to the cooking water so that the pasta will not stick together.
- Another method is to place a layer of macaroni in the casserole dish then sprinkle a layer of cheese on top, crumbled bacon bits and finely chopped scallions.
- The macaroni should only be boiled for 5 minutes, the drained.

- The casserole should hold 3 layers with a topping of breadcrumbs.

COMMON ASIAN NOODLES

- The preparation of Asian noodles will depend on the type of noodle. Some are cooked in large amounts of boiling water, while others may be fried or used with a dipping sauce.
- After noodles are fried they should be drained in a brown paper bag, shaking the bag to be sure that the majority of the loose fat has been absorbed.
- Asian noodles are frequently made in advance and then re-heated when needed.
- When re-heating noodles the best method is to place the noodles in a metal colander and sit them over a pot of boiling water.

Chinese Egg Noodles

- The best quality should be made with flour and eggs.
- Watch the label for a food coloring being used in the less expensive brands. They are not very good.
- Can be purchased either thick or thin.

Mung Bean Noodles

- Made from mung bean starch
- They are very thin and usually entwined in the package.

Rice Noodles

- These can be purchased fresh from a Chinese market and some specialty supermarkets.
- They are usually sold in sheets and can be cut into the width required for that particular dish.

Soba Noodles

Soba noodles are so popular in Japan that there are 6,000 soba noodle factories and over 40,000 stores that only sell soba noodles.

- These are made from buckwheat flour and considered a delicacy in Japan.
- They look like long spaghetti noodles and are served in a broth.
- Has an excellent flavor and high nutritional content.

Somen Noodles

- Very thin Japanese wheat noodles that are made with a small amount of oil incorporated into the dough.
- Use in cold dishes and salads or with dipping sauce on the side.

Udon Noodles

- These are sturdier noodles made from wheat and are very chewy.
- Usually used in soups.
- One of the most consumed noodle in Japan.

SPECIALTY PASTA DISHES

Lasagna

- Place a small amount of oil in the cooking water to prevent the noodles from sticking together.
- Sauce Bolognese is normally used for this dish with the addition of other spices as desired.
- Place a thin layer of tomato sauce on the bottom of the pan before placing the noodles in.
- Always under-bake the noodles since they will continue to cook in the casserole and will turn to mush.

Always leave the lasagna in the oven for 30 minutes after it is done to allow the layers to settle. It will be tastier and much easier to cut.

- Lasagna can be frozen if placed in aluminum foil and should always be reheated from the frozen state. Spoon some tomato sauce over the top when reheating.

Noodle Kugel

- Nuts are optional but are usually not added. Raisins are a must.
- Make sure that the noodles are the wide ones and drained well before pouring the melted butter on top.
- The egg yolks should be beat into the sugar before adding your favorite spices. Then add the mixture to the noodles.
- The egg whites should then be beaten until stiff and folded into the noodle mixture.
- The mixture is placed into the casserole dish in 3 layers with raisins sprinkled on top of each layer.

For the best results, all the steps need to be completed as fast as possible.

- If you want to remove the noodle kugel and place it on another dish, be sure and butter the inside of the dish and sprinkle the inside with bread crumbs mixed with a small amount of sugar.

Spaghetti Bolognese

- Do not use spaghettini for this dish.
- If your recipe calls for celery, try using celeriac or celery root, which are more flavorful and fragrant.
- Continue using the same pan and do not wash it between cooking different parts of the recipe. Just wipe the pan with paper towel.
- The shortening should be a combination of oil and butter. If you use olive oil always add a small amount of canola to increase the smoke point.
- The size of the meat should be about the size of peas.
- In Italy chicken livers are usually added, which provide a great flavor.
- Beef consommé is usually used as the base liquid.
- If you want to freeze the sauce, do not add any cream.
- To de-frost the sauce, use a water bath for the best results and to retain the flavor.
- The cheese for this dish should be FRESHLY grated Parmesan or Romano cheese.

Classic Old Fashioned Spaghetti Sauce Recipe

4 tablespoons of extra virgin olive oil
1 teaspoon of Canola oil
³/₄ cup red onion, chopped
2 cloves of garlic, chopped
1 large carrot, chopped
3 large stalk of celery, chopped
1 pound of lean ground round
¹/₂ cup Chianti (optional)
4 large ripe tomatoes, skinned, seeded and chopped
4 tablespoon fresh thyme
5 cups of brown stock
Add salt and ground black pepper as desired

Place the olive and canola oil in a large pan over medium heat and sauté the onions for about 5 minutes but do not allow them to burn. Add the carrot, garlic and celery and sauté for another 5 minutes. Add the ground beef and cook until the meat is well browned, then stir in the tomato, wine (optional), thyme and brown stock. Lower the heat and simmer for 50 minutes. Add the salt and pepper as desired.

Ravioli

- Be sure that the ravioli are well sealed so that the stuffing will not leak out.
- One of the biggest problems is that most people want to overstuff the ravioli.
- If the dough is hard to seal, just add 1 teaspoon of milk to the dough when you are making it.

Be sure that all stuffing mix is fully cooked and seasoned before placing it into the ravioli.

- The stuffing should be cool when you are stuffing the ravioli.
- Ravioli dough is available in most supermarkets.
- Wontons may be used in place of the typical ravioli dough. They are usually sold in the produce department of most supermarkets.

CHAPTER 21

SUBSTITUTIONS WITHOUT COMPROMISE

SUBSTITUTIONS THAT REALLY WORK

- If your using a cookbook and it was published in England, the following information will be very useful since many of the common cooking ingredients are called by different names.

BRITISH FOOD	AMERICAN FOOD
Plain Flour	All-Purpose Flour
Wholemeal Flour	Whole Wheat Flour
Strong Flour	Bread Flour
Single Cream	Light Cream
Double Cream	Whipping Cream
Castor Sugar	Granulated Sugar (10X)
Demerara Sugar	Brown Sugar
Treacle Sugar	Molasses
Dark Chocolate	Semi-Sweet Chocolate
Sultanas	White Raisins
Courgettes	Zucchini
Swedes	Turnips
Gammon	Ham

ACTIVE DRY YEAST (one package)

Use 1 cake compressed yeast.

AGAR-AGAR

Use unflavored gelatin.

ALLSPICE

Allspice was discovered by Columbus in 1494 in Jamaica and is the fruit of the evergreen pimiento tree.

$1/4$ teaspoon cinnamon & $1/2$ teaspoon ground cloves or $1/4$ teaspoon nutmeg for baking only or black pepper other than baking.

ANISE (use equivalent amount)

Use fennel, dill or cumin.

APPLES

One cup of firm chopped pears and one tablespoon of lemon juice.
1 pound of apples = 4 small, 3 medium, or 2 large or $2^3/4$ cups sliced.

ARROWROOT

Use all-purpose flour, just enough to thicken, should take a few tablespoons.

BAKING POWDER (one teaspoon, double-acting)

$1/2$ teaspoon cream of tartar plus $1/4$ teaspoon of baking soda; or
$1/4$ teaspoon baking soda; plus $1/2$ cup of sour milk, cream, or buttermilk.
Must take the place of other liquid or 4 teaspoons of quick-cooking tapioca

BAKING POWDER (one teaspoon, single-acting)

$3/4$ teaspoon double-acting baking powder

BASIL (dried)

Use tarragon or summer savory of equal amounts or thyme or oregano.

BAY LEAF

Use thyme of equal amounts.

BLACK PEPPER

Allspice in cooking providing salt is also used in the dish.

BORAGE

Cucumber.

BRANDY

Use cognac or rum.

BREAD CRUMBS (¼ cup, dry)

¼ cup cracker crumbs or ½ slice of bread, may be toasted or crumbled;s or
¼ cup rolled oats or ¼ cup of matzo meal or ¼ cup of sifted flour; or
¼ cup of corn flakes or ¼ cup shredded potatoes (meatloaf) or ¼ cup matzo
meal.

BULGUR

Use equal amounts of cracked wheat, kasha, brown rice, conscious, millet or
quinoa.

BUTTER (in baking)

Use hard margarine or shortening **- DO NOT USE OIL IN BAKED PRODUCTS**
1 pound = 2 cups
1 cup = 2 sticks
2 Tablespoons = ¼ stick or 1 ounce
4 Tablespoons = ½ stick or 2 ounces
8 Tablespoons = 1 stick or 4 ounces

BUTTERMILK

Use one cup of milk plus 1³/₄ tablespoons of cream of tartar or equivalent of sour cream.

CAKE FLOUR

Use 1 cup of all-purpose flour minus 2 tablespoons.

CAPERS

Use chopped green olives.

CARAWAY SEED

Fennel seed or cumin seed.

CARDAMOM

Use cinnamon or mace.

CAYENNE PEPPER

Use ground hot red pepper or chili powder.
Store cayenne pepper in the refrigerator and it will maintain its flavor and color longer.

CHERVIL

Use parsley or tarragon (use less) or anise (use less).

CHIVES

Use onion powder (small amount) or leeks or shallots (small amount).

CHOCOLATE, BAKING, UNSWEETENED (one ounce or square)

3 tablespoons of unsweetened cocoa plus 1 tablespoon of butter or
3 tablespoons of carob powder plus 2 tablespoons of water.

CHOCOLATE, BAKING, UNSWEETENED (one ounce pre-melted)

3 tablespoons of unsweetened cocoa plus 1 tablespoon of corn oil or melted Crisco

CHOCOLATE, SEMI-SWEET (6 ounces of chips or squares)

Use 9 tablespoons of cocoa plus 7 tablespoons of sugar plus 3 tablespoons of unsalted butter.

CILANTRO

Use parsley and lemon juice or orange peel and a small amount of sage or lemon grass with a small amount of mint.

CINNAMON

Use allspice (use a small amount) or cardamom.

CLOVES (ground)

Use allspice or nutmeg or mace.

CLUB SODA

Use mineral water or seltzer.

CONFECTIONER'S SUGAR

Use $1^3/4$ cup of confectioner's sugar to replace 1 cup of granulated sugar.

CORNMEAL

Use grits (corn) or polenta.

CORNSTARCH

Flour: a few tablespoons for thickening, usually no more than two.

CORN SYRUP (one cup, light)

$1^1/_4$ cups granulated sugar or 1 cup granulated sugar plus $^1/_4$ cup of liquid.

CREAM CHEESE

Use cottage cheese mixed with cream or cream with a small amount of butter or milk.

CREME FRAICHE

Use sour cream in a recipe or $^1/_2$ sour cream and $^1/_2$ heavy cream in sauces.

CUMIN

Use $^1/_3$ anise plus $^2/_3$ caraway or fennel.

DILL SEED

Use caraway or celery seed.

EDIBLE FLOWERS (garnish)

Bachelor buttons, blue borage, calendula petals, chive blossoms, mini carnations, nasturtiums, pansies, rose petals, snapdragon, or violets.

EGGS, WHOLE (one)

2 tablespoons water plus 2 tablespoons of flour plus $^1/_2$ tablespoons of Crisco plus $^1/_2$ teaspoon of baking powder; or 2 yolks plus 1 tablespoon of water or 2 tablespoons of corn oil plus 1 tablespoon of water; or
1 teaspoon of cornstarch plus 3 tablespoons of water if part of a recipe
1 banana (best for cakes and pancakes); or 2 tablespoons of cornstarch or arrowroot starch or $^1/_4$ cup of tofu (blend with liquid ingredients before adding to any dry ingredients).

EVAPORATED MILK

Use light cream or half-and-half or heavy cream.

FLOUR (thickeners, use up to 2-3 tablespoons only)

Use Bisquick, tapioca (quick cooking), cornstarch, arrowroot (use small amount), potato starch, mashed potato flakes, or pancake mix.

GARLIC (equivalent of 1 clove)

$1/4$ teaspoon of minced, dried garlic or $1/8$ teaspoon of garlic powder or $1/4$ teaspoon of garlic juice or $1/2$ teaspoon of garlic salt (omit $1/2$ teaspoon salt from recipe).

GHEE

Use clarified butter.

GRANULATED SUGAR

Use 1 cup of granulated sugar to replace $1 3/4$ cup of confectioner's sugar.

HONEY (one cup in baked goods)

Use 1 $1/4$ cups granulated sugar plus $1/4$ cup water.

JUNIPER BERRIES

Use a small amount of gin.

LEMONGRASS

Lemon or lemon rind; or verbena; or lime rind.

LEMON JUICE

Use $1/2$ teaspoon of white vinegar for each teaspoon of lemon juice, unless the flavor is required.

LOVAGE

Use celery leaves.

MARJORAM

Use oregano (use small amount); or thyme; or savory.

MASA HARINA

Use corn flour.

MASCARPONE

Use cream cheese, whipped with a small amount of butter.

MEAT

Use Tempeh (cultured soybeans provides a chewy texture); or Tofu (after it has been frozen); or Wheat gluten.

MILK, EVAPORATED

Use light cream; or half and half; or heavy cream.

MILK (in baked goods)

Use fruit juice plus $1/2$ teaspoon of baking soda mixed in with the flour.

MILK (one cup)

$1/2$ cup evaporated milk plus $1/2$ cup of water; or
3 tablespoons of powdered milk: plus 1 cup of water. If whole milk is called for add 2 tablespoons of butter.

MOLASSES (one cup)

Use 1 cup of honey.

NUTMEG

Use allspice; or cloves; or mace

NUTS (in baked goods only)

Use whole bran.

OREGANO

Use marjoram; or rosemary; or thyme (fresh only).

PANCETTA

Use lean bacon (cooked) or very thin sliced ham.

PARSLEY

Use chervil or cilantro.

POLENTA

Use cornmeal or grits (corn)

POULTRY SEASONING

Use sage plus a blend of any of these: thyme, marjoram, savory, black pepper, and rosemary.

POWDERED SUGAR

See confectioner's sugar.

ROSEMARY

Use thyme; or tarragon; or savory.

SAFFRON (⅛ teaspoon)

Use 1 teaspoon dried yellow marigold petals; or 1 teaspoon of azafran or 1 teaspoon safflower; or $1/2$ to 1-teaspoon turmeric (adds color).

SAGE

Use poultry seasoning; or savory; or marjoram or rosemary.

SELF-RISING FLOUR (one cup)

Use 1 cup all-purpose flour plus 1 teaspoon of baking powder, $1/2$ teaspoon of salt, and $1/4$ teaspoon of baking soda.

SHALLOTS

Use small green onions; or leeks; or standard onions (use small amount); or scallions (use more than is called for).

SHORTENING (one cup in baked goods only)

Use 1-cup butter or 1 cup hard margarine.

SOUR CREAM (one cup)

Use 1 tablespoon of white vinegar plus sufficient milk to make 1 cup. Allow the mixture to stand for 5 minutes before using or use 1 tablespoon of lemon juice plus enough evaporated milk to make 1 cup; or use 1 cup of plain yogurt if it is being used in a dip or cold soup: or use 6 ounces of cream cheese plus 3 tablespoons of milk; or use $1/3$ cup of melted butter plus $3/4$ cup of sour milk for baked goods.

TAHINI

Use finely ground sesame seeds.

TARRAGON

Use anise (use small amount) or chervil (use larger amount) or parsley (use larger amount) or a dash of fennel seed.

TOMATO PASTE (one tablespoon)

Use 1 tablespoon of ketchup or $1/2$ cup of tomato sauce providing you reduce some of the other liquid.

TURMERIC

Use mustard powder.

VANILLA EXTRACT (in baked goods only)

Use almond extract or other extracts that will alter the flavor.

VINEGAR

Lemon juice in cooking and salads only or grapefruit juice, in salads or wine, in marinades.

YOGURT

Sour cream or creme fraiche or buttermilk or heavy cream or mayonnaise (use in small amounts).s

COMMON LIQUID SUBSTITUTIONS

- The following substitution may be used for liquids that are not available at the time the recipe is being prepared. However, it is always better to use the ingredients called for in the recipe for the best results.

LIQUID INGREDIENT	ADEQUATE SUBSTITUTION
1 cup barbecue sauce	1 cup ketchup + 2 tsp. Worcestershire sauce.
1 cup broth	1 bouillon cube dissolved in 1 cup of water.
1 cup butter	1 cup vegetable shortening + 2 Tbsp. water.
1 cup buttermilk	1 Tbsp. lemon juice + balance of cup in milk then allow it to stand for 5 minutes before using or add 1 Tbsp. of vinegar to 1 cup of evaporated milk and allow to stand for 5 minutes before using.
1 cup chili sauce	1 cup tomato sauce + $\frac{1}{2}$ cup sugar + 2 Tbsp. vinegar.
1 cup corn syrup	$\frac{3}{4}$ cup sugar + $\frac{1}{4}$ cup water.
1 cup creme fraiche	$\frac{1}{2}$ cup sour cream + $\frac{1}{2}$ cup heavy cream.
1 egg	1 banana or 2 Tbsp. cornstarch or arrowroot starch or $\frac{1}{4}$ cup tofu blended into liquid ingredients well.
1 cup evaporated milk	Equal amount of light or cream or half and half.
1 cup heavy cream	$\frac{3}{4}$ cup whole milk + $\frac{1}{3}$ cup of butter.

1 cup light cream	1 cup milk + 3 Tbsp. butter.
1 cup ketchup	1 cup tomato sauce + 4 Tbsp. sugar + 2 Tbsp. vinegar + $1/4$ tsp. ground cloves.
1 cup honey	$1 1/4$ cups granulated sugar + $1/4$ cup water.
1 tsp. lemon juice	1 tsp. of vinegar.
1 cup molasses	1 cup honey.
1 cup whole milk	4 Tbsp. dry whole milk + 1 cup water or 1 cup buttermilk + $1/2$ tsp. baking soda.
1 cup non-fat milk (skim)	4 Tbsp. nonfat dry milk + 1 cup water.
1 cup sour milk	1 Tbsp. lemon juice or vinegar + additional milk to fill 1 cup, allow to stand for 5 minutes.
2 drops of hot pepper sauce	A dash of cayenne or red pepper
2 tsp. tapioca	1 Tbsp. all-purpose flour (more if. desired)
1 cup tomato juice	$1/2$ cup tomato sauce + $1/2$ cup water.
1 Tbsp. tomato paste	1 Tbsp. tomato ketchup.
1 cup tomato puree	6 ounce can of tomato paste + 6 ounces of water.
1 Tbsp. Worcestershire sauce	1 Tbsp. soy sauce + dash hot sauce.
1 cup wine	1 cup apple juice or apple cider or 1 part of vinegar, diluted in 3 parts of water.
1 cup yogurt	1 cup buttermilk or sour cream.

EXTRACTS AND ESSENCES

LIQUID INGREDIENT	ADEQUATE SUBSTITUTION
Angostura Bitters	Orange Bitters or Worcestershire sauce
Anise Extract	Anise Oil (only use 50%)
Cinnamon Extract	Cinnamon Oil (only ¼ as much)
Ginger Juice	Place minced ginger in cheesecloth and squeeze out the juice.
Oil of Bitter Almonds	Almond Extract (use 50% more)
Peppermint Extract	Peppermint Oil (use ¼ as much)
Rose Water	Rose Syrup (2-3 drops)

OILS AND COOKING SPRAYS

Almond Oil	Walnut Oil or Extra Virgin Olive Oil
Canola Oil	Corn Oil or Safflower Oil
Clarified Butter	Butter (foods may overbrown)
Coconut Oil	Canola Oil or Corn Oil
Corn Oil	Canola Oil or Soybean Oil
Ghee	Clarified Butter or Canola Oil
Grapeseed Oil	Avocado Oil (very high smoke point)
Peanut Oil	Corn Oil or Canola Oil
Schmaltz	No known substitute when prepared right
Soybean Oil	Corn Oil

THESE LIQUIDS DO MEASURE UP

60 drops	=	5 ml. or 1 Tsp.
3 Tsp.	=	1 Tbsp.
2 Tbsp.	=	30 ml. or 1 fl. oz.
8 Tbsp.	=	½ cup
5 Lg. Eggs	=	1 cup
2 Tbsp. butter	=	1 oz.
1 oz.	=	30 grams
Juice of 1 orange	=	5-6 Tsp.

CHAPTER 22

DESSERTS AND CANDY MAKING TIPS

DESSERTS, CANDY & CHOCOLATE

CANDY

- One of the most important factors in cooking candies is to follow directions to the letter.
- Always use a heavy pan that conducts heat well. A poor pan will easily scorch and burn candy.
- Never use fructose in hard candy, it has the tendency to retain moisture.
- When making candy, chefs always use a pan larger than they need to avoid sugary syrups boiling over.
- The temperature recommended is very important and a higher temperature to speed up a procedure will not produce good results.
- Temperature must be controlled when cooking syrup since the lower the temperature the softer the candy. The higher the temperature the harder the candy.
- Candy recipes are very precise and they cannot be doubled to make a larger batch to save time.

When boiling syrup the sugar may tend to crystallize. To resolve this problem, just put a pinch of baking soda in the syrup while it is cooking to reduce the acidity.

- When adding water to a candy recipe, always add very hot water for the best results and a clearer candy.
- Cane sugar is best for candies; blended sugars will cause candies to become sticky.

- Most candies do not freeze well and never taste the same. Hard candy may crumble when thawed and jellies become granular.
- Candy will store well in as airtight a container as possible for about 3 weeks.
- Different candies should be stored separately.
- If you have a problem with candy boil over, just place a wooden spoon across the top of the pot. A better method, however, to reduce the risk of catching the spoon on fire is to just rub a thin layer of oil about 1-2 inches down the inside of the pot from the top.

Remember; to always wash off any spoon you use to stir syrup with before using it again. Crystals tend to cling and crystallize on the spoon and can damage the syrup.

- Best not to make candy if the weather is rainy or if the humidity is over 50%. If you must cook under these conditions the temperature should be increased by about two degrees above recommended.
- The best temperature to make chocolates, divinity, fudge and hard candy is between 62°-68°F with low humidity.
- Marshmallows are made from corn syrup, albumen, granulated sugar and gelatin beaten into a soft spongy consistency.
- Marshmallows are best stored in the freezer. Dip in hot water for a few seconds to thaw and separate.
- If you are going to make taffy, try not to use molasses or it may boil over easily. If you do use it, use a large pot.
- Make sure that when you are melting sugar you do so over low heat and be sure that ALL the sugar crystals have melted. If any crystals have clung to the sides of the pot and did not melt this will cause a problem.

If you have a problem with sugar melting, cover the pot and allow the steam to melt the rest of the crystals.

- When using sugar to prepare syrups, remember that sugar has the tendency to attract moisture from the air and thus keeps foods moist.
- Cakes are lighter because the sugar slows the gluten from becoming stiff.
- Sugar has the tendency to lower the freezing point of most liquids, which keeps ice cream in a state of a semi-solid.
- When using sugar on meats it will help retain the natural moisture.

EASY TO PREPARE SUGAR SYRUPS

Thin sugar syrup
One cup of granulated sugar added to two cups of water.

Medium sugar syrup
One cup of granulated sugar added to one cup of water.

Heavy sugar syrup
One cup of granulated sugar added to ³/₄ cup of water.

Thick sugar syrup
One cup of granulated sugar added to ¹/₂ cup of water.

In a small saucepan, add the sugar to the water and stir gently over low heat. Do not allow the mixture to boil until the sugar is completely dissolved. When boiling begins, stop stirring and continue to boil (uncovered) for about 1 minute. Flavorings can be added either before or after cooking. If you overcook the syrup, just add ¹/₄ cup of boiling water and cook again.

THREAD STAGES OF SUGAR SYRUP

- The thread stage is used to determine the actual temperature of the sugary syrup. In order for the candy to set up it must crystallize into sugary syrup. Cook the syrup in a small saucepan over medium heat until it reaches the desired temperature. If you do not have a thermometer, the following will be useful:

Thread Stage
230° F. to 234° F. (110° C. to 112.2° C.):
Syrup will form a soft light thread.

Soft Ball
234° F. to 240° F. (112.2° C. to 115.6° C.):
Syrup will form a small ball that will flatten out by itself when removed.

Firm Ball
244° F. to 248° F. (117.8° C. to 120° C.):
Syrup will form a firm ball that tends to flatten out when pressed between your fingers.

Hard Ball
250° F. to 265° F. (121.1° C. to 129.4° C.):
Syrup will form a hard ball that has just a little give to it when squeezed.

Soft Crack
270° F. to 290° F. (132.2° C. to 143.3° C.):
Syrup tends to separate into hard threads that are bendable.

Hard Crack
300° F. to 310° F. (148.9° C. to 154.4° C.):
Syrup will separate into threads, which are hard and very brittle.

Caramelized Sugar
310° F. to 338° F. (154.4° C. to 170° C.):
Syrup will become a golden color.

- When sugar is cooked above 350° F. (176.7° C.) will turn black and burn.
- When making sugar syrup, always watch the bubbles since they tend to become smaller as the syrup thickens. If the bubbles get too small before it thickens, better start over.

Caramel

- Caramel sauce is prepared from sugar and water. The mixture is cooked until it is a dark brown color.
- Caramel candy is prepared from sugar, milk or cream, honey or corn syrup and butter.

CHOCOLATE

Chocolate is made from the cacao bean. The majority of the world's cacao beans come from West Africa. The largest producers are Ghana, the Ivory Coast and Nigeria. The earliest known plantations; were started by the Mayans in 600AD in the Yucatan Peninsula. The word "chocolate" is derived from the Mayan "xocolatl."

CHOCOLATE SAUCE/SYRUP

- When preparing chocolate sauces there are a number of tips that you should be aware of. The following will help you obtain the perfect sauce:
- If a liquid is used in the recipe, always melt the chocolate in the liquid, not separate for the best results. Use low heat and stir continuously.
- The microwave is excellent for melting chocolate. Just place the chocolate in a large measuring glass and cook until melted, while keeping an eye on it to be sure it doesn't cook too much.
- Most chefs melt chocolate in a double boiler over simmering (not boiling) water.
- Always use the type of chocolate called for in a particular recipe and always use the highest quality chocolate you can find.
- Ganache is one of the finest blends of chocolate sauce you will ever taste when made properly. It consists of melted semi-sweet chocolate, heavy cream and unsalted butter. It is definitely not a healthy food since it is high in fat, cholesterol and calories.

Ganache Recipe

In a small saucepan heat 1 cup of heavy cream and 2 tablespoons of butter to boiling. Place a 12 ounce bag of chocolate semi-sweet morsels into a medium bowl and pour the hot butter cream mixture over the chocolate and stir until smooth. When it is cool, it will remain somewhat soft and should not harden.

Grandma's Hot Fudge Heaven Sauce Recipe

4 ounces of bittersweet chocolate (4 squares)
12 ounce can of quality evaporated milk
3 tablespoons of salted butter
2 1/2 cups confectioner's sugar
2 teaspoons of pure vanilla extract

Combine the chocolate, sugar and evaporated milk on the top of a double boiler with simmering water in the bottom. Stir occasionally until the chocolate has melted completely. Remove from the heat and whisk in the pure vanilla and butter until the mixture is smooth. Enjoy!

Chocolate Cherry Delight Sauce Recipe

$1/4$ cup quality unsweetened cocoa powder
$1/2$ sweet cream
$1/3$ cup Karo® syrup
$1/2$ cup granulated sugar
2 teaspoons real vanilla extract
$1/4$ pound of salted butter
2 ounces of bittersweet chocolate (2 squares)
1 tablespoon of a quality cherry Brandy (optional) or use
maraschino cherry juice

Using a small saucepan, whisk the cocoa and sugar together on medium heat. Slowly, add the cream (or half-and-half), the Karo® syrup (or any corn syrup), butter and chocolate. Stir continuously until the mixture comes to a boil and is smooth. Remove the sauce and immediately add the cherry brandy or cherry juice and the vanilla. Best to serve the sauce hot or at least warm.

Chocolate Peppermint Cream Sauce Recipe

4 ounces of bittersweet chocolate (4 squares)
$1/2$ cup granulated sugar
$1/4$ pound of unsalted butter
1 cup of heavy cream
1 teaspoon of a good quality peppermint extract

The chocolate can be melted in a double boiler over simmering water (not boiling). As soon as the chocolate is melted, add the sugar and butter. After you have stirred them in add the cream and allow the mixture to remain on low heat over direct heat for 3-5 minutes and just simmer. Remove the sauce from the hot burner and add in the peppermint extract slowly, while continually stirring.

- Tempering chocolate is the process of melting it, cooling it, and then melting it again. This process produces a more lustrous, glossy and stable mixture and is called for in many chocolate recipes. This is an exact science to obtain the right consistency and takes some practice.
- However, there is a "quick-tempering" method that utilizes a small amount of oil that will speed the process up considerably. The end product will be a little thinner, but will not make a difference in most recipes and decorative uses.

The quick-tempering method:
Use 1 tablespoon of vegetable oil, (preferable a neutral oil such as Canola or safflower) clarified butter is often used by some candy chefs, even a solid shortening. Stir 1 tablespoon of the oil into every 3 ounces of melted chocolate you use over low heat. Quick-tempered chocolate will only hold up for 2-3 days, but the candy is usually long gone before that.

Chocolate Sauce

- If too much heat is applied to chocolate sauce it will burn or clump up.
- Chocolate is best melted in a double boiler with the water simmering, not boiling.
- Only use the type of chocolate called for in the recipe; do not substitute.
- Buy the best quality chocolate; there is a difference.
- When making chocolate sauce you need to use a heavy saucepan to control the heat more easily.

Chocolate-Covered Fruit

- Use the best brand of bittersweet chocolate and melt it to dip fruit into for a great dessert.
- Place a toothpick into each piece of fruit, dip it, and then place it on a cookie sheet in the refrigerator to harden.

Coating Chocolate

- Normally used in candy making.
- Has a high percentage of cocoa butter, giving candy a hard, shiny finish.
- This is a special chocolate that is hard to use unless you are experienced.

Cocoa Powder

- Dried and powdered chocolate liquor with at least half of the cocoa butter removed.

The "Dutched" variety has alkali added to make it darker and less acidic.

- Some of the cocoa powders that are used for cooking have sugar added.
- The best quality will be the unsweetened variety.

Confectioner's Chocolate

- Not really chocolate. Made from vegetable oil instead of cocoa butter.

Couverture (covering)

- This special kind of chocolate contains more cocoa butter than standard chocolate.
- The cocoa butter content is usually between 33%-38%.
- Used for coating truffles and similar confectionery products.
- Commonly used in "enrobing" or "hand-dipping."

Chocolate Fondue

- Chocolate fondue makes a great dessert treat, just mix 8 ounces of chocolate chips with $1/2$ cup of whipping cream. Melt in a double boiler and stir until it is smooth. Remove from the heat and mix in $1^1/4$ teaspoon of pure vanilla extract. Dip grapes or strawberries in the fondue.

Chocolate Mousse

- For a different treat, try pouring $1/4$ cup of Grand Marnier into the egg yolk and chocolate mixture just before it begins to thicken.

Chocolate Pudding

- When making pudding from scratch, mix together the water and cornstarch very thoroughly and set it aside.
- Mix the other ingredients in a large saucepan. Mix the sugar, cocoa and salt stirring well with a wooden spoon, then mix in the warm milk and make a smooth paste.
- Place the saucepan over medium heat and bring to a boil while stirring continually for 2-3 minutes before adding the chopped chocolate. Stir until all has melted and is smooth.
- Gradually add the heavy cream and the cornstarch mixture (be sure it is well mixed) and stir for about 5-6 minutes or until it thickens and boils.
- Make sure that you stir around the bottom on the pot as it cooks with the wooden spoon to avoid lumps.
- After you pour the pudding into the individual cups, place a piece of plastic wrap directly on top of the pudding to prevent skin from forming.

If you would like coffee-flavored pudding, substitute 1 tablespoon of coffee liqueur or Kahlua for the vanilla extract.

- Toasted nuts can be added to provide a different taste treat.

Melting Chocolate

- When you are melting chocolate, water droplets along with excess condensation and high temperatures may cause the chocolate to stiffen prematurely. To alleviate this problem, just add 1 teaspoon of corn oil to the pan and stir. More oil can be added if needed to assure the proper consistency.
- When melting chocolate, spray the inside with an oil spray to make it easier to remove all the chocolate.
- If you need to grate chocolate, make sure you allow it to warm to room temperature first to make the job easier.

Make sure that no water gets into chocolate when it is melting or it may cause the chocolate to harden and clump up.

- If chocolate does get hard and clumps up, just add 1 tablespoon of corn oil for every 6 ounces of chocolate and re-heat while stirring until it becomes smooth again.
- If you scorch chocolate even the slightest bit discard the batch.
- Chocolate squares that are wrapped in paper can be melted in the paper.
- If a white coating appears on chocolate it is because the chocolate has been around moisture and the moisture has drawn the sugar to the surface and crystallized it.
- If you are preparing a recipe that calls for melted chocolate, remember to always melt the chocolate in the liquid for the best results. Use low heat and stir continuously.
- The microwave does a good job of melting chocolate.
- Chocolate is best melted in a double boiler over simmering water not boiling water.
- Chocolate should be cooled at room temperature before you add it to cookie dough or any cake batter.

Help! My chocolate had a seizure

- If your chocolate turns from a shiny, smooth liquid to a dull, very thick paste it has what is called a "chocolate seizure." Seizing happens when you do not follow instructions to the letter. The following are the most common problems that cause seizure:

- The temperature got too hot and it was not stirred continually.
- Milk and white chocolate are more susceptible to seizing.

  Moisture got into the pot. Even a small amount of moisture from a metal spoon can cause a seizure. Use a wooden spoon.

- Fondue chocolate can change if too much moisture gets into the fondue pot from the fruit that is being dipped in.
- Never add cold cream or milk; be sure it is the same temperature as the chocolate.
- Even large amounts of liquid can be added to chocolate as long as the liquid is the same temperature or has at least been warmed.

Milk Chocolate

- Contains chocolate liquor, cocoa butter, sugar, milk solids and vanilla.
- Best for eating and not for baking.

Semisweet or Bittersweet Chocolate

- Chocolate liquor that has sugar, cocoa butter and vanilla added.
- Bittersweet chocolate has a little less sugar than semisweet chocolate.
- Semisweet chocolate morsels can be substituted for semisweet chocolate in all recipes.
- To make bittersweet chocolate, use 1 ounce of unsweetened chocolate and mix it with 4 ounces of semisweet chocolate.

Unsweetened Chocolate

- Contains about 50% cocoa butter in the chocolate liquor.
- Does not contain sugar or any other added ingredients.
- This is not to be confused with bittersweet chocolate.

Unsweetened Baking Chocolate (Premelted)

- Liquid blend of cocoa and vegetable oil. Best to use the standard unsweetened chocolate.

White Chocolate

- Contains no chocolate liquor and is not really chocolate.
- This is made from cocoa butter, sugar, milk solids and flavorings.
- Quality white chocolate is at least 100% cocoa butter.

HOT CHOCOLATE (COCOA)

- The basic formula for great cocoa is to place $2^1/_2$ teaspoons of unsweetened cocoa, $2^1/_2$ Tablespoons of granulated sugar and a pinch of salt in a saucepan, then add $^1/_2$ cup of cool tap water and place over medium heat. Cook until thick, then slowly add $1^3/_4$ cup of milk while stirring continuously. Do not allow the cocoa to boil.
- If you would like foamy cocoa, just beat it slightly with an electric beater.
- To spice it up a little, just add $^1/_2$ teaspoon of peppermint schnapps.
- Cocoa does not mix well with water and tends to remain in suspension for only a short period of time. The heat from the water will cause the particles to remain in suspension only as long as the drink is hot. As the drink cools, a percentage of the particles will fall to the bottom of the cup.
- When mixed with hot milk, however, the fat in the milk tends to hold the chocolate better in suspension.
- A great drink in the summer is to take a cup of ice, a cup of whole milk and 3 tablespoons of a quality cocoa and place it into a blender until the ice cubes are gone. Makes a great chocolate chiller. Ice 4 can be added in place of the milk if you prefer.

Recipe for homemade hot chocolate

1 pint heavy cream
$^1/_4$ cup whole milk
6 ounces semi-sweet chocolate bits(finely grated)
1 tsp. vanilla (not imitation)

Using a double boiler, melt the chocolate; then slowly stir in the cream, vanilla and milk. Continue to heat the mixture to a point just below boiling, stirring continually. Serve topped with whipped cream.

- Mixes should only be used to prepare hot, chocolate drinks. They contain milk or cream powder and sugar or a substitute.
- Only pure cocoa or "real" chocolate should be used when recipes call for cocoa powder or chocolate.
- There are new chemicals being added to some cocoas used for hot drinks. These new ingredients are called texturing agents and are tapioca-based products that will help keep the cocoa powder in suspension better providing you a smoother, more enjoyable drink. The new product is called Textra™ and is manufactured by National Starch Company and actually gives the product a mouth feel similar to that of fat, without the fat calories.
- Hot chocolate does have caffeine; however, it only has about 1/10th the amount found in a cup of regular coffee.
- The better grades of hot chocolate powders are sweetened with sugar; however, there is a sugar-free hot chocolate available that uses Nutrasweet™. The amount of sugar is low in a hot chocolate and the real sugar is preferred to an artificial sweetener.
- Most European cocoas are less sweet than the American varieties. Europeans prefer a cocoa that does not have the sweet taste so that they can enjoy the flavor of the chocolate more.
- White, hot chocolate is hot chocolate without the "chocolate liquor," which makes real chocolate "real." It does have a smooth, creamy flavor and is a favorite of many hot chocolate connoisseurs.
- If you purchase one of the better brands of cocoa powder, such as Mont Blanc, it should last for at least a year and be fresh.
- A new item from the Sunbeam Company is now being sold called the "Cocomotion." The Cocomotion is a European-designed machine that is capable of heating, aerating and blending 4 cups worth of hot chocolate in 10 minutes. The machine has a clear plastic chamber that allows the children to view the mixture being prepared. The unit is priced at $49.95, which includes a recipe book.
- If you want to eliminate the skin forming on top of your hot chocolate, just beat the drink for a few seconds until it gets frothy.
- Try mixing a teaspoon of cornstarch and a pinch of salt in a small amount of water and adding it to the pot of hot chocolate to improve the taste and texture.

Fudge

The word "fudge" was originally used to denote a negative act or to cheat. The term was picked up, however, by college women in the early part of the 20th century to pertain to the fact that they were going to "fudge" and eat candy to help them gain the 15 pounds that was expected of a freshman to gain during their freshman year. The term relating to the 15 pounds was first used at Wellesley and Vassar colleges and the candy was called "Wellesley fudge" and "Vassar fudge."

- Plastic or rubber spatulas may melt if the fudge gets too hot and should not be used.
- Raw sugar is not the best sugar for fudge.
- The best chocolate is Hershey's for fudge.

Fudge is made from three ingredients; sugar, liquid (usually milk), chocolate and flavoring if desired.

- Corn syrup and honey do not produce good results.
- If you use any other nut except walnuts, only use $^3/_4$ cup instead of 1 cup.
- It is OK to make fudge when it is snowing since the humidity is usually low. If it is a wet, heavy snow the humidity will be too high.
- Powdered sugar should not be used in fudge.

- Brown sugar can be used to replace white sugar but only up to $^1/_2$ of the total sugar used in the recipe.
- If you want to use milk chocolate only use half milk chocolate and half semi-sweet chocolate.

- When making fudge you need to continue with all procedures until completely done.
- A variety of extracts can be added to fudge to produce great flavors. Some of the favorites include mint, lemon, vanilla, orange and maple, however, only add $^1/_4$ teaspoon of an extract to fudge

- Always use a wooden spoon to mix fudge and mix until it starts to become firm before adding any raisins or nuts. Metal spoons get too hot.

The basics of fudge making

- The mixture of milk, sugar and butter are brought to a boil
- The boil must be held for 5-10 minutes to reduce the amount of water and supersaturate the sugary slurry.

  If you live at sea level, you will have less trouble with your fudge setting up than people who live at high altitudes or in humid climates.

- If you use semi-sweet chocolate bits, the milk will make the taste similar to milk chocolate.
- If you use milk chocolate as your base the fudge may be too milk chocolate unless it is to your liking.
- Using milk chocolate will make very sweet fudge, which many people do not like.
- Nuts, cherries or raisins can be added after the fudge is finished cooking and is ready to be cooled.
- If you do not add any nuts or raisins a 9 X 9-inch pan will do.

- Insulated pots may cause the fudge to cool too slowly.
- If fudge is wrapped as airtight as possible it can be frozen for about 12 months.
- Fudge can be poured into a lightly buttered glass dish or a tin foil lined pan that has been lightly buttered.
- The texture of fudge will become creamier if allowed to remain at room temperature for the first 18 hours after it was poured into the pan.

Fudge won't set up?

- If you have a problem with fudge setting up, just add 1 teaspoon of cornstarch when you start mixing in the ingredients.
- Divinity fudge tends to attract moisture and cannot be made on humid days.
- Placing the fudge in the refrigerator may harden it temporarily, but when it gets back to room temperature it will start to soften again.

Too much butter is a common problem.

- If the water content is too high it won't set properly.
- Poor grades of margarine that have been substituted for quality butter will also cause the problem.

PAULETTE'S FUDGE RECIPE

5 ounces of quality unsalted butter (stick)
2³/₄ cups of granulated sugar
²/₃ cups of evaporated milk (not condensed milk)
12 ounces of semi-sweet chocolate chips or bits
7 ounce of quality marshmallow crème
³/₄ cup of fresh walnuts (chopped)
¹/₄-¹/₂ cup of raisins (good quality)
1 teaspoon of pure vanilla extract (best quality)

Use a 13 X 9-inch pan or equivalent and grease it lightly with the butter wrapper. Mix the sugar and milk in a 3-quart saucepan, stir continually and bring to a boil. The butter should be added after you mix the sugar into the milk and after it starts to boil. Boil gradually and start with a medium heat and then go to high.

Do not allow crystallization around the inside top of the pot. Wipe clean.
Boil for about 7-8 minutes on medium-high heat. Should be a rolling boil.
Use a candy thermometer and boil until the temperature reaches 235°F.
Remove from heat and stir in butter.
Chocolate chips, marshmallow and vanilla should be in a separate <u>heat-safe</u> bowl.
Carefully pour the hot butter, sugar and milk mixture over the chocolate chip mixture and stir until combined.
Add any remaining ingredients or raisins and mix well, then pour into pan.
The fudge should be cooled at room temperature and should set up perfect. Slice as soon as it sets up but is not completely solid.

DESSERTS

Baked Alaska

Baked Alaska was invented by Benjamin Thompson around 1800 in Massachusetts. He studied the resistance of egg whites to heat and was able to place a crust on top of ice cream. The dish was originally known as "omelette surprise" and then "Alaska-Florida Cake." The dessert was originally prepared and served at Delmonico's Restaurant in New York City by Chef Charles Ranhofer in 1867.

- The sponge cake used must be trimmed to 1 inch in thickness.
- The cake cannot be covered with more than 3 inches of ice cream.
- Freeze the cake and ice cream until solid.
- The egg whites must be beat until stiff before adding 1 teaspoon of pure vanilla, $1/2$ teaspoon of cream of tartar and $2/3$ cup of granulated sugar.
- The frozen ice cream/cake is removed from the freezer and the egg whites are spread in swirls around the ice cream and shaped into a dome.
- Bake in a pre-heated oven at 500°F just until the top of the dome is golden brown, which should only take about 3 minutes.
- The dessert must be served immediately.

Frozen Desserts

- To remove a frozen dessert from a mold, just place a very hot towel around the mold for a few seconds.

Tiramisu

Originated in the Italian provence of Tuscany and was originally pre-pared for the Grand Duke Cosimo de'Medici III and called "duke's soup." The dish did not gain popularity in the United States until the 1980's. The original tiramisu that is still served along the banks of the canals in Venice is composed of ladyfingers, lightly moistened with marsala and espresso, then layered with sweetened egg yolks and enriched mascapone cheese. It is sold chilled with a light dusting of cocoa powder.

- Make sure that the egg yolks and confectioner's sugar and mixed together until they are just pale and thick.

- Then beat in 1 tablespoon of the liqueur and sweet Marsala, then add the mascarpone cheese and only beat until smooth and somewhat thick.
- In another bowl combine the coffee or espresso and 1 tablespoon of the liqueur. Place 3 ladyfingers into the bottom of the glasses you are using, then slowly drizzle the coffee mixture over them.

Ladyfingers are sold in different sizes. Usually, 2 6-ounce packages will be enough for two layers.

- Spoon in half of the mascarpone mixture and sprinkle with grated milk chocolate.
- Repeat the layers of ladyfingers, coffee and mascarpone mixture and chocolate and refrigerate for about 2 hours before serving.

CHAPTER 23

SWEETENERS & JELLIES

NATURAL SWEETENERS

Brown Sugar

- May be purchased in either light or dark granulated forms.
- The lighter the brown sugar the lighter the flavor. The darker the more molasses flavor it will have.
- Store brown sugar in the freezer and it will not harden or cake up.
- When you measure brown sugar, make sure that you pack it firmly into the measuring spoon or cup.

Never use "liquid" brown sugar in recipes as a substitute for granulated brown sugar.

- Always purchase brown sugar in a plastic bag. Unless it is very fresh, it will be partially caked if purchased in a box.
- If you must store brown sugar in the cupboard, be sure and add a small piece of fresh white bread to the package and replace it weekly.
- When substituting brown sugar for white sugar in a recipe, be aware that the baked goods will be somewhat more moist and may have a slight butterscotch flavor.

Corn Syrup

The most common liquid sweetener produced from a mixture of starch granules derived from corn, which are then processed with acids or enzymes to convert it into heavy sweet syrup. The corn syrup is then artificially flavored and used for literally thousands of products including; pancake syrups, candy making, ice creams, etc. The fact that corn syrup tends to retard crystallization makes it a good choice for candy, preserves, and frostings. Corn syrup does not store well and should be used by the date on the label.

- When a recipe calls for corn syrup and does not specify whether dark or light, always use light.
- Dark corn syrup has a stronger flavor and will add color to a dish.
- Since corn syrup has the ability to retard crystallization, it is excellent for icings, jellies and most candies.

Corn syrup will provide a chewy texture, which granulated sugar will not do.

- Honey is sweeter than corn syrup. If a recipe calls for honey, use honey.
- If you don't have corn syrup in the house, just use $1^{1}/_{4}$ cups granulated sugar plus $^{1}/_{4}$ cup of cool water to equal 1 cup of light corn syrup.

Confectioner's Sugar (powdered)

- Will usually be labeled 10X. The more "X's" on a sugar bag, the finer the sugar.
- There is a difference in confectioner's sugar when it is sifted. When you sift 1 pound of the sugar it will equal $4^{1}/_{2}$ cups, however, if you don't sift it, it will be only 4 cups.
- Always keep a shaker of confectioner's sugar handy when you need to "dust" cookies or a pastry.
- If you are going to sprinkle confectioner's sugar on a cake or cookie, make sure that they are cool and dry before sugaring it.

Granulated Sugar

- Superfine sugar is the finest degree of granulated sugar, which has been powdered in a blender or food processor.
- Superfine sugar dissolves very quickly and is excellent when making meringue and as a sweetener for cold beverages.
- Granulated sugar can be replaced with superfine sugar in recipes equally.
- Granulated sugar may be processed from sugar cane or sugar beets.
- To prepare superfine sugar, blend sugar cubes or granulated sugar in a blender or food processor into a powder.

Honey

Honey was first mentioned in the old writing of the Sumerians, Babylonians, the Hittite code, the sacred writings of India and the writings of the Egyptians. Palestine is often called the "land of milk and honey." Honey was also used as a sweetener by the Egyptians. By the 11th century, the Germans were sweetening their beer with honey and honey was introduced to the American Colonies in 1638.

TYPES OF HONEY

Whole Comb

- This is an unprocessed form, which comes directly from the hive and can be purchased with the large waxy pieces floating in the raw honey.
- The comb contains many unopened honey cells from which the raw honey is removed from cells as they are broken open when harvested.

Raw Honey

- Honey that has not been heat processed and is in the original form when harvested from the honey comb.
- This product may contain insect parts and debris from the hive.

Filtered Honey

- Raw honey that has been heated just enough to allow the honey to pass through filters to remove the debris impurities.
- The heat is low enough to allow the honey to retain almost all of its nutrient values.

Liquid Honey

- Liquid honey is heated to higher temperatures than any other processed honey so that it can be easily filtered.
- It is a lighter color and the flavor is somewhat milder than other types of honey because of the heat processing.
- The honey does not crystallize as easily as most other types of honey, however, many nutrients are lost in the processing.

Spun Honey (crystallized)

- This type of honey is not only heat processed, but has a good percentage of its moisture removed to make it creamy and easy to spread.
- This honey lacks most nutrients that are associated with honey. It is just a sweet treat.

Honey Facts

- The highest quality honey will be labeled "100% pure unfiltered," "raw," or "uncooked." This honey: will not be nutrient depleted by the heat processing.
- Honey is a unique sugar in that it is the only food that will not grow bacteria. Remember, when using honey, it is twice as sweet as granulated sugar.
- Crystallized honey can be liquefied by just placing it into the microwave for about 1 minute depending on the size of the jar and the wattage of the microwave.
- Never allow honey to boil or get too hot since it will break down and must be discarded.
- One pound of honey = 1 $\frac{1}{3}$ cups.
- Honey that is produced from certain geological areas may contain substances that are harmful to the human body. Farmers call this honey "mad honey." Bees that obtain nectar from flowers such as the rhododendron, azalea, and laurel family may cause symptoms of numbness in the extremities, vomiting, and muscle weakness. These are rarely fatal but will cause a bit of discomfort for a few days.
- Honey should never be given to babies since their digestive system is too immature to handle the botulism bacillus if it is present and they tend to develop a form of infant botulism. Use only pasteurized honey, never honey that has not been pasteurized for children under 1-year of age.
- Honey storage is very important and honey should be stored in as airtight a

container as possible since the sugars are "moisture attracting" and will absorb water from the air very easily especially if the humidity is over 60%.

- If the water content of honey goes above 17% the honey and yeast will activate, the honey will ferment, and the sugars will change to alcohol and carbon dioxide.
- Honey tends to crystallize easily causing the glucose to be released from the sugars. Heating the honey slightly will force the glucose back into the sugar molecule and return the honey to a liquid.
- The flavor of the different honey may make it difficult to cook with. Some are sweeter than others and some take on the flavor of the flower, herb or weed source.
- Onc cup of honey can be replaced in a recipe with $1^1/_4$ cup of granulated sugar and $^1/_4$ cup more of the liquid recommended in the recipe.
- Corn syrup, maple syrup or molasses can be used to replace honey in a recipe.
- If you would like to use honey instead of granulated sugar in a recipe, use $^1/_3$ cup of honey, reduce the liquid by 2 tablespoons and add $^1/_4$ teaspoon of baking soda to replace $^1/_2$ cup of granulated sugar.

Honey has the tendency to over-brown certain baked goods when it is used to replace sugar. Best to lower the temperature by about 25°F to compensate.

- If you are going to use honey to bake with, always choose the mildest-flavored, which is white or golden honey.
- When honey is added to a batter, it should be added in a slow stream with continuous stirring.
- When honey is added to bake goods, the baked goods will remain moist for a longer period of time.

Maple Syrup

- The "sap run" is one of the more interesting mysteries that nature has recently shared with us. Pure maple syrup is the product of the rock maple tree, which is the only tree that produces high quality syrup. The sap is only collected in the spring providing ideal conditions exist. The amount of syrup available is dependent on the leaves converting the right proportions of sunlight, water, and carbon dioxide into sugar. Sap is only collected from the first major spring thaw until the leaf buds begin to burst. If the sap collection is not discontinued at this point the syrup will have a bitter flavor.

- Conditions must be near perfect to have a good "sap run." The winter must be severe enough to freeze the trees roots, the snow cover must extend to the spring to keep the roots very cold, the temperature must be extreme from day to night, and the tree must have excellent exposure to adequate sunlight. To produce sap the tree needs to have stored sugar from the previous season in the trunk, especially in specialized cells known as "xylem" cells. Transport tubes are formed in the tree from both live and dead cells in which the xylem normally carries water and nutrients from the tree's root system to the leaves and trunk.

- In early spring when the rock maple tree thaws, the xylem cells tend to pump sugar into specialized xylem vessels, the transport tubes are now activated and the increase in sugar content in the xylem vessels creates a pressure that draws water into the vessels, increasing the water pressure. As the pressure increases, the xylem cells become more active and start to release waste products and carbon dioxide. The carbon dioxide gas level in the water tends to decrease with the rise in spring temperature, the trunk of the tree warms causing the gas pressure and water to build up in the xylem tissues forcing the sap to run and be collected.

- Maple tree sap is about 3% sucrose with one tree averaging about 10-12 gallons of sap per spring season. To produce one gallon of "pure maple syrup" it requires 35 gallons of sap. The final syrup is composed of 62% sucrose, 35% water, 1% glucose and fructose, and 1% malic acid. The more the syrup is boiled during processing, the darker the syrup becomes due to a reaction between the sugars and proteins.

MAPLE CANDY TREAT

- This treat goes back hundreds of years, except our great grandmothers didn't have the convenience of a microwave oven. The following ingredients will be needed:

> 3 Cups of crushed ice
> $^1/_2$ Cup of "real" maple syrup (imitation only if you must)

Place the maple syrup into a microwave-safe bowl and cook on high power for 4-6 minutes depending on the wattage. The syrup must be at a hard stage and very hot (be careful) when it is removed. Place the crushed ice in about a 6 X 8 shallow glass dish and using a wooden spoon, spoon the syrup over the crushed ice. When the hot syrup comes into contact with the crushed ice it will turn into hard strands of maple sugar, linking all the sugar molecules together. Remove the strands (with a fork), which will be fairy hard, allow them to cool, then place them into individual pieces of plastic wrap.

- When a product is labeled "maple sugar" it must contain a minimum of 35% "real" maple syrup.
- Try to find a product where the color is very, light. the lighter the color, the higher the quality. Maple syrup is best stored in the refrigerator after it is opened to retain its flavor and retard the growth of mold. If it granulates, just warm it up slightly. It should last about 1 year and is best used at room temperature or slightly heated.
- Read the label well! Make sure it doesn't say: "maple flavored," "maple-blended," or use the word "imitation."
- The real thing is rare and does contain an excellent blend of natural nutrients, especially iron and calcium. The typical pancake syrup is almost pure corn syrup and artificial maple flavoring.
- Pure maple syrup will have a better flavor than artificial maple syrup and should always be used when maple syrup is called for in a recipe.
- When using maple syrup in a recipe always be sure and allow it to warm to room temperature if it has been refrigerated.
- Watch for the presence of mold on the lid. If any appears discard the entire container.
- Maple syrup can be substituted for honey in a recipe.

Molasses

On a very unseasonably warm day in January 1919, a large tank of molasses burst open in the North End of Boston, Massachusetts. Over 2 million gallons of sticky molasses syrup flowed down city streets at a speed of 35-40 miles per hour, carrying everything in its path along with it. Pedestrians, horses and buggies were not spared and slid along with the tide of molasses.

- Molasses is produced from sugar cane that goes through a complex processing, removing all nutrients, resulting in a white sugar. It is basically the by-product of the refining of sugar. The residue that remains after processing, is the actual blackstrap molasses. Unsulfured molasses is actually produced to make molasses and not the results of the processing to make sugar.
- Unsulfured molasses has a lighter, cleaner flavor than sulfured. Blackstrap molasses is collected from the top layer and is higher in nutrients than any other type of molasses. It is an excellent source of iron, calcium, and potassium.
- If a recipe calls for dark molasses, you can use light molasses without a problem.

When you bake with molasses you will need to reduce the temperature by 25°F or the food may over-brown.

- Try coating a measuring spoon with spray vegetable oil before measuring molasses to obtain a more accurate measurement.
- Molasses has a degree of acidity that can be neutralized by adding 1 teaspoon of baking soda to the dry ingredients for every cup of molasses the recipe calls for.
- Molasses is best when used in gingerbread and baked beans.
- Cane syrup may be confused with molasses, but is really cane juice that has been boiled down to make the syrup.
- Treacle is another sweetener that is similar to molasses, but is slightly different and is a more pale golden brown color.

Raw Sugar (turbinado)

- Refined sugar that is almost exactly like refined white sugar, except with the addition of molasses for color.
- Has no advantage over normal refined sugar except the price is higher. As with all sugar it can be labeled "natural" to make you think that it is better for you.

Sugar Substitutes

- Sugar substitutes cannot be used in baked goods with good results.
- Equal tends to breakdown and lose its sweetening power when heated.

ARTIFICIAL SWEETENERS

Acesulfame K

- Non-caloric sweetener, which is sold under two brand names, "Sunette" or "Sweet-One."
- It will provide sweetening and cannot be metabolized by the body, but passes through and is excreted.
- It has an advantage over Equal in that it can be used for high temperature baking and cooking.
- It is about 200 times sweeter than sugar and commonly used commercially in chewing gums, beverage mixers, candies, puddings, and custards.

Alitame

- Sweetener produced from two amino acids (proteins) and has 2,000 times the sweetness of sugar.
- It is metabolized by the body with almost no caloric value.
- It is a good all around sweetener that may be used in most recipes and baked goods.

Aspartame (Nutrasweet, Equal)

- Caution must be taken when Aspartame is heated since a percentage may turn into methyl alcohol. It is not recommended for use in baked goods and any drink that requires a liquid being brought to the boiling point. Recent negative study results by leading universities and the Arizona Department of Health Sciences were regarded by the FDA as "unfounded fears."

Cyclamates

- May be found again in baked goods and other products.
- The FDA reversed a decision and is now allowing the use of this artificial sweetener. However, it would still be best to read the label and try and avoid most artificial sweeteners.

L-Sugars

- Artificial sweetener that contains no calories or aftertaste and is available to replace a number of other sweeteners.
- Can be substituted cup for cup for granulated sugar in recipes and may be available shortly.

Saccharin

- This sweetener has been around since 1879 and is 300 times sweeter than sugar.
- Used in many common products such as mouthwashes and lipsticks.
- Presently, it is under additional testing by the FDA. Products that do contain saccharin must have a warning label stating that saccharin may be hazardous to your health.

Stevia

- This sweetener is new to the United States but has been used in South America and Japan for a number of years as a calorie-free sweetener.
- Stevia is an herbal extract from a member of the chrysanthemum family that is being sold in health food stores as a "dietary supplement."
- Since it is a natural herbal product, the Dietary Supplement Act of 1994 applies and the product was allowed into the country. However, the FDA is still not sure of any potential problems that might arise since testing is not conclusive at present.
- The extract is concentrated and is 200-300 times sweeter than table sugar. It is being used for cooking and may leave a licorice flavored aftertaste.

Sucralose

- Refined from common table sugar but has been concentrated to where it is 600 times sweeter with no calories.
- Sucralose is a very stable product in foods and carbonated beverages sold in Canada under the brand name "Splenda." Splenda can be used for high temperature cooking and will retain its sweet taste.

JELLIES & PRESERVES

- If you replace sugar in jams and jellies, use half as much honey as you would sugar. Two cups of honey will replace 4 cups of sugar. You will also have to cook the jelly a little longer.
- When using honey in preserves or jellies, always use liquid honey and powdered pectin.
- Never make jelly or preserves if the humidity is over 50% or if it is a rainy day.

Jellies should never be placed in the freezer or they will lose their consistency and become granular.

- Best to prepare jelly in small batches since large batches use large quantities of juice and need an extended boiling time, which results in a loss of flavor.
- Jelly should always be boiled rapidly. When jelly is boiled slowly, the pectin in the fruit juices may be destroyed.

There are a number of reasons why crystals form in jelly.

1. Crystals may form if too much sugar is used. Test the fruit juice with a Jelmeter (sweetness tester) to be sure that you have the proper proportions of sugar.
2. Crystals can form if there is sugar that has not been dissolved and is stuck to the sides of the saucepan. Make sure that you wipe the sides of the pan clean and free of crystals with a damp rag before you fill the jars.
3. If you are making grape jelly, the grape juice you are using may have tartrate crystals in it. To resolve this, just extract the grape juice and allow the tartrate crystals to settle down. This can be accomplished: by refrigerating the grape juice overnight and the straining the juice through a fine sieve to remove the crystals.
4. Crystals can also be formed from cooking the mixture too slowly or too long. The juice should be cooked at a rapid boil and when it reaches the jellying point, removed from the heat.

- When jelly is poured into the jars directly from the pot, keep the pot very close to the top of the jar or as the jelly is poured, slowly air may become trapped in the hot jelly and form bubbles. Pour as fast as you can safely. If you see bubbles in the jelly, discard the jelly.

One of the most common problems when preparing jelly is that the jelly is too soft. The more common reasons for this are as follows:

1. Overcooking the fruit to extract the juice. This lowers the pectin level.
2. Using too much water when extracting the juice. Follow directions more closely.
3. Used the wrong proportions of sugar and juice.
4. Concentrations are too low from undercooking.
5. The fruit was too low in acid content. A small amount of lemon juice may be needed.
6. Making too large a batch. Never use more than 4-6 cups of juice for each batch.

• If your jelly is too dark, it may have been overcooked and the sugar burnt. Boiling too long will also cause a dark color.

Sometimes jelly tends to "weep." This is caused by too much acid, which reduces the effectiveness of the pectin. Acidity levels when preparing jelly is very important.

• Temperature fluctuations will also cause jelly to become weepy.
• Make sure that the fruit you are using is fully ripe. If the fruit is not ripe the jelly may be cloudy.
• Cloudiness can also be caused by forcing the fruit through the strainer instead of allowing it to drip naturally.
• If your jelly is too stiff and tough you have probably overcooked it. Jelly should be cooked to a temperature of 220°F or 8° more than the boiling point of water. It should flow from a spoon in a sheet.
• Too much pectin or too little sugar will make the jelly tough.
• When adding pectin you should use only ³/₄ cup of sugar to every 1 cup of juice for the majority of fruits.

CHAPTER 24

CONDIMENTS

Hot Pepper Sauces

- When handling hot peppers, always wear light rubber gloves and be careful not to touch your eyes. The chemical capsaicin in peppers can be very irritating to your skin and especially your eyes. The same chemical is used in police pepper sprays. One drop of pure capsaicin diluted in 100,000 drops of water is still strong enough to blister your tongue.
- One of the most common hot sauces is salsa. These sauces are very popular in Mexico and most of South America. They may be served either hot or cold.
- To reduce the hotness, remove the seeds and the ribs then wash the peppers in cold water.
- If you really want fire hot, try Mad Dog Liquid Fire Hot Sauce. Just use it a drop at a time or it will take your toupee off and send it flying. The product contains jalapeno peppers and African Bird's Eye chili pepper. There are a few other secret ingredients and I think it's best we don't know what they are.
- Salsa can be frozen; however, it must be uncooked and freshly prepared. Drain as much liquid off as you can from the tomatoes or a layer of ice will be formed on the top.

Tabasco Sauce

Only three ingredients go into producing the most popular hot sauce in the world: they are fiery, hot Tabasco peppers, vinegar and salt. Sales total over 76 million bottles annually. The Tabasco pepper seeds were originally planted in the United States on Avery Island, Louisiana around 1865 and the product produced today is still using peppers planted from the first strain. The salt used in Tabasco Sauce is from the same island. The peppers need to be fermented for 3 years before they can be used in the sauce. Tabasco was first marketed in 1868.

Hot Peppers

- The following peppers have been graded as to their level of hotness. A grade of 10 will knock your socks off and curl your toes, 6-9 will only knock your socks off, and below 6 will still give you a pretty good kick, but are palatable for most people. If your mouth is on fire, try to drink a small amount of milk or beer, since both will neutralize the hot bite. Most dairy products will work well. Peppers are graded on a Scoville Scale for their level of hotness. The hottest pepper is the Habanero at a 200,000-300,000 Scoville unit rating.

Pepper	Grade	Scoville
Habanero	10+	(200,000-300,000)
Thai Piquin	10	(100,000)
Jalapeno	9	(85,000)
Cayenne	8+	(50,000)
De Arbol	8	(25,000)
Hungarian Wax	7	(20,000)
Serrano	6+	(12,000)
Cherry	6	(7,500)
Cascabel	5	(5,000)
Ancho	3+	(1,500)
Anaheim	3	(1,000)
Pimiento	2	(500)
Peperoncini	1	(100)

HOT! HOT! HOT!
NEED MILK!
MUY PRONTO!

South of the Border Jalapeno Vinaigrette Recipe

³/₄ cup extra virgin olive oil (cold processed)
1 tablespoon quality yellow mustard
2 cloves of finely chopped garlic
¹/₄ cup red wine vinegar
1 teaspoon finely chopped jalapeno peppers (remove seeds and ribs and rinse in cold water)
¹/₄ cup minced fresh cilantro
Add salt and ground black pepper to taste

Thoroughly mix all the ingredients together and allow the mixture to stand at room temperature for about 30 minutes. Refrigerate if not used immediately, but allow the mixture to return to room temperature before using.

- If you like to prepare spicy, somewhat hot mustard sauce to place on beef sandwiches, try mixing 1 teaspoon of white horseradish with 3 teaspoons of American mustard.
- To prepare mustard butter, just blend 3 tablespoons of American mustard with ¹/₂ cup unsalted room temperature butter. If you want super-hot, use Chinese mustard.

Ketchup (catsup)

Ketchup was originally called "ketsiap" and was invented by the Chinese in the 1600's. It was used as a sauce for fish and was composed of fish entrails, vinegar and hot spices. The sauce was exported to Malayan's who sold the sauce to English sailors during the 1700's. In 1792 the sauce was altered and tomatoes were added and it was renamed "catsup." The sauce became popular in the United States in 1830 and H.J. Heinz started producing the commercial product in 1870.

Cranberry Ketchup Recipe

4¹/₂ cups fresh cranberries (frozen if necessary)
2 cups of apple cider vinegar
1¹/₂ cups of red onions, chopped
2 cups pure water
3¹/₄ cups granulated sugar
1 tablespoon powdered cinnamon
¹/₂ tablespoon ground cloves
1 tablespoon ground allspice
1¹/₄ tablespoon celery seed
1 teaspoon ground black pepper
³/₄ teaspoon sea salt
¹/₂ teaspoon quality dry mustard
1 cup dry white wine (optional)

Combine the cranberries, onions, wine and water in a large saucepan and place over medium heat. Cook until the cranberries pop and no further then allow the mixture to cool slightly. Place the mixture in a blender and puree. Return the puree to the saucepan and add in the balance of the ingredients. Simmer the mixture over low heat for 25 minutes or until it starts to thicken, stirring frequently. Allow the mixture to cool and use or freeze.

Marinades (general)

- You can reduce the marinade to intensify the flavor and use it as a sauce.
- Some of the meat tenderizing foods that contain acids and can be used in marinades are papaya, pineapple, lemon juice, cider vinegar, lime juice and kiwi.
- The most common seasonings used in marinades are salt, black and red pepper, garlic and onions.
- Marinades are usually prepared with one or more acidic foods, which are used to soften the food, allowing the flavors to be more easily absorbed.
- They are usually thin liquids; however, most utilize an oil as a carrier of the flavorings into the food. Marinades may be used for as little as 30 minutes and as much as 2-3 days depending on the type of food and the recipe.
- Marinades will provide a small amount of moisture to a piece of meat; however, one of the major components of a marinade is acid. Acid will reduce the ability of the meat to retain its natural moisture when the meat is cooked. In some meat, the addition of the marinade will balance off this process and you

will not notice any dryness.
- Most marinades are used to both flavor the food as well as tenderize it.
- The number of seasonings used in marinades is endless and really depends on a person's taste.
- Metal of any type will cause the foods to have an off-flavor.

Marinated meats should be at room temperature when they start cooking.

- Many chefs use a plastic bag to apply the marinade to meats and fish. Just pour the marinade into the bag, add the food and seal it up well with a rubber band, plastic strap or metal tie. The bag can easily be turned occasionally to be sure that all areas of the food are well marinated.
- For great garlic marinade mix together $1/4$ cup of virgin olive oil, 4 cloves of crushed garlic, 4 tablespoons of cider vinegar, 5 tablespoons of parsley, $1/2$ cup of red wine and 1 tablespoon of finely, chopped red onion.

- Always marinade foods in a glass container since you will be using an acid medium.

If you use marinade for basting that was used for the food you are cooking, be sure and boil it first.

- Chicken needs only about 3-4 hours in the marinade or it will lose flavor.
- Meats should not be marinated for more than 3-4 hours, or the meat may have a tendency to dry out when being cooked from the acid in the marinade.
- Never marinade fish for more than 30 minutes in a delicate, flavored marinade.
- The length of time a piece of meat remains in the marinade will depend on the thickness of the meat and the strength of the marinade.

- Always remember to allow your roast to rest for 10 minutes after you remove it from the oven so that the liquids that are left can return to the surface of the roast.
- Sometimes a chef will simmer the marinade after removing the food, thus reducing it and concentrating the flavors and use the marinade as a sauce. One note of caution; if the marinade was used for raw meats of any kind or raw fish, it would be best not to use the marinade for a sauce unless it is boiled.

Garlic Marinade

¹/₄ cup extra virgin olive oil (cold pressed)
1 cloves of garlic, crushed
1 tablespoons apple cider vinegar
1 tablespoons of parsley
¹/₂ cup dry red wine
1 tablespoon finely chopped red onion

Combine all the ingredients in a bowl and mix thoroughly before placing the marinade into a plastic bag with the food. This marinade is best for meats, however, it does make a tasty chicken marinade.

Mustard

The mustard we know today can be traced back to 1726, and was produced by Adam Bernhard Bergrath in Dusseldorf. He combined strong brown mustard seeds with a milder yellow seed and added vinegar, water and salt. One of the finest quality mustard's produced in the world is made by Appel & Frenzel under the name Lowensenf Mustard.

If mustard is called for in a recipe, best to use standard American mustard unless some other mustard is recommended. There is a flavor and potency difference in mustards, especially German and Chinese mustards.

- Dijon mustard has a flavor range that needs to be taken into consideration when using it in a recipe. The flavor and potency ranges from mild to hot.
- A common combination is mayonnaise mixed with mustard. Use 3 teaspoons of Dijon mustard mixed with $^1/_2$ cup of standard mayonnaise.

Old Fashioned Mustard Sauce Recipe

3 tablespoons of quality mustard
1 cup heavy cream
3 tablespoons pure water
1$^1/_2$ teaspoons fresh cornstarch

Mix the mustard and heavy cream in a small pan and bring the mixture to a boil with the heat on high. Mix the water and cornstarch in a separate pan and stir until it becomes a smooth paste, then add it to the mustard sauce and bring to a boil, stirring continuously, as soon as it starts to boil, stop the cooking process and serve.

Soy Sauce

- Soy sauce is one of the most popular condiments in the world.
- It is prepared from roasted soybeans and wheat (or barley) which have been fermented.
- The Chinese claim that ketchup was originally produced from a Chinese soy sauce recipe.

There are four varieties of soy sauce

- Light soy sauce that we normally see in the supermarkets.
- Dark soy sauce, which is not as salty but has a very strong flavor.
- Chinese black soy sauce, which is very thick and the color of blackstrap molasses.
- Japanese tamari soy sauce, which is very dark, thick and has a lower salt content that the Chinese variety.

- Kikkoman International, Inc.: is the largest producer of soy sauce worldwide.
- Their latest product is a clear soy sauce that can be used in recipes without altering the color of the food. The company also produces soy sauce that is preservative-free and reduced-sodium, both available in either powered or liquid forms.

STEAK SAUCE

A-1 Steak Sauce

- The ingredients are: tomato puree, high fructose corn syrup, distilled vinegar, corn syrup, salt, raisins, spices, orange base (combination of orange, lemon and grapefruit juices), orange peel, dried onion and garlic, xanthan gum and caramel color.

New Steak Sauce

Grande Gusto™ is a new flavor enhancer that has been approved by the FDA and contains all-natural flavor and has no yeast or MSG.

Vinegar

- Vinegar is commonly produced from ethyl alcohol utilizing the bacteria, acetobacter, which feeds on the alcohol, converting it into acetic acid (vinegar).
- Vinegar, however, can be made from a number of other foods, which is the preferred variety to use such as, apples or grains.

Vinegar tends to stimulate the taste buds and make them more receptive to other flavors.

- The varieties of vinegar are endless depending on the food that is used to produce it. It is a mild acid called "acetic acid."
- The actual amount of acid in vinegar varies from 4-7 percent with the average being 5 percent. Common types include apple cider vinegar, plain white distilled, red and white wine, barley, malt, rice, and balsamic.
- The acetic acid content of vinegar: is referred to by "grains". A 5 percent acetic acid content is known as 50-grain vinegar. The 50-grain means that the product is 50% water and 50% vinegar.
- 6-7 percent vinegar will keep foods fresher longer because of the higher acid content. Vinegar will have a shelf life and retain its effectiveness for about 18 months.
- Studies have found that excessive use of vinegar, which contains a mild acid may cause digestive problems, liver disorders, ulcers and destroy red blood cells prematurely. In moderation there should be no problem, however, if you can substitute apple cider vinegar in a recipe it would be healthier.
- Vinegar has the tendency to lose its pungency when heated. For this reason, when you add vinegar to a dish, it should only be added when you remove the dish from the heat.
- If the level of acidity in vinegar is not desired, just add the vinegar while the dish is cooking and the acidity will dissipate.
- If you purchase a better quality wine, cider or malt vinegar, they may be used for a starter if the vinegar has not been filtered or pasteurized. Bacteria or "mother" may form on the surface, then sink to the bottom. If this occurs, the "mother" can be used to prepare another batch of vinegar similar to a sourdough starter.
- One method of tasting vinegar is to place a square sugar cube into the vinegar for about 5 seconds then suck out the vinegar. It is best not to try and taste more than 4-5 different varieties before drinking a small amount of pure mineral water to clear your taste buds.

If you over-sweeten a dish, try adding a small amount of vinegar until the flavor is more to your liking.

- When vegetables become slightly wilted, they can be revived, by placing them into a vinegar and water bath. Make sure the water is ice cold.

Apple Cider Vinegar

- Produced from whole apples that have been ground into pulp, then cold-pressed and fermented in wooden barrels. It can be used in salad dressings, pickling and any dish that calls for white vinegar. Be sure and purchase a good brand since some apple cider vinegar is produced from apple cores and peelings and poorly processed. The best flavoring herb combination is dill, garlic and bay.
- Apple cider vinegar contains malic acid, which is actually friendly to the human digestive process.

Balsamic Vinegar

The first historical reference to balsamic vinegar was in 1046 when it was used by Emperor Enrico III of Franconia as a disinfectant.

- Most of the common, commercial balsamic vinegar is produced in Italy and aged 3-12 years before being sold. The aging produces mellow, brown vinegar that is relatively sweet. Most of the common and some of the gourmet balsamic vinegar is produced from the unfermented juice of the Trebbiano grape.
- The grape juice is boiled down until it is fruity syrup and then aged in wooden barrels for at least 6 years. Some balsamic vinegar may be 50 to 100 years old and still be usable. The age of the balsamic vinegar will determine the price.
- It is one of the best cooking vinegar and is great for a salad dressing, bringing out the flavor of many vegetables.
- Gourmet balsamic vinegar: artesian-made and commercial. True balsamic vinegar is more of a liqueur than vinegar and is almost like syrup. True balsamic vinegar can only be produced in the provinces of Modena and Reggio in northern Italy. Artisan-made balsamic vinegar can be traced back over 1,000 years.

Gourmet balsamic vinegar cannot contain any wine vinegar. The aging process is complex and the juice must be passed down through a series of progressively smaller wooden barrels, which are kept in a cool, dry location.

- These special wooden barrels have small holes in their tops, which encourages evaporation, thus allowing the flavors to concentrate. This process also allows special enzymes to assist in the production of complex flavors.

- The vinegar must be aged between 12 and 20 years and the cost for a $^1/_2$ ounce bottle is between $60.00 and $250.00. The best brands to purchase are Malpighi, Cavalli, Mamma Balducci and Giusti.

Cane Vinegar

- Produced from sugar cane extract and water that has been fermented. The acid level of cane vinegar is just barely within the legal limits of 4% acidity.
- Can only be purchased in some oriental groceries and is mainly used in the Philippines.

Champagne Vinegar

- This is really not made from champagne, but from the grapes that are used to make champagne. These include Chardonnay and Pinot Noir. The methods used are the same methods that are used to produce wine vinegar. Acidity levels; in champagne vinegar is relatively high and runs around 6%. Most have excellent flavors and are usually used in delicate sauces. Flavoring herbs are lemon balm, lemongrass and lemon zest.

Coconut Vinegar

- Tends to leave an aftertaste and has a very low acidity level of 4%. May only be found in Asian grocery stores. Frequently used in Thai cooking.

Distilled Vinegar

- May be prepared from grain, wood pulp or oil by-products. Distilled vinegar has a somewhat harsh flavor and acidity level of 5%. Usually used in commercial processing of pickles and related foods. Best used for cleaning purposes around the house. Distilled White Vinegar.

Fruit Vinegar

- Prepared using good quality cider vinegar, which has fruits such as strawberries, peaches, or oranges added.

Herb Flavored Wine Vinegar

- Produced from white wine or a quality cider vinegar with the addition of any herb that is compatible.
- The most popular herbs are basil, rosemary, dill, chive and oregano.

Tarragon wine vinegar is commonly used by chef's, for shellfish dishes, and poultry.

- Rosemary wine vinegar is excellent with lamb dishes.

Malt Vinegar

- Originally prepared using soured beer and was called "alegar" in Europe.
- Traditionally it is used on fish and chips in England. Presently it is produced from malted barley and grain, mash, which is fermented and then combined with wood shavings, then placed into large vats with a vinegar, bacteria.
- Acidity levels; in malt vinegar is normally 5%.
- The best flavorings are a combination of tarragon, whole cloves and garlic. Malt Vinegar

Raspberry Vinegar

- Produced by soaking raspberries in white wine providing the vinegar with a pleasant fruity flavor.
- Commonly used with pork dishes, poultry, as a salad dressing, and on fruits. Vinegar can be produce from almost any fruit; however, the flavor of raspberry vinegar seems to be the most acceptable for a large majority of the public.

Rice Vinegar

- The Chinese have produced rice vinegar for over 5,000 years.
- It has a mild, somewhat sweet taste and is produced from rice wine or sake.
- This is very robust vinegar that is somewhat bitter.

The Japanese produce rice vinegar that is sweeter and much milder using cooked rice.

- The Japanese rice vinegar is capable of neutralizing lactic acid in the body, which may relate to increasing endurance levels for athletes.

Sherry Vinegar

- This is very mellow vinegar with a somewhat nutty flavor.
- A more expensive vinegar; it is produced similar to the methods of producing balsamic vinegar.
- Acidity levels in sherry vinegar is 6-7% and the oil blends especially well with olive oil in salad dressings.
- Chefs use the vinegar to de-glaze pans.
- The best flavoring combination is Thyme, rosemary, oregano and basil.

Wine Vinegar

- Wine vinegar is produced from white, red or rose wine and is common vinegar for salad dressings.
- White wine vinegar is milder than the red and goes well with fish and lighter dishes.
- The best flavoring combination for red wine vinegar is Rosemary, savory sage, bay leaf, garlic and basil.
- The best flavoring combination for white wine is dill, tarragon, basil and lemon balm.

VINEGAR SUBSTITUTES

Apple Cider Vinegar	Wine Vinegar
Balsamic Vinegar	Sherry Vinegar
Champagne Vinegar	Apple Cider Vinegar
Raspberry Vinegar	Red Wine Vinegar
Red Wine Vinegar	Balsamic Vinegar
Rice Vinegar	Apple Cider Vinegar
White Vinegar	Apple Cider Vinegar (canning only with at least 5% acidity)

Worcestershire Sauce

- John Lea and William Perrins invented Worcestershire Sauce in England in 1835 by accident. They were managing a small drug store in Worcester, England when a customer, Lord Marcus Sandys asked them to reproduce his favorite Indian sauce that he had liked when he was in Bengal. They mixed up a batch of sauce prepared from vegetables and fish but didn't like the aroma it gave off and placed the mixture in their cellar for storage.
- While cleaning the cellar two years later they accidentally found the mixture and were surprised at the taste. Lea & Perrins Worcestershire Sauce is now one of the most popular steak sauces in the world

- The recipe has barely changed from the original one using anchovies layered in brine, tamarinds in molasses, garlic in vinegar, chilies, cloves, shallots and sugar to sweeten it up.
- The mixture must still age for two years before being sold. The solids are filtered out and preservatives and citric acid added.

CHAPTER 25

COFFEE AND TEA

THE STORY OF COFFEE

- The coffee tree is believed to have originated in Central Africa where the natives would grind the coffee cherries into a powder and mix it with animal fat. Then they would roll it into small balls, which they would take with them on long journeys or hunting trips. Raw coffee is high in protein (until it is diluted with water) and when combined with fat provides adequate calories and a stimulant.

- According to literature, the Arabs were the first to actually drink the beverage. The coffee beans were protected to such a degree that the Arabs would not allow them to be exported under the threat of death. However, in 1660 some of the coffee seedlings were smuggled into Holland and then transported to Brazil in 1727 where the warm climate and soil conditions were more favorable

- Coffee trees require at least 70 inches of rainfall annually so that the tree can produce at least 2,000 coffee cherries, which only makes one pound of coffee. The United States consumes about 50% of the world's coffee production, which amounts to about 400 million cups per day. Eight out of every 10 adults drink at least one cup of coffee every day.

WHERE DID "CUP OF JOE" ORIGINATE FROM

- Alcoholic beverages used to be allowed on board U.S. Naval vessels. However, this practice was discontinued when Admiral Josephus "Joe" Daniels became Naval Chief of Operations. He discontinued all alcoholic beverages with the exception of special occasions. The seamen then took to drinking their second choice beverage, coffee and nicknamed coffee, "a cup of Joe" as a bit of sarcasm directed at the Admiral.

ESPRESSO COFFEE

Espresso coffee was the result of the invention of the Pavoni espresso machine. These were the first used but were only capable of producing about 150 cups per hour. Since this was not sufficient to serve larger crowds, a bigger version called the "La Victoria Arduino" machine was invented which was capable of producing about 1,000 cups per hour. This is the reason for the size of some of the older machines. These early machines, however, had the tendency to over-extract and pull too much coffee out of the grounds, scalding the coffee and producing a somewhat bitter espresso.

The machines that are now in use utilize a horizontal water boiler, which allows the steam and water to mix more efficiently. The steam and hot water is forced through the coffee under high pressure, producing an excellent tasting cup of espresso with good strength and taste.

- Espresso is prepared by "rapid infusion" which forces the coffee through almost boiling water. A high-quality dark, fine, gritty ground (never powdered) coffee should be used.
- The darker the coffee, how dense it is packed and the amount of water being forced through will determine the strength of the final product.
- Always use the recommended amount suggested by the manufacturer of your machine, never less.
- Espresso should never be served with cream.
- For the best-tasting espresso: purchase the beans that you will be using from an Italian grocery store.

TYPES OF ESPRESSO

Cappuccino

- Combine one shot of strong espresso with very hot steamed milk and top, it with a layer of frothy milk.

Café Au Lait

- Use very strong coffee (no espresso) and add steamed milk.

Caffe Mocha

- Use one shot of espresso topped with hot chocolate froth.

Caffe Latte

- Use one shot of espresso combined with 4 ounces of steamed milk providing a head of foam.

Espresso

- Should be prepared with a "very" fine ground.

Latte

- Use a small amount of espresso on top of a glass of steamed milk.

Macchiato

- Use one shot of espresso, and place a very small amount of foam on top.

Coffee Preparation Facts

- The size of the grind does make a difference, both in taste and the caffeine content. Espresso should be made with a fine ground, while Turkish coffees need an even finer ground.
- The majority of American coffee is ground into a "drip grind" providing the maximum, surface area, which makes the richest coffee and never bitter. However, if the grinds are micro-fine, the water will take longer to filter through and this will result in an increase of tannins (polyphenols), which produce a bitter taste.

Brewing Coffee

- When coffee beans are ground, a large percentage of their surface is exposed to the air, thus allowing the breakdown of the flavor components and their rapid destruction. The process is called oxidation and takes its toll on all surfaces of every food when you expose their delicate innards to the air.
- Another problem that can occur is that the longer the ground up bean is stored, the more carbon dioxide is going to be lost, which also contributes to the aroma and flavor of the bean. If you do grind up more than you can use, store the remainder in a well-sealed container in the refrigerator and use as soon as possible.

Making the Perfect Cup

- There are a few factors that you need to be aware of when preparing the perfect cup of coffee:

  - The freshness of the ground beans, always grind the beans just before you are ready to use it.
  - How long ago the bean was roasted. Is the coffee bean fresh?
  - Cleanliness of the brewing equipment.
  - The quality of the bean.
  - The quality of the water.

- Never use water that has been previously boiled and cooled to make coffee.
- Make sure that the coffeepot is clean and that there is no sign of even a hint of soap scum remaining.
- The temperature must be between 185°-205°F for the best results.
- If the temperature is too low the coffee will not release enough caffeols and if the temperature is too high, the tannins take over and the coffee is too acidic.

If you add a pinch of baking soda to a cup of coffee, it will reduce the acidity level.

- A glass or porcelain pot is best. Metal pots are not recommended for a really good cup of coffee.
- Percolators make bitter coffee by boiling coffee for too long a period.
- Never use hot tap water, may have contaminants.
- A coffee warmer only retains the top flavor for about 30 minutes.
- Cream has the tendency to curdle when added to a high acidic coffee. Just place a pinch of baking soda in the cream and this will eliminate the problem.

CAFFEINE CONTENT

BEVERAGE	PER 8 OUNCE SERVING
Espresso	.350-400mg
Drip Coffee	.178-200mg
Percolated	.80-156mg
Instant Coffee	.90-112mg

TEA

Tea was probably first consumed in China around 2737 BC when the Chinese Emperor Shen Nung was boiling his drinking water and some leaves from the Camellia sinensis plant accidentally dropped into his pot. The tealeaf was then commonly used to flavor water, which had a somewhat off taste after being boiled to purify it. The Emperor felt that the new beverage gave him added energy and called the new beverage the "vigor of the body."

Tea was introduced to Japan by the Chinese and was immediately hailed as a beverage of choice. Presently, the Island of Ceylon is the world's leading grower of quality tea. The tea is still picked by hand and an experienced picker is capable of picking 35-40 pounds of tealeaves per day.

Tea Facts

- One of the original teapots was more of a solo pot called a Yixing (E-ching). These small pots can be found in all different shapes. They may be in the shape of a vegetable or flower and were made from red clay that was only found in the Yunnan province of Mainland China. The Chinese only used a pot for one tea variety, which protected the pot from absorbing different flavors.
- The red clay tended to hold the heat, keeping the flavor in and the tea hot for a long period of time. Since the clay did not conduct the heat well to the exterior of the pot, the outside was cooler and could be handled easily.
- There are also small individual cups that are available in many different sizes and shapes. One of the more popular is the Chinese style "guywan" cup which has a lid to keep the tea hot while the infusion process is taking place

releasing flavor into the water.

- A quality teapot is crucial to enjoying the full flavor of the tea. Someone who really enjoys tea will never place a teabag in a cup and place it in the microwave.
- The following are temperatures that tea should be brewed at according to tea experts on two continents.

MAJOR VARIETIES OF TEAS

Green Tea

- Green tea is mainly produced in China, Japan, India and Taiwan. Green is the natural color of green tea since oxidation does not effect the chlorophyll content of the tealeaf and the tea is not fermented.
- The manufacturing process has only three stages; first the tealeaf is steamed to inactivate the enzymes and prevent fermentation and oxidation. Second, the leaves are rolled and dried over and over until they are crisp. This releases the juices, which are then held by the leaf. Third, repeated controlled stirrings then produces a stable, well-hardened tea that has retained its flavor and essential elements. The final product contains only 3% residual moisture, therefore is not capable of any further changes.
- Chinese green teas are graded by age and style, with the finest being Gunpowder produced from tiny balls that are made from very young or at least medium-aged leaves.
- Next best is called, Young Hyson and finally, Imperial. The quality of Japanese green tea is graded as follows: Extra Choicest, Choicest, Choice, Finest, Fine, Good Medium, Good Common, Nibs, Fanning and Dust. Indian green tea is graded: Fine Young Hyson, Young Hyson, Hyson No. 1, Twankay, Sowmee, Fanning and Dust.
- The Encyclopedia of Chinese Teas lists 138 different varieties of green teas and 12,500 sub groups. However, only about 500 varieties are really recognized.

The following are some of the more common varieties of Chinese green teas

Pouchong

- Used frequently to prepare jasmine tea.
- The leaves are oxidized to a greater extent than most green tealeaves, which allows the leaf to retain the flavor of jasmine better.
- The jasmine flower has been imported from Persia for 1,000 years to flavor the tea.

Ching Cha

- This variety; is grown in Mainland China and includes some of the more famous and best tasting green teas such as Pi Lo Chun and Tai Ping Hou Gui.

Chumee

- Grown in Yunnan province and has a somewhat plum flavor.
- Care needs to be taken so as not to over-brew, which is easily done.

Dragonwell

- This one of the favorite teas of Mainland China. It has a sweet, fresh taste and there are eight grades of Dragonwell with the highest grade called Qing Ming.

Fmerald Tips

- A Dragonwell type of tea that is grown in an area, which borders the Dragonwell growing area.
- The quality is not as good; however, it is still a good quality tea.

Gunpowder

- First tea ever exported from China to Europe and is the most popular Chinese tea in Europe.
- If the tea "pellets" are fresh, they will resist pressure and not easily crush.

The following are some of the more common varieties of Indian green teas

Assam

- The most plentiful tea in India accounting for $^1/_3$ of all tea produced.
- The tea is grown to produce a strong aroma and flavor and only a small quantity is grown for green tea.

Darjeeling

- This tea is grown on the southern slopes of the Himalayan Mountains near Nepal.
- This variety has been called the champagne of teas and the finest grown in India. However, very little of the tea is produced as green tea.
- If you are lucky enough to find "single-estate" Darjeeling green tea you will enjoy an unusual cup of tea.

The following are some of the more common varieties of Japanese green teas

Bancha

- The most common tea sold in Japan.
- The green Bancha is actually somewhat bitter and not one of the better green teas.

Fukuiju

- A higher quality green tea with a pleasant aftertaste.

Gyokuro

- The highest quality green tea produced in Japan and is very fragrant and flavorful.
- It is sometimes mixed with lower grade teas to enhance their flavor and aroma.

Spiderleg

Another of the high quality green teas that has an excellent aroma and flavor. Occasionally found with a cherry aroma.

Green tea:
should be brewed between 180°F. to 200° F.(82.2° C. to 93.3° C.)

Oolong tea:
should be brewed between 185°F. to 205° F. (85° C. to 96° C.)

Black tea:
should be brewed between 190° F. to 210° F. (87.8° C. to 98.9° C.)

- Green teas should have a greenish-golden color. If the color of green tea is a somewhat brownish-yellow color this indicates that the tea is old or was produced from low-grade leaves. A good rule of thumb is the lighter the color, the higher the probability that it is a quality green tea.
- The better quality teas should be brewed at a lower temperature since they will release their flavor more readily. The higher temperatures used in the lower quality teas tends to stimulate the release of the flavors.

The following steps will lead you through the process of making the perfect cup of tea:

1. Use the best grade of tea that you enjoy.
2. Use pure quality cold water and bring it to a top boil. Only use the water when it is bubbling rapidly. Never use water from a hot water under sink unit.
3. Rinse the teapot with the hottest water possible or use boiling water. The teapot should be warm before you add the tea.
4. When pouring the boiling water into the teapot, take the kettle to the teapot to assure that the water will be as hot as possible.
5. Brew the tea for 3-5 minutes depending on your taste and the type of tea. Most teas should never be brewed for more than 5 minutes.
6. Make sure that the brewing tea is kept as hot as possible as it is brewing.
7. Always have a removable tea leaf strainer that is easily removable to eliminate the tea leaf residues. Always stir the tea after removing the infusion.
8. If the tea cools after you pour it, it would be best to brew another batch and not try to re-heat it.

- The problem most people have when trying to make a strong tea is that it usually turns out bitter. Never increase the steeping period; always add more tea leaves. The longer the leaves remain in the hot water, the more polyphenols are released, thus producing a bitter tea.

- The reason why you would keep a cover on a cup or pot of steeping tea may seem simply that it keeps the heat in. However, another very important reason is that it traps the steam and dampens any tealeaves that are floating on the top, thus extracting their flavor.

- Loose tea should always be stored in a cool, dry location.

Humidity and heat will reduce the quality of the tea significantly. A sealed container works well allowing as little oxygen to come into contact with the loose tea.

- Containers should only be large enough to hold the tea and be opaque, since the light can have a negative effect as well. A large container will retain too much oxygen and may cause undue oxidation to take place.

- Teabags should be stored in the container they are purchased in and also stored in a cool; dry location.

CAFFEINE CONTENT OF TEAS

- One pound of tea contains 205 grains of caffeine. The primary effects from the caffeine in tea lasts from 15-45 minutes depending on the individual sensitivity level to caffeine.

BEVERAGE	PER 8 OUNCE SERVING
Green Tea (5 minute brew)	35mg
Black Tea (1 minute brew)	24mg
Black Tea (3 minute brew)	41mg
Black Tea (5 minute brew)	50mg
Iced Tea	34mg
Instant Tea	28mg
Decaffeinated Tea	~10mg or less

TEA FACTS

- The best organic tea comes from the oldest gardens in Darjeeling, the Makaibari Tea Estates. They grow the finest certified pure organic teas in the world. One of their most popular teas is the Makaibari Green, which has a taste of Darjeeling; however, it is still a green tea.

A pound of tea has almost twice the caffeine content than a pound of coffee. Tea goes farther making about 180-200 cups, compared to coffee only making about 40 cups. The taste of tea that is made with the equivalent measure of a coffee scoop would be too powerful to drink.

- The better the quality of the tea, the less you have to use per cup. Poor quality tea may take up to one teaspoon per cup to give the desired taste, while the higher quality green teas may only take half that much.
- Your typical supermarket teas may be a blend of 60 different teas and most people will never know what a good cup of tea really tastes like.
- Never drink hot tea from a Styrofoam cup with lemon added. The two acids, citric and tannic will react with the heat and eat a hole through the cup leaving a puddle on your desk and adding a number of carcinogens into the tea from the Styrofoam. If you don't believe it, try it for yourself. It only works with hot tea and lemon.
- Tea is the second most consumed beverage in the world.
- If you want test the freshness of tea, just close your fist very tightly around a small amount of tea or a tea bag and breathe in as you release your fingers. The aroma should be sweet and somewhat grassy. If you do not smell a strong aroma, the tea is probably old and should be thrown out.
- There is nothing wrong with purchasing a quality tea in a tea bag. They come in an odorless, tasteless filter paper that is very convenient and not as messy as loose tea.

The mistake most people make is not using very hot, almost boiling water and then allowing the bag to remain in the water until the desired flavor is achieved. To dunk the teabag a number of times defeats the purpose of the teabag and does not result in a quality cup of tea. The water needs time to absorb the flavor and the cup should have a cover on it while it is steeping.

- The color of tea can tell you a lot about the tea even before you drink it.
- Black tea should not have any greenish tint to it or it is indicative of an under-withered, over-fermented tea.
- The tea that was originally imported by England tended to be a bit astringent and this was not an acceptable quality, so the English tried adding a small amount of milk which reduced the astringency caused by the higher tannic acid content. The milk protein would bind with the tannic acid.
- Another benefit is that by reducing the tannins, the tea became less constipating. Problems did arise, however, when the tea with the added milk had less aroma and flavor than they were used to. The habit stuck and a large number of the English still prefer their tea with milk.

• When pouring hot tea into a good china cup, it would be a wise move to place the spoon in first. The spoon tends to absorb the heat first and you will not risk cracking the cup. Many of the cracks are micro-cracks and cannot be seen for many years. If they do appear, just boil a small amount of milk and pour it into the cup. Allow it to stand for about 20 minutes and the milk protein will seal the micro-cracks. Another method is to rinse the cup under very hot tap water before adding the tea or coffee.

Almost any herb can be placed in a tea infuser and placed in your soup or stew to add the flavor of the spice without allowing the spice to fall apart and then be more difficult to retrieve. The infuser can even be used to stir your dish with while the flavor of the spice is being released.

- To remove the stains left by tannins, place $^1/_2$ cup of borax into a teapot full of boiling water, remove from the heat and allow to stand overnight. Clean thoroughly before using.
- If your tea is cloudy, just add a pinch of baking soda to the teapot.
- Ice cubes used for iced tea or coffee should be made from the tea or coffee. Ice tea is diluted to a great degree and loses up to 40% of its flavor from the ice cubes.

Cloudiness is common in iced tea but can be eliminated if you just allow the tea to cool to room temperature before placing it into the refrigerator.

- If the tea is still cloudy, try adding a small amount of boiling water to it until it clears up. A number of minerals are released when the tea is brewed which results in the cloudiness.
- When making herbal tea and it is in the form of a flower or a leaf, an infusion ball may be used to make the tea. Place $^1/_4$ to $^1/_2$ teaspoon of the crushed herb into the infusion ball and pour boiling water into the cup or pot, allowing it to steep for 10-15 minutes depending on the desired level of potency.
- If you are using one of the milder herbs, use $^1/_2$ to 1 teaspoon of the herb for the best results.
- If you make tea from the bark, seeds or the root of the herb, it would be best to use the decoction method. To prepare one pint of tea, just place 1 ounce of the herb in $1^1/_2$ pints of pure water and boil for 30 minutes. Whenever possible use a teabag!

CHAPTER 26

MEXICAN COOKING

CLASSIC MEXICAN FOODS

CHILIES RELLENOS (stuffed chilies)

- Use fresh vegetable oil heated to 350°F when frying rellenos.

  Roasted peppers are somewhat slippery and should be placed on a kitchen towel when you are working with them.

- The best chili for rellenos is poblano chilies. The flavor is excellent and they are not too spicy, hot.
- The poblano chili also has wide sides and very thick flesh, which makes them easy to stuff.

CHILI POWDER

- Authentic Mexican chili powder is made from the following: 3 tablespoons of ancho chili powder, 1 teaspoon of freshly ground black pepper, 1 tablespoon of ground cumin, 2 teaspoons of dried oregano, 1 teaspoon of ground coriander and 1 teaspoon of coarse salt.
- Place all the ingredients into a jar with a lid and shake well.

EMPANADA

- Dissolve 1 package of fresh yeast into $^1/_2$ cup of lukewarm water.
- Cut 4 tablespoons of unsalted butter into 4 cups of all-purpose flour, then add 1 teaspoon of salt and 1 tablespoon of granulated sugar.
- Pour the yeast into the flour mixture and prepare dough.
- The dough should be rolled into thin sheets and then cut into rounds.
- The filling can be mincemeat or a fruit preserve.
- They are folded according to your recipe directions and then fried.

FLAN

- The vanilla pod that is called for in most recipes should be somewhat flexible when purchased or it will not be fresh.
- The caramel should be cooked very slowly and watched carefully and should be a dark coffee color when finished.
- Bake flan at a low oven temperature, usually 325°F for about 1 hour.
- The center of the custard should just barely jiggle when touched: to be fully cooked and the edges should be firm.

  If small bubbles appear, you have overcooked the flan.

- A watery texture is also a sign of overcooking.
- Cooking the flan in a water bath or French *bain marie*, is the ideal method of cooking flan.
- To prepare chocolate flan, increase the eggs in the recipe by one and stir in 3 ounces of slivered bittersweet chocolate into the milk mixture just before it boils.

FRIED PLANTAINS

- Banana pancakes are best made with plantains. Just mash them and add them to your batter.
- Make sure that the plantains are fully ripe before adding them to any dish.
- Normally, plantains are sliced and lightly fried for about 2-3 minutes on each side in a small amount of oil and served as a breakfast side dish.
- They are commonly served fried on top of Mexican rice.

GUACAMOLE

- A small amount of lemon juice should be added to guacamole to retard the browning.
- Make sure that the avocados used for guacamole are very ripe.
- Never over mash avocados, guacamole is supposed to be a little chunky.
- Tomatoes add too much liquid and should not be used in a good guacamole.

Never put garlic in guacamole, it alters the flavor.

- Use jalapenos if you want it real spicy and hot or poblanos if you want it medium to somewhat mild.
- If you heat guacamole, it will turn bitter.

MENUDO

Traditionally menudo was served on Sunday mornings as a cure for hangovers from Saturday night. Originally it was prepared from tripe, green chili peppers, hominy and special seasonings. It was served with lime slices and tortillas. The only drawback was trying to eat tripe first thing in the morning.

- Traditional Mexican stew is composed of tripe (stomach lining), chilies and hominy.
- Make sure that you remove any visible fat and wash it well in cold water before you cook tripe.
- Most of the tripe sold in supermarkets in the United States is partially cooked, which begins the tenderizing process.

Tripe should be off-white and should be cooked the same day it is purchased.

- Ancho chilies are the chili of choice when preparing menudo.
- In Mexico, a calf's foot is added to the pot to provide a rich gelatinous stew. You may have to go to a Mexican meat market to get the calf's foot.

MOLE

- This sauce is of Mexican origin and can probably be traced back to the Aztecs who used chocolate to sweeten dishes. However, originally a mole sauce was any sauce that contained hot chili peppers. The sauce is traditionally served with poultry dishes, but can be found on almost any dish in a Mexican restaurant.
- Mole is actually a stew composed of sauce thickened with toasted chilies, nuts and seeds from the region.
- Some mole contain chocolate, however, the chocolate flavor is not really desired and is usually hidden. Chocolate can be left out of the recipe.
- If your recipe calls for raisins, you can substitute any dried fruit.

Standard Mexican Mole Sauce Recipe

1 tablespoon of extra virgin olive oil (cold pressed)
$^1/_2$ teaspoon of canola oil
$^1/_2$ cup red onions, sliced
2 large ripe tomatoes, peeled, seeded and diced
3 Poblano chilies: remove seeds, ribs, skin and cut up
4 cloves of fresh garlic, sliced
$^1/_4$ cup regular or seasoned bread crumbs
$^1/_2$ cup roasted peanuts, finely chopped
$^1/_4$ teaspoon powdered cinnamon
$^1/_2$ teaspoon ground black pepper
1 cups chicken stock
2 ounces of chopped quality unsweetened chocolate
1 tablespoon toasted sesame seeds
Add salt as desired

Place the chilies, nuts, tomatoes, breadcrumbs and onion in a blender or food processor and chop them up on a fine setting. Be sure not to make mush, just chop them up fine. Place the mixture in a medium bowl and stir in the black pepper, cinnamon, salt and chocolate. Place a medium-sized pan over medium heat and heat the olive and Canola oil for 2 minutes, then whisk in the bread crumb mixture and allow to simmer for about 5-7 minutes or until the chocolate has melted and the mixture has thickened.

Add the chicken stock and simmer for about 15-20 minutes or until the mixture is very hot and thick, but workable. Add the sesame seeds and the sauce is finished. This sauce should be served as soon as it is prepared for the best results.

QUESADILLAS

- Make sure that the cheese does not overwhelm the tortilla since this is a common mistake, trying to make it too cheesy.
- If you add vegetables or meat, be sure that you cook them first and add them before the final cooking of the quesadilla.

MEXICAN RICE

- Long-grain rice is recommended for most Mexican dishes.
- Make sure that the rice is rinsed well before cooking it to remove excess starch or the rice may become somewhat sticky.
- If rice does become mushy: spread it out on a cookie sheet and allow it to dry out.
- If your recipe calls for toasted rice, do the toasting in a skillet, not in the oven for the best results.
- A spoon should never be used to stir rice as it is slightly cooling before serving. Use a fork and be very gentle or you will damage the rice.
- A small amount of salsa is commonly added to rice before serving.

REFRIED BEANS

The term "refried beans" was actually an error in translation from the Mexican "frijoles refritos, meaning "well-fried beans." In 1957 when a cookbook on Mexican-American cooking was printed they were called "refried beans."

- The tastiest bean is the small black bean for making refried beans.
- Basically, these beans are softened, mashed and fried in fat, commonly lard.
- True refried beans need the pork flavor derived from the lard, but any fat will do.
- Bacon drippings can replace lard, but there isn't a big difference in the fat content.
- To have a true authentic flavor of Mexican refried beans, you will need to find a sprig of epazote. Add the epazote to the beans while they are cooking for the last 10-15 minutes.

Epazote as well as fennel seed has the ability to neutralize the complex sugar in the beans that causes flatulence.

- Epazote is a weed that can be found along the roadside in the Los Angeles area and throughout the Southwest.

SALSA

- Removing the ribs and seeds will reduce the potency of the capsaicin, which is the hot chemical in the peppers.

Classic Red Chili Salsa Recipe

1 large ripe tomatoes, peeled, seeded and chopped
3 ancho or casabel chilies: remove stems, seeds and ribs, chopped up fine
8 scallions, do not use dark green stem, chopped
3 tablespoons of extra virgin olive oil (cold pressed)
¹/₂ cup minced fresh coriander
4 tablespoons of red wine vinegar
Add salt and ground black pepper as desired

Using a medium, mixing bowl, add all the ingredients and stir well. Place a piece of plastic wrap over the bowl and place in the refrigerator for at least 8-10 hours, which will allow the flavors to blend well.

TACOS

- The tortillas should be warmed by rapidly dropping them into a shallow pan of water, then immediately on a grill or very hot sauté pan for about 30 seconds on each side to just soften them.
- They should then be stacked and wrapped in a damp towel and placed into aluminum foil. They should then be allowed to remain for about 30 minutes before being used to make a taco.

Fish Taco

- The best fish for fish tacos is salmon, bass, snapper or halibut.
- Drizzle of lime on a fish taco makes all the difference.
- Before placing fish on a taco, be sure and place a thin bed of lettuce on the taco first, then the fish on top.

Taco Sauce Recipe

2 can whole tomatoes, chopped
1 cup green chili, chopped
1 whole Tamed™ Jalapeno, chopped
2 teaspoon cumin
1 teaspoon oregano
1 red onion, chopped
1 teaspoon salt

Place tomatoes, onions and green chili in a large saucepan with juice from the tomato cans, add all spices and simmer for 1½ hours.

TAMALE

- The dried corn husks should be soaked in hot water for 8 hours.
- After you dry the husks on paper towel, cut out a 9-inch square from a piece of aluminum foil to use for each tamale.
- To fill the tamale, place the husk lengthwise on a flat surface with the narrow end pointing away from you, then spread about 2-3 tablespoons of filling down the center. Allow about 2 inches with no filling at the top of the husk.
- Fold the sides over first, then the ends to completely enclose the filling.
- The tamale is then placed on the aluminum foil square, and the foil is folded to enclose the tamale.

The flavor of lard is necessary for authentic tamales, but should be used in moderation for special occasions only.

- One-half cup of lard is all that is necessary for 12 tamales, which provides about the same level of pork fat as one slice of bacon.
- Tamale dough is sold in many supermarkets making it easy to make great tamales.
- Tamales can be steamed if you prefer with good results.
- If you would like to sweeten tamales, add the following to your recipe: ½ teaspoon of ground cinnamon, ¼ teaspoon cloves, ¼ teaspoon nutmeg and ½ cup of raisins.

Banana Leaves

- Banana leaves are a common wrapper for tamales in many South American countries.
- If you are going to use banana leaves, be sure and heat them briefly in a dry frying pan for a few seconds each to soften them.
- The leaves need to be cut into 9-inch squares.

TORTILLAS

- To prepare a cheese tortilla, just place the tortilla on a piece of paper towel and space small cheese strips on it then roll up the tortilla move it to one end of the paper towel and roll it up in the paper towel. Microwave on high for 17 seconds.

Flour Tortilla Recipe

4 cups of all-purpose flour
1 teaspoon of salt
2 cups of water

Place all the ingredients into a bowl and mix well. Put a small amount of oil on your hands and knead the dough. Cover the bowl and allow it to stand for 15 minutes. Lightly flour a rolling pin and wooden board, then shape the dough into 24 small round balls and flatten each out on the board. Roll the dough with a circular motion to keep it round. Place the tortillas on a medium-heat griddle after it has warmed up and cook until barely brown, which only takes about 30-40 seconds. Turn over and just cook the other side for a few seconds. Brush the tortilla with salted butter and stack. Cover with a towel until ready to serve.

TORTILLA CHIPS

- Cut a round tortilla in half, and then thinly slice them across the width to make strips.
- If you want to make chips, cut the tortillas in half, then cut them into 4 wedges.
- Use a large, heavy pot and place vegetable oil in to a depth of about 2 inches. Heat the oil to 375°F.

Make sure that a piece of tortilla bubbles and rises to the surface. That is the point when the oil is ready.

- Fry small batches for the best results and then remove the chips with a slotted spoon.
- Chips should be lightly seasoned while still warm so that they will retain the seasoning.

TOSTADO

- For the best tostado ever, all the ingredients need to be seasoned and prepared separately.
- Meat that is used should be moistened with your dressing before being added.
- By flavoring every ingredient before placing it on the tostado, you assure that every bite will be flavorful.
- The refried beans should be spread out on top of the fried tortilla shell in all directions and to the edges if possible.
- Tostados are the perfect way to use leftovers.
- Tostado shells are available in most supermarkets.

QUINONA PUDDING

- Quinona is a grain grown in Mexico and South America and is one of the best grain (or vegetable) sources of protein.

> *2 large eggs*
> *1 cup non-fat milk*
> *¹/₂ cup fresh quinona*
> *¹/₄ cup rolled oats*
> *1 cup cooked brown rice*
> *3 tablespoons of brown sugar*
> *1 teaspoon almond extract*
> *¹/₂ cup dried figs, chopped*
> *¹/₄ cup raisins*

Place the quinona into a large bowl and rinse thoroughly several times with cold water. If any grains float to the top, discard them. Using a medium saucepan, place the quinona in 1 cup of water and bring to a slow boil over medium heat. Cover the saucepan: reduce the heat and simmer for 15 minutes or until the grain is somewhat transparent. Remove the pan from the heat and allow it to cool for a few minutes.

Using a medium-sized bowl, place the eggs in and beat them. Add the quinona, figs, rice and oats while continually stirring. Transfer the mixture to a baking dish with high sides and add boiling water to about ¹/₂ inch from the top, then place the dish in a 375°F. (190.5 C.) oven for 45 minutes or until the top is a golden brown and serve.

CHAPTER 27

COOKING WITH HERBS & SPICES

COOKING WITH HERBS & SPICES

The difference between herbs and spices is that herbs are the fragrant leaves of plants that do not have a woody stem and spices are barks of trees, berries, roots and fruits. Spices may also be the stems of certain trees, plants and vines. Pre-ground herbs and spices will not have the full rich aroma or flavor of the fresh ones.

- The definition of "Cajun Style" cooking refers to cooking a dish that contains: onion/onion powder/dehydrated onion, garlic/garlic powder/dehydrated garlic/, white pepper, red pepper and freshly ground black pepper.
- When you need to increase the amount of food in a recipe and are not sure if you should increase the seasonings in the same proportion as the original recipe called for, the answer is never increase the seasonings to the full degree.
- If you double the recipe, increase the seasonings only by 1½, if you increase by three times, only increase two times the original. If the recipe is a complicated one it would be best to make two batches.

Never increase sugar in tomato sauce dishes.

- Never increase salt more than a pinch or two at the most.
- Place the spices in a 350° F. oven spread out on a cookie sheet for 3-5 minutes or until they release their aroma. Remove from the oven and use as is or grind them up.
- Herb stems can be used in soups, stocks and sauces that have to simmer for a long period of time. Herb stems have less chlorophyll and will not color the dish, but will provide adequate flavor.

Allspice

- The flavor is similar to that of cinnamon, cloves, and nutmeg and is sold in both whole and ground forms.
- The spice is used in pickling, meats, fish, baked goods, relish, puddings, and fruit preserves.
- Allspice is a common herb and can be found in number of ready-to-serve foods such as, hot dogs, soups, and baked beans.
- Used by bakers in spice cakes and cookies.
- Common spice in apple pies.

Anise Seed

- Usually sold as anise seeds and can be found in licorice candy, cookies, pickling, and in soft drinks.
- Used to make Anisette and can replace ginger in some recipes. Rabbits love the taste of licorice.
- Used more and more in breads.

Basil

- Common seasoning for fish, meat, tomato dishes, soups, stews, pizza sauce, dressings, and used on salads.
- Basil that is grown in the United States is called "sweet basil." Best to store fresh basil in the refrigerator in a slightly moistened plastic bag. It should retain its flavor and aroma for about 4 days.

  Basil tends to lose much of its flavor after about 15 minutes of cooking and should be added about 10 minutes before the food is done for the best results.

- There are a number of varieties of basil which include lemon and cinnamon basil which have green leaves and opal basil which has purple leaves.
- Most Italian dishes have basil.

Bay Leaf

- Usually sold as whole leaves and commonly used in stews, sauces, soups, French dressing, dill pickles, meat dishes, veal, and poultry. Also, used in numerous ready-to-serve foods.

- Never crumble up a bay leaf when using it in a recipe and stir gently so as not to break the bay leaf up.

Bay leaves grown in California are one of the strongest.

- Favorite herb for pot-roast.
- The Turkish variety of bay leaf has a milder flavor than the California variety and is wider and shorter.
- Being used more in rice puddings and custards than ever before.

Bee Balm

- Has a somewhat lemony flavor and is used in soups.

Borage

- The young leaves are excellent in salads and string beans.

Capers

- Normally sold either whole or pickled in brine. Commonly used on smoked fish, chicken dishes, eggs, or veal.

Caraway Seeds

- Somewhat similar flavor to licorice (anise) and are harvested at night before the dew evaporates.
- The majority sold in the United States is imported from the Netherlands and commonly used in rye bread, cookies, organ meats, dips, cabbage, sauerkraut, soft cheese spreads, sweet pickles, sauerbraten, and French dressing.
- Excellent in cooked winter squashes.

Cardamom Seed

- Member of the ginger family with a slight lemon flavor. Best used in pickling, pastries, grape jellies, hot dogs, pumpkin dishes, sweet potatoes, and Asian dishes.
- Usually imported from India and sold whole or ground.
- Commonly used in spice cakes.

Cayenne Pepper

- A common spice also called capsaicin or red pepper. Sold in crushed, ground, or whole forms.
- Commonly used in curries, relishes, salsas, chili products, most Mexican dishes, Italian and Indian foods, sausages, and dressings.

Should be added by the pinch for the best results.

Celery Seed

- Sold in the seed form and as celery salt and used in soups, stews, salad dressings, fish dishes, salads, pickling, and many vegetable dishes.
- Celery flakes are made from dehydrated leaves and the stalks and used in the same dishes.
- Excellent in macaroni, coleslaw and potato salads.

Chervil

- Imported from France and used in salad dressings and anything that you would use parsley for.
- Commonly used in fish, shellfish and chicken dishes.

Chili Peppers

- The best method of preparing chili peppers for use in recipes is to first roast them. Just use a long handled fork on top of the stove and singe them until the skin blisters.
- Place the hot peppers on a cloth and cover them allowing them to steam making the skin relax and easily pull away allowing the seeds and veins to be removed.

The pulp will be very spicy but the seeds and veins will be even hotter.

- Try not to use too many of the seeds unless you desire a hot fiery dish.

Chili Powder

- Prepared from a combination of cumin seed, hot chili peppers, oregano, salt, cayenne pepper, garlic, and allspice. This will give you a jolt if you are not used to it. Have a glass of milk ready.

Chives

- Chives have a light onion flavor and are commonly used in to flavor dips, sauces, soups, baked potatoes, or to replace onion flavor in a recipe.
- Chives should be cut up only just before you are ready to use them to preserve their vitamins and minerals. Heating chives will also cause a big loss of nutrients.
- Frozen chives retain a larger percentage of their flavor than dried chives.
- Commonly used in cream soups.

Cilantro

- Sold as fresh coriander, looks like parsley and is commonly used in Mexican dishes and in salad dressings and salsa.
- To keep cilantro fresh, just remove the fresh leaves from the stem and place them on a piece of barely moist paper towel in a single layer. Roll the paper towel up and wrap it in plastic wrap or a baggie, making sure as much air as possible is removed. Store in the refrigerator and the cilantro should stay fresh for at least 3-5 days.

Cinnamon

- The "real" cinnamon is from the laurel tree.
- The ground form is used for baked goods, ketchup, vegetables, apple butter, mustards, and spiced peaches.

Cinnamon sticks are the most potent form of cinnamon.

- If you are going to flavor with cinnamon it doesn't take very much to obtain a good flavor. In many soups and marinades it only takes a pinch or two.

- To prepare cinnamon sugar, just add 1 tablespoon of ground cinnamon to $1/2$ cup of granulated sugar.
- Excellent on acorn squash and sweet potatoes.

Clove

- Usually sold as whole cloves.
- A strong spice used in moderation in baked beans, pickling, ham roasts, sweet potatoes, baked goods, puddings, mustards, soups, hot dogs, sausages, and barbecue sauces.
- Commonly used by placing in onions and added to stews for flavor.
- Excellent with sweet potatoes and squash.

Coriander Seed

- Relative of the carrot family, it has a sweet musk flavor.
- The seed or ground form is used in gingerbread, cookies, cakes, biscuits, poultry stuffing, pork, spiced dishes, pea soup, and cheese dishes.
- When using the fresh herb, be sure and add it just before serving or the flavor will be lost.

Cumin Seed

- Used mainly in its ground form in curry, chili powder, soups, stuffed eggs, fruit pies, stews, soft cheeses, and chili con carne.

Curry Powder

- Curry powder is a blend of at least 20 spices, herbs, and seeds. Ingredients may include chili peppers, cloves, coriander, fennel seed, nutmeg, mace, cayenne, black pepper, sesame seed, saffron, and turmeric.
- Small, hot, bitter seed.
- The yellow color comes from the turmeric.
- Usually used in Indian cooking, poultry, stews, soups, sauces, and meat dishes.
- Can be purchased in two mixtures, standard and Madras. Madras is very spicy and hot.

If you place curry powder in a saucepan with a small amount of butter and heat it for about 45 seconds it will have a better flavor.

- Unless you are used to using curry powder start off with a small amount.
- If you are going to add curry powder to a dish, be sure and eat the food soon after. The longer the food sits, the more potent the curry powder becomes.

Dill

- Sold in whole or ground seed form or as a fresh herb.
- The seeds and herb are used for pickles.
- Provides an excellent flavor for many sauces.
- Usually used in cottage cheese, chowders, pickling, soups, sauerkraut, salads, fish, meat sauces, potato salad, green apple pie, and spiced vinegar.
- Great for livening up egg salad.
- Shrimp in dill sauce is a world favorite.

Dried Herbs

- Herbs can be dried in a microwave on paper towel for about 2-3 minutes depending on the amount of herbs to be dried.
- Dried herbs do best when stored in as airtight a container as possible and refrigerated.
- Dried herbs that are sold in the supermarket are usually more potent than fresh herbs, however, they do not retain their potency very long.
- When storing herbs always date the package or container.
- Herbs will retain their potency for about 4-6 months before starting to lose it.

The rule of thumb when using dried herbs to replace fresh herbs is 1 teaspoon of dried herbs for 1 tablespoon of fresh herbs.

- If you are going to replace leaf herbs with dried, use $1/2$ the amount of dried herbs.
- The potency of dried herbs; can be intensified by crushing them with your fingers before using them.
- If you are planning to use dried herbs in a cold salad dressing or sauce, you can obtain better flavor by first mixing the herbs in hot water to moisten them and allowing them to remain for about 10 minutes before draining and drying them on paper towel.

Epazote

- Pungent herb commonly used in Mexican cooking with beans.

Fennel

- The flavor is similar to anise but is somewhat sweeter.
- Usually used in pork dishes, baked squash, Italian sausage, sweet pickles, fish dishes, candies, cabbage, pastries, oxtail soup, and pizza sauce.

When you choose fresh fennel, make sure you choose clean, crisp bulbs that are not browning.

- The stalks and greenery should be removed before using. Fennel bulbs and the base may be used raw in salads.
- Used in most Scandinavian breads.

Fenugreek

- The aroma is similar to curry powder and is mainly used to make imitation maple syrup, and a digestive aide as a tea.

Fresh Herbs

- When purchasing fresh herbs, be sure they look fresh and have a pleasant aroma.
- Make sure that there is no wilting or off colors on the herbs.
- Never store fresh herbs near a heat source or even a microwave exhaust fan.
- Wash and dry herbs before using them.

Fresh herbs usually are more potent than processed herbs and you may want to use less to obtain the same results as with processed herbs.

- Over seasoning with fresh herbs may ruin a dish and reversal may be impossible.
- When using fresh herbs to flavor a dish, allow the dish to remain for at least 1-2 hours to give the herb time to flavor the dish.
- Fresh herb potency may be lost to heat very quickly and should be added to cooking dishes during the final 15-20 minutes of cooking time.
- Herb butter can be prepared by adding about $1\frac{1}{2}$ tablespoons of finely chopped herbs to $\frac{1}{2}$ pound of room temperature softened unsalted butter.
- Herb butter should be kept refrigerated and allowed to soften at room temperature before serving.

Garlic

- There are several varieties of garlic:
    Simoneti and Burgundy are mild garlic varieties.
    Inchelium, Red and Locati are medium potency garlic.
    Metachi and Chinese Purple are the strongest garlic
- Read the label before you buy a garlic product. Garlic products should contain an antibacterial or acidifying agent such as phosphoric acid or citric acid. If this is not on the label the product must be sold and stored at under refrigeration at all times.
- Make sure the garlic bulbs are firm with dry skins and no brown or soft spots

Never buy garlic if it has green shoots.

- If a clove of garlic is removed without damaging it, it will not have a smell or taste.
- Garlic only has taste and smell when damaged.
- The minute garlic is crushed or damaged in any way the chemicals inside mix together resulting in the taste and aroma.
- The fresher the garlic, the better the flavor.
- When using older garlic, be sure and remove the inner green core or the garlic will have a stronger, somewhat unsavory flavor.
- When a recipe calls for "green garlic" it is referring to a very young white garlic bulb with long green stems.
- Garlic butter has a very short shelf life and should be used up or discarded. I can be kept refrigerated for only 14 days.
- If you have too much garlic in a dish, just add some parsley. The parsley will absorb the garlic, then discard the parsley.
- The more garlic is processed, crushed or pureed, the more flavor will be released.
- Whole garlic cloves or quarters will only release a small percentage of its flavor
- Garlic should never be frozen or it will lose potency.
- Garlic cloves will peel easily if the cloves are separated from the bulb and placed into boiling water for 30-40 seconds then immediately immersed into ice cold water.

Garlic skins are very strong and may clog a garbage disposal.

- When using a garlic press, you can place the whole garlic in and the meat will be released leaving the skin in the press.
- Salt has the tendency to absorb garlic juice when you are chopping or minc-

ing garlic if you want to keep things dry.

- Sprinkle a small amount of salt that will be used in the recipe on garlic when mincing and the garlic will not stick to the knife
- If a garlic clove is damaged with a nick from a knife it has to be used or discarded since it will develop mold very quickly

Rub a garlic clove on the inside of a salad bowl or the inside of a pan you are going to cook in for a light flavor of garlic.

- Garlic turns bitter and has an off odor if cooked too long.
- If you are heating a dish to a high temperature for a prolonged period of time, garlic should be added during the final 10-15 minutes.
- To obtain a small amount of garlic flavor in a cooked dish, just add the garlic (in a piece of cheesecloth) at the beginning of the cooking process and then remove it after 2-5 minutes depending on the potency you desire.
- If garlic is slow-cooked the flavor is released and it can be cooked longer without turning bitter.

The more you cook garlic, the more flavor and aroma are lost because the more allicin is broken down.

- Roasting garlic results in garlic becoming soft, having a pleasant sweet flavor and turning golden brown.

- To eliminate the odor of garlic after you consume it, just chew a small amount of fennel or parsley.
- To eliminate the odor of garlic from your hands, just rinse in a small amount of lemon juice or place a small amount of salt on a lemon slice and rub on your hands.
- To eliminate the odor of garlic from a cutting board, just clean the area with a paste of baking soda and warm water.
- Garlic vinegar can be made by placing 2-3 fresh cloves in a pint of white vinegar and allowed to stand for 2 weeks in the refrigerator.
- Garlic, when processed, is more perishable than most other herbs and should be used or discarded.
- If you want to place garlic in a stew for a short period of time, just place it in a tea infuser for easy removal. You can also place a toothpick in the clove.
- When sautéing garlic and onions, always sauté the onions first and then add the garlic just before you finish or the garlic will become bitter.
- Garlic can be stored at room temperature in a cool, dry location for 1-2 months.

For the strongest garlic flavor, crush unpeeled garlic clove in a garlic press and sauté until it is just golden brown.

- When sautéing garlic in oil the garlic should be placed into the oil when you add the oil and never into oil that has already heated or it may burn the garlic and turn it bitter.
- To prepare garlic butter, peel and blanch 4 cloves of garlic, then pound them in a bowl with $1/4$ pound of unsalted butter (softened at room temperature) then pass the mixture through a fine sieve.
- To make garlic oil, blanch 15 cloves of garlic, drain them and pound in a mortar until it is a fine paste, add $1 \, 1/3$ cups of extra virgin olive oil, mix thoroughly, then pass the mixture through a muslin cloth.
- Garlic powder can be prepared by drying the cloves slowly in the oven, peel and pound them with a mortar, then place them back in the oven to dry further. Pound them again until they are reduced to a fine powder then pass through a fine sieve. Pound any remaining pieces again and pass through the sieve.

Roasting Garlic

1. Peel away the majority of the outer skin, leaving about 3 layers.
2. Make sure that you cut off the top, just enough to expose the cross-section of the cloves.
3. Place the bulbs in a baking dish and very lightly pour some extra virgin olive oil on top to keep the cloves from burning and provide some flavor.
4. Try sprinkling a different herb on top of each bulb for a different flavor treat.
5. The dish should be covered and baked at 3750F for 30 minutes.
6. Remove the lid or tin foil and allow the bulbs to bake for an additional 6-7 minutes to give then a nice crisp top.
7. The longer you roast, the more mild the garlic will become.

Ginger

- Fresh ginger will have a totally different flavor from dried ground ginger and cannot be substituted for the ground.
- The skin on gingerroot should be peeled carefully so as no to remove any of the meat that is just under the skin. This is the most flavorful part of the gingerroot.
- Never add ginger to a gelatin dish or the gelatin will not set up unless the ginger is cooked first.

Chefs may add a piece of gingerroot to a wine bottle and use it to flavor stir-fry dishes or sauces.

- Common spice used in curry, fruit dishes and many baked goods such as gingerbread.
- Candied ginger can be prepared with sugar syrup and then coated with coarse sugar.
- Japanese cooking uses pickled ginger as a condiment. Pickled ginger is usually preserved in rice vinegar.
- Sometimes grated and used in marinades.

Ground Spices

- When spices are ground too much of their surface is exposed to the damaging effects of oxygen and the spices lose their aroma and flavor very quickly.
- If you plan on grinding your spices, then purchase small quantities. These

spices will be more potent than the ground spices you purchase in boxes, packages or small jars.

- Spices should be stored in a well-sealed container in a cool, dry location and make sure you date the container.

The flavor of certain spices can be intensified by roasting. Whole all-spice berries, white and black peppercorns can be roasted at 350°F for 8-10 minutes before grinding with excellent results.

- If you plan on making a large purchase of a spice it would be best to store it in the refrigerator. Most will last for 4-6 months if sealed well.

Hyssop

- Has a somewhat mint flavor.
- Young leaves may be used in salads.

Juniper Berries

- Usually used in making gin.
- Used occasionally in sauerkraut and marinades.

Lemon Grass

- Can be used when preparing vinaigrette and is common in Indonesian and Near Eastern cooking.

Lemon Balm

- Has sweet lemon flavor.
- Used in soups, salads, jellies, and on fruits.

Lovage

- Has taste like celery.
- Commonly used in salads, stocks and soups.

Mace

- Mace is the dried out husk of the nutmeg shell. It is sold in ground form and used in pound cake and chocolate dishes.
- In its whole form it is used in jellies, beverages, pickling, ketchup, baked beans, soups, deviled chicken, ham spreads, and French dressing.
- A favorite in spice cakes.

Marjoram

- Related to the oregano family with a sweet nutty flavor. It can be purchased in leaves and is imported from France, Chile, and Peru. Usually combined with other herbs and used in soups, Greek salad, potato dishes, stews, poultry seasoning, sauces, and fish dishes.

Mint

- Tomatoes go very well with mint and small amounts of chopped mint should be added to tomato dishes for a new taste sensation.
- When you purchase mint, be sure that none of the leaves look wilted or are discolored or the flavor will be poor.
- Peppermint has bright green leaves with purple-tinged stems, spearmint leaves, will be a gray-green and the flavor will be milder than peppermint.
- Commonly used in tabbouleh and other grin dishes.

Mint Flakes

- These dehydrated flakes of the peppermint and spearmint plants have a strong sweet flavor. Grown in the United States and Europe and used to flavor lamb dishes, fish, stews, soups, peas, sauces, desserts, and jellies.
- For an instant breath freshener, try chewing a few mint leaves.

Mustard Seeds

- Yellow or white seeds will produce mild mustard, while the brown seeds produce the more spicy variety.
- Powdered mustard has almost no aroma until mixed with a liquid.
- Mustard has hundreds of uses and is one of the popular spices worldwide. Most mustard will last about 2 years if kept under refrigeration.

If a recipe calls for a particular type of mustard, it would be best to use that one. Using the wrong mustard will make a difference in the taste desired.

- Mustard oil, which is pressed from brown mustard seeds is extremely hot and sometimes used in Chinese or other oriental dishes

Types:

American Mustard

- The typical hot dog mustard is produced from a mild yellow mustard seed, sweetener, vinegar, and usually colored with the herb turmeric. It has a fairly smooth texture.

Chinese Mustard

- Found in small ceramic dishes in all Chinese restaurants. It is produced from powdered mustard, water, and strong vinegar. The sweetener is left out and the mustard will only retain its bite for 1-2 hours.

Dijon Mustard

- Originated in Dijon, France. Produced from brown mustard seeds, white wine, unfermented grape juice and a variety of seasonings. It has a smooth texture and is usually a grayish-yellow color.

English Mustard

- This mustard is produced from white and black mustard seeds, a small amount of flour, and turmeric for coloring. This is one of the hottest mustards sold.

German Mustard

- Produced from a variety of mustard seeds. The color varies and the flavor is somewhat mild due to a small amount of sugar used in the production.

Nutmeg

- A relatively sweet spice that is available in ground form and imported from the East and West Indies.
- Commonly used in sauces, puddings, as a topping for custards, creamed foods, eggnogs, whipped cream, sausages, frankfurters, and ravioli.
- The most pungent is the freshly ground nutmeg. Special nutmeg graters are sold in kitchen specialty shops.

If you are going to use nutmeg and going to grate your own, be aware that freshly ground is much more potent than canned or ground.

- The outer covering of nutmeg seed is used to make the spice mace.

Oregano

- A relative of the mint family and may be found by the names origanum and Mexican sage.
- Commonly sold in leaf or ground forms. A common herb on Italian specialties such as pizza and spaghetti sauces. Try oregano on a grilled cheese sandwich and you will never eat another one without it.
- Commonly used in Mexican and Greek cooking.

Paprika

- The best paprika is Hungarian paprika and can be purchased in varieties that range from mild to very hot. The very hot can be compared in potency to cayenne pepper.
- The milder variety, red sweet, is grown in the United States.
- It is commonly used in a wide variety of dishes such as cream sauces, vegetables, mustards, salad dressings, ketchup, sausages, dips and fish dishes.
- Makes an excellent powdered garnish.

Parsley

- Make sure that the parsley you are using is bright green with no signs of wilting.
- Parsley can be revived if it becomes wilted by placing the parsley in a bowl of ice water (with ice cubes) in the refrigerator for 45 minutes.
- Parsley can be sliced with scissors fast and easy. Make sure that the leaves are dry.

Flat-leaf Italian parsley is the most flavorful parsley

- Parsley can be dried in the microwave then crumbled.
- Parsley should not be cooked since it tends to destroy a high percentage of its vitamins and minerals.
- Parsley should only be sliced or chopped just before you use it to preserve the flavor. To store parsley, sprinkle it with cold water, wrap it in a piece of paper towel, place it in a plastic bag and store in the refrigerator.

Pepper, Black and White

- Black peppercorns will have a stronger flavor than white or green peppercorns.
- Freshly ground pepper will lose its flavor fairly quickly since you are exposing a large surface of the peppercorn to oxygen.

White pepper is used to season light or white sauces and other dishes where the black color is not desired.

- If you prefer to use already ground pepper, try adding a few black peppercorns to the box or shaker to improve the flavor and aroma.

Poppy Seeds

- Has a rich, nut-like flavor and used in salads, cookies, pastry fillings, Indian dishes, and baked goods.

Poultry Seasoning

- Commonly used in poultry dressings and soups.
- The major ingredients are sage, thyme, marjoram, and Savoy.

Rosemary

- A sweet, fragrant and spicy herb, with a very pungent aroma. Imported from Spain and Portugal and used in stews, meat dishes, dressings, and Italian foods.
- Commonly used by chefs over mushrooms and roasted potatoes.

Saffron

- This is one of the more difficult herbs to acquire as well as being the most expensive herb in the world at $800 per pound.
- It is extracted from the stigma of a flowering crocus and is only imported from Spain.
- It should be used in moderation and is normally used in dishes that contain poultry, special baked goods and rice dishes.

It requires 14,000 hand picked crocus stigmas to produce one ounce of saffron.

- Saffron's color strength will determine the level of flavor and aroma. The best quality saffron is sold in saffron threads and not the powder.
- When working with saffron, it is best never to use a whisk, since the threads will become entwined in the whisk. Also, wooden utensils will absorb saffron and should be avoided.
- Saffron quality is measured in "coloring strength" with the best strength being between 246-256. It is possible to purchase saffron with strength of only 110 but this will be an inferior product.
- Saffron should never be purchased with a level below 190 degrees. To use saffron properly the threads should be soaked to infuse the saffron before adding it to a recipe.

Saffron is not lost to boiling water much like many herbs. Saffron will continue to release flavor and aroma for at least 12 hours after you place it in a dish. This is why most recipes that recommend saffron advise you to allow the dish to sit overnight for the best flavor.

- Saffron threads should never be added to boiling water or directly into a dish. When a recipe calls for saffron, it is best to use the threads and crush them just before using.
- This is an expensive herb that can be cut with turmeric if you so desire, but the results will not be as good.
- Saffron can be activated to produce a stronger flavor by mixing it in a very small amount of very hot water and letting it stand for 8-10 minutes before using it.
- Excellent in risotto.
- Saffron is water soluble and should not be added to fat.

Sage

- A very strong herb that is a member of the mint family and available in leaf or ground form.
- Commonly used in veal dishes, stews, soups, pork products, stuffing, salads, fish dishes, and pizza sauces.
- Sage contains a number of essential oils, such as thujone, camphor and eucalyptol.
- Used in poultry seasoning.

Salt (sodium chloride)

- When salt is processed, the native minerals are stripped away and it is then enriched with iodine and dextrose to stabilize it, sodium bicarbonate to keep it white, and anti-caking agents to keep it "free-flowing."
- When you add too much salt to a dish, try repairing it by adding 1 teaspoon of apple cider vinegar and 1 teaspoon of sugar.

Morton's Special Salt is one of the only salt varieties that have no additives.

- Salt is used in almost every food that is processed and is one of the best preservatives.
- When preparing food and seasoning with salt the recommended amounts for certain dishes are:

  1 teaspoon for soups and sauces
  1 teaspoon for raw meat dishes
  1 teaspoon for every 4 cups of flour (dough)
  1 teaspoon for every 2 cups of liquid used in cooked cereals

- 40% of regular table salt is sodium; Lite salt has only 20% sodium content.
- For thousands of years, salt has been used to preserve foods by inhibiting microbial growth.
- Salt has the ability to draw liquids from tissues and freeing water that is bound by breaking down proteins. The mechanism involves salts ability to create a concentration of "ions" (electrically charged particles) outside of the bacteria and mold cells encompassing the microbe drawing out its water and either drying it up and killing it or slowing down its replication. It is the drying out feature of salt that makes it such a good preservative.

Kelp can be ground up and used in a shaker to replace salt. It only contains 4% sodium and the taste is very close.

- It is necessary to read labels and be aware that many foods contain ingredients that contain sodium, such as MSG. Many spices also contain sodium as a normal part of their makeup.
- The following are some spices and flavorings that are sodium-free:

ALLSPICE	ALMOND EXTRACT	BAY LEAVE
CARAWAY SEEDS	CINNAMON	CURRY POWDER
GARLIC	GINGER	LEMON EXTRACT
MACE	MAPLE EXTRACT	MARJORAM
MUSTARD POWDER	NUTMEG	PAPRIKA
PARSLEY	PEPPER	PIMIENTO
ROSEMARY	PEPPERMINT EXTRACT	SAGE
SESAME SEED	THYME	TURMERIC
VANILLA EXTRACT	WALNUT EXTRACT	VINEGAR

- The majority of the salt used in the United States is mined from salt deposits that were laid down thousands of years ago and are readily accessible.

TYPES OF SALT

Canning Salt

- This is really pure salt and only salt. It is only found in canning sections of the supermarket.

CHEF'S SALT

1 cup of salt
1 Tbl. Spanish paprika
1/4 tsp. celery salt
1 tsp. ground black pepper
1/4 tsp. ground white pepper
1/4 tsp. garlic salt
If you use garlic powder, just a pinch will do.

Ice Cream Salt

- Produced from large chunks of salt and is used for home ice cream making. It is also used to ice down large kegs of beer.
- This is normally not food grade salt.

Kosher Salt

- Has an excellent flavor and texture as well as being additive-free.
- Kosher salt has larger salt crystals and a more jagged shape, which means that they will cling to food better.
- Because of its characteristics, kosher salt has the ability to draw more blood from meats, since kosher meats must be as free from blood as possible to meet the strict Jewish dietary laws.

Pickling Salt

- A fine-grained salt that is additive-free and used in the preparation of pickles and sauerkraut.

Rock Salt

- A poorly refined salt that has a grayish appearance with large crystals. Combines with ice to make ice cream.

Sea Salt

- Has a fresh flavor and is available in fine or coarse-grained varieties.
- It is usually imported and preferred by chefs.
- Sea salt; as its name implies, is acquired by allowing salt water to accumulate in pools and having the sun evaporate off the water leaving a stronger flavored salt with a few more trace minerals than table salt.
- There is not that big of a difference to pay the extra price for sea salt.

Iodized and Non-Iodized Salt

- This is the standard table salt with iodine added or excluded.
- Most table salts have a non-caking, agent added. Very fine-grained: making it free flowing.

Savoy

- Has a slight peppery flavor and is a member of the mint family.
- Commonly sold in leaf and ground forms and is primarily used to flavor eggs, meats, poultry, and fish.

Sesame Seeds

- Has a rich, nut-like flavor and high oil content. Commonly used as a topping for baked goods and in halvah.

Sichuan Peppercorns

- Sold as whole peppercorns.
- Used mainly in Chines and Asian dishes.

Tarragon

- Has a strong flavor similar to licorice. It is native to Siberia with the majority imported from Spain and France.
- Commonly used in sauce béarnaise, meat-dishes, salads, herb dressings, and tomato casseroles.
- Frequently used in mayonnaise.

Thyme

- Has a strong, very spicy flavor and is available in leaf and ground forms.
- Commonly used in tomato-based soups, stews, sauces, chipped beef (an old army favorite), mushrooms, sausages, clam chowder, herb dressings, and mock turtle soup.
- Chefs use thyme in pates.

Turmeric

- Imported from India and Peru and used in chicken, pickles, meat dishes, dressings, curry powder, Spanish rice, relishes, and mustards.
- Common ingredient in curry powder, mustard and pickles.

Vanilla

- Always use "pure" vanilla extract," there is no substitute that will compare.
- If you are going to use a vanilla bean in a dish, slit it lengthwise with a pointed knife and a piece of the bean to flavor the dish. Remove the bean before serving.
- When adding a vanilla bean to a recipe, always add it toward the end of the cooking time since it will lose its flavor if heated too much.

Mexican vanilla may be contaminated and should be avoided.

- The vanilla pod is the only food produced by a plant member of the orchid family.
- The reason "real" vanilla is so expensive is that it is hand pollinated when grown commercially. In the wild it is pollinated by only one species of hummingbird. Since they are so expensive to grow and over 75% of the bean is grown in Madagascar where the pods are actually branded with the growers brand because of "vanilla bean rustlers" stealing the crop.
- Pure vanilla extract can only be made by percolating the bean similar to making coffee.
- Imitation vanilla is produced from the chemical vanillin, which is a by-product of the wood pulp industry.

CHAPTER 28

VEGETARIANISM

General Overview

- An ever-increasing segment of the American public is choosing not to eat meat. In 2000 there were approximately 15 million vegetarians in the United States and increasing every year. This food trend is pursued for a variety of reasons, such as considering it wrong to kill animals, a waste of natural resources by using large quantities of grain to feed beef and hogs, religious beliefs or just to lead a healthier lifestyle.

- While vegetarianism is a way of achieving a healthier diet for many of us, it is a radical change and one that is not easily adhered to. There are sufficient studies and evidence to support them that provide us with the proof that even a modified vegetarian diet can be beneficial and result in a healthier, longer life.

- One of the major concerns among non-vegetarians who wish to consider changing to vegetarianism is that they will lack adequate protein. There are, of course, many excellent vegetable and grain sources that are capable of supplying all your amino acid (protein) needs.

- One of the best plant sources of protein is the soybean, from which many products are presently produced and are readily available in your local supermarkets. These soy products contain 30-40% protein and many are closer to meat protein than vegetable protein, even when examined under amino acid pattern analysis.

- The question also arises regarding the lack of vitamin B_{12} in a vegetarian diet, since vitamin B_{12} is normally found in animal products. However, most vegetarians do eat some dairy products, which provide them with adequate levels of vitamin B_{12} eliminating the problem.

If you are planning to change you dietary patterns and become a vegetarian, it would be wise to purchase a book on vegetarianism and learn to do extensive meal planning, especially for the first 6 months.

TYPES OF VEGANS

True vegetarians

will never consume any food from an animal source, not even dairy products. They normally need supplementation to obtain B12.

Lacto-vegetarians

will include dairy products but no eggs in their diet.

Lacto-Ovo vegetarians

will include dairy products and eggs in their diets but will not eat any meats, poultry or fish.

Ovo vegetarians

will eat eggs and no other dairy product or animal product of any kind.

Pesco-vegetarians

will eat fish, dairy products and eggs but will not eat any poultry or meats.

Vegetarian Facts

- Meat is really not needed for a healthy diet.
- B_{12} is usually taken as a supplement; however, some forms of Brewer's yeast may contain B_{12}. Tempeh and sea vegetables may contain vitamin B_{12}.
- Most vegetarians do eat some dairy products, which all contain vitamin B_{12}.
- Most vegetarians have lower cholesterol levels and less coronary problems than meat eaters do.
- Vegetarians have fewer cases of colon cancer and digestive problems.
- They tend to have a lower incidence of cancer.

Soy products contain a high level of phytoestrogens, which scientists now think will reduce the risks of breast and prostate cancer. However, studies are not conclusive regarding the benefits of soy.

- Iron and zinc are not easily absorbed by true vegetarians and may have to be supplemented.
- Beans and rice are considered to be a "complete" protein because they contain all the essential amino acids.
- Good sources of calcium are dark, green leafy vegetables.
- Vegetarian products made from soybeans have a lower fast content and still provide an excellent source of protein.
- Most vegetarian foods, however, do contain too much sodium.
- When preparing vegetarian dishes, try and avoid soy sauce if possible since this seems to be the source of most of the sodium.
- Iron can be derived from dried beans, spinach, chard, beet greens, blackstrap molasses, bulgur, and prune juice to name just a few sources.

VEGETARIAN SOY & WHEAT PRODUCTS

Aburage (deep-fried tofu)

- Soy product used to prepare inari sushi. Available only in oriental markets.

Bean Stick

- Made from barley instead of soybeans and not as pungent as ones that are made from red miso.

Cheese

- Cheese produced from soy will soon be appearing at all markets as a specialty food. Soy cheese is lactose and cholesterol-free as well as low in saturated fat.

Miso

Originated in China and was probably invented by Buddhist Monks around 700AD. Commercial production started around 1674 in Japan. Presently, Japan produces over 600,000 tons annually by 1,600 miso manufacturers.

- High in protein, isoflavones, and antioxidants.
- Miso has high sodium content and is used more as a condiment and flavoring agent.

- Found in Japanese food markets and health food stores.
- Miso is a combination of soybeans and a grain. It has very little fat and is usually used as a seasoning for soups, dips and stews.
- The darker varieties are saltier than the lighter-colored varieties.
- The "dark" miso is strong flavored as well as salty.
- The "red" and "yellow" miso is milder.
- The "white" miso is sweet.
- Awase miso is a combination of red and white and is one of the more popular varieties.
- Adding miso to soups and stews must be done close to the end of the cooking cycle since the flavor is easily lost.
- Miso combines and blends easily with most foods, especially soups and stews.

Seitan:

- Prepared from wheat gluten and may be called "wheat meat."
- Contains a very high level of protein and does not have to be cooked.
- Seitan can be sliced and replace meat loaf in a sandwich.

Soy Milk

- Extracted from soybeans and consumed by people who have an allergy to cow's milk.
- Usually found supplemented with vitamin D and B12.
- Commonly found flavored with chocolate.

Tempeh

- Made from whole cooked soybeans that are infused with starter bacteria then allowed to ferment. This produces a product that is very dense and chewy with a nutty flavor. Can be fried, grilled, or used for veggie burgers.
- Because of the fermentation process, it contains one of the only vegetable sources of vitamin B12.
- It can be prepared as hamburger or meatloaf with excellent results.
- It is also broken into small pieces and fried with vegetables.

TSP or TVP (textured vegetable protein)

- Made from compressing soy flour.
- Excellent source of calcium and because of its consistency is used as a replacement for hamburger meat in many recipes.

- Try replacing 30-50% of your ground beef with TSP next time you make a meatloaf.

Tofu (bean curd)

Tofu has been a popular Chinese food for thousands of years and was invented when sea, water (sea salt), which contains calcium sulfate (a coagulant) accidentally spilled into a pot of heating soy milk causing it to curdle. The silken Japanese variety is more popular than the firm variety.

- Tofu is a curd that is prepared by boiling soybeans in water then grinding the beans into a paste and adding calcium sulfate to coagulate the curd, making it a better source of calcium than raw soybeans. It can also be prepared from soybean milk.
- Most Japanese and Chinese tofu is made without the addition of the calcium sulfate instead they use an acid such as lemon juice or vinegar.
- The protein in bean curd is 90% digestible, which is close to milk.
- The curds are compressed into blocks then stored in water under refrigeration or vacuum-packed.
- If you purchase tofu that is not in a package, be sure and change the water it is stored in daily.
- Low-fat tofu is now being sold that will last for 3-5 days from the "sell date" and possibly 2 weeks if it is very fresh when purchased.
- If you are going to freeze tofu, then it should be frozen as soon as it is purchased in its original water and container. It can be frozen for about 2 months at 0^0 F. After it is thawed it will, however, be a little bit more fragile and will disintegrate unless added to dish just before serving.
- Can be purchased in soft, silken, regular, medium or firm varieties.
- Tofu products may vary significantly regarding nutritional content. It is best to read the labels.
- Nigari tofu is very firm.
- Chinese tofu is firmer and sweeter than the Japanese tofu.
- Sold in cakes of tofu in the supermarket.
- Tempeh or TVP can substitute for tofu in recipes.
- Prepared from curdled soy milk.
- Tends to take on the flavor of whatever food it is mixed with.
- Best to purchase tofu that has been packaged. When it is allowed to stand in water it may attract bacteria from the air and may be easily contaminated.
- The texture will vary and will be sold in either soft, firm or extra firm varieties.

Tofu is very perishable and should be refrigerated as soon as possible. If purchased in water, the water needs to be changed when you bring it home. The water must cover the tofu and must be changed daily.

- Tofu can be frozen for 2-3 months.
- Unless tofu is added to dishes that require stirring it should be added toward the end of the cooking cycle since it tends to fall apart easily.
- Soft tofu can be whipped in a blender and used to increase the protein level in custard and puddings.

CHAPTER 29

LOW-CALORIE COOKING

LOW-CALORIE COOKING

- The majority of recipes do not need the amount of fat that the recipe calls for to achieve a great-tasting dish. Most dishes contain a "fat point," which is the point that there is sufficient fat in the dish to make the recipe work. The excess fat can usually be replaced with some other ingredient such as applesauce or a lower fat cheese or milk.

- When chefs are asked to alter a dish they frequently use fruit or vegetable purees to add moisture and flavor to certain dishes. Just match the flavor with the dish and this works great. In many dishes the puree can easily replace the oil to a certain degree.

When eggs are called for and are only used as a binder to hold foods together, egg whites can be used without the yolks. Even partially discarding some of the yolks will make a difference in the fat and cholesterol content of a recipe.

- If a food is labeled "fat-free", it can still have .05 gram of fat per serving
- If a food is labeled "low fat", it can have no more than 3 grams of fat per serving.
- If a food is labeled "lean", it can have 10 grams of total fat, 4 grams of which can be saturated.
- If the food is labeled "lite" or "light", it must contain $1/3$ fewer calories than the original higher calorie version.

Bacon

- A good alternative to regular bacon is Canadian bacon. The fat content is about one-third that of regular bacon.
- Imitation bacon prepared from chicken and turkey are good alternatives but lack the flavor.
- Many imitation products may contain MSG or very high salt levels.
- Pre-cooked bacon is also available and is lower in fat.
- Cook bacon in a pan with a rack so that the fat drips down and the bacon does not cook in its own fat.

Breads

- Many bread companies are now producing thinly sliced bread with 40 calories per slice.
- Bagels are still low calorie if they are not the giant ones.
- It usually is not bread that is high calories but the toppings we put on.
- Diet breads are very common in supermarkets. Most reduce the fat content and use a fat substitute or sell you a wafer-thin slice.
- Breadcrumbs can be made from diet breads.

Cheeses

- Fat-free and low fat cheeses taste relatively good; much better than they did when they originally came out.
- Most low fat cheeses can replace regular cheese in most recipes without a problem.
- If dips are seasoned well, low fat cottage cheese or sour cream can easily be used.

Low fat Cheese Sauce Recipe

¹/₂ cup white wine
2 Tbsp. fresh Parmesan cheese, finely grated
¹/₂ cup chopped scallions (light green and white parts only)
3 cloves of minced garlic
1 large red, yellow or green bell pepper, chopped fine (seeded and ribbed)
¹/₂ cup finely grated part-skim milk mozzarella cheese
¹/₄ cup low fat, small curd cottage cheese
Add salt and ground black pepper to taste

Using a medium saucepan over medium heat. Heat the wine to a point just below boiling, then add the garlic and simmer for 1 minute. Add the scallions and bell pepper and sauté for another 5 minutes stirring frequently. Place the three cheeses in a blender and puree; then slowly add the puree and whisk. Makes an excellent low fat pasta or vegetable sauce served warm.

- To retain the flavor in cheese dishes, try using 1part regular cheese to 4 parts of low fat or fat-free cheese.

Desserts

- Cocoa powder can provide chocolate flavor with almost all the cocoa butter removed.
- Fruit purees are used frequently in many low fat cookbooks to provide sweetness and take the place of sugar.
- Either a smaller amount recommended in the recipe or using a low-calorie jelly can make a big difference.
- Some fruit juices that are unsweetened are still relatively sweet and can be used to replace sugar.
- Sweet dessert sauces can be made with evaporated milk instead of cream.
- Fruit-flavored yogurts can be used for toppings and in some baked goods.
- Chocolate desserts in many instances can substitute prune puree for the fat.
- Applesauce works great as a substitute in snack cakes.
- Phyllo dough is excellent for low-calorie desserts.

LOW FAT CHOCOLATE SYRUP

New low fat chocolate syrup has hit the markets, which has the flavor and taste of the real thing and 5 times less fat. The product is produced by New-Market Foods of Petaluma, California and consists of brown-rice syrup, honey, molasses and cocoa. The topping is syrupy and buttery and found in health food stores.

Eggs

- Egg substitutes can be used and most are made from egg white and soy. They work great in omelets, mayonnaise, and many baked goods.
- Eggs do have fat but are not really a high fat or high calorie food.
- Eggs are a good source of protein and an inexpensive one.
- Egg whites alone still provide a good quality protein without the fat from the yolk.

Frying

- Many foods that are pan-fried may be fried in a small amount of oil that is sprayed into the pan. Especially if you are using non-stick cookware.
- This book contains many tricks to limit the amount of fat absorbed when deep-frying foods.

Mashed Potatoes

- For low fat mashed potatoes, add two garlic cloves to the boiling potatoes; then mash them into the potatoes with non-fat milk.
- To give them a little more body reduced-fat milk can be used.
- Sweet potatoes have more nutrition but have more calories as well.

Meats

- All visible fat should be removed, which will make a difference in flavor.
- If you are good at seasoning, you can overcome the taste differences in using lower fat meat cuts.

Pancakes/Waffles

- The toppings are usually the problem, which can be solved by using a sugar-free preserve topping.
- Non-stick surface grilled should be used.

Poultry

- For fried chicken, remove the skin befor breading and fry in a small amount of oil.
- White meat is leaner and has fewer calorics and fat.

Sauces

- Fat-free yogurt can be substituted with excellent results in many sauces, unfortunately you will have to experiment with your recipe.

  Non-fat and reduced-fat milks can be used in most sauces and baked goods with good success.

- Non-dairy creamers can be used in most recipes, but be sure and use the plain in all instances.

Sausage

- There are many sausages that are made from chicken or turkey that are seasoned very well.
- The sodium content in most sausages is still very high.
- Many sausage products still contain high levels of MSG.

REDUCED FAT COOKING TECHNIQUES

Braising   can be done after dry frying in a non-stick pan that has been lightly sprayed with a vegetable spray.

Dry frying is simply to fry in a pan on the stovetop instead of a deep-fat fryer using a non-stick pan and vegetable spray oil. Heavy iron skillets work best.

Frying   methods are mentioned in this book with the foods that they relate to such as French fries and doughnuts, both of which can be fried in oil and still reduce the calories.

Grilling   usually does not add any fat, but it is always best to spray the grill with a vegetable spray to avoid the food sticking.

Roasting   should be done by placing the roast on a rack in the roaster or at least place celery stalks under the roast to keep it away from the drippings.

Stir-frying can be done with a vegetable spray, but it would be best to cook small batches for the best results.

LOW FAT, BAKED "FRIED FISH"

It is possible to prepare low fat "fried fish" without using all the fat to fry the fish in. Just dredge them in seasoned flour; dip the fish in egg yolk that has been beaten with a small amount of water and then coat them with breadcrumbs. Then place the fish in a shallow baking pan that has been lightly greased or sprayed with a vegetable spray. Dot the fish with small dollops of butter or margarine and bake for 6-10 minutes per inch of thickness or until the flesh is opaque.

HEALTHY RESTAURANT EATING

Chinese

Soup Choices: Wonton or hot and sour soup
Main Courses: Vegetable dishes cooked in a Wok (stir-fried), white rice, chow
  1
Stay Clear Of: Anything fried, especially egg rolls and breaded fried anything,
Sweet and sour dishes are high calorie and any dish sautéed in
large amounts of oil such as Szechwan style foods.

Italian

Soup Choices: Minestrone.
Main Courses: Any grilled lean meats, seafood, or vegetable
dishes without creams, pasta with marinara sauce.
Stay Clear Of: Antipasto, garlic bread, dishes topped with cheeses, breaded
and fried foods.

French

Soup Choices: Broth or vegetable soups
Main Courses: Any grilled lean meats or seafood, stews with a tomato base
ands

  vegetable dishes without cream sauces.
Stay Clear Of: French onion soup unless they leave the cheese topping off,
pate, anything in butter sauce, croissants, au fromage or au
gratin dishes.

Mexican

Soup Choices: Corn tortilla soup.
Main Courses: Bean and rice dishes without cheese, chicken fajitas without
cheese, corn tortilla or taco.
Stay Clear Of: Flour tortilla and chips, cheese sauces, guacamole, beef dishes,
fried tortilla dishes, enchiladas, burritos.

Fast Food Chains

Breakfast: Recommended are scrambled eggs, English muffin with no butter, orange juice.

Lunch: Smallest single burger with no cheese or sauce, Carl's Jr. or Roy Rogers roast beef sandwich, baked fish, rotisserie chicken with a salad at Kenny Rogers Roasters, salads with low-cal dressing, small single layer cheese pizza with vegetable toppings, Wendy's chili, Jack-In-The-Box Club Pita.

Stay Clear Of: Everything else.

CHAPTER 30

FOOD SAFETY

FOOD SAFETY

- Studies keep going on and on regarding the safety of cutting boards. Plastic cutting boards were then thought to be the best since they were less porous than wood, However, in a 1996 study the Wisconsin's Food Research Institute reported that wooden cutting boards may be best and bacterial levels were low after only a few minutes. The studies are continuing and all we can suggest is that if you cut up any meat product, clean the board thoroughly with very hot soapy water immediately afterwards. A new study in 1995 completed by the federal government Center for Food Safety and Applied Nutrition showed that only one out of four people wash their cutting boards after cutting or preparing raw meats and poultry.

- Dishrags and sponges should be placed in the wash or dishwasher every day. Paper towels are safer to use in most instances. Can openers are the number one germ spreader.

- Salmonella food poisoning is on the rise and in 2000 almost 47,500 cases of salmonella poisonings were reported (how many were not?) in restaurants. Most of these cases were caused by human error and many have been associated with restaurant and employee cleanliness. There are 1800 strains of salmonella, most of which will cause food poisoning.

- A large majority of food poisonings are related to the "pot luck" type of event. These are usually a result of poor temperature controls of the foods containing egg, dairy, or meat products.

- Imported lead crystal decanters may cause an excessive amount of lead to be consumed if you store wine or vinegar in them for any length of time. A number of fluids can leach the lead out of crystal and into the product.

- Never purchase a can or jar if there is any sign of damage or a bulge. When you open a can or jar always smell the contents to see if there is any off-odor and check the top for mold. Food can also be contaminated rather easily by tasting the foods from a container with a utensil that has been in your mouth.

- Recent studies are showing that plastic may be altered over time and release chemicals into the foods when foods are stored or cooked in them. Dr. Fredrick Vom Saal is conducting the studies at the University of Missouri and testing has already shown that mice are having a few reproductive problems. The FDA still insists that plastic is safe. The future may bring a new-coated plastic that will never be able to leach out any chemical and if it does, the color will change.

- Never drink from a glass that has been stored upside down over a bar. Smoke and other contaminants are able to get into the glass and remain there.

- Food-borne illnesses will make over 7,000,000 Americans ill in 2001 according to the Center for Disease Control. However, a more accurate total is probably closer to 85,000,000. Approximately 10,000 people will die from food-borne illnesses in 2001. The majority of the cases are relatively mild and most people get over the illness in about 2-3 days. However, almost 10,000 of these cases are fatal with most of the fatalities caused by meat and poultry.

- If you can see the cooks in a restaurant and any of them are smoking it would be wise to leave as soon as possible. Saliva contamination from smokers touching the cigarette then the food is relatively common.

- If you have leftovers in the refrigerator for more than 36 hours they should be re-cooked. Refrigerator temperatures are usually not cold enough to slow down bacterial growth for any longer period of time, especially on meat products.

- When working with raw meat or poultry for barbecuing, never use the same plate or utensil that touched the raw food. Placing the cooked food back on the same plate that held the raw food has caused many people to get food poisoning.

- If you make chili with beef, be sure and reheat it to a temperature of 160^0 F. before serving it.

- Recently, a supermarket placed barbecued birds from the oven onto a pan that had held fresh chicken without washing the pan. Every barbecued chicken was contaminated with Salmonella typhimurium and caused food poisoning at a picnic.

- Sulfites in foods for the most part are becoming a chemical of the past, especially after salad bars that were using the chemicals to retard the browning killed a number of people and brought on an untold number of asthmatic attacks. Occasionally, however, they seem to still appear in a few processed food products. The ones to watch out for are the following:

Sodium metabisulfite	Sodium sulfite	Sodium bisulfite
Potassium metabisulfite	Potassium bisulfite	Sulfur dioxide

FOOD CANNING FACTS

- When canning anything, the jars should always be sterilized regardless of the method used. The only exception is when you cook the foods in the jars, then the jars do not need sterilization, but should be thoroughly washed.
- No preservatives, additives, or artificial colorings should ever be added to a home canned product. Always wipe the outside of all jars with white vinegar before storing to reduce the risk of mold forming on any food that wasn't cleaned off well.
- As long as the seal is intact frozen home-canned goods are still safe to eat providing the seal is intact. However, as with all fresh frozen foods the taste and texture may change.
- If you see a black deposit on the lid after you open a canned food it is usually nothing to worry about (as long as the jar seal is intact). The mold-looking deposits are actually caused by tannins in the food or by hydrogen sulfide released by the foods when processed.
- Foods high in starch such as corn, Lima beans, and peas need to be packed loosely since they tend to expand during after being processed. Fruits and berries should be packed solidly due to shrinkage and the fact that their texture does not stop the heat penetration.
- If you see a jar that has a cloudy liquid, the food is probably spoiled. Be very cautious, these jars should be disposed of without being opened. Spores can be released that may be harmful.
- When you open any canned food, check the liquid and make sure that it is not cloudy. Cloudiness in many liquids indicates spoilage.
- If you have any doubts about foods, it is best to throw them out without tasting them. There are, however, a number of reasons foods may become cloudy and still be good such as different sizes of foods causing the breakdown of the smaller pieces, hard water, salt containing impurities and additives.
- Pickles may frequently become cloudy due to the fermentation process and this is not harmful.
- Pure apple cider vinegar is the best to use when pickling. It has a 4-5% acidity level.
- If you don't want your pickles to become soft, make sure that the vinegar has adequate acidity and that enough is used. Also, keeping the pickles in the refrigerator will help them remain hard.
- As long as the seal is intact, canned foods can last for many years. Nutrient content will be diminished, however, to a great degree.
- After canning the food, tap the top, you should hear a clear "ringing note."

If the food is touching the top, this may not occur, but as long as the top does not move up and down, the food does not have to be reprocessed.

- Canned foods need to be stored in a cool, dark location.   Summer heat may cause a location to develop enough heat to damage the canned foods. Heat causes dormant bacteria to become active and multiply.
- Research will have become high-tech by 2001 when it comes to the transfer of genes into plants. At present the rate of transfer is about 1 in 1,000 is all that can be achieved. By transferring genes in a micro-gravity atmosphere the rate of transfer more than doubles.
- Always slowly thaw frozen fruits in the refrigerator. The fruit will have time to absorb the sugar as it thaws.
- A small piece of string placed on top of the warm wax before sealing a jar of preserves will make it easier to remove the wax.

DINING OUT

- If you order a dish made from custard, whipped cream, or has a cream, filling, be sure they are served cool to the touch. These are all supposed to be refrigerated desserts.

- If the server touches the top of your water glass, either ask for a new glass or ask for a straw with your water when you first order.

- Check the cream for your coffee. If it has small white objects floating around it has been left out to long and is starting to go sour. If it is not cool don't use it.

- If the menu, server's uniforms, or bathrooms are dirty get out while the goings good.

Radiation Exposed Foods

- It is still the feeling by many scientists and doctors that radiation exposed foods are not as safe to eat as foods that have not been irradiated. The companies that plan to irradiate the foods, of course, do not share this view. It is felt that exposure will destroy the nutritional quality of foods, especially vitamins A, C, E, K and some B's. Certain amino acids and enzymes will also be destroyed. Studies have shown that radiation exposed foods can cause the following problems in lab animals:

Chromosomal damage	Testicular tumors
Reduced rate of offspring	High infancy mortality
Sperm-count reduction	Mutagenicity

CONSUMER NUTRITION SAFETY HOTLINE 1-(800) 366-1655

GOVERNMENT FILTH IN FOOD FACTS

- The "Filth in Food" guidelines; are controlled by the FDA. The following levels of contamination (insects, etc) if found in food would be the cause for the FDA to take legal action to remove the food from the supermarket. However, the following is just a small sample of foods and contaminants, there is a complete manual listing all foods available from the U.S. Government Consumer Affairs office in Washington.

The following is just a sample taken from the Consumers Affairs Booklet:

Apricots

- Canned, average of 2% insect infested or damaged.

Coffee Beans

- If 10% by count are infested or insect damaged or show evidence of mold.

Citrus Juice (canned)

- Microscopic mold count average of 10%. Drosophila and other fly eggs: 5 per 250ml. Drosophila larva: 1 per 250ml. If average of 5% by count contain larvae.

Peaches (canned)

- Average of 5% wormy or moldy fruit or 4% if a whole larva or equivalent is found in 20% of the cans.

Popcorn

- One rodent pellet in one or more sub-samples or six 10-ounce consumer-size packages, and 1 rodent hair in other sub-samples; or 2 rodent hairs per pound and any rodent hairs in 50% of the sub-samples' 20 gnawed grains per pound and rodent hairs in 50% of the sub-samples.

Asparagus (canned)

- 15% of the spears by count infested with 6 attached asparagus beetle eggs or egg sacs.

Broccoli

- Frozen, average of 80 aphids or thrips per 100 grams.

Tomato Juice

- 10 fly eggs per $3^1/_2$ oz or 5 fly eggs and 1 larva per $3^1/_2$ oz or 2 larva per $3^1/_2$ oz

Raisins

- Average of 40mm sand and grit per $3^1/_2$ oz or 10 insects and 35 fly eggs per 8 oz of golden bleached raisins.

Wheat

- One rodent pellet per pint or 1% by weight of insect-damaged kernels.

Brussels Sprouts

- Average of 40 aphids per $3^1/_2$ oz.

Flour

- The FDA allows wheat flour to contain approximately 50 insect parts per 2 ounces of flour. These are harmless and won't affect your health.

COMMON FOOD POISONING BACTERIA/VIRUS

ORGANISM	SOURCE	SYMPTOMS APPEAR	TYPICAL DURATION
SALMONELLA	Undercooked, raw poultry, eggs, beef, pork, raw milk	12-48 hours	1-4 days
CAMPYLOBACTER JEJUNI	Raw poultry & milk	2-7 days	1-2 weeks
STAPHLOCOCCUS AUREUS	Improperly handled cooked food.	1-6 hours	12-24 hours
CLOSTRIDIUM PERFRINGENS	Improperly handled meats & foods only kept warm.	8-15 hours	6-24 hours
CLOSTRIDIUM BOTULINUM	Improperly canned foods, raw honey.	18-48 hours	1-7 months
BACILLUS CEREUS	Cooked grains & vegetables left at room temperature.	1-15 hours	6-24 hours
CAMPYLOBACTER	Undercooked chicken.	1-5 hour	12-24 hours
SHIGELLA	Contaminated food with feces from very young children.	36-72 hours	4-8 days
ESCHERICHIA COLI	Ground meat, raw milk, organic vegetables.	5-48 hours	3 days-2 wks
NORWALK VIRUS	Fecal contaminated food or hands.	35-40 hours	2 days
VIBRIO	Raw shellfish	12 hours	2-4 days
LISTERIA	Processed meat, deli-type salads, under, aged cheese.	3-12 hours	2-7 days

CAUTION

- Symptoms of food poisoning will vary depending on the level of the germ or viruses ingested. Symptoms usually include chills, stomachache, nausea, muscle aches, and diarrhea. If diarrhea occurs shortly after a meal it is usually a sign of food poisoning. If you experience any abnormal symptom or even feel that you have eaten a contaminated food, contact your doctor immediately.

- Every day 22,000 people get sick from eating foods that are contaminated in the United States.

HEALTH HAZARDS IN OUR EVERYDAY PRODUCTS

ALUMINUM CONTAMINATION

- This mineral can affect the absorption of calcium, magnesium, phosphorus, selenium, and fluoride. One of the problem products seems to be aluminum, containing antacids. Excessive intake can be harmful.

ENVIRONMENTAL CONTAMINANTS

Cooking Vessels	Antacids	Deodorants
Industrial Utensils	Lab Equipment	Aluminum Foil
Water Supplies	Aluminum Cans	Bronze Paint
Cables/Wiring	Air/Wastes	Beer
Alum	Nasal Sprays	Toothpaste
Cigarette Filters	Dental Amalgams	Smoke
Pesticides	Vanilla Powder	Baking Powder
Emulsifiers	Medicines	Foods
Coal Burning	Milk Equipment	Table Salt
Packaging Material	Soil	Refining

OVEREXPOSURE SYMPTOMS

Skin Reactions	Fatigue	Gastric Upset
Heart Problems	Aching Muscles	Flatulence
Psychosis	Hyperactivity	Senility
Osteoporosis	Rickets	Kidney Problem
Memory Loss	Emphysema	Back Pain

LEAD CONTAMINATION

ENVIRONMENTAL CONTAMINANTS

Urban Atmosphere	Enamels	Batteries
Gasoline Additives	Newsprint	Foundries
Machine Shops	Paints	Printing
Ceramic Glazes	Solder	Insecticides
Cigarette Smoke	Plaster	Ammunitions
Hair Coloring	Putty	Lead Pipes
Wines (lead caps)	Plating	Glass
Old Paints	Mascara	Toothpaste

OVEREXPOSURE SYMPTOMS

Headache	Depression	Dizziness
Confusion/Fatigue	Disorientation	Anxiety
Irritability	Nervousness	Insomnia
Drowsiness	Weak Muscles	Gout
Aching Muscles	Abdominal Pain	Ataxia
Memory Loss	Hypertension	Weight Loss
Constipation	Seizures	Hyperactivity
Loss of Appetite	Crying	Withdrawal

CADMIUM CONTAMINATION

ENVIRONMENTAL CONTAMINANTS

Cigarette Smoke
Galvanized Pipes
Drinking Water
Instant Coffee
Smelting of Zinc
Processed Meats
Process Engraving
Paint Manufacturing
Fungicide Manufacturing
Welding Metal
Rubber Carpet Backing

Cisterns
Candles
Batteries
Motor Oils
Auto Exhaust
Shellfish
Electroplating
Rust-proofing
Jewelry Making
Soil
Plastic Tapes

Silver Polish
Iron Roofs
Auto Tires
Air Particles
Incineration
Cola Drinks
Plastics
Soldering
Pigments
Sewage Sludge
Solders

OVEREXPOSURE SYMPTOMS

Fatigue
Iron Deficiency Anemia
Teeth Discoloration
Pain in back and legs
Increased Mortality

Liver Damage
Loss of Smell
Hypertension
Arthritis
Dyspnea

Emphysema
Renal Colic
Bone Softening
Cancer
Glucosuria

MERCURY CONTAMINATION

ENVIRONMENTAL CONTAMINANTS

Water Based Paints	Thermometers	Floor Waxes
Dental Amalgams	Batteries	Camera Film
Fabric Softener	Ointments	Antiseptics
Pharmaceuticals	Cosmetics	Plastics
Florescent Lamps	Canvas	Pesticides
Chemical Fertilizers	Burning Coal	Adhesives
Fish/Shellfish	Body Powders	Talc

OVEREXPOSURE SYMPTOMS

Anxiety	Irritability	Drowsiness
Loss of Self Confidence	Nervousness	Shyness
Lack of Self Control	Depression	Weight Loss
Loss of Appetite	Insomnia	Tremors
Memory Losses	Ataxia	Dermatitis
Hearing Losses	Speech Problems	Renal Damage
Muscle Weakness	Paralysis	Vision Problem

HEALTH AROUND THE HOME

Kitchen

- A recent survey showed that over 50% of people never wash the cutting board after using it to prepare a meat product before using the board for another type of food. There are more germs in the kitchen than any other room in the home.

Bathroom

- Only 50% of adults wash their hands after using the toilet.

Nursery

- Children can have as many as 7 colds per year caused by germs spread from playing with toys that other children have handled. Stuffed toys can become germ catchers and need to be cleaned.

GLOSSARY

ACACIA (gum Arabic)
Chemical that is used to stabilize and clear the wine.

ACETIFICATION
The aroma of wine as it ages.

ACID
A sour tasting substance that is soluble in water.

ACIDULATED WATER
A number of fruits and vegetables turn brown easily and need to be sprayed with a solution of a mild acid found in fruits called ascorbic acid (vitamin C). To prepare acidulated water, just mix 1 part of lemon or lime, juice to 5 parts of water and place the mixture in a bowl or spray bottle.

ACRID
Substance that produces a hot, irritating sensation.

ACQUIRED BOUQUET
The aroma of the wine as it ages.

AGE
Allowing meat to hang, bringing out the flavor after the animal is killed.

ALCOHOL
This is the amount of ethyl alcohol (ETOH) in a beverage obtained by the process of fermentation and subsequent distillation.

ALCOHOL CONTENT

If the content is less than 14%, the wine may be labeled "Table Wine." The accuracy is allowed to within 1.5% either way. If the alcohol content is over 14%, the percentage must appear on the label.

AL DENTE

This is an Italian term meaning "to the tooth." It is used to describe the pasta when it has been cooked to the stage that is has a slight resistance when you bite down on it.

ALKALI

Substance that is capable of neutralizing an acid. Sodium bicarbonate is a good example.

ALKALOIDS

An irritant that may produce hallucinations and may be poisonous. Some will affect the nervous system while others may just have an astringent effect.

ALPHA ACID

The most important compound found in hops. It provides the beer with the bitter flavor.

ALLEMANDE

A thick sauce made from meat stock with egg yolks and lemon juice.

AMYLASE

Enzyme which converts carbohydrates to malt sugars. They are released from the germination of the barley and assist in the breakdown of the wort.

ANALGESIC

Substance that reduces pain.

ANGELICA

This is a sweet aromatic herb whose candied stems are used in cake decorating and to flavor alcoholic beverages.

ANGLAISE

Typical English dish that is boiled or roasted.

ANTIPASTO
An Italian word for an assortment of appetizers, such as, cold cuts, olives, pickles, peppers, and vegetables.

ANTISEPTIC
A substance that is capable of preventing the growth of or destroying bacteria.

APHRODISIAC
A substance that is capable of improving sexual potency and desires.

ARIBICA
This is the species of tree that produces the "Coffee Aribica" coffee. These trees may be grown in different countries; however, the name was given to the particular species by a European botanist when he was categorizing the trees and flora of the Arabian Peninsula.

ARROWROOT
A fine powder that is produced from dried root stalks of a subtropical tuber. It is used to thicken soups, sauces, and pastes. Has $1^1/_2$ times the thickening power of flour.

ASPIC
Gelatin made from concentrated vegetables and meat stocks. Usually contains tomato juice.

A BUERRE
Either "with" or "cooked in butter."

AU GRATIN
Usually refers to a dish that has a browned covering of bread crumbs and usually mixed with cheese and butter.

AU JUS
Meat juices that are the result of a cooking process. Usually de-fatted before serving.

AU SEC
Until it is dry.

AUTOLYSIS
A breakdown of the yeast cells inside sparkling wine bottles after the secondary fermentation takes place.

ANTIOXIDANT
Substance: that has the capability of protecting another substance from being destroyed or damaged by oxygen.

APERITIF
An alcoholic beverage such as sweet vermouth, dry sherry, or champagne served before a meal to stimulate the appetite.

ASTRINGENCY
Drying or puckering sensation in the mouth, which is usually caused by tannins.

ASTRINGENT
These are compounds that are capable of drawing skin or other soft tissue together. They are used to close the pores of the skin and block toxins from entering surface cells.

AVIDIN
A protein that is found in egg white that will inactivate biotin.

AVERAGE FLOUR VALUE
This is derived from four factors: the color of the flour, loaves per barrel, the size of the loaf, and the quality of the bread as compared to any given flour shipment.

B

BAIN-MARIE
A pan of hot water used to keep foods warm and reduce the risk of curdling.

BAKE
Cooking foods by allowing air to circulate around them.

BAKING CHOCOLATE
This is also called bitter or unsweetened chocolate and is pure chocolate liquor that has been extracted from the cocoa bean. Usually has lecithin and vanilla added for flavor and to keep it in a usable suspension.

BARBECUE
Cooking over natural wood or charcoal on a grill surface.

BARDING
This is the process of covering meats or fowl with added fat to keep the flesh moist, It is usually done to meats that only have a small fat covering and is accomplished by basting the meat with any fat source.

BAGGY
The term is usually applied to an off-taste in coffee that is produced from a weak roast and or one that may have been stored for too long a period in poor conditions.

BASTE
Keeping foods moist while they are cooking by spooning liquid on them. A bulb baster is normally used for this purpose.

BEAN THREADS
Translucent threads that are produced from the starch of mung beans. These are also known as Chinese vermicelli or glass noodles. They may be found in oriental markets.

BEANY
Coffee that has not been roasted to its fullest and will not have the complete aroma that it should have.

BÉARNAISE SAUCE
Sauce made from egg yolk, vinegar, Tarragon, butter and chives.

BEAT
Combining ingredients rapidly producing a smooth mixture.

BÉCHAMEL SAUCE
White sauce that is prepared from flour, butter, milk and special seasonings.

BEER
Beer is a beverage that is produced through alcoholic fermentation of hops, yeast, malt, and water. Proteins used in the production of the beer will determine how long the "head" will last.

BENTONITE
Wyoming clay substance that is safe to add to wine to remove the grape proteins that remains in solution. The proteins contain a positive charge and the bentonite has a negative charge, which attracts the protein. The protein-bentonite compound precipitates to the top for easy removal. Proteins will cause cloudiness in wine.

BENZYL PEROXIDE
Fine powder that is mixed into the flour in very small amounts to bleach the flour.

BEURRE MANIE
Combining equal amounts of softened butter and flour and then added to soups or sauces as a thickener.

BEURRE NOIR
Butter that is heated until the color is dark brown then flavored with vinegar.

BEURRE NOISETTE
Butter that is heated until the color is a light brown.

BIGARADE
Food that has been cooked in orange juice.

BIND
Adding an ingredient that will assist in holding other ingredients together, such as an egg.

BISQUE
Rich, creamy soup made from fish or game. May also refer to a frozen dessert.

BITTER
A taste that is caused by a combination of quinine, caffeine and possibly other alkaloids. The bitterness is isolated at the back of the tongue.

BITTERS
These are spirits that are flavored with fruits or botanicals. They all tend to have a somewhat bitter taste.

BLANCH
Process of plunging food into boiling water usually to remove the skin from fruits and vegetables or to kill bacteria prior to freezing.

BLANC MANGE
A thick, corn starch type of white pudding.

BLACK BEANS
Coffee beans that have fallen to the ground before they are harvested. When used, they will cause a poor tasting coffee.

BLEND
Combining ingredients together to form a desired consistency.

BODY
The thickness of beer perceived as mouth feel. The level of carbonation can also affect the mouth feel.

BOIL
Heating water to 212^0F at sea level. Water bubbles rapidly when boiling.

BOILED ICING
Made by beating cooked sugar syrup into egg whites that have been firmly whipped. The mixture is then beaten until it is smooth and glossy. Also known as Italian meringue.

BOLOGNESE
Recipes that originated in the Bologna, Italy area. A common spaghetti sauce is called Bolognese.

BONE
Using a special "boning" knife to remove bones from meats and fish.

BORDELAISE
Brown sauce with red wine, shallots, pepper and herbs. Often garnished with marrow.

BOTANICALS
Flavorings derived from fruits or flowers that are used in neutral spirits when producing gin or a liqueur.

BOUILLON

Bouillon was invented by the Duke of Godfrey in 1089 at his castle at Bouillon, Belgium. The Duke became the first European King of Jerusalem.

This is a concentrated stock that has been clarified and usually made from bones and meat or poultry.

BOUILLABAISSE

Originated in France and was prepared from any fish that were not sold when the fishing fleet came home.

A French soup/stew, that is prepared using different types of fish and vegetables.

BOURRIDE

A type of fish soup that has been bound together with garlic mayonnaise.

BRACHISH

A poor taste in coffee that produces a salty or alkaline sensation. This is usually the result of inorganic residues caused by excessive heating after the coffee is already brewed.

BRAISE

Browning meats in a saucepan in fat over high heat: then covered and usually cooked in the oven in a small amount of liquid. Usually used for tougher cuts of meat.

BREAD

Coating placed on foods. Usually involves dredging or coating with bread-crumbs.

BREATHE (wine term)

The process of allowing air to mix with wine. This may be done by leaving the cork out of the bottle or by decanting. This process allows unpleasant odors to escape.

BRINY

A term used to describe coffee that has been over-roasted.

BRIX SCALE
This is a measurement of the density of sugar that has been dissolved in water to prepare syrup. The scale is designed to provide a measurement of the amount of water, which will determine whether the syrup is at a low or high density level. The instrument used to accomplish this is called a saccharometer.

BROIL
Cooking with very intense heat usually on a grill or under a broiler.

BROTH
A clear soup, that is produced from simmering meats, poultry and vegetables in water.

BROWN
Cooking food quickly in a broiler, pre-heated oven or very hot pan.

BROWN SAUCE
Gravy: that is prepared using onions, beef broth, butter, flours, vegetables and seasonings.

BRUNOISE
A generic term referring to a food that contains finely diced vegetables.

BRUT
The driest Champagne sold. Should have no sign of sweet taste.

BUD
The top unopened tender leaf of tea plant.

BULK HEADING
This pertains to the pressurizing of beer storage during the secondary fermentation process, which results in the desired level of carbon dioxide that is dissolved in the beer.

BUNG
The hole in a keg of beer used for filling and emptying is called a bung or bunghole.

BURDOCK ROOT

Traditional ingredient used in American root beers. Burdock root has been used as a blood cleanser for hundreds of years. The herb is common to most of the United States.

C

CAKE BREAKER

A comb with 3-4 inch long metal teeth that is used to slice angel food and chiffon cakes. Cuts the cakes cleanly instead of tearing them, which a knife will do.

CAKE LEVELER

U-shaped metal frame that is used to cut cakes into even horizontal layers. It stands on plastic feet and has a thin, very sharp, serrated cutting blade. Adjust to any size slice. The cake is pushed against the blade and will cut cakes up to 16 inches in diameter.

CARAMELIZING

Browning of sugar by heating.

CARAMEL RULERS

Also called chocolate rulers. They are used to contain the hot chocolate or caramel as they cool. They are usually 20-30 inches in length with $1/2$-inch stainless steel or chrome bars. The bars are lightly oiled or dusted with corn, starch to keep the product from sticking and are placed on a marble working counter. The hot mixture is then poured into the center of the mold.

CARBON DIOXIDE

Colorless odorless gas that is noncombustible. Used commonly as a pressure, dispensing agent in gassed whipped creams and carbonated beverages. Also, used as dry ice in the frozen food industry. Has been used in stage productions to produce harmless smoke or fumes. However, it may cause shortness of breath, nausea, elevated blood pressure, and disorientation if inhaled in lager quantities.

CASEIN

The main protein in cow's milk is used as a water absorbing powder with no odor. It is used as a texturizer for a number of dairy products including ice cream and frozen custards. Used in hair preparations to thicken thin hair and as an emulsifier in cosmetics.

CHEESECLOTH

Natural white cotton cloth, which is available in either fine or coarse weaves. It is lint-free and maintains its shape when wet. Primarily used for straining jellies or encompassing stuffing in turkeys.

CHELATING AGENT

Compound that has the capability of binding with and precipitating trace metals from the body. The most common agent is EDTA (ethylenediamine tetraacetic acid).

CHEVRE CHEESE

Any cheese made from goat's milk, usually found coated with an herb or ash.

CHIBOUST CREAM

Vanilla pastry cream with a very light texture produced by adding stiffly beaten egg whites.

CHICORY

A taste that is somewhat sweet, yet is a bit bitter and even acidic. .

CHINOS

Cone-shaped strainer made of metal with a long handle and hooks to edge of pot. Mesh comes in different sizes.

CHOCOLATE BLOOM

This has also been called "fat bloom." The bloom is actually accomplished when the cocoa butter and the chocolate separate during cooking and the cocoa butter floats to the top and crystallizes. The streaks of fat look like the bloom of a plant, hence the name. As soon as the chocolate melts, the cocoa butter goes back into the mixture.

CHOCOLATE LIQUEUR

This not real liqueur, but a liquid that is extracted from the cocoa bean, then used in the manufacture of chocolate.

CHOU PASTE

The French name for special pastry dough used in cream puffs and chocolate eclairs.

CHOWDER
Thick soup prepared using cream, fat, vegetables and a type of fish base.

CLARIFICATION
The process of removing small particles of suspended material from a liquid. Butyl alcohol is used to remove particles from shampoos. Traces of copper and iron are removed from certain beverages and vinegar.

CLARIFICATION EQUIPMENT
Centrifuges are used to speed up the clarification of beer. This normally done during the secondary phase of fermentation when the yeast cells sink to the bottom. When they sink, they trap and carry with them the haze-producing factors such as proteins and hop resins.

CLOTTED CREAM
May also be known as Devonshire cream in recipes. It is a thick, rich, scalded cream that is made by slowly cooking and skimming cream or unpasteurized milk. The thickened cream floats to the surface and is removed after the cream cools. It is traditionally served with scones in England.

COAGULATION
Process: by which proteins will become firm when heated.

COCKLE
Very small mollusk that resembles a clam. May be sold either shucked or canned.

COCONUT CREAM
Dried coconut meat is squeezed out and the layer that rises to the top of the milk is called the coconut cream. Coconut cream is used in many oriental recipes.

CODDLE
Poaching that is performed in slowly simmering water.

COFFEE ACIDITY
This is a normal characteristic of coffee. An expert coffee taster can recognize three variables in acidic tastes: 1) natural and desirable, 2) sour and undesirable, 3) too acidic with a bite and puckering sensation.

COFFEE ALKALINITY
A coffee taste: that is defined by a sensation of dryness toward the back of the tongue. This is usually produced by the presence of alkaloid compounds.

COLLAGEN
A protein found in all vertebrates.

CONDENSER
The part of a still that is responsible for liquefying the alcohol vapors.

CONGENERS
Refers to the flavorings and aromas that are the result of the organic compounds being broken down by the fermentation and distillation processes. The more a beverage is distilled, the fewer congeners it will contain and the more pure the beverage will be.

COLLOIDS
These are proteins and tannins that produce a haze in beer and need to be removed. Stabilization compounds are added to the mixture, which attach to the colloids and make it easy to remove them.

CONDENSED MILK
Canned milk which is produced by evaporation and then sweetened with sugar.

CONSOMMÉS
Strong brown stock soup that is clarified and usually prepared from two types of meat or poultry and meat combined.

CRACKLINGS
Crisp, browned pieces that remain in the bottom of the pan after fresh pork fat is rendered into lard. May be added to a number of dishes, especially beans, corn bread, or vegetables.

CREAM
Beating foods until they become light and fluffy. Commonly sugar, butter and shortening.

CREAM ALE
American beer that has a high level of carbonation. Usually fermented with both ale and lager yeast.

CREAM SOUPS
Usually prepared using a vegetable soup base with the addition of cream or butter and milk.

CRÈME ANGLAISE
French for a rich custard sauce that is poured on cakes and fruit desserts.

CRÈME FRAICHE
This is actually the French version of heavy cream and is made by mixing 2 tablespoons of sour cream (or 1 teaspoon of buttermilk) to 1 cup of whipping cream. The mixture is shaken and left to sit at room temperature for 24 hours or until it is thick. It should then be covered and refrigerated.

CURDLE
Heating milk until it starts to separate and lumps begin to form.

CUSTARD
A mixture of milk and eggs, that is usually prepared in a double boiler or oven.

CUTIN
The process of adding fat into a flour mixture with a pastry blender or other mixing utensil.

D

DASH
Usually refers to 1/16th of a teaspoon.

DECANTING
Removing the sediment before pouring. Pour the wine through a piece of cheesecloth until you start seeing the sediment. Unfiltered wine may need decanting. Decanting a red wine will allow possible undesirable chemical to be released into the air. Decanting may also be done by pouring the wine carefully from the bottle into a carafe.

DECOCTION
An herbal tea made from the seeds, bark or roots of a plant. The ingredients need to be boiled for a period of time to release the herbal extracts.

DE-GLAZE
The process of adding a liquid to remove and dissolve the residues remaining on the bottom of a pan.

DEGREE DAYS
Is a measurement of total heat days during the summer season and measured by the actual accumulation of heat, which determines the speed of growth and is figured on the average daily temperature within each 24-hour period.

DEMULCENT
Thick or any creamy substance usually oily, that is used to relieve pain and inflammation in mucosal membranes. One of the common demulcents is gum acacia.

DEXTRIN
A sugar produced by the reaction of starch and the malt.

DISTILLING
The process of releasing and capturing vapors from a liquid. The vapors are then put through a condenser, which re-liquefies the vapors into a more potent alcoholic beverage.

DIURETIC
An herb or compound that is capable of increasing the flow of urine.

DOCKER
This is a tool made for making holes in pastry dough, especially puff pastries so that steam can escape as the dough is baking. It looks like a paint roller with protruding metal or plastic spikes.

DOLLOP
A small amount dropped by a spoon. Usually refers to whipped cream or sour cream when only a small amount is added to the top of a dish.

DREDGE
Lightly coating foods with flour or breadcrumbs.

DRY-HEAT COOKING
The heat is conducted to the food without the use of moisture.

E

EGG WASH
Prepared from a whole egg or portion of an egg, such as the yolk or white and beaten together with milk, cream or water. Usually brushed on top of baked goods to produce an even browning.

ENZYME
A protein substance that is manufactured by living cells and is active in regulating and causing chemical reactions to occur in living organisms. An enzyme does not change itself, but causes reactions to progress to the next step.

EMULSIFIER
A commonly used substance used to stabilize a mixture and to ensure the proper consistency. One of the most common emulsifier is lecithin, which will keep oil and vinegar in suspension. Cosmetics use stearic acid soaps, which include potassium and sodium stearates.

ESTERS
Produced from the combination of acids and alcohol to form a more volatile substance, providing alcoholic beverages their unique aroma.

ETUVER
Cooking or steaming a food in its own juices.

EXTRACT
A compound that is extracted from a liquid. In beer production the extract is malt extract and is extracted during the process of mashing. When it is dissolved in water, it is then called wort.

F

FANNINGS

A leftover from the manufacturing of tea that is sometimes used in low-priced teabags. If the color of the tea comes out quickly and is dark, the tea probably has some fannings or dust added.

FERMENTATION

The breakdown of starch (grains) using certain enzymes that speed up the reaction. The end product may depend on the particular enzyme that is used. If the enzyme diastase is used, the end product will be maltose.

FERMENTED COFFEE

This refers to a taste abnormality in the bean, causing a sour sensation on the tongue. Enzymes in the green bean have converted the sugars to acids.

FILE POWDER

A spice used by Cajun chefs is made from ground sassafras leaves to thicken as well as adding a thyme-like flavor to gumbos. The spice tends to become stringy when boiled and needs to be added just before serving.

FLAMBÉ

Pouring brandy or other liqueur over a food and igniting it.

FLOATING ISLAND

A dessert made from chilled custard and topped with a special "poached" meringue. The custard usually contains fruit and the meringue is occasionally drizzled and combined with a thin stream of caramel syrup.

FLUMMERY

A soft custard-like dessert that is served over berries or other types of fruit. Resembles a thickened fruit sauce.

FLUTE

Decorating the edges of a pastry or pie shell in a scalloped design sometime performed with your fingers.

FOCACCIA

Italian yeast bread that resembles a deep-dish pizza crust with a bread-like texture and is usually topped with a variety of toppings.

FOLD
Mixing two ingredients or more together. Without stirring or using a beater. Usually accomplished by placing a rubber spatula under the mixture and gently turning.

FONDANT
Sugary syrup that is usually cooked until it is a soft ball, then kneaded until creamy.

FORCING TEST
A method of determining what the shelf life will be for the beer. It employs a method of artificial aging using specific alternating temperature changes.

FORTIFIED WINES
Wines with an alcohol content; that has been raised to 17-24% by adding brandy or a neutral alcohol. These are usually dry sherry and cream sherry.

FRAPPE
A beverage or slushy dessert that is made with crushed ice and usually with liquor poured over it.

FRENCH ROAST
If the coffee is said to have a "French Roast," it means that the coffee was roasted long enough to release the natural oils in the bean, allowing them to rise to the surface. Provides a "roasted" flavor that can be easily identified.

FRICASSEE
Cooking foods gently usually in liquid and sometimes vegetables after they have been browned.

FRITTER
Small pieces of meat or vegetable dipped in a batter and deep-fried.

G

GELATIN
Jelly-like substance used as a thickening agent and derived from the bones and connective tissue of animals. Gelatin can also be derived from seaweed and is called agar-agar.

GENE
Biological unit of inheritance, which is part of the genetic material, DNA, which contains the genetic information that is needed to produce a single protein.

GLACE
Coating foods with sugary, syrup usually cooked to the "cracked" stage.

GNOCCHI
A small Italian dumpling made from potatoes and 100% seminola flour. They may be found in many shapes from squares to balls and usually served as an appetizer in better Italian restaurants.

H

HARD LIQUOR
Beverage with high alcohol content, usually measured in "proof."

HARICOT
A term used to describe a thick meat stew.

HOGSHEAD
Refers to a container that is used to ship wine in large quantities. Usually has a capacity of 60 gallons.

HOLLANDAISE SAUCE
Sauce that is prepared with egg yokes, lemon juice and butter.

HORS D'OEUVRE
Very small canapé that is served either hot or cold.

HYGROSCOPIC
Substance that readily absorbs moisture.

HYDROMETER
Instrument used to measure dissolved solids such as sugar or Brix of a solution.

HYDROLYZED
To be placed into water form.

I

ICE WINES
A relatively rare wine that can only be produced in certain years when the grapes have been frozen on the vine. The level of sugar at harvest must be at least 35^0 Brix with a residual sugar content of at least 18%.

INFUSE
To allow flavoring or herb to remain in a boiling liquid.

INFUSER
Small metal ball that is used to hold the loose tea when it is placed into a cup or pot.

INFUSION
The process of including a flavor into an alcoholic beverage so that it will remain a permanent part of the beverage.

ITALIAN ROAST
Coffee beans that have been roasted darker than the French Roast and very popular in many countries that produce coffee.

J

JAGGERY
This is also known as palm sugar and is semi-refined sugar, which is produced from the sap of the Palmyra palm tree. It may also be made from Hawaiian sugar cane. It looks like a coarse, crumbly, brown sugar with a strong flavor, and is sold in cakes. It is mostly used in Asian and Indonesian dishes.

JULIENNE
Slicing fresh vegetables into small strips of uniform sizes.

K

KEG
A sealed metal barrel, that holds 15.5 gallons of beer. Also, referred to as half a barrel or "pony keg."

KERATIN
Protein that is taken from grinding hooves, horns, feathers and the hair of animals.

KNEAD
Working dough in the palms of your hands after all the ingredients have been added on a floured surface.

L

LEAVENING
A chemical placed in baked goods to make them lighter and more porous by causing the release of carbon dioxide gas during cooking.

LEES
The residues of yeast, fruit skins, or other extraneous matter leftover after fermentation. These leftovers are sometimes used to produce pomace brandy.

LIMOUSINE
A type of oak that originates in a forest near Limousine, France. This is considered the best wood for producing oak barrels and casks to mature Cognac and other spirits.
Contains approximately 1.5 % alcohol.

M

MALT BEER
This is a top-fermented dark beer, which has a high extract content of about 12% using caramelized sugar. It is higher in calories than most beer and has only a 1% alcohol content.

MANDOLINE
A tool used for slicing vegetables that has four adjustable blades.

MARYANN PAN
Also known as the "shortcake pan." It is a shallow, round, aluminum pan that looks like a tart pan. It has fluted sides and is made with a deep hollow area around the edges making the center look like it is raised. Used mainly for sponge cakes and pastry shells.

MIREPOIX
Mixture of diced carrots, celery and onions that have been sautéed in butter.

MOIST-HEAT COOKING
The heat is conducted to the food by water or other type of liquid.

MULL
When you mull a drink it means that you are heating the drink and adding spices.

N

NUTELLA
Smooth paste prepared from chocolate and hazelnuts.

O

ORGANIC WINE
Produced from grapes that were grown where there were no fertilizers or pesticides used. The vineyard must be free of contaminants for at least one year before a harvest. The wine that is produced must also be free of any additives, especially sulfites.

P

PAN-BROIL
Cooking uncovered in a skillet without the use of any fat.

PAPILLOTE
Food is wrapped in parchment or foil so that the food is steamed in its own moisture.

PAR-BOIL
The food is partially cooked in simmering liquid or boiled.

PAR-COOK
To cook the food partially by any method.

PARCH
Browning with a dry heat.

PAVLOVA
Unique dessert invented in New Zealand made of marshmallows and meringue.

pH
This refers to the scale to measure acidity and alkalinity. The pH is actually the hydrogen (H) ion concentration of a solution. The small p is for the power of the hydrogen ion. The scale used to determine the level of acidity or alkalinity of a product or solution is measured with the number 14 as the highest level and 7 as a neutral point where the acidity and alkalinity are balanced. Water is 7, and if the number goes above 7 the solution is considered to be alkaline. If the number falls below 7 then the solution is considered to be acidic. Human blood has a pH of 7.3, Vinegar and lemon juices are 2.3, and common lye is 13.

PHYLLO DOUGH
Very thin pastry dough; usually sold in one pound cartons. Sold fresh in the Middle East and sold frozen in the United States. Must be kept wrapped, otherwise the dough will dry out rapidly.

PIPING GEL
A transparent substance that is prepared from sugar, waters vegetable gums, benzoate of soda and corn syrup. It is usually used to write on cakes and pastries.

PIQUANT
Refers to any food that has a sharp flavor, usually used to describe cheeses.

POUTINE
French fries combined with cheese curds and covered with gravy.

PROOF
Testing yeast to check whether it is still active.

PUREE
Strained and blended cooked vegetables or fruits to produce a thick liquid. Usually done in a blender or food processor.

Q

QUENELLE
A small, delicate, round dumpling made from finely chopped fish or meat in a flour and egg mixture. They are poached and served as an appetizer with a rich sauce over them.

R

RACLETTE
A Swiss cheese snack prepared by placing a piece of cheese near a flame so that it will remain soft enough to scrape a small amount of the cheese off and use it as a spread on bread or boiled potatoes as the meal progresses.

REDUCE
Thickening or concentrating a sauce by boiling it down, thus lessening the volume and intensifying the flavor.

RENDER
Liquefying solid fat over low heat.

RENNIN
An enzyme found in calve stomachs.

RICE STICK
This is an almost transparent Oriental noodle that is flavorless. It is made from rice flour and may be sold as rice noodles or rice vermicelli. They will expand to 8-10 times their original volume and are usually cooked in liquid or deep-fried.

ROBUSTA
Coffees that contain high caffeine content and are somewhat bitter. The coffee does not have a strong coffee aroma.

ROCKY MOUNTAIN OYSTERS
Lamb or cattle testicles that are breaded and then deep-fried. Originated in the Rocky Mountain States.

ROSE WATER
Pleasant oil that is distilled from rose petals. Commonly used to scent pastries and confections and frequently found in Turkish candies.

ROUX
A mixture of butter (or any oil) and flour that is browned and used as a thickener or flavoring agent for soups and stews.

RUSK
Slice of bread that is crisp and used as a cracker. The bread is baked then sliced very thin and allowed to dry out and is browned.

S

SAUTÉ
Cooking in a small amount of oil until the food has browned.

SCRAPPLE
Bits and pieces of leftover pig, mixed with cornmeal and spices then usually served in a tomato sauce.

SEQUESTRANT
Substance that will absorb iron and prevents chemical changes that would affect the flavor, texture, and the color of foods. Sodium is an example that is used for water softening.

SHELF STABLE
This is a term that is used to describe foods that have been sterilized, then sealed in airtight plastic bags, containers, or special paper foil. This is a type of preservation of food that does not require refrigeration or freezing and sometimes referred to as aseptic packaging. The most popular products to be sold in this manner are dairy products, puddings, and sauces.

SIMMER
Cooking food in a liquid at a temperature that is just below boiling. The liquid being simmered should be lightly bubbling.

SORBET
A frozen dessert that never contains eggs or heavy cream.

SOUR
A normal flavor that is caused by acids in the coffee created by the presence of either one or all of the following compounds: tartaric acid, citric acid or malic acid.

SUET
This is semi-hard fat found in the loin and kidney areas of beef and pork. Occasionally beef suet will be used to make mincemeat.

SWEAT
Cooking slowly in fat without browning, usually in a covered pan.

T

TAMARI
Type of Japanese soy sauce that is naturally fermented and is usually free of wheat with an excellent flavor of its own.

TAMIS
A screen that is stretched over a round frame used for straining liquids. Commonly used for straining mousses and vegetable purees. The food is forced through the tamis with a spatula.

TANNIN
A substance found in the seeds and stems of grapes. It has astringent properties and is important in the aging process of wine. As wine ages the level of astringency will diminish and the wine develops more of its own characteristics.

TEMPER
To balance a cool ingredient before adding it to a hot ingredient, thus avoiding curdling or separation.

TERASI
Shrimp paste prepared with a variety of spices depending on which Asian country prepares it.

TINCTURE
Usually referred to an extraction of the herbs in a solution of vinegar or alcohol. The preferred vinegar is apple cider vinegar.

TOXIN
Organic poison that is produced in or on living or dead organisms.

TARRY
A burnt flavor that is the result of in the holding process after the coffee has been brewed caused by the condensation and burning of the coffee proteins.

TWIGLETS
A cracker snack food: that is shaped like a twig. Contains cheese and yeast extract.

U

ULLAGE
The bottle fill level.

V

VINTAGE WINE
This means that the wine came from an excellent harvest and will be more expensive. Vintage wines that are labeled "prestige" are the highest quality wines.

VOLATILE OIL
A complex chemical compound that is capable of producing the aroma and taste of herbs. Usually obtained from the fresh plant.

W

WAFTING
The process of waving your hand over a dish toward your nose in order to smell the aroma.

WHISK
Beating with a wire loop beater. Excellent for blending ingredients, especially sauces.

WHITE WINE
Produced using red grapes and processing them quickly without extracting any of the color.

Y

YEAST

A block of yeast is composed of a million one-celled fungi that will multiply at a fast rate, especially if given their favorite food sugar and a moist warm environment. Yeast turns the sugar into glucose, which in turn produces alcohol and carbon dioxide. Yeast should be tested before being used to be sure it is alive and active.

Z

ZEST

The oil found in the outer yellow or orange rind of citrus fruits.

CONVERSION CHART

U.S. WEIGHTS AND MEASURES

1 pinch = less than $\frac{1}{8}$ teaspoon
1 Tbls. = 3 tsp. = $\frac{1}{2}$ ounce liquid
2 Tbls. = 1 ounce, liquid or dry
8 ounces = 1 cup = 16 Tbls. = $\frac{1}{2}$ Lb.
2 cups = 16 ounces = 1 pint
1 quart = 2 pints
8 tbls. = 4 ounces = $\frac{1}{2}$ cup = 1 stick butter
1 cup pre-sifted all-purpose flour = 5 ounces
1 cup granulated sugar = 8 ounces
1 cup brown sugar = 6 ounces
1 large egg = 2 ounces = $\frac{1}{4}$ cup = 4 tbls.

TEMPERATURE CONVERSION

Fahrenheit		Centigrade
0°F		-17.7°C
32°F	Water Freezes	0°C
68°F	Room Temperature	20°C
100°F	Water Simmers	96.1°C
212°F	Water Boils	100°C
350°F	Baking	177°C
500°F	Broiling	260°C